COGNITIVE PROCESSES
in STEREOTYPING and
INTERGROUP BEHAVIOR

COGNITIVE PROCESSES
in STEREOTYPING and
INTERGROUP BEHAVIOR

edited by
DAVID L. HAMILTON
University of California, Santa Barbara

LEA

LAWRENCE ERLBAUM ASSOCIATES, PUBLISHERS
1981   Hillsdale, New Jersey

Lawrence Erlbaum Associates, Inc., Publishers
365 Broadway
Hillsdale, New Jersey 07642

Library of Congress Cataloging in Publication Data
Main entry under title:

Cognitive processes in stereotyping and intergroup
   behavior.

   Bibliography: p.
   Includes index.
   1. Social interaction—Addresses, essays, lec-
tures. 2. Stereotype (Psychology)—Addresses, essays,
lectures. 3. Cognition—Addresses, essays, lectures.
I. Hamilton, David L.
HM291.C586   302   80-29408
ISBN 0-89859-081-7

Printed in the United States of America

Contents

v

Preface

In the spring of 1975 I delivered a talk at the Carnegie Symposium on "Cognition and Social Behavior." I opened that talk with the observation that "it is difficult to think of a topic in social psychology that has more obvious and important societal implications and yet has yielded less progress toward increasing our knowledge and understanding than research on stereotypes." After briefly bemoaning this apparent stagnation, I attempted in the remainder of that address to summarize some then-recent findings that suggested to me that "this state of affairs may be changing." The common ingredient in the research I discussed was a focus on the role of cognitive processes in stereotyping and intergroup behavior. Although the cognitive orientation to these topics had a long history, this new work was exciting because it developed this approach in new ways, often borrowing on principles and methods from cognitive psychology.

These new lines of development, the beginnings of which were apparent in 1975, have continued and expanded in the intervening years. A number of research programs developed, and by 1977 work by several of us had progressed to that point that we (Hamilton, Rothbart, Snyder, Taylor) could present some of our findings in a symposium at the APA Convention in San Francisco. The research programs of these and other researchers have continued to develop and to extend the cognitive approach in new directions and to new issues.

This volume brings together contributions by several of the authors whose research has contributed significantly to the recent advances in our understanding of the role of cognitive processes in stereotyping and intergroup behavior. All of these chapters were written specifically for this volume. While each chapter reflects a cognitive approach to its subject matter, a broad range of topics, issues, and contexts is addressed by this collection of authors. In an introductory chapter

Ashmore and Del Boca present an historical overview of psychological research on stereotyping, discussing historical trends in this literature and summarizing the conceptual orientations which have guided research in this area. This chapter not only provides useful background information for the reader but also presents a broader context within which the current cognitively oriented research, on which the remaining chapter focus, can be viewed. Each of the next six chapters (by Ashmore, Taylor, Hamilton, Rothbart, Snyder, and Wilder) reports on integrative program of studies bearing on some aspect of the relationship of cognitive functioning to stereotyping and/or intergroup behavior. Each of these chapters, then, is rich in empirical findings. In addition, however, these authors have gone beyond simple summaries of their results. They have integrated their work with relevant research by others and have discussed both the theoretical and practical implications of their findings. In Chapter 8, Rose provides a thoughtful analysis of psychological processes that come to bear on intergroup interactions, focusing on the cognitive and dyadic processes mediating intergroup contact. The final two chapters, by Pettigrew and Hamilton, discuss the contributions of these authors in the context of previous research on stereotyping and intergroup behavior and with an eye toward future directions for a cognitively-oriented approach to these topics.

I am grateful to a number of persons for their assistance as this volume was being put together. My primary gratitude, of course, is to the authors of these chapters, not only for the excellence of their contributions, but also for their responsiveness to my editorial suggestions and promptings. Several of them also provided valuable advice as this project was developing. Larry Erlbaum and Art Lizza of Lawrence Erlbaum Associates have been very helpful throughout this endeavor. Finally, I thank my family—Susan, Brad, and Jessica—for the support, tolerance, and inspiration they have given me.

DAVID L. HAMILTON
University of California, Santa Barbara

COGNITIVE PROCESSES
in STEREOTYPING and
INTERGROUP BEHAVIOR

1

Conceptual Approaches to Stereotypes and Stereotyping

Richard D. Ashmore
Frances K. Del Boca
Livingston College, Rutgers–The State University

This volume presents an analysis of stereotyping and intergroup behavior from a cognitive perspective. While no single unified theory is articulated, the authors of the chapters that follow do share a cognitive orientation. The purpose of the present chapter is to place this orientation within the context of other social scientific approaches to the study of stereotypes. Three separate, yet highly interrelated, aspects of stereotype research and theory will be examined. First, a history of the stereotype concept is presented. Here we discuss the significant events and trends of the past that condition present and likely future efforts in this area. Second, the various meanings ascribed to the term *stereotype* are considered. Implicit as well as explicit and operational as well as conceptual definitions are reviewed in order to explicate both areas of agreement and disagreement regarding how the construct ''stereotype'' is best defined. Finally, we discuss the basic orientations taken by social scientists in seeking to understand stereotypes. Although not sufficiently explicit or complete to be called ''theories,'' three perspectives are clearly discernible—sociocultural, psychodynamic, and cognitive. The elements and implications of each of these three orientations are described.

HISTORY OF STEREOTYPE RESEARCH AND THEORY

The word *stereotype* was coined in 1798 by the French printer Didot to describe a printing process involving the use of fixed casts of the material to be reproduced. Approximately a century later psychiatrists began to use the related term *stereotypy* to denote a pathological condition characterized by behavior of ''per-

sistent repetitiveness and unchanging mode of expression [Gordon, 1962, p. 4]."
It is important to note that psychiatry adopted the word "stereotypy," not
"stereotype," and that stereotypy referred to fixity of behavior, both topographi-
cally (i.e., "unchanging mode of expression") and temporally (i.e., "persistent
repetitiveness"). The related notions of "fixed," "unchanging," and "persistent" point to one of the major themes, usually referred to as "rigidity," in
stereotype research and theory.

It was not until 1922 and the publication of Lippmann's *Public Opinion* that
the term "stereotype" was brought to the attention of social scientists. That
Lippmann is the father of "stereotype" as a social scientific concept is acknowledged in all historical accounts (cf. Brigham, 1971; Cauthen, Robinson, &
Krauss, 1971; Fishman, 1956; Gordon, 1962; Jones, 1977; LaViolette & Silvert,
1951) and is indicated by the clear recognition accorded him in the earliest
research reports on this topic (e.g., Katz & Braly, 1933; McGill, 1931; Rice,
1926). Perhaps because he was a journalist and not a scientist, Lippmann did not
provide a single explicit definition of "stereotype." He did, however, set forth a
number of ideas regarding stereotypes. These ideas are reflected in later conceptualizations and many seem startlingly contemporary.

Certainly the most often quoted phrase from *Public Opinion* is "pictures in
our heads." This phrase is the second half of the title of Chapter 1, which begins,
"The World Outside and the. . . ." It is here that Lippmann presented his basic
thesis: Humans do not respond directly to external reality (i.e., "the world
outside") but to a "representation of the environment which is in lesser or
greater degree made by man himself [p. 10]." He called this a "pseudoenviron-
ment" or "fiction." Lippmann assumed that "reality" was too complex to be
fully represented in the individual's "pseudo-environment" and argued that
stereotypes serve to simplify perception and cognition. In essence Lippmann
used the term "stereotype" very much as contemporary cognitive psychologists
use the term *schema* (e.g., Neisser, 1976), and social psychologists use the term
social schema (cf. Taylor & Crocker, 1981). Although a variety of definitions
have been proposed, most researchers would probably agree that a schema is a
cognitive structure that influences all the perceptual–cognitive activities that
together are labeled "information processing" (e.g., perceiving, encoding, storing, retrieving, decision making) with respect to a particular domain. For
Lippmann, in other words, stereotypes were cognitive structures that help individuals process information about the environment: "This is the perfect
stereotype. Its hallmark is that it precedes the use of reason; is a form of perception, imposes a certain character on the data of our senses before the data reach
the intelligence [1922, p. 65]."

Lippmann did not, however, conceive of these cognitive structures as neutral.
A whole chapter was devoted to the topic "Stereotypes as Defense." The theme
of this chapter is captured in one simple sentence: "The systems of stereotypes
may be the core of our personal tradition, the defenses of our position in society

[p. 63]." Thus, stereotypes were cognitive structures that were integral parts of the individual's personality and served to explain or rationalize her or his social standing. With regard to this latter point it is significant to note Lippmann's description of Aristotle's first book of *Politics:* "with unerring instinct he understood that to justify slavery he must teach the Greeks a way of *seeing* their slaves that comported with the continuance of slavery [p. 64]." Other authors have offered similar explanations of stereotypes as societal-level phenomena—stereotypes explain the relationship between social groups (cf. Ashmore & Del Boca, 1976). For example, in slave-holding societies, the slave is generally depicted as "childlike" and, thus, his subservient position is best for master, slave and society.

While Lippmann was most concerned with explicating the role of stereotypes in shaping public opinion, he did make one suggestion regarding how these cognitive structures are acquired: "In the great blooming, buzzing confusion of the outer world we pick out what our culture has already defined for us, and we tend to perceive that which we have picked out in the form stereotyped for us by our culture [p. 55]." Thus, according to Lippmann, individuals do not necessarily develop stereotypes through some approximation of the slow and effortful process of scientific hypothesis testing. Rather, they frequently incorporate, as part of their way of cognitively organizing the world, the "folkways" of their cultural group.

Most of the major themes of later research and theory are evident in Lippmann's discussion of stereotypes. Of particular importance, he presented the basic themes of the three orientations to the study of stereotypes discussed in the concluding section of this chapter. The cognitive perspective is clearly foreshadowed by Lippmann's distinction of "pseudo-environment" from "environment" and his emphasis on how stereotypes simplify the environment to make it more psychologically manageable. Although he did not accept the Freudian underpinnings of what later became the psychodynamic position, Lippmann did see stereotypes as related to personality or identity and as serving "defensive" functions. Lippmann also anticipated the sociocultural orientation by: (1) suggesting that stereotypes rationalize existing societal arrangements; and (2) pointing to society as the source of many of our individual "pictures in the head."

How did this rich conceptualization influence social scientists? As a partial answer, we have indicated in Table 1.1 the number of articles and books concerned with stereotypes that have been abstracted in the *Psychological Abstracts* from its inception in 1927 to 1977. As Table 1.1 suggests, Lippmann's immediate influence was not great.[1] From 1927 to 1933 the term *stereotype* appeared only three times in the *Psychological Abstracts:* McGill (1931), Litterer

---

[1]The table of contents of the *Psychological Index,* which was the predecessor to the *Psychological Abstracts,* made no reference to "stereotype" during the period from 1922 to 1927.

TABLE 1.1.
Number and Rate of Stereotype Entries Appearing in Psychological Abstracts and Sociological Abstracts Per Year

Psychological Abstracts								Sociological Abstracts			
Year	Volume	Number of "Stereotype" Entries[a]	"Stereotype" Entries Per 1,000 Abstracts	Year	Volume	Number of "Stereotype" Entries[a]	"Stereotype" Entries Per 1,000 Abstracts[b]	Year	Volume	Number of "Stereotype" Entries	"Stereotype" Entries Per 1,000 Abstracts
1927	1	0	0	1953	27	2	0.2	1953	1	0	0
1928	2	0	0	1954	28	6	0.7	1954	2	3	3.2
1929	3	0	0	1955	29	13	1.4	1955	3	0	0
1930	4	1	0.2	1956	30	6	0.7	1956	4	0	0
1931	5	1	0.2	1957	31	10	1.1	1957	5	1	1.0
1932	6	0	0	1958	32	8	1.3	1958	6	2	1.5
1933	7	2	0.3	1959	33	21	1.9	1959	7	6	3.6
1934	8	1	0.2	1960	34	12	1.4	1960	8	4	2.2
1935	9	1	0.2	1961	35	15	2.0	1961	9	6	2.6
1936	10	0	0	1962	36	14	—	1962	10	15	5.1
1937	11	5	0.8	1963	37	16	1.9	1963	11	14	3.7

12	1938	4	0.6
13	1939	0	0
14	1940	0	0
15	1941	7	1.3
16	1942	4[c]	0.8
17	1943	3	0.7
18	1944	4	1.0
19	1945	1	0.3
20	1946	2	0.4
21	1947	4	0.9
22	1948	1	0.2
23	1949	3	0.5
24	1950	1	0.2
25	1951	5	0.6
26	1952	2	0.3

Year		Entries	Per 1,000
1964	38	12	1.1
1965	39	21	1.3
1966	40	15	1.1
1967	41	32	1.9
1968	42	25	1.3
1969	43	8	0.4
1970	44	16	0.7
1971	45,46	53	2.3
1972	47,48	50	2.1
1973	49,50	89	3.6
1974	51,52	93	3.6
1975	53,54	119	4.7
1976	55,56	164	6.6
1977	57,58	203	7.5

Year		Entries	Per 1,000
1964	12	7	1.2
1965	13	5	1.2
1966	14	6	1.2
1967	15	9	1.6
1968	16	16	2.7
1969	17	7	1.2
1970	18	12	2.0
1971	19	16	2.5
1972	20	16	2.2
1973	21	0	0
1974	22	3	0.4
1975	23	17	2.2
1976	24	15	2.1
1977	25	49	5.9

[a] Also "Stereotypy" and "Stereotyped Attitudes." From 1974 to 1977 two headings were used for stereotype studies—"Stereotyped Attitudes" and "Stereotyped Behavior." For these years the entries in the table refer only to the former category.

[b] Entries per 1,000 for 1962 not computed because the total number of entries not known.

[c] There were actually five entries; one (Meenes, 1942) was an abstract for a paper presentation. The same data were reported in an article abstracted in Volume 17 (Meenes, 1943).

(1933), and Meltzer (1932). Inspection of these articles reveals three other relevant sources (Rice, 1926, 1928; Rice & Waller, 1928). All of these early investigations—except that by Meltzer (1932), which was concerned with "stereotypy" as a psychiatric or clinical phenomenon—shared a common conceptualization: If stereotypes are "pictures in the head" that shape perception of reality, then they must aid individuals in recognizing members of various social groups. And this shared conceptual approach gave rise to a common methodology: Photographs of individuals were presented to subjects who were asked to guess the occupations of the persons depicted. Evidence of stereotypes was of two types. First, stereotypes were assumed to exist if the perceivers were correct more often than would be expected on the basis of chance. Second, even when subjects were not accurate, their responses were said to be "stereotyped" when there were above-chance levels of agreement regarding the occupations of the pictured individuals.

While Lippmann introduced the concept to social scientists, it was Katz and Braly (1933) who conducted the classic empirical study of stereotypes. Princeton undergraduates were given a list of 84 trait adjectives (e.g., *brilliant, neat, physically dirty*) and asked to indicate those items that were "typical . . . characteristics" of each of 10 different ethnic groups. The stereotype of each group was operationally defined as the set of adjectives most frequently assigned to that group. For example, the stereotype of Turks included *cruel* (54%), *very religious* (30%), *treacherous* (24%), and *sensual* (23%). The adjective checklist procedure and the aggregate analysis introduced by Katz and Braly have served as the model for the majority of stereotype studies conducted since 1933.

Although not so explicitly, Katz and Braly (1933) had a significant impact on two other aspects of social scientific approaches to stereotypes. First, in discussing their results they noted the parallel between the stereotype of certain groups as revealed by the checklist procedure and: "the popular stereotype to be found in newspapers and magazines [p. 285]." This connection, plus the use of agreement or consensus to define stereotypes, suggests that stereotypes were considered to be, in large part, sociocultural or group-level phenomena.

Second, Katz and Braly linked stereotypes to attitudes and prejudice. The introduction to their article is concerned almost exclusively with attitudes and prejudice; the word "stereotype" occurs only once and even then does not refer to a set of beliefs about the characteristics of a particular group. The stereotype-prejudice connection was further developed in a second article entitled "Racial Prejudice and Racial Stereotypes" (Katz & Braly, 1935). This paper is concerned primarily with prejudice; stereotypes were analyzed only in terms of their implications for the evaluation of ethnic groups. In their final sentence, Katz and Braly (1935) virtually equated stereotypes and prejudice: "Racial prejudice is thus a generalized set of stereotypes of a high degree of consistency which includes emotional responses to race names, a belief in typical characteristics associated with race names, and evaluation of such traits [pp. 191–192]."

Allport (1935) further established the prejudice–stereotype link in his classic chapter on attitudes:

Attitudes and Prejudices or Stereotypes. Attitudes which result in gross over-simplification of experience and in prejudgments are of great importance in social psychology. . . . They are commonly called biases, prejudices, or stereotypes. The latter term is less normative, and therefore on the whole to be preferred [p. 809].

He also clearly articulated the view that stereotypes are bad. While this is implied in associating the term with prejudice, Allport specified some reasons why stereotypes might be regarded as bad. As is clear in the previous quote, he felt that stereotypes are oversimplified and thus to some extent incorrect. Further, stereotypes were considered to be rigid, and they were thought to impair perception and cognition.

The connection established between stereotypes and prejudice, in conjunction with the introduction of the adjective checklist, significantly altered the character of stereotype research in the years following the publication of Katz and Braly's (1933, 1935) articles. As indicated by Table 1.1, there was a small but steady stream of stereotype studies in the late 1930s and in the 1940s. Whereas some of these were concerned with stereotypy and stereotyped behavior as phenomena in clinical and experimental psychology, most dealt with stereotype as a social psychological construct. Unlike the earliest studies, however, racial, ethnic, and national groups were the major targets used in research. Verbal group labels (e.g., "Germans") replaced pictured individuals as stimuli and the adjective checklist became the major response format.

In 1950, Adorno, Frenkel-Brunswik, Levinson, and Sanford published *The Authoritarian Personality*. In this monumental two-volume work, they set forth a psychodynamic theory of prejudice. According to this theory, negative inter-group attitudes are rooted in a particular personality syndrome that is labeled the antidemocratic or authoritarian personality. One component of this syndrome is "stereotypy" or the tendency to think in terms of rigid, black-and-white categories. By implication, stereotypes are rigid beliefs about social groups. This certainly is not inconsistent with the position articulated by Allport. Adorno and his collaborators, however, provided an explanation for rigidity–prejudice and its attendant stereotypes fulfill a personality need.

The Authoritarian Personality generated a great deal of research (cf. Kirscht & Dillehay, 1967); however, it did not affect significantly either the amount or the nature of research on stereotypes. As can be seen in Table 1.1, the rate of stereotype publications remained relatively constant during the early and mid-1950s. The methods used to study stereotypes and the questions addressed in research also changed little. Indeed, Gilbert's (1951) well-known replication of the original Katz and Braly (1933) investigation at Princeton, published just one year after *The Authoritarian Personality,* typifies the stereotype research conducted at this time.

The rate of stereotype publications increased slightly in the late 1950s and remained relatively stable in the 1960s. This pattern is evident in both the *Psychological Abstracts* and in the *Sociological Abstracts,* which was first published in 1953 (see Table 1.1). Inspection of the empirical studies published during this period indicates that psychologists continued to concentrate on stereotypic conceptions of racial, ethnic, and national groups and to rely on the Katz and Braly adjective checklist. Sociologists studied the same targets and used the same checklist procedure popular in psychology; however, more emphasis was placed on social structural targets (e.g., social classes, occupations), and there was a greater tendency to study stereotypic images portrayed in the mass media (e.g., in newspapers and magazines). In both psychology and sociology, methodological critiques were rare. In 1965, Ehrlich and Rinehart criticized the adjective checklist technique. As with earlier critiques (e.g., Eysenck & Crown, 1948), however, this did little to alter the course of stereotype research.

Although there was little innovation in terms of the empirical investigation of stereotypes, a number of theoretical articles did appear in the literature. In psychology, Vinacke (1957), for example, argued that stereotypes should be regarded as cognitive structures no different from other concepts and proposed that principles derived from the study of cognition be applied to understanding stereotypes. In sociology, LaViolette and Silvert (1951) presented a conceptual critique of stereotype research, and Fishman (1956) suggested that the investigation of stereotypes be tied to the study of normal psychological and sociological phenomena such as language and communication.

Despite the appearance of these and other conceptual treatments of stereotypes, it was not until the end of the 1960s that a theoretical article significantly affected social scientific thinking and research regarding stereotypes. In a paper entitled, "Cognitive Aspects of Prejudice," Tajfel (1969) offered an alternative to the idea that stereotypes are derived from the deep-seated personality needs of prejudiced persons and presented the outline of a cognitive approach to understanding the social psychology of intergroup conflict: "the etiology of intergroup relations cannot be properly understood without the help of an analysis of their cognitive aspects, and . . . this analysis cannot be derived from statements about motivation and about instinctive behavior [p. 81]." In terms of their impact on the conduct of research, the ideas Tajfel presented in this and subsequent papers (e.g., Tajfel, 1970) appear to have had their strongest influence on the investigation of intergroup behavior, particularly intergroup discrimination (cf. Brewer, 1979, Wilder, in this volume). The effect of Tajfel's formulation on stereotype research per se has been, until very recently, more modest. Variants of the Katz and Braly procedure have continued to dominate the empirical study of stereotypes in the 1970s. It is perhaps ironic that, in addition to Tajfel's article, the year 1969 marked the publication of the second replication at Princeton of the original Katz and Braly study (Karlins, Coffman, & Walters, 1969).

By the end of the 1960s, the relatively stable rate of stereotype research had produced a considerable body of empirical findings. Much of the accumulated data were concerned with ethnic group stereotypes and two reviews of this literature were published in 1971 (Brigham, 1971; Cauthen et al. 1971). In addition to summarizing the available evidence, both reviews sharply criticized the existing state of research and theory concerning ethnic stereotypes. Like other critiques before them, however, these reviews had little effect on the actual conduct of stereotype research.

With the 1970s came a large increase in the absolute number and rate of abstracts dealing with stereotypes. In the 1960s, a yearly average of 1.4 per 1,000 entries in the *Psychological Abstracts* dealt with stereotypes; by 1977 this rate had jumped to 7.5 abstracts per 1,000. The parallel rates for the *Sociological Abstracts* were 2.3 and 5.9, respectively (see Table 1.1). This increase in stereotype research in the 1970s is almost completely attributable to investigations of how women and men are perceived. In 1968 only one sex stereotype study appeared in the *Psychological Abstracts;* a decade later in 1977, 159 abstracts, fully 78% of the entries under ''Stereotyped Attitudes'' concerned beliefs about the personal attributes of women and men. By 1977, 45% of the stereotype entries in the *Sociological Abstracts* dealt with sex.

The single sex stereotype article to be abstracted in the 1968 *Psychological Abstracts* was an important one. In this article Rosenkrantz, Vogel, Bee, Broverman, and Broverman (1968) reported the development of an instrument for assessing sex-role stereotypes. This Sex-Role Questionnaire (SRQ) consists of bipolar adjective scales (e.g., *aggressive–not at all aggressive*). Respondents are asked to indicate where the average adult female and average adult male would fall on each scale. The use of bipolar rating scales in the SRQ represented a refinement of the traditional adjective checklist method of assessing stereotypes. Rather than simply indicating whether a given group did or did not possess a particular personal quality, respondents rated the *degree* to which each attribute characterized each sex. Sex stereotypic attributes were operationally defined as those items for which a clear majority of subjects (75%) rated one particular sex more highly than the other. Thus, female and male stereotypes were defined in terms of consensual beliefs regarding perceived sex differences in personality. The SRQ has been used in a large number of studies, and the conclusions reached by the originators of this technique (Broverman, Vogel, Broverman, Clarkson, and Rosenkrantz, 1972) have become the ''conventional wisdom'' regarding sex stereotypes.

The preceding historical review suggests four major conclusions about the efforts of social scientists to understand stereotypes. First, stereotypes are not the province of any single academic discipline or subdiscipline; rather, the terms

"stereotype," "stereotyped," and "stereotyping" have appeared in the literatures of clinical, experimental, and social psychology as well as in sociological
writings. This review has been most concerned with stereotype as a social
psychological construct, and the remainder of this chapter is concerned solely
with stereotypes about social groups. Here it is important to note, however, the
difference between stereotype as a concept in clinical and experimental psychology and the social psychological usage of the term. As indicated previously,
psychiatrists and clinical psychologists prefer the word "stereotypy," which
they employ to describe behavior that is fixed in form or emitted repeatedly.
Although a variety of meanings of stereotypy appear in experimental psychology, it is most commonly used, according to Schroeder (1970): "to refer to
invariant repetition of a fixed response or response chain [p. 340]." Both the
clinical and experimental usages, then, seem to center on *behavior,* whereas in
social psychology stereotypes are associated with *attitudes.* This distinction is
clear in the *Psychological Abstracts,* where in recent years there have been two
separate headings, "Stereotyped Behaviors" and "Stereotyped Attitudes."

Second, from Katz and Braly (1933) to the most recent investigations of
beliefs about women and men, stereotypes have been treated in conjunction with
prejudice. Researchers of widely varying conceptual orientations agree that there
is an association between stereotypes and prejudice. Katz and Braly (1933), who
represent a sociocultural position, Adorno et al. (1950), who epitomize the
psychodynamic orientation, and Tajfel (1969), who exemplifies the cognitive
perspective, would all agree that stereotypes are related to prejudice and are
important ingredients in understanding intergroup relations.[2] It should be noted
that contemporary social scientists do not equate stereotypes and prejudice as did
many researchers in the late 1930s and early 1940s. Rather, stereotypes are
generally regarded as equivalent to or part of the cognitive component of intergroup attitudes (cf. Allport, 1958, chapter 12; Ehrlich, 1973, chapter 2; Harding,
Proshansky, Kutner, & Chein, 1969, p. 4; McGuire, 1969, p. 155).

The linking of stereotypes to prejudice has clearly influenced stereotype research and theory. Prejudice is regarded as a "social problem" (cf. Rose, 1970,
p. 571; Harding et al., 1969, pp. 1–2). It is bad to be "prejudiced," and, by
implication, it is bad to hold stereotypes. As a consequence of this view,
stereotypes have been treated as "special," at times even bizarre or pathological
phenomena, and work on stereotypes has proceeded in isolation from basic
research and theory in psychology and sociology. (The stereotypes-as-bad theme
is explored more fully later.)

Third, stereotypes of a wide variety of social groups have been studied—
adolescents and the aged, heroes and criminals, college men and congressmen,
beautiful people and those with various types of stigmata. Most work, however,

---

[2]This assumption has persisted even though there is scant empirical evidence that prejudice and
stereotyping are correlated (Brigham, 1971, pp. 26–28; Jones, 1977, pp. 61–62).

has been concerned either with racial–ethnic–national groups or with females and males. In part, this emphasis can be traced back to the social-problem view: Racism and sexism are widely regarded as significant social problems. Ethnic group studies predominated until recently, but sex stereotype research has far outstripped work on other targets in the 1970s.

The final conclusion to be drawn from the foregoing historical analysis is perhaps the most important: Past attempts to understand stereotypes have been shaped more by methodological factors than by conceptual analysis. The overwhelming majority of publications concerned with stereotypes have been descriptive, (i.e., "*x* group of perceivers holds the following beliefs about the characteristics of group *y*"). And, most of the descriptive studies have used the Katz and Braly (1933) adjective checklist procedure. As Harding and his colleagues (1969) put it, this methodology: "has completely dominated the field since its introduction [p. 7]." The accumulation of descriptive studies has occurred in the absence of consensus among researchers about a number of important conceptual questions regarding stereotypes.[3]

Five decades ago Rice and Waller (1928) concluded their article on stereotypes with the following paragraph:

> A number of questions concerning stereotypes seem worth mentioning. Of whom do we have stereotypes? How are they formed? Do they disappear upon intimate acquaintance with members of a particular group? How do they enter into the formulation of political attitudes? Are stereotypes really representative of social types? Do we have stereotypes of pictures, or of roles? Photographic, or dramatic, stereotypes? What is the relation of pictorial stereotypes to stereotyped ideas [p. 185]?

Twenty-three years later LaViolette and Silvert (1951) concluded that: "it appears that the attributes of stereotypes have not been examined critically by social psychologists. In fact we may call their characteristics 'claims' rather than established attributes [p. 260]." And, in 1971 Brigham began his review of the ethnic stereotype literature by noting that stereotype researchers seldom considered such important conceptual questions as: What is a stereotype? What is the function of stereotypes?

Why has stereotype research been so little affected by the conceptual–theoretical treatments?[4] Kuhn's (1962, 1970, 1977) analysis of scientific progress suggests an answer. According to Kuhn (1970), scientists are members of

---

[3]The extant literature is also suspect on more strictly methodological grounds (Brigham, 1971, pp. 24–25).

[4]In addition to the works noted in the preceding review, theoretical discussions of stereotypes have been presented by the following authors: Allport, 1958, Chapters 10–13; Asch, 1952; Brown, 1965; Campbell, 1967; Ehrlich, 1973, Chapter 2; Gardner, 1973; Gardner, Kirby, & Finlay, 1973; Gordon, 1962; Jones, 1977; Kretch & Crutchfield, 1948; Mackie, 1973.

"scientific communities" that comprise: "the practitioners of a scientific specialty . . . (who) have undergone similar educations and professional initiations [p. 177]." Members of a scientific community share a "disciplinary matrix." Of the many components of a particular disciplinary matrix, three "are central to the cognitive operation of the group [1977, p. 297]": *symbolic generalizations, models,* and *exemplars.* Symbolic generalizations are logical expressions such as $E = mc^2$, whereas models denote the metaphors preferred by practitioners of a specialty (e.g., the notion of "Economic Man"). Exemplars are "concrete problems with their solutions [1977, p. 306]." They are the specific instances of basic research methods that students of a particular discipline are taught. As Kuhn notes, exemplars imply a great deal about the phenomenon being studied and play a significant role in defining the "puzzles" that scientists attempt to solve. In fact, the power of examplars is that they serve as substitutes for explicit rules specifying how research should be conducted. It is our belief that the Katz and Braly (1933) adjective checklist technique is the exemplar for stereotype researchers. In the next section we discuss how this exemplar has shaped the definition of stereotypes. At this point the question is: Why has the checklist been such a successful exemplar? There appear to be several contributing factors: (1) The adjective checklist is easy to administer and score. (2) It can be extended almost indefinitely (e.g., the stereotype of any target can be assessed) and poses many puzzles (e.g., do stereotypes change over time?). (3) Although the checklist (as most often used) does commit one to defining stereotypes in terms of agreement across respondents, it is neutral on other points of contention regarding stereotypes.

In summary, there is considerable agreement that stereotypes are important, and a good deal of research has been directed at stereotypes. Unfortunately, Brigham's (1971) assessment of the ethnic stereotype literature is equally valid for stereotype research more generally: "In spite of the volume of research on ethnic stereotypes that has been carried out for the last 40 years, there seem to be relatively few 'advances in knowledge' that have been made about stereotypes and stereotyping [p. 29]." One step toward making progress is the recognition that the Katz and Braly procedure constrains research. A second step is to make explicit some of the conceptual questions that this exemplar has obscured. Two such questions are: What is a stereotype? How should stereotypes be studied? These questions are addressed in the next two sections of the paper.

WHAT IS A STEREOTYPE?

The most central conceptual question confronting stereotype researchers concerns definition: What is a stereotype? While agreeing on most of the defining features of stereotypes, investigators have exhibited some important differences in the way in which they have defined their major construct. The primary goal of this section is to make explicit both areas of agreement and of disagreement. A second goal is to demonstrate that current differences of opinion regarding the meaning of the term "stereotype" can be reformulated as questions for empirical research and that such reformulation offers promising possibilities for furthering our understanding of stereotypes and intergroup behavior.

As indicated in the foregoing, the most commonly studied stereotype targets have been ethnic–racial–national groups and, more recently, women and men. In order to determine how stereotype researchers have defined their central construct, we inspected the two bodies of research that deal with these targets. Brigham's (1971) review represents the most comprehensive survey of the ethnic stereotype literature to date.[5] On the basis of Brigham's (1971) discussion of the "Meaning of 'Stereotype' in Psychology [pp. 17–19]," Table 1.2 was constructed. Table 1.2 clearly indicates one major disagreement about how the concept "stereotype" should be defined. Approximately one half of the authors listed in Table 1.2 (see the last four columns) consider a stereotype to be bad by definition, while the remainder (see the first two columns) do not include this value judgment in their specification of the term's meaning. Although somewhat less dramatically, Table 1.2 illustrates one point on which there is virtually unanimous agreement: An ethnic stereotype is a cognitive construct. As the sample definitions in Table 1.2 indicate, an ethnic stereotype is a generalization about or an impression of an ethnic group. More specifically, there is agreement that an ethnic stereotype is a set of beliefs about the personal attributes of the members of a particular social category. (While some authors [e.g., Brigham, 1971] use "stereotype" to refer to the attribution of a single trait to a group, most researchers consider the term to denote the full set of attributes associated with a particular target.) Although seldom included in conceptual definitions (and thus not to be seen in Table 1.2), most stereotype measures include only personality traits (e.g., *dirty, kind, aggressive*). In practice, then, the content of stereotypes as personal attributes has been restricted to trait adjectives. In sum, researchers disagree about whether a stereotype is by definition bad, but they agree that an ethnic stereotype is a set of cognitions that specify the personal qualities (especially personality traits) of members of an ethnic group.

How have investigators interested in the topic of sex stereotypes defined their major concept? In a recent review of this literature (Ashmore & Del Boca, 1979), we found that there was not much concern with the issue of definition. However, when researchers have defined "sex stereotype," there has been considerable agreement about the meaning of the term. The definition offered by Rosenkrantz et al. (1968), originators of the aforementioned Sex-Role Questionnaire is quite typical of those that appear in this literature: "The existence of sex-role stereotypes, that is, consensual beliefs about the differing characteristics of men

---

[5]Cauthen et al. (1971), who reviewed the same literature, focused primarily on the conclusions that could be drawn from the empirical research on ethnic stereotypes.

TABLE 1.2.
A Taxonomy of Psychological Meanings of the Construct "Stereotype" Derived from Brigham's (1971) Analysis

Stereotype Not Defined as Bad, rather it is . . .		Stereotype Defined as a Bad Generalization/Category/Concept, Because it is . . .			
Generalization[a]	Category/Concept[b]	Incorrectly Learned[c]	Overgeneralized	Factually Incorrect	Rigid
"Stereotyping may be defined as the tendency to attribute generalized and simplified characteristics to groups of people in the form of verbal labels, and to act towards the members of those groups in terms of those labels [Vinacke, 1949, p. 265]."	"A stereotype is commonly thought of as involving a categorical response, i.e., membership is sufficient to evoke the judgment that the stimulus person possesses all the attributes belonging to that category [Secord, 1959, p. 309]."	"Unlike other generalizations . . . *stereotypes are based not on an inductive collection of data, but on hearsay, rumor, and anecdotes*—in short, on evidence which is insufficient to justify the generalization [Klineberg, 1951, p. 505; quoted by Brigham, 1971, p. 18]."	". . . *a stereotype is an exaggerated belief associated with a category* [Allport, 1958, p. 187]."	"A stereotype is a fixed impression, which conforms very little to the fact it pretends to represent, and results from our defining first and observing second [Katz & Braly, 1935, p. 181]."	"stereotypy . . . the disposition to think in rigid categories [Adorno, et al., 1950, p. 228]."

Abate & Berrien, 1967	Harding et al., 1954	Lippman, 1922	Schoenfield, 1942	Lippman, 1922	Kerr, 1943
Blake & Dennis, 1943	Sanford, 1956	Sanford, 1956	Zawadski, 1948	Prothro & Melikian, 1954	Meenes, 1943
Brown, 1958, 1965[a]	Saenger & Flowerman, 1954	Zawadski, 1948	Bogardus, 1950	Klineberg, 1951	Bogardus, 1950
Child & Doob, 1943	Simpson & Yinger, 1965	Bogardus, 1950	Wedge, 1966		Sanford, 1956
Diab, 1962, 1963[a]	Vinacke, 1957	Fishman, 1956	Krech, Crutchfield, & Ballachey, 1962		Simpson & Yinger, 1965
Edward, 1940			Gilbert, 1951		Katz & Braly, 1935
Sherif & Sherif, 1969			Campbell, 1967		Katz & Stotland, 1959
Sinha & Upadhyay, 1960[a]			Rokeach, 1968		Sinha & Upadhyay, 1960
Fishman, 1956[d]					Rokeach, 1960
Mann, 1967a & 1967b[d]					Scott, 1965
Schumann, 1966[d]					
Vinacke, 1956[d]					
Mead, 1956[d]					

Note. The full reference for the above works can be found in Brigham (1971).

[a] *"Generalization of unspecified validity* ... In this view any generalization is a stereotype [Brigham, 1971, p. 17]."

[b] *"Categorizations and concepts* ... Some writers speak of stereotypes as the use (or misuse) of categories [Brigham, 1971, p. 18]."

[c] Stereotypes as "Products of a 'faulty' thought process. [Brigham, 1971, p. 18]."

[d] These authors "do not consider validity irrelevant, but recognize that classing stereotypes as *overgeneralizations* implies the existence of a criterion of validity.... (but) such a criterion has seldom been available [Brigham, 1971, p. 18]."

and women in our society [p. 287]." According to these definitions, sex stereotypes, like ethnic stereotypes, comprise sets of beliefs about the characteristics of social groups. In addition, however, researchers have usually restricted the content of these sets of beliefs in two ways: (1) sex stereotypes are limited to beliefs about women and men that are widely shared; and (2) sex stereotypes include only those attributes that are thought to differentiate women from men.

Despite the differences that exist within and between the sex and ethnic stereotype literatures, then, there is agreement among researchers that stereotypes are cognitive structures that comprise the perceived or assumed characteristics of social groups. Thus, we propose the following as the core meaning of the term "stereotype": *A set of beliefs about the personal attributes of a group of people.* It is important to note that we are not proposing a single *best* conceptual definition of the stereotype construct; rather, we are attempting to state explicitly the essential defining features of the term *as it has been used by social scientists.*

What differences of opinion does this core definition obscure? As Table 1.2 clearly indicates, there is considerable disagreement in the ethnic stereotype literature about whether stereotypes are by definition bad. Inspection of the sex stereotype literature raises two additional questions. Should the term stereotype apply to the beliefs that an *individual* holds about a particular group, or should the term be reserved for beliefs that are *consensual* or culturally shared? Are stereotypes best conceptualized as those traits thought to be *characteristic* of a particular social group, or as those attributes that are believed to *differentiate* a target group from other groups (e.g., "Russians are aggressive; we are peace loving.")?

Stereotypes have been defined as "bad" for one or a combination of the following reasons: A stereotype is a set of beliefs that is incorrectly learned, overgeneralized, factually incorrect, or rigid (see Table 1.2). While stereotypes may well have any or all of these characteristics, the proposed sources of "badness" should not be incorporated into the definition of the term "stereotype" for three reasons. First, it is not parsimonious to add this value judgment to the substantive specification of what a stereotype is. Although parsimony should not be the only value to be optimized in defining scientific terms, in the present case there is little to be gained and much to be lost by making badness a point of definition (for dissenting views see Asch, 1952; Brigham, 1971).

Second, and more importantly, defining stereotypes as bad leads to the inference that stereotypes and stereotyping refer to cognitive structures and processes that are deviant, bizarre, or pathological. This view—like the tendency to associate stereotypes with prejudice previously discussed—serves to isolate stereotype research from areas of psychology and sociology that deal with the "normal" processes involved in the perception of individuals and groups (e.g., person perception, social stratification). The stereotype researcher assumes that "basic" research and theory are irrelevant to her or his interests. If stereotypes are bad by definition, there is little reason to assess the extent to which they are similar to or different from other cognitive and interpersonal phenomena. There may well be something "special" or "different" about beliefs regarding social groups; however, this is best regarded as an empirical, rather than a conceptual, issue. The third argument against defining stereotypes as bad is closely related to the second. The stereotypes-as-bad notion has not only cut off stereotype research from possibly relevant "basic" research and theory, it has also led researchers to assume rather than study the alleged reasons for badness. This can be seen by briefly reviewing the evidence concerning each of these reasons.

Are stereotypes incorrectly learned? Unfortunately, no sure answer can be given since this question has been seldom studied. There has been little research directed at understanding how children acquire sex stereotypes (cf. Del Boca & Ashmore, 1980), and the same is true regarding ethnic stereotypes (cf. Brigham, 1971; Cauthen et al., 1971). Cauthen and his colleagues make this point quite dramatically: "Only one study sheds light on the learning of stereotypes [p. 107]." Other relevant studies have appeared in the 1970s, but even these do not assess directly the process of stereotype acquisition.[6] As is discussed more fully in the section on the sociocultural orientation to the study of stereotypes, a great deal of work has been done to document the "stereotyped content" of the mass media, but little attention has been paid to the question of how this content influences the beliefs of individuals. Generally, it is assumed that people simply absorb the stereotypic portrayals. Although it is likely that people do learn from the media, how this process occurs seems an important question for research. Taking this perspective generates more specific questions. Two examples: Are there individual and subgroup differences in learning stereotypes from the media? With regard to television, does the type of program (particularly "entertainment" versus "documentary" versus "news") affect stereotype acquisition?

The hypotheses that stereotypes are overgeneralized or completely invalid also have not been tested. LaPiere (1936) is often cited as evidence that stereotypes are inaccurate. Although the publication does point out discrepancies between perceptions of Armenians and the actual behaviors of members of this group, a fuller report of this research (LaPiere, 1930) indicates that the stereotype of Armenians was accurate regarding several traits (Mackie, 1973). While other instances of stereotype accuracy can be cited (e.g., Mackie, 1973, pp. 434–435), Brigham (1971) is correct in stating that: "with reference to the actual distribution of traits within ethnic groups, empirical evidence is exceedingly scan-

---

[6]It is important to note that even if evidence were available on how people acquire stereotypes, the "incorrect learning" view requires some standard for differentiating correct from incorrect learning. Although social scientists could develop a rule or standard for identifying "incorrect learning," we believe that more is to be gained by focusing research attention directly on the stereotype acquisition process itself.

ty. . . . Thus, in most cases, no criteria are available for assessing the factual validity of an ethnic generalization [p. 17]."

Although there is certainly a great deal of research directed at measuring sex differences, it is quite difficult to use this literature to test the validity of sex stereotypes. In a widely cited book, Maccoby and Jacklin (1974) conclude that sex differences "are fairly well established" for only four variables: (1) visual–spatial ability; (2) mathematical ability; (3) verbal ability; and (4) aggressive behavior. In her critique of the Maccoby and Jacklin book, Block (1976) discusses data suggesting that females and males differ significantly on several other psychological variables. While Block's argument is more convincing than that put forth by Maccoby and Jacklin, the sex-differences literature is not useful as a criterion for evaluating the validity of sex stereotypes. The findings are not stable, and interactions, not sex main effects, are the rule. Further, it is not clear exactly how mean differences between the sexes can be used to test the truth or falsity of sex stereotypes. What level of statistical significance is required to establish a "real" sex difference? Does the existence of an interaction (e.g., age × sex) invalidate a significant sex main effect?

As with their other alleged evils, there is at present little evidence regarding the rigidity of stereotypes. The etymology of the word implies that a stereotype must be "fixed" or "rigid," but just what this means for stereotypes as social psychological phenomena has been a matter of some confusion. The term, "rigidity" has, in fact, been given two related but distinct meanings in discussions of stereotypes (cf. Fishman, 1956; LaViolette & Silvert, 1951). First, stereotypes have been regarded as rigid because they are believed to be persistent over time. Researchers note, for example, the stability of stereotypes across three successive generations of Princeton college students (Gilbert, 1951; Karlins et al., 1969; Katz & Braly, 1933). In these terms, rigidity is less a psychological (individual-level) than a sociological (group-level) aspect of beliefs regarding social groups. Fishman (1956) and, more recently, Brigham (1971) have argued that stereotypes are rigid in terms of persistence only if they remain unchanged in the face of actual changes in the groups in question or in the nature of the interaction between them. This type of temporal stability has not, however, been observed. Rather, stereotypes appear to be related to intergroup relations, and, as Fishman (1956) has stated: "The former are only as rigid as the latter, and since the latter may or may not be rigid, this must also be the case with respect to the former [p. 38]."

Second, rigidity has also denoted a psychological quality of the individual perceiver. Many of those who define stereotype rigidity in this way come from a psychoanalytic tradition. As will be discussed more fully later, these writers speak of "stereotypy"; in these terms, rigidity implies both an undifferentiated view of social groups and a set of beliefs that is impervious to new information. Rigidity is not so much an attribute of stereotypes as a characteristic of the person who holds the stereotype. In their attempts to understand rigidity of thinking as an individual difference or personality variable, psychologists have developed a myriad of concepts (e.g., intolerance for ambiguity) and measuring devices (e.g., the Water Jar test). Numerous studies have been conducted in an effort to demonstrate an empirical relationship between this style of thought and prejudice (cf. Ehrlich, 1973; Kirscht & Dillehay, 1967). Little attention, however, has been directed at assessing the relationship between rigidity of thinking and the nature of beliefs the individual holds about social groups (see, however, Gordon, 1962).

The second difference of opinion concerning how best to define the term "stereotype" centers on the issue of consensus. There is general agreement among those interested in perceptions of the sexes that stereotypes are shared beliefs. This idea is not restricted to the sex stereotype literature. (It was not apparent in the aforementioned review of the ethnic stereotype literature because we followed Brigham, who was only concerned with stereotype as a psychological concept.) Regardless of the target, most sociologists view a stereotype as: "*those folk beliefs about the attributes characterizing a social category on which there is substantial agreement* [Mackie, 1973, (p. 435)]." Should the term stereotype be applied only to those beliefs about social groups that are widely shared?

Elsewhere (Ashmore & Del Boca, 1979) we have argued that the term "stereotype" should be reserved for the set of beliefs held by an individual regarding a social group and that the term "cultural stereotype" should be used to describe shared or community-wide patterns of beliefs. (Others [e.g., Gordon, 1962; Karlins et al., 1969; Kretch & Crutchfield, 1948; Secord & Backman, 1964] have made similar proposals.) Here we wish only to make two points regarding the issue of consensus. First, consensus has become part of the conceptual definition of stereotype in large part because of the manner in which the construct is most often operationalized and not from theoretical analysis.[7] That is, the Katz and Braly technique, which is the exemplar for stereotype research, implicitly builds consensus into the meaning of the term. While it is true that techniques for assessing individual belief systems are not widely available, it seems unwise to tailor conceptual definitions to fit convenient, often used methods. Second, two different concepts have been referred to as "stereotypes," and it is essential that these concepts be distinguished. Distinguishing "stereotype" from "cultural stereotype" facilitates communication and raises significant questions for research (e.g., Are there differences in the degree to which individuals adopt cultural stereotypes?).

The final area of disagreement regarding the meaning of the term "stereotype" concerns the question: Are stereotypes best conceptualized as beliefs regarding the personal attributes that serve to *differentiate* a particular group

---

[7]Gardner et al. (1970) concede that this is true but argue that there are good theoretical reasons for defining stereotypes as consensual beliefs. (See also Gardner, 1973; Gardner et al., 1973.)

from other groups? As noted earlier, sex stereotypes typically have been defined in terms of assumed or perceived sex differences. Ethnic stereotypes, on the other hand, generally have been defined, both conceptually and operationally, in terms of the characteristics that are most frequently ascribed to a target group. Recently, however, McCauley, Stitt, and Segal (1980) have proposed that all stereotypes be regarded as: "generalizations about a class of people that distinguish that class from others [p. 197]."

Some investigators (Pleck, 1977; Sherriffs & McKee, 1957) have argued that this approach may lead to the inclusion in the stereotype of attributes that, although differentiating among groups, actually are ascribed to a particular group rather infrequently. Similarly, traits that are attributed with a high degree of frequency, but fail to distinguish among groups, may be excluded from the stereotype. This problem need not be restricted to beliefs about social groups that are widely shared (i.e., what are here termed cultural stereotypes); a parallel argument can be made at the level of the individual perceiver. For example, a particular trait may be thought to occur in each of two groups rather infrequently and, at the same time, be seen as more likely in one group than in the other (e.g., 20% of Group A are thought to possess a particular quality whereas only 5% of Group B are believed to have the same trait).

In our view, the degree of association between a particular trait and a social group should not be the sole determinant of whether that trait is included in an individual or a cultural stereotype. Differentiating traits, even if they tend to be ascribed with a relatively low degree of frequency, should be regarded as elements of a stereotype. Indeed, it seems likely that such traits are functionally important in terms of both individual and cultural stereotypes. If stereotypes are used to anticipate the behavior of others in social interaction, it seems probable that, for the individual perceiver, differentiating traits maximize a stereotype's predictive utility. With regard to cultural stereotypes, traits that are thought to discriminate various categories of people are probably related to positions these groups occupy in society.

Stereotypes should not, however, be restricted to trait elements that are assumed to distinguish various groups, for two reasons. First, it is likely that those attributes that are thought to differentiate a target group from other groups constitute a relatively small proportion of the traits that actually make up the individual's "picture in the head" for, or the cultural stereotype of, that group. Further, it is likely that the meaning of nondifferentiating traits varies as a function of the complete set of beliefs about a social group. For example, Saenger and Flowerman (1954) found that both Jews and Americans were judged to be *aggressive* but that: "The gestalt 'Jewish aggressiveness' differs from the gestalt 'American aggressiveness' [p. 223]."

Second, defining stereotypes in terms of perceived differences between groups requires the specification of a particular comparison group for each stereotype, a task that is neither simple nor straightforward. McCauley and his associates (McCauley et al., 1980) have dealt with this problem by assuming that individuals use "humans in general" as a baseline for evaluating the characteristics of social groups. It is certainly likely that perceivers possess beliefs about "humans in general," and such beliefs may influence the ascription of traits to social groups. It is unlikely, however, that "humans in general" is the sole, or even primary, "contrast category" for beliefs about specific groups. McCauley and his colleagues acknowledge that "for stereotypes that exist in mirror-image pairs . . . it is convenient to focus on how the two mirror-image groups differ from each other rather than focusing on how each group differs from all the world's people" (p. 199). While some of the mirror-image pairs offered by McCauley et al. seem clear (e.g., "female" vs. "male"), these authors do not specify any rules for identifying "mirror-image pairs" nor for predicting when a perceiver will base his or her stereotype (as differentiating attributes) of a particular group on a comparison with "humans in general" or with some specific group of humans. Two important questions for research would seem to be: What are the contrast categories for various stereotypes? What factors determine which of several possible contrast categories is employed by a perceiver?

This review of definitional issues suggests three conclusions regarding the meaning of "stereotype" as a social psychological construct. First, there is agreement that a stereotype is a set of beliefs about the personal attributes of a social group. Second, personal attributes are most often operationally defined as personality trait adjectives. Although traits are an important part of how adults "think about" people and groups (cf. Goldberg, 1978), they are certainly not the only elements of the "pictures in our heads" concerning social categories. Several additional types of personal attributes seem worthy of attention. Elsewhere we (Ashmore & Del Boca, 1979) have argued that stereotype elements can be divided into two broad classes—identifying and ascribed. Identifying attributes are the cues that a perceiver uses to identify a person as an instance of a particular social category (e.g., dark skin and kinky hair for the social category, "Negro" or "Black"). Contemporary stereotype researchers seldom assess identifying attributes even though the earliest empirical stereotype investigations (e.g., Rice, 1926) were concerned with identification. With respect to ascribed attributes, researchers need not be restricted to trait adjectives. "Pictures in the head" regarding social groups are also likely to include feelings aroused by the group and its members as well as expected patterns of behavior (cf. Ashmore & Del Boca, 1979).

The final conclusion concerns differences of opinion—there is considerable disagreement among researchers about: (1) whether or not stereotypes are bad by definition; (2) whether stereotypes are individual or consensual sets of beliefs; and (3) whether stereotypes include characteristic or differentiating personal attributes. These disagreements, however, need not hinder progress in understanding stereotypes and intergroup relations. If, as has been suggested above, these issues are treated as questions for research, they can, in fact, facilitate social scientific approaches to stereotypes.

ORIENTATIONS TO THE STUDY OF STEREOTYPES

How should stereotypes be studied and a theory of stereotyping be developed? Since the Katz and Braly (1933) adjective checklist procedure has been the primary tool for conducting stereotype research, it is tempting to conclude that stereotypes should be studied by means of self-report measures designed to assess agreement concerning what are thought to be the typical or characteristic traits of social groups. However, the preceding discussion of history and definitions suggests that social scientists are far from unanimous in their views about how best to develop a theoretical framework for and conduct research on stereotypes. Although these differences of opinion can be variously grouped, three basic orientations can be identified—sociocultural, psychodynamic, and cognitive.

This section is devoted to a discussion of each of these perspectives. The primary goal is to describe further the context of the cognitive orientation that is presented in the remaining chapters of this volume. A secondary aim is to make each of the three positions as explicit as possible. In the words of Shaw and Costanzo (1970): these are "general approach(es) to the analysis and interpretation of behavior [p. 8]." They are not "theories"; rather, they are frames of reference that guide, often quite implicitly, the conduct of research. The explication of these perspectives will be facilitated by returning to Kuhn's (1962, 1970, 1977) framework for describing the "doing" of science. As noted previously, members of a scientific community share a disciplinary matrix that has three primary components: symbolic generalizations, exemplars, and models. Symbolic generalizations are rare in social psychology and thus will be of no help in understanding the three orientations to the study of stereotypes. As noted earlier, an exemplar is a particular method of data gathering, analysis, and interpretation. While the Katz and Braly (1933) adjective checklist has been the dominant exemplar for stereotype researchers, the three orientations differ in their reliance on this technique and in terms of their use of other methods.

The final component of a disciplinary matrix is the set of beliefs Kuhn (1970) labels "models." These beliefs: "supply the group (of researchers) with preferred or permissible analogies and metaphors [p. 184]." The sociocultural, psychodynamic, and cognitive orientations are characterized by quite different underlying models. Since these models have seldom been made explicit, they are best described as tacit assumptions. Two related sets of assumptions can be identified and phrased in terms of questions: (1) What is the *nature* of individual human beings and of human society? (2) What *functions* do stereotypes serve at both an individual and societal level? These two questions will be used to structure discussion of the three points of view that have characterized stereotype research.

The Sociocultural Orientation

The roots of the sociocultural position can be traced to Lippmann's (1922) observation that many stereotypes are provided by one's culture. Though not explicitly, Katz and Braly (1933) established the foundation for the sociocultural orientation by building consensus into the operational definition of stereotype. Again quite implicitly, Katz and Braly (1935) further developed this position by linking stereotypes with *patterns* of prejudice that are relatively consistent across time and region of the country. Such consistency is assumed to derive from culture. The recent upswing in sex stereotype research involves an almost total, though generally implicit, commitment to a sociocultural perspective—sex stereotypes are assumed to be part of the same cultural pattern that specifies sex roles and sex-role standards.

While the sociocultural orientation has never been fully articulated (see, however, Fishman (1956) and Gardner, Rodensky, & Kirby (1970) for partial expositions), it is instructive to make it explicit. Society is the focus of attention for those taking this perspective: Stereotypes (here, cultural stereotypes) are part of a society's nonmaterial culture. At the individual level, the preferred metaphor is "man (or woman) the good citizen." Individuals are socialized into a particular culture, and, through social rewards and punishments, led to act in accordance with cultural dictates. Further, by accepting cultural stereotypes, individuals reinforce and thereby help to perpetuate the existing cultural pattern.

What models underlie this orientation? With regard to the assumed nature of society, two forms of the sociocultural viewpoint can be identified. The first is built around a Parsonian structuralist–functionalist conception of society. Society is characterized by consensus, and individual conduct is determined by "institutionalized patterns." The second form, generally labeled the "conflict perspective" (cf. Bowker & Carrier, 1976), rests on a quite different view: Society comprises groups with different values and interests and these groups are in competition with one another. As Wrong (1976) has so clearly shown, both structuralism–functionalism and many variants of the conflict perspective involve the same two assumptions regarding human nature: Humans internalize social values and norms and are largely motivated to seek social approval by conforming to these values and norms. These two forms of the sociocultural position differ in this respect only in terms of what values and norms are internalized and acted upon. In the structuralist–functionalist view, a single cultural pattern is accepted throughout a society. Conflict theorists, on the other hand, assume that individuals incorporate the belief system of their particular sub-group. (Some conflict theorists, however, maintain that individuals play an active role in "the social construction of reality [cf. Wrong, 1976, pp. 51–52].)

What functions are stereotypes assumed to serve by those who accept the sociocultural orientation? At both the individual and societal level, the sociocultural approach assumes that stereotypes serve utilitarian and value-expressive functions (cf. Katz, 1960, 1968). For society, the structuralist–functionalist view is that stereotypes specify the nature of various social groups, both within and outside the society, and thus support norms about how these groups and individual group members are expected to behave and how they should be treated. For example, the cultural stereotype of "used-car salesmen" specifies that they are *aggressive* and *shady;* hence, they are expected to try to "put one over" on customers and are generally not held in high esteem. The conflict perspective holds that stereotypes justify or rationalize existing patterns of intergroup relations. For example, the belief that the poor are *lazy* and *incompetent* legitimizes existing differences in economic well-being and helps the nonpoor to justify resistance to public policies that are designed to alter the economic status quo (cf. Ashmore & McConahay, 1975, Chapter 3). At the societal level, stereotypes also serve a value-expressive function (e.g., negative images about the mentally retarded reinforce cultural values concerning intelligence and self-reliance). For the individual, expressing stereotyped beliefs is an affirmation of part of a system of beliefs that one accepts as one's own. And, by expressing these shared views the individual gains social acceptance.

What kind of research is fostered by the sociocultural perspective? The most frequent type of study is a simple demonstration that a set of perceivers agree about the characteristics of some target group or groups. This emphasis is clear in our own review of the sex stereotype literature (Del Boca & Ashmore, 1980). It is probably even more true of research on ethnic stereotypes. As Brigham (1971) has stated with regard to this literature: "A voluminous amount of research effort has been directed toward the assessment of stereotypes. . . . Most researchers have used the Katz and Braly experimental framework in toto [p. 20]."

Far less frequently, there are attempts to demonstrate that similar stereotypes are held by people of varying demographic characteristics. For example. the first conclusion stated by Broverman and her colleagues (1972) regarding their program of sex stereotype research is: "A strong consensus about the differing characteristics of men and women exists across groups which differ in sex, age, religion, marital status, and educational level [p. 61]." Implicitly these investigators have adopted the structuralist–functionalist form of the sociocultural orientation. Consistent with this approach is research aimed at demonstrating the persistence of cultural stereotypes over time. The Princeton studies (Gilbert, 1951; Karlins et al., 1969; Katz & Braly, 1933) are the clearest examples of such research.

Those implicitly or explicitly adopting a conflict view are also most concerned with consensual beliefs about social groups. As might be expected, research in this tradition relates such beliefs to intergroup relations, particularly to changes in the nature of intergroup interdependence. Certainly the most negative form of interdependence is war, and several studies have shown that armed conflict between nations significantly alters stereotype attributions (cf. Ehrlich, 1973, pp. 35–36). Although conflict theorists are concerned with international disputes, their distinctive contribution concerns group conflict within a particular society. Elsewhere we (Ashmore & Del Boca, 1976, pp. 76–77) have presented an analysis of the history of black–white relations in the United States from what is essentially a conflict perspective.

One very popular type of research stimulated by the sociocultural orientation is the analysis of various socialization channels in order to demonstrate stereotyped content. Sex stereotypes have been found in, among other places, women's magazines (Friedan, 1963), TV commercials (MacArthur & Resko, 1975), children's readers (Saario, Jacklin, & Tittle, 1973) and marriage manuals (Gordon & Shankweiler, 1971). Friedman (1977) was able to identify over 1,000 books and articles relevant to sex stereotypes and the mass media. Considerable research has been done also on the images of other social groups (e.g., Blacks) in both the mass media and in educational materials (Ehrlich, 1973, pp. 32–34).

While such research can demonstrate that stereotypes are part of a cultural pattern, there has been remarkably little research addressing the question of how children are influenced by socialization agents. As noted above, there is simply very little research on how children acquire stereotypes. Reviews of the effects of the mass media (Greenberg & Mazingo, 1976; Maccoby, 1964; Stein & Friedrich, 1975; Weiss, 1969) reveal little empirical evidence on how stereotypic media images of social groups are translated into the "pictures in the heads" of individual perceivers. Most researchers seem to assume that the members of the mass media audience simply "absorb" what is portrayed by the media. Again, both the structuralist–functionalist and conflict forms of the sociocultural orientation share the assumption that the media and other socializing agents directly and effectively teach prevailing cultural stereotypes. In the former, however, this is seen simply as part of "socialization," whereas conflict theorists prefer the term "manipulation theory [Ben-Horin, 1977, pp. 17–19]."

The Psychodynamic Orientation

The psychodynamic orientation to the study of stereotypes actually embraces a wide diversity of approaches. These approaches are clearly united, however, by an overriding interest in intergroup relations and prejudice and the view that prejudice exists in the service of personality (or societal) integration. Stereotypes and stereotyping are a secondary concern, primarily of interest because they are related to prejudice and personality.

Two forms of the psychodynamic orientation can be distinguished: psychoanalytic reductionism and psychosocial theories of prejudice. (See Billig, 1976, Chapters 2-5, for a detailed discussion of the various psychoanalytic theories of intergroup relations.) Psychoanalytic reductionists adhere to the tenets of Freud's individualistic psychology and seek to explain prejudice solely in terms of the unconscious dynamics of the individual. Psychosocial theories of prejudice (Billing's "Theories of Society and Personality"), on the other hand, attempt to consider the role of sociocultural factors in the etiology of prejudice. This second form of the psychodynamic orientation includes interpersonal theories and ego psychology as well as psychoanalytic formulations that emphasize the dialectical interplay between psychological and social variables.

Psychoanalytic reductionists explain prejudice in terms of the unconscious instinctual nature of humans, particularly the aggressive instinct. Stereotypes are dealt with only indirectly; the specific content of the stereotypes that are associated with particular target groups is of little concern. Derogatory beliefs regarding the objects of prejudice are generally thought to derive from the operation of two defense mechanisms, displacement and projection. Outgroup hostility is a result of displaced aggression; stereotypic beliefs are projections onto the group that serve to justify or rationalize the hostility directed against the group.

Psychosocial theories tend to place less emphasis on the role of instinctual forces in the etiology of prejudice. Probably the most richly elaborated and influential of these theories is presented in *The Authoritarian Personality* (Adorno et al., 1950). As noted previously, the authoritarian personality syndrome is thought to predispose the individual to antidemocratic ideology (including a generalized antipathy toward outgroups). This syndrome comprises a number of interrelated dimensions of personality, including "stereotypy." In the context of the authoritarian personality, stereotypy retains the same connotations it had acquired from its earlier usage as a psychiatric term. According to Adorno et al. (1950) stereotypy represents a generalized "tendency mechanically to subsume things under rigid categories [p. 44]." Thus, for example, rigid categories of "good" and "bad" or "strong" and "weak" are thought to pervade the prejudiced individual's thinking about people and events. With respect to social groups, stereotypy leads to gross overgeneralization—perceptions of group members are invariant with no recognition of individual differences.

What metatheoretical models underlie the psychodynamic perspective on stereotypes and stereotyping? With respect to human nature, the various theories embraced by this basic orientation tend to share the two major assumptions of Freud's original theory. First, human thought and behavior are assumed to be intrapsychically determined. And second, the most important features of adult personality are believed to be determined by the manner in which the individual resolves the psychological conflicts that arise in the first few years of life. Human beings are viewed as closed energy systems propelled by unconscious sexual and aggressive drives. The impulses associated with these drives push for expression and inevitably conflict with the demands of reality or the constraints of the superego. Prejudice with its attendant stereotypes serves as one means of reducing the tension generated by the resulting intrapsychic conflict. Thus, prejudice and stereotypes fulfill what Katz (1960, 1968) has referred to as an "ego-defensive" function. Ego psychologists posit a variation on this theme. As suggested by Bettelheim and Janowitz (1964): "The search for identity, and with it the search for ego strength and personal control, might very well involve as a detour the desire to find one's identity, or to strengthen it, through prejudice [p. 57]."

Proponents of the psychodynamic position view society as a force that thwarts the expression of libidinal impulses. Beyond this basic agreement, the different forms of this orientation tend to make different assumptions concerning the nature of society. For the psychoanalytic reductionist, all societal phenomena are explicable in terms of psychological factors. According to Billig (1976): "all social forms are explained . . . with respect to unconscious and instinctual forces. In this way the id constitutes the ultimate explanatory variable [p. 45]."

Although all psychosocial theories agree that society plays an important role in the development of prejudice and its associated stereotypes, there are fundamental differences among theories in terms of their conceptions of the nature of society. Proponents of ego psychology have tended to adopt implicitly a structuralist–functionalist view. Society is seen as an independent entity to which individuals are thought to accommodate their instinctual natures, finding and adapting to their own places within a culture. The learning of particular ingroup/outgroup attitudes is part of the acculturation process. Thus, ego psychology considers the influence of sociocultural factors on the individual; however, it neglects to examine the factors that shape social structure itself. Other psychosocial theories of prejudice have emphasized the dialectic interplay between individual psychology and sociocultural factors. In particular, two of the authors of *The Authoritarian Personality* (Adorno and Sanford), have linked authoritarianism specifically to the economic and political conditions of Nazi Germany (see Billig, 1976, Chapter 4, for a fuller discussion of these points).[8]

What research has been generated by the psychodynamic orientation? Adherents of this perspective have produced an impressive volume of empirical research. It is important to note again, however, that this research is largely directed at determining the etiology of prejudice, not at explicating the nature of stereotypes. Psychoanalytic reductionists have produced a massive quantity of case study reports. Most of these deal with patients undergoing psychoanalytic treatment and seek to explain prejudice in terms of the psychodynamics of the

---

[8]Dr. Richard J. Butsch first brought to our attention that Adorno—contrary to the view of most social psychologists—was as much or more a Marxist as a Freudian (see Jay, 1973, Chapter 7).

individual. The primary exemplar for these researchers, then, is the in-depth clinical interview.

A great deal of work also has been done by researchers who adhere to the psychosocial form of the psychodynamic orientation. *The Authoritarian Personality,* itself a massive research effort, spawned hundreds of studies. The majority of these have used a correlational approach to identify the antecedents and consequences of authoritarianism as a personality syndrome (see Kirscht & Dillehay, 1967). In terms of stereotypes and stereotyping, a number of studies have examined the relationship between various forms of "rigidity of thinking" (stereotypy) and prejudice, but, as noted earlier, little attention has been paid to the relationship between such individual differences in cognitive style and the content and organization of beliefs regarding social groups.[9]

The Cognitive Orientation

Although almost all researchers agree that a stereotype is a concept or a set of beliefs, stereotypes usually have been regarded as cognitive structures that are somehow "special"; that is, the term stereotype has been reserved for sets of beliefs that are different in some important way from the concepts individuals hold about nonstereotyped objects. What seems to be most distinctive about the contemporary cognitive orientation to stereotypes and stereotyping (as represented by the present volume) is a view of these phenomena as "nothing special," as not essentially different from other cognitive structures and processes.

What is the "something special" about stereotypes represented in many earlier writings on this topic? As the preceding discussion of definitions indicates, stereotypes of social groups often have been regarded as distinctive because of some irrational factor: They are invalid or overgeneralized, they are acquired incorrectly, or they do not change in the face of contrary evidence. Even in cases where the term is not *defined* as bad or bizarre, writers have often seemed to suggest implicitly that these phenomena are somehow special.

This view of stereotypes as special implies that, in most cases, human conceptions of people and events arise directly from individual experience, that they represent experience with no loss of information, and that beliefs change readily in the face of new information even if that information contradicts previous experience. Most earlier writers, then, appear to have entertained a view of human beings as immanently rational creatures, capable of objectively processing and evaluating information. When people seemed to fail in this respect (i.e., when they held stereotypes), such failure was explained either by motivational

---

[9]In addition to these bodies of research, the psychodynamic orientation has produced a considerable number of studies dealing specifically with the frustration-aggression hypothesis. As with other research guided by this perspective, these studies have focused more on prejudice than stereotypes (cf. Billig, 1976, Chapter 5).

factors or by assuming that the available information was "biased." These two explanations, of course, correspond to the psychodynamic and sociocultural orientations, respectively.

The cognitive orientation to the study of stereotypes takes a different view of human nature. According to this perspective, the human capacity for processing information is limited; that is, the basic rationality of humans is "bounded" (Carroll & Payne, 1976). Hence, apparent breakdowns in perception and cognition need not be attributed to motivational factors or inadequate available information. Further, cognitive limitations make humans susceptible to systematic biases in processing information about people and events, and these biases contribute significantly to the formation and maintenance of stereotypes regarding social groups.

How did the developing cognitive orientation to stereotyping and intergroup behavior emerge in social psychology? First, it is important to note that many features of this approach are not, in fact, entirely new. Some of the current views regarding stereotypes were anticipated by earlier writers. Lippmann's (1922) primary point that "reality" is too complex to be fully comprehended and responded to can be seen as the core of the contemporary cognitive orientation. Kretch and Crutchfield presented a cognitive theory of social perception as early as 1948. Vinacke (1957) suggested that stereotypes should be conceptualized as concepts and proposed that principles derived from the study of cognition be applied to understanding stereotypes. Both Allport (1958) and Secord (1959) expressed ideas regarding stereotypes and the process of categorization that are remarkably similar to those advanced in the present volume.

Although these and other early authors expressed ideas similar to those that characterize the orientation presented in this volume, they failed to redirect thinking and research regarding stereotypes and stereotyping. The watershed in terms of the establishment of the new cognitive position appears to be the publication in 1969 of Tajfel's "Cognitive Aspects of Prejudice." Whereas much of the earlier writing concerned with the cognitive aspects of stereotypes had been largely conceptual, Tajfel articulated his viewpoint and presented an impressive set of empirical data to support his argument.

The state of theory and research in psychology provided fertile ground for the emergence of this new orientation. Social psychologists had for some time been growing disenchanted with the attitude construct as the primary means for understanding intergroup relations. (Wicker's [1969] widely cited critique of the attitude–behavior link appeared in the same volume of the *Journal of Social Issues* as Tajfel's paper.) Moreover, a "crisis" was developing in the field of social psychology. Even though social psychologists had developed an impressive body of theory, methods, and empirical results, critiques of the field began to be published in the late 1960s (e.g., McGuire, 1967; Ring, 1967), and these continued into the 1970s (e.g., Israel & Tajfel, 1972). As often happens when scientists begin to lose faith in a prevailing paradigm, many investigators began looking outside the discipline of social psychology for new conceptual and methodological approaches. Also, psychology as a whole was experiencing a shift in perspective, with greater emphasis in a number of subfields on the cognitive contribution to human behavior (e.g., McKeachie, 1976). Finally, cognitive psychology itself was abandoning the "computer model" of the human being as an information-processing machine (cf. Neisser, 1976). The emerging view of "bounded rationality" facilitated the development of the cognitive–social orientation to stereotypes and stereotyping.

As noted in the foregoing, the metatheory that underlies the orientation presented in this volume centers around the notion that humans are cognitive creatures. Although conceived as having a limited information-processing capacity, human beings are seen as intrinsically motivated by "intelligent" concerns. Woman (or man) is a scientist, albeit a fallible one, seeking to make sense out of a complex environment. Stereotypes serve a "knowledge function" (Katz, 1960, 1968). That is, they help the human organism to reduce and make more manageable the complexity of the social world. Although stereotypes aid the perceiver in this respect, they are still implicitly regarded as bad. Basically, they are seen as undesirable because they represent cognitive "shortcuts" and may lead to their own fulfillment.

Those adopting a cognitive perspective have attempted to reformulate conceptual questions regarding stereotypes and develop new research strategies. Questions are currently being restated so that the theory and methods of cognitive psychology may be brought to bear on the topic of stereotypes. Emphasis is placed on how information about individuals and groups is attended to, encoded, and retrieved rather than on the content of beliefs regarding specific social groups. Finally, a much greater emphasis is placed on the cognitive and behavioral consequences of stereotyping.

Comment on and Critique of Orientations

Two general comments are necessary with respect to the preceding description of the three orientations to the study of stereotypes. First, these orientations have been for the most part implicit. Most workers have taken a strictly empirical approach. The foregoing analysis should be seen as an attempt to make explicit the assumptions underlying the extant literature and not as a reflection of the literature itself. Second, the three orientations have not been "equal partners." The sociocultural view has been dominant. It is preferred by most sociologists. The majority of contributors—regardless of disciplinary affiliation—to the burgeoning sex stereotype literature assume, often tacitly, that sex stereotypes are consensual beliefs. Although it has not generated a large literature directly concerned with stereotypes, the psychodynamic perspective has been the dominant psychological approach to intergroup relations. The cognitive orientation has received the least attention.

As should be expected given the complexity of human beings, each of the three orientations has both strengths and weaknesses as a general approach to the study of stereotypes. The sociocultural perspective is strong in explicitly recognizing that the human being is a social animal, that the beliefs of individuals must be related to societal factors. The research implicitly guided by this orientation, however, suffers from a lack of concern with exactly how cultural belief systems are translated into individual belief systems. Workers adopting a sociocultural view seem to have assumed that this translation process is simple and that all members of a particular society acquire the same set of beliefs. Neither of these assumptions seems tenable.

The psychodynamic and cognitive orientations are strong just where the sociocultural is weak, at the level of the individual. The psychodynamic view clearly acknowledges that thoughts about social groups are related to feelings about those groups. Further, this general approach directs attention to individual differences in stereotype acquisition and stereotyping. The psychodynamic orientation, however, has not given due attention to the perceptual–cognitive factors involved in intergroup relations. The cognitive perspective is directly concerned with such factors, and, of the three general approaches, it is the most process oriented.

CONCLUSION

In summarizing the foregoing discussion of the history of stereotype research and theory it was observed that very little progress had been made in understanding this important phenomenon. A great deal of research has been conducted but little has been added to social scientific "knowledge" regarding stereotyping and intergroup behavior. The value of past research was attenuated, in large part, because workers persisted in the use of convenient methods and failed to consider significant conceptual issues. When such issues were raised they were not tied to methods of data gathering and analyses. As a consequence the theoretical pieces that did appear had little impact on the conduct of stereotype research.

We believe that cumulative additions to social scientific understanding of stereotypes are most likely to derive from the following two-part strategy. First because each of the three orientations represents only "part of the blindman's elephant," it is necessary to seek connections between these perspectives. Second, each orientation should be developed and elaborated. In the past these perspectives have been implicit. Thus, they have not been "pushed" to see just how much they can account for. The present volume sets forth the cognitive position clearly and relatively completely. Progress in understanding stereotypes and stereotyping would benefit greatly from a similar clarification of the other two perspectives. Explication of the individual orientations will make it easier to implement the first part of the suggested strategy (i.e., seeking connections between the orientations) and ultimately to integrate the sociocultural, psychodynamic, and cognitive viewpoints into a more complete picture of stereotypes and intergroup behavior.

ACKNOWLEDGMENTS

The authors acknowledge the helpful comments of Richard J. Butsch, David L. Hamilton, Shelley E. Taylor, Mary Lou Tumia, and Geoffrey M. White on an earlier draft of the manuscript.

REFERENCES

Adorno, T. W., Frenkel-Brunswik, E., Levinson, D. J., & Sanford, R. N. *The authoritarian personality*. New York: Harper and Row, 1950.

Allport, G. W. Attitudes. In C. Murchison (Ed.), *Handbook of social psychology*. Worcester, Mass.: Clark University Press, 1935.

Allport, G. W. *The nature of prejudice*. Garden City, N.Y.: Doubleday and Company, 1958.

Asch, S. E. *Social psychology*. Englewood Cliffs, N.J.: Prentice-Hall, 1952.

Ashmore, R. D., & Del Boca, F. K. Psychological approaches to understanding intergroup conflict. In P. Katz (Ed.), *Towards the elimination of racism*. New York: Pergamon Press, 1976.

Ashmore, R. D., & Del Boca, F. K. Sex stereotypes and implicit personality theory: Toward a cognitive-social psychological conceptualization. *Sex Roles*, 1979, *5*, 219-248.

Ashmore, R. D., & McConahay, J. B. *Psychology and America's urban dilemmas*. New York: McGraw-Hill, 1975.

Ben-Horin, D. Television without tears: An outline of a socialist approach to popular television. *Socialist Revolution*, 1977, *7*, 7-35.

Bettelheim, B., & Janowitz, M. *Social change and prejudice*. New York: The Free Press, 1964.

Billig, M. *Social psychology and intergroup relations*. New York: Academic Press, 1976.

Block, J. H. Issues, problems, and pitfalls in assessing sex differences: A critical review of *The psychology of sex differences*. *Merrill-Palmer Quarterly*, 1976, *22*, 283-308.

Bowker, G., & Carrier, J. (Eds.). *Race and ethnic relations: Sociological readings*. New York: Holmes & Meier, 1976.

Brewer, M. B. In-group bias in the minimal intergroup situation: A cognitive-motivational analysis. *Psychological Bulletin*, 1979, *86*, 307-324.

Brigham, J. C. Ethnic stereotypes. *Psychological Bulletin*, 1971, *76*, 15-33.

Broverman, I. K., Vogel, S. R., Broverman, D. M., Clarkson, F. E., & Rosenkrantz, P. S. Sex-role stereotypes: A current appraisal. *Journal of Social Issues*, 1972, *28*, 59-78.

Brown, R. *Social psychology*. New York: The Free Press, 1965.

Campbell, D. T. Stereotypes and the perception of group differences. *American Psychologist*, 1967, *22*, 817-829.

Carroll, J. S., & Payne, J. W. (Eds.). *Cognition and social behavior*. Hillsdale, N.J.: Lawrence Erlbaum Associates, 1976.

Cauthen, N. R., Robinson, I. E., & Krauss, H. H. Stereotypes: A review of the literature 1926-1968. *Journal of Social Psychology*, 1971, *84*, 103-125.

Del Boca, F. K., & Ashmore, R. D. Sex stereotypes through the life cycle. In L. Wheeler (Ed.), *Review of personality and social psychology* (Vol. 1). Beverly Hills, Calif.: Sage Publications, 1980.

Ehrlich, H. J. *The Social psychology of prejudice.* New York: John Wiley & Sons, 1973.

Ehrlich, H. J., & Rinehart, J. W. A brief report on the methodology of stereotype research. *Social Forces,* 1965, *43,* 564-575.

Eysenck, H. J., & Crown, S. National stereotypes: An experimental and methodological study. *International Journal of Opinion and Attitude Research,* 1948, *2,* 26-39.

Fishman, J. A. An examination of the process and function of social stereotyping. *Journal of Social Psychology,* 1956, *43,* 26-64.

Friedan, B. *The feminine mystique.* New York: W. W. Norton, 1963.

Friedman, L. J. *Sex role stereotyping in the mass media: An annotated bibliography.* New York: Garland Publishers, 1977.

Gardner, R. C. Ethnic stereotypes: The traditional approach, a new look. *The Canadian Psychologist,* 1973, *14,* 133-148.

Gardner, R. C., Kirby, D. M., & Finlay, J. C. Ethnic stereotypes: The significance of consensus. *Canadian Journal of Behavioral Science,* 1973, *5,* 4-12.

Gardner, R. C., Rodensky, R. L., & Kirby, D. M. Ethnic stereotypes: A critical review. *Research Bulletin No. 157.* University of Western Ontario, July, 1970.

Gilbert, G. M. Stereotype persistence and change among college students. *Journal of Abnormal and Social Psychology,* 1951, *46,* 245-254.

Goldberg, L. R. *Language and personality: Developing a taxonomy of personality descriptive terms.* Unpublished manuscript, 1978.

Gordon, M., & Shankweiler, P. J. Different equals less: Female sexuality in recent marriage manuals. *Journal of Marriage and the Family,* 1971, *33,* 459-466.

Gordon, R. *Stereotypy of imagery and belief as an ego defense.* London: Cambridge University Press, 1962.

Greenberg, B. S., & Mazingo, S. L. Racial issues in mass media institutions. In P. Katz (Ed.), *Towards the elimination of racism.* New York: Pergamon Press, 1976.

Harding, J., Proshansky, H., Kutner, B., & Chein, I. Prejudice and ethnic relations. In G. Lindzey & E. Aronson (Eds.), *Handbook of social psychology* (Vol. 5) (2nd ed.). Reading, Mass.: Addison-Wesley, 1969.

Israel, J., & Tajfel, H. (Eds.). *The context of social psychology: A critical assessment.* London: Academic Press, 1972.

Jay, M. *The dialectical imagination.* Boston: Little, Brown and Co., 1973.

Jones, R. A. *Self-fulfilling prophecies: Social, psychological and physiological effects of expectancies.* Hillsdale, N.J.: Lawrence Erlbaum Associates, 1977.

Karlins, M., Coffman, T. L., & Walters, G. On the fading of social stereotypes: Studies in three generations of college students. *Journal of Personality and Social Psychology,* 1969, *13,* 1-16.

Katz, D. The functional approach to the study of attitudes. *Public Opinion Quarterly,* 1960, *24,* 163-204.

Katz, D. Consistency for what? The functional approach. In R. P. Abelson, E. Aronson, W. J. McGuire, T. M. Newcomb, M. J. Rosenberg, & P. H. Tannenbaum (Eds.), *Theories of cognitive consistency: A sourcebook.* Chicago: Rand McNally and Company, 1968.

Katz, D., & Braly, K. Racial stereotypes in one hundred college students. *Journal of Abnormal and Social Psychology,* 1933, *28,* 280-290.

Katz, D., & Braly, K. W. Racial prejudice and racial stereotypes. *Journal of Abnormal and Social Psychology,* 1935, *30,* 175-193.

Kirscht, J. P., & Dillehay, R. C. *Dimensions of authoritarianism.* Lexington, Ky.: University of Kentucky Press, 1967.

Klineberg, O. The scientific study of national stereotypes. *International Social Science Bulletin,* 1951, *3,* 505-515.

Kretch, D., & Crutchfield, R. S. *Theory and problems in social psychology.* New York: McGraw-Hill, 1948.

Kuhn, T. S. *The structure of scientific revolutions*. Chicago: University of Chicago Press, 1962.

Kuhn, T. S. *The structure of scientific revolutions* (2nd ed.). Chicago: University of Chicago Press, 1970.

Kuhn, T. S. *The essential tension: Selected studies in scientific tradition and change*. Chicago: University of Chicago Press, 1977.

LaPiere, R. T. *The Armenian colony in Fresno County, California: A study in social psychology*. Ph.D. dissertation, Stanford University, 1930.

LaPiere, R. T. Type-rationalizations of group antipathy. *Social Forces*, 1936, *15*, 232-237.

LaViolette, F., & Silvert, K. H. A theory of stereotypes. *Social Forces*, 1951, *29*, 257-262.

Lippmann, W. *Public opinion*. New York: Harcourt, Brace, Jovanovitch, 1922.

Litterer, O. F. Stereotypes. *Journal of Social Psychology*, 1933, *4*, 59-69.

Maccoby, E. E. Effects of the mass media. In M. Hoffman & L. Hoffman (Eds.), *Review of child development research*. New York: Russell Sage, 1964.

Maccoby, E. E., & Jacklin, C. N. *The psychology of sex differences*. Stanford, Calif.: Stanford University Press, 1974.

Mackie, M. Arriving at "truth" by definition, the case of stereotype inaccuracy. *Social Problem*, 1973, *20*, 431-447.

McArthur, L. Z., & Resko, B. G. The portrayal of men and women in American television commercials. *The Journal of Social Psychology*, 1975, *97*, 209-220.

McCauley, C., Stitt, C. L., & Segal, M. Stereotyping: From prejudice to prediction. *Psychological Bulletin*, 1980, *87*, 195-208.

McGill, K. H. The school-teacher stereotype. *Journal of Educational Sociology*, 1931, *4*, 642-650.

McGuire, W. J. Some impending reorientations in social psychology: Some thoughts provoked by Kenneth Ring. *Journal of Experimental Social Psychology*, 1967, *3*, 124-139.

McGuire, W. J. The nature of attitudes and attitude change. In G. Lindzey & E. Aronson (Eds.), *Handbook of social psychology* (Vol. 3) (2nd ed.). Reading, Mass.: Addison–Wesley, 1969.

McKeachie, W. J. Psychology in America's bicentennial year. *American Psychologist*, 1976, *31*, 819-833.

Meenes, M. A comparison of racial stereotypes of Negro college students in 1935 and in 1942. *Psychological Bulletin*, 1942, *39*, 467-468.

Meenes, M. A comparison of racial stereotypes of 1935 and 1942. *Journal of Social Psychology*, 1943, *17*, 327-336.

Meltzer, H. Personification of ideals and stereotypes in problem children. *American Journal of Orthopsychiatry*, 1932, *2*, 384-399.

Neisser, U. *Cognition and reality*. San Francisco: W. H. Freeman and Company, 1976.

Pleck, J. H. Males' traditional attitudes toward women: Conceptual issues in research. In J. Sherman & F. Denmark (Eds.), *The psychology of women: Future directions in research*. New York: Psychological Dimensions, 1979.

Rice, S. A. Stereotypes, a source of error judging human character. *Journal of Personnel Research*, 1926, *5*, 267-276.

Rice, S. A. *Quantitative methods in politics*. New York: Alfred A. Knopf, 1928.

Rice, S. A., & Waller, W. Stereotypes. *Papers and Proceedings of the American Sociology Society*, 1928, *22*, 180-185.

Ring, K. Experimental social psychology: Some sober questions about some frivolous values. *Journal of Experimental Social Psychology*, 1967, *3*, 113-123.

Rose, P. The development of race studies. In G. W. Shepherd, Jr. (Ed.), *Race among nations: A conceptual approach*. Lexington, Mass.: Heath Lexington Books, 1970.

Rosenkrantz, P. S., Vogel, S. R., Bee, H., Broverman, I. K., & Broverman, D. M. Sex-role stereotypes and self concepts in college students. *Journal of Consulting and Clinical Psychology*, 1968, *32*, 287-295.

Saario, T. N., Jacklin, C. N., & Tittle, C. K. Sex role stereotyping in the public schools. *Harvard Educational Review*, 1973, *43*, 386-416.

Saenger, G., & Flowerman, S. Stereotypes and prejudicial attitudes. *Human Relations*, 1954, *7*, 217–238.

Schroeder, S. R. Usage of stereotyping as a descriptive term. *Psychological Record*, 1970, *20*, 337–342.

Secord, P. F. Stereotyping and favorableness in the perception of Negro faces. *Journal of Abnormal and Social Psychology*, 1959, *59*, 309–315.

Secord, P. F., & Backman, C. W. *Social psychology*. New York: McGraw-Hill, 1964.

Shaw, M. E., & Costanza, P. R. *Theories of social psychology*. New York: McGraw-Hill, 1970.

Sherriffs, A. C., & McKee, J. P. Quantitative aspects of beliefs about men and women. *Journal of Personality*, 1957, *25*, 451–464.

Stein, A. H., & Friedrich, L. K. Impact of television on children and youth. In E. M. Hetherington (Ed.), *Review of child development research* (Vol. 5). Chicago: University of Chicago Press, 1975.

Tajfel, H. Cognitive aspects of prejudice. *Journal of Social Issues*, 1969, *25*, 79–97.

Tajfel, H. Experiments in intergroup discrimination. *Scientific American*, 1970, *223*, 96–102.

Taylor, S. E., & Crocker, J. Schematic bases of social information processing. In E. T. Higgins, P. Hermann, & M. P. Zanna (Eds.), *The Ontario Symposium on Personality and Social Psychology* (Vol. 1). Hillsdale, N.J.: Lawrence Erlbaum Associates, 1981.

Vinacke, W. E. Stereotyping among national-racial groups in Hawaii: A study in ethnocentrism. *Journal of Social Psychology*, 1949, *30*, 265–291.

Vinacke, W. E. Stereotypes as social concepts. *The Journal of Social Psychology*, 1957, *46*, 229–243.

Weiss, W. Effects of the mass media of communication. In G. Lindzey & E. Aronson (Eds.), *Handbook of social psychology* (Vol. 5) (2nd ed.). Reading, Mass.: Addison-Wesley, 1969.

Wicker, A. W. Attitudes versus actions: The relationship of verbal and overt behavioral responses to attitude objects. *Journal of Social Issues*, 1969, *25*, 41–78.

Wrong, D. H. *Skeptical sociology*. New York: Columbia University Press, 1976.

2 Sex Stereotypes and Implicit Personality Theory

Richard D. Ashmore
Livington College, Rutgers—The State University

As noted in Chapter 1, there has been a dramatic increase in sex stereotype research over the past decade. There has not, however, been a corresponding rise in our understanding of how women and men are perceived. According to many secondary sources, the accumulated research presents a clear picture—there is a set of attributes that are consensually regarded as typical of females and another that is agreed to be typical of males. (The list of male stereotypic traits is often summarized by such terms as "competent," "rational," and "assertive," while the female stereotype is said to indicate "warmth" and "expressiveness.") Our review of the sex stereotype literature (Ashmore & Del Boca, 1979) leads us to question this conclusion. Two points illustrate the confusing state of research on beliefs about the sexes. First, as stated by Cowan and Stewart (1977): "the perception of the stereotypic male and female appear to be determined to a large extent by the instrument used to structure that expressed perception [p. 214]." Second, even the same measuring device does not lead to the same results. For example, Petro and Putnam (1979) used the Sex-Role Questionnaire developed by Rosenkrantz, Vogel, Bee, Broverman, and Broverman (1968) but obtained quite different results from the original study.

These and other inconsistencies can, in part, be traced to "methodological factors" (e.g., different subject samples, different rules for identifying stereotypic items) or actual changes over time in how the sexes are perceived (e.g., perhaps sex stereotyping is on the decline). A significant part of the problem, however, is the lack of conceptual analysis. Sex stereotype research has been, and continues to be, instrument driven. The goal of most studies is simply to obtain, using one of a small number of measuring devices, a list of "male" traits and a second list of "female" traits. This cataloguing approach is generally

37

extended by: (1) using "new" samples (e.g., teachers, social workers); and/or (2) correlating stereotyping with demographic (e.g., age, sex) or personality (e.g., self-concept, assertiveness) variables. Although such research adds somewhat to our knowledge of sex stereotypes, my collaborators and I believe that significant increases in understanding how women and men are perceived will require more attention to conceptual issues.

This chapter reports a line of research that takes as its starting point explicit answers to two of the most central conceptual questions concerning stereotypes: What is a stereotype? What is the function of stereotypes in social perception and interpersonal behavior? I begin by explaining how we have answered these questions. In the second section of the chapter, an implicit personality theory formulation of the "sex stereotype" construct is proposed, and the specific studies generated by this conceptual framework are presented. The final section of the chapter is devoted to a discussion of the implications and possible extensions of this conceptualization.

DEFINITION AND FUNCTION OF STEREOTYPES

In Chapter 1 it was asserted that most social scientists would agree in considering a stereotype to be "A set of beliefs about the personal attributes of a group of people." To this core definition my collaborators and I add the notion of structure. Sex stereotypes, which are the primary focus of this chapter, are defined as: "*the structured sets of beliefs about the personal attributes of women and of men*" (Ashmore & Del Boca, 1979, p. 222). The notion of structure is included in this definition for two related reasons. First, in theoretical treatments, if not in empirical investigations, stereotypes have been considered to be cognitive structures that shape perception of individuals and groups (cf. Funk, Horowitz, Lipshitz, & Young, 1976). This was clear in Lippmann's (1922) original discussion of stereotypes (see Chapter 1), and Cauthen, Robinson, and Krauss (1971) make the point quite directly: "The purpose of stereotype research is to investigate the picture or cognitive structure that we act upon as if it were real [p. 104]." Second, it is unlikely that people think of social groups in terms of simple lists or catalogues of attributes as is implied by most extant assessment devices. For example, subjects in two of the major investigations of sex stereotypes (Rosenkrantz et al., 1968; Sherriffs & McKee, 1957) supplied 159 personal attributes that they considered to differentiate the sexes. Common sense suggests that we don't think about women and men (or other social categories) in terms of such a long list. Rather, this list must be organized in some way. Research in cognitive and in social psychology supports this commonsense view: Our perception of and thoughts about both people and things are structured and meaningful (i.e., the units of perception and cognition are interrelated in a systematic fashion [cf., Schneider, Hastorf, & Ellsworth, 1979, p. 15]).

Our position with respect to the function of stereotypes is congruent with the cognitive orientation covered in Chapter 1. As discussed more fully elsewhere (Ashmore & Del Boca, 1979), humans are viewed as "naive scientists" (cf. Heider, 1958; Kelly, 1955). Individuals do not respond passively to external contingencies; rather, they actively attempt to "make sense" out of a complex environment. As with the trained researcher, the naive scientist is concerned with description, prediction, and explanation. With respect to the domain of people, description involves discrimination of various groups of people (e.g., "women" and "men") and organization of information regarding these groups (e.g., "Women are softer than men"). The predictions of the naive personologist most often take the form of interpersonal expectancies (e.g., "She will want me to drive"). And the naive scientist seems to be motivated to explain why people behave the way they do (e.g., "He got a low grade on his painting because most men just aren't artistically inclined"). The foregoing should not be taken to mean that we conceive of humans as always living up to some model of the scientific ideal. [Discussion of factors accounting for deviations from objective appraisal of the social environment are postponed until the concluding section of the chapter (see also Ashmore & Del Boca, 1979, especially pp. 241–244).] It is further assumed that humans respond to the world as they construe it. That is, an individual's conduct is guided by the way in which she or he believes the world to be. As noted in Chapter 1, this point was made quite nicely by Lippmann (1922)—we respond not to "reality" but to the "pictures in our heads" that we have constructed to represent that reality. According to the present view, then, stereotypes function on the one hand to summarize and organize knowledge about social groups and on the other to guide behavior with respect to groups and individual group members.

AN IMPLICIT PERSONALITY THEORY FORMULATION OF SEX STEREOTYPES

Progress in understanding sex stereotypes has been hampered not just by the tendency to avoid conceptual analysis but also by the rather widespread assumption that stereotypes are aberrant or pathological in nature. As do others who share a cognitive orientation, my collaborators and I believe that stereotypes are normal, though frequently undesirable phenomena. This assumption allows one to relate stereotypes to basic social science research and theory. Any complete theory of stereotypes will be tied to a variety of content areas in psychology, sociology, and other disciplines. Because our first goal was to understand stereotypes as cognitive structures involved in the perception of individuals and groups, we began by relating them to the social psychological construct, "implicit personality theory." In the broadest sense, stereotypes are "about" the categorization and perception of people; implicit theories of personality are "about'' the same thing. Hastorf, Schneider, and Polefka (1970) state this connection quite explicitly: "Implicit personality theories are, in the final analysis, stereotypes we hold about other people [p. 46]."

The present framework is based on reformulating the construct "stereotype" in implicit personality theory terms. The various definitions of "implicit personality theory" share four features. First, "implicit personality theory" is a hypothetical construct. Second, "implicit personality theory" denotes a cognitive structure. Third, implicit theories of personality contain elements (i.e., attributes of personality) and relations (i.e., inferential relations between these elements). Finally, the naive personologist is often not aware of his or her "theory of personality," and most individuals are seldom required to elaborate fully their "theories." Thus, these theories are termed "implicit" to contrast them with the more fully elaborated and consciously developed theories of personality psychologists. "Implicit personality theory," then, can be defined as: *A hypothetical cognitive structure, often held nonconsciously, that comprises the attributes of personality that an individual believes others to possess and the set of expected relations (i.e., inferential relations) between these attributes.*

The defining features of "implicit personality theory" directly parallel the components of stereotype as here defined. That is, both terms denote hypothetical cognitive constructs that comprise elements and relations. The parallel can be made explicit by reformulating the definition of sex stereotypes proposed above in "implicit personality theory" terms, "*The structured sets of inferential relations that link personal attributes to the social categories female and male* (Ashmore & Del Boca, 1979, p. 225)."

According to this definition, sex stereotypes—and, by extension, beliefs about ethnic groups and other social categories—are but one aspect of an individual's overall cognitive scheme for making sense out of other people (i.e., one aspect of the individual's "implicit theory of personality"). At the same time, this definition involves an expansion of the concept of "implicit personality theory" as it is most often studied. Specifically, it adds "social categories" as important elements of implicit theories of personality. A social category is considered to be: "a rule or set of specifications that a perceiver uses to classify people as similar" (Ashmore & Del Boca, 1979, p. 280).

To date, most research on the structure of person perception has used trait adjectives. While traits are clearly significant in our thinking about the social environment, they are certainly not the only cognitions we have concerning other people. In the concluding section it is suggested that feelings and expected behaviors are also part of implicit theories of personality. At this point, however, it is simply argued that implicit personality theories are most fruitfully considered to comprise "social categories" as well as "attributes of personality." Four reasons are advanced in support of this contention. First, attributes and categories are different, both conceptually and phenomenologically. Gordon (1968) makes both points quite clearly: "The relevant *categories* denote the 'kind of thing' the object is, whereas the *attributes* describe the object in terms of qualities that differentiate it from others of its kind. . . . The category–attribute dichotomy is not a logical problem for the individual. He knows that everyone is characterized by both sets of references at once [pp. 117–118].'' Second, social categories are linked to social identities and roles (i.e., to proper ways of behaving) and are thus personally and interpersonally important. Third, open-ended descriptions of self and others often contain references to category membership (cf. Gordon, 1968; Fiske & Cox, 1979). And finally, categories play an important role in perceptual and cognitive processes. Although there is much debate about the structure and function of categories, most cognitive psychologists agree that ''category concepts'' play a major role in the organization of memory. In addition, there is evidence suggesting that ''category concepts'' are more helpful in retrieving information from memory than are attributes (cf. Glass, Holyoak, & Santa, 1979, p. 351).

The primary aim of this section is to demonstrate the utility of conceptualizing sex stereotypes in terms of implicit personality theory. An important consequence of the present formulation is that research and theory in the area of person perception become available for the study of stereotypes. The three studies to be described in this section involve the application of implicit personality theory methods to assess sex stereotypes. There are two basic approaches to uncovering an individual's implicit theory of personality: personality description and trait inference (cf. Rosenberg & Sedlak, 1972). The personality description approach requires the respondent to ascribe attributes of personality to specific other people. Using the trait inference method, the investigator presents a single trait or set of traits, which is usually said to describe a particular person, and then asks the subject to make inferences about the presence of other traits. The first two studies to be described are extended replications of the classic investigations employing these two approaches—Rosenberg, Nelson, and Vivekananthan's (1968) analysis of the multidimensional nature of personality impressions using personality description and Asch's (1946) trait inference experiments exploring the central trait effect. In both cases, sex of target was added to the original design. In the third study, the same methods were used as in the first study except that respondents were asked to describe other people, using traits that had been found to be ''sex stereotypic'' in previous research that employed conventional approaches to assessing sex stereotypes.

The Sorting Study: A Personality Description Approach to the Assessment and Representation of Sex Stereotypes

In the original Rosenberg et al. (1968) study, subjects were asked to use a trait sorting method (see the following for details) to describe other people, and multidimensional scaling was used to provide a geometric representation of the inferential relations among the traits. In this first study, Ashmore and Tumia (1980) replicated this data-gathering procedure and then asked subjects to indicate the sex of each of the people they had described. This addition allowed computation of an indirect index of the strength of association between each trait and the social categories female and male. Direct ratings of the traits were obtained also on three sex-related psychological properties (e.g., Male–Female) in a manner quite similar to that most commonly used to assess sex stereotypes (e.g., Rosenkrantz et al., 1968; Williams & Bennett, 1975). This provided a means for comparison of the present Indirect Female–Male property with these procedures.

The sorting task data were subjected to both multidimensional scaling and hierarchial clustering. These methods of analysis are good ways of uncovering and representing cognitive structure (cf. Shepard, Romney, & Nerlove, 1972). They provide different types of structural representations and imply that perceivers use different perceptual or decision-making strategies. The multidimensional scaling algorithm seeks to position objects (in the present case, the trait adjectives used to describe people) in an n-dimensional space such that the distances between points in the space best fit the input distances between objects (here derived from the sorting task). By representing the traits as points in a continuous Euclidean space this approach implicitly assumes that perceivers respond to the traits (and the people described by these traits) in terms of shades of difference along underlying dimensions (e.g., good–bad). An alternative model for depicting cognitive structure is "categorical" or "typological" (Rosenberg & Sedlak, 1972). Typological representations are obtained through clustering algorithms that partition the objects of interest into homogeneous subsets or "clusters." In this model it is tacitly assumed that perceivers simply make binary decisions regarding objects. In the present case, for example, traits and people are either "in" (a member of) or "not in" (not a member of) a particular cognitive category.

Although multidimensional scaling and hierarchical clustering can be thought of as alternatives to be tested against one another (see, for example, Jones & Ashmore, 1973), it is probably more often the case that they will complement one another. Human memory involves multiple, crosscutting categorizations of the same information (cf. Cohen, 1977). Thus, it is unlikely that a single means of representing cognitive structure will be *the correct one* (see also Forgas, 1976, p. 208, on this point). Furthermore, the scaling and clustering algorithms take different paths to representing structure (cf. White, 1978, pp. 339–340). Multidimensional scaling configurations are obtained by means of a "top-down" strategy. In positioning the points in the n-dimensional space the distances between *each object and all others are considered simultaneously for all of the objects being studied.* As a consequence, scaling representations account quite well for the overall structure of the relations among objects and for large differences between objects. Hierarchical clustering is based on a "bottom-up" strategy. It *begins by grouping the most similar items* and constructs the complete structure by building on these early clusters. Clustering, then, is most useful in representing small differences between objects, or what might be called "local structure." In the present case, the use of these two methods makes it possible to uncover and represent the overall cognitive structure associated with the social categories female and male and to explore the possibility of local structure associated with sex of target. The identification of such sex-linked clusters of attributes or traits would be evidence that perceivers not only organize their impressions of others in terms of the broad categories "female" and "male" but also perceptually discriminate types of women and men (i.e., gender subcategories [cf. Ashmore & Del Boca, 1979, pp. 232-233]).

Method and Analysis.   The data-gathering procedures and analyses are described in some detail because: (1) they are quite a departure from the methods used in most stereotype research (see, however, Funk et al., 1976, and Jones & Ashmore, 1973); and (2) the same approach is used in the third study to be reported later.

The subjects were female and male white middle-class college students. Each subject completed the same sorting task used originally by Rosenberg and his associates (1968). Subjects were given 66 slips of paper, each with a trait name (e.g., *warm, intelligent*), and asked to sort them into piles such that traits that co-occur in the same person would be in the same pile. Subjects were told that: "one way to make these judgments is to think of a number of people you know. . . . A category will then correspond to a person" (Rosenberg et al., 1968, p. 285). Upon completing the sorting task subjects were asked to identify each pile as either "female" or "male" and as either a "liked" or a "disliked" person.

The sorting data were converted into a half matrix of distances between each of the possible pairs of 66 traits. Essentially, the derived distance score, which is termed the "disassociation measure," is based on the assumption that traits that often occur together or with some third trait are psychologically similar or close, whereas traits that are rarely sorted into the same category are psychologically dissimilar or distant (see Rosenberg et al., 1968, pp. 285-286, for computational details and rationale).

The sorting data were used also to derive two indirect property scores for each of the traits. The Indirect Female–Male score for a particular trait was simply the proportion of subjects who sorted the trait into a pile that they subsequently labeled as "male." A high score thus indicated a close inferential relation between the trait and the social category male while a low score indicated that the trait was closely related to the social category female. Indirect Dislike–Like property scores were calculated in an analogous manner. These two properties are said to be "indirect" because the respondent's attention was drawn to the sorting task itself; the labeling of the piles in terms of sex and liking was done after the sorting and in an offhand manner. Thus, these scores were based on relatively unobtrusive procedures.

In contrast to the nonreactive nature of the Indirect Female–Male measure, direct ratings were obtained from an independent sample of subjects on the following three sex-related properties: Male–Female, Typical of Males–Not Typical of Males, Typical of Females–Not Typical of Females. Thus, subjects were asked to locate each trait along a sex-related continuum. Such ratings are analogous to the adjective checklist and rating scale techniques that are most commonly used to assess sex stereotypes. In the former, subjects assign each trait to the category male or female; in the latter approach, respondents are asked to locate the average adult male and female along various bipolar adjective scales.

Direct ratings of the traits were available from previous research for five additional properties: Evaluation (good–bad), Potency (hard–soft), Activity (active–passive), Social Desirability (good–bad in social activities), and Intellectual Desirability (good–bad in intellectual activities) (Rosenberg & Jones, 1972b).

Results: Multidimensional Scaling. The half matrix of disassociation scores between traits was used as input to Kruskal's (1964a, 1964b, 1967) MDSCAL (Version 3) computer program. A measure of badness of fit (called ''stress'') suggested that the two-dimensional configuration provided an adequate representation of the input distances for both female and male sorters.[1] Inasmuch as inspection and formal comparison of configurations based on female and male sorting data indicated that they were quite similar, only the two-dimensional configuration based on the sorting data for both sexes is considered hereafter.

In order to give meaning to, or ''interpret,'' the scaling results, the trait properties were fit to the two-dimensional configuration by means of linear multiple regression (see Rosenberg et al., 1968, for details). This procedure yields a multiple R, which indicates the degree to which the scores for a particular property fit the configuration. In addition, the beta weights can be used to position an axis for the property in the space. Fig. 2.1 presents the two-dimensional configuration with the fitted axes for Social and Intellectual Desirability as well as the Indirect Female–Male (*not* directly rated Male–Female) and Potency properties. These properties were chosen because they best described the overall meaning of the configuration and indicated the inferential relations between the social categories female and male and attributes of personality.

The meaning of the two-dimensional configuration is best understood in terms of two relatively orthogonal dimensions: ''social evaluation'' and ''potency.'' That is, good versus bad in social activities and hard versus soft are here rela-

---

[1]As in the original Rosenberg et al. (1968) study, the stress values indicated that either a two- or three-dimensional configuration was acceptable. Also as in the original study, analysis of the three-dimensional configuration suggested that the Activity property accounted best for the third dimension but that conclusions based on the two-dimensional configuration did not have to be amended.

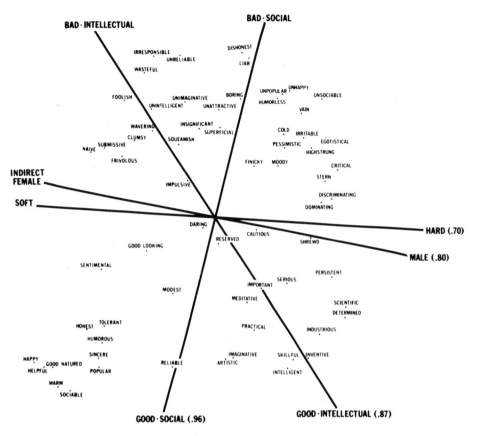

FIG. 2.1. Sorting Study: Two-dimensional configuration of the 66 traits showing best-fitting axis of the Social Desirability, Intellectual Desirability, Potency, and Indirect Female-Male properties. (Each number in parentheses represents the multiple correlations between projections on the axis and the property values.) [Ashmore & Tumia, 1980, p. 511; reprinted with permission of the publisher, Plenum Publishing Corporation.]

tively unrelated or independent cognitive continua. The social evaluation dimension is represented by the Social Desirability property that runs roughly from the top to the bottom of Fig. 2.1. This dimension also includes the Evaluation and Indirect Dislike–Like properties. (These dimensions are not plotted, since they fell quite close to the Social Desirability axis and can thus be thought of as cognitive distinctions quite similar to that of good versus bad in social activities.) The potency dimension is represented by the Potency property in Fig. 2.1. In terms of quality of fit, the Social Desirability, Evaluation, Indirect Dislike–Like properties all had very high multiple Rs indicating that for the present subjects "social evaluation" was an important dimension in cognitively organizing the traits and the people described by the traits. The fit of the Potency property was lower but still good enough to justify the conclusion that hard versus soft was a significant distinction for the respondents.

The Indirect Female–Male property fits the configuration quite well—not as well as the social evaluation properties but better than Potency. This high degree of fit clearly shows that the traits were used in a consistent fashion to describe female and male targets. It further suggests that the respondents' overall impressions of other people were clearly influenced by the sex of those people. The positioning of the fitted axis for the Indirect Female–Male property near Potency indicates the nature of this pattern: The social category male was associated with traits high in Potency (i.e., "hard" traits), whereas "soft" traits were assigned to females. Thus, it is possible to summarize the sex stereotypes of the present subject sample as "female = soft, male = hard."

The fit of the directly rated sex-related properties to the configuration showed an interesting pattern. The Typical of Males property fitted the configuration quite well and fell close to the Intellectual Desirability property. Thus, as can be seen in Fig. 2.1, traits such as *intelligent* were viewed as typical of males, while *foolish* and other traits in the upper left-hand portion of the configuration were judged as not typical of males. For the present sample, then, the judgment that a trait was typical versus not typical of males was closely related to the perception of whether the trait indicated that a person would be good versus bad in intellectual activities.

The Male–Female and Typical of Females properties did not fit the configurations well.[2] In other words, the direct judgments of the traits in terms of male versus female and typical versus not typical of females were not consistently related to the way in which the traits were used to organize cognitively impressions of the personalities of other people.

The seemingly inconsistent pattern displayed by the directly rated sex-related properties argues for caution in the use and interpretation of obtrusive or reactive assessments of sex stereotypes. The fact that Typical of Males fitted the configuration better than Male–Female, which, in turn, fitted better than Typical of Females suggests that self-reports about the qualities of females are most problematic. Whether due to social desirability (i.e., it is "sexist" to "stereotype" women) or to sincere unclarity about what is typical of females (i.e., recent media coverage may portray a wide variety of women) it seems that the *direct* question, "What is a female?," is not easy for college students to answer.

---

[2]In part, this lack of fit is due to the fact that the raters tended to judge most traits near the neutral point (i.e., 4 on a 1 to 7 scale) on both property scales. For example, on the Typical of Females property, males and females each gave 36 traits a rating of 4. Note that raters were not reluctant to use the full 1 to 7 rating scale for the Typical of Males property and that the quality of fit for this property was quite good.

Results: Hierarchical Clustering.   The "typological" representation of the sorting data was obtained by means of Johnson's (1967) complete-linkage method of hierarchical clustering. This method partitions the objects (in this case, traits) into independent (i.e., nonoverlapping) groupings on the basis of the disassociation scores. The clustering algorithm begins with each object in its own grouping or cluster (since the distance from an object to itself is assumed to be 0). The requirement for any two objects being considered equivalent (i.e., in the same cluster) is then relaxed (i.e., a small but nonzero disassociation score is allowed for grouping items together). This process goes on until all items are joined into one cluster. The clustering is hierarchical in that groups of items once clustered remain together throughout the analysis and are merged with other items or clusters to form higher level clusters.

The disassociation measures were analyzed separately for female and male sorters (see Ashmore & Tumia [1979] for details). The two resulting tree diagrams were similar but not enough so to justify collapsing over sex of sorter as was done for the multidimensional scaling analysis. In order to interpret the categorical structures, the same psychological properties used in the scaling analysis were fitted to the two tree diagrams by means of a series of parallel but separate analyses of variance (Rosenberg & Jones, 1972a). At each level of clustering the ratings for a particular property can be partitioned into between-cluster and within-cluster sums of squares. As stated by Rosenberg and Sedlak (1972): "The F ratio based on this partitioning reveals the extent to which the property in question is an appropriate interpretation of cluster differences at this particular level of clustering. The optimal level of clustering for a property is the one for which the F ratio has the smallest p-value [p. 270]." At this level the property maximally discriminates among the means of the clusters. Each tree was partitioned at the points where each of the properties achieved its minimum p-value (i.e., at the points where each property is optimal in differentiating the trait clusters). This is illustrated in Fig. 2.2, which presents the partitioned tree diagram for female perceivers. Two examples from the figure indicate how to read the tree diagram: (1) Indirect Female–Male reached its minimum p-value very early in the clustering process. It was maximally differentiating among clusters when the δ-measure distance for forming clusters was .32. At this point the traits are partitioned into 30 groupings. Reading from the top of the figure, the first cluster extends from *good-natured* to *helpful* and the last cluster contains only *unpopular* and *unattractive*; (2) Indirect Liking was the final property to achieve its minimum p-value for females. It discriminated best when the traits had been grouped into three large clusters.

The hierarchical clustering results support the multidimensional scaling analysis. The major conclusions from the scaling were that: (1) social evaluation and female versus male are significant and relatively independent dimensions of implicit personality theory; and (2) the distinction between the social categories female and male is similar to the personality trait distinction soft versus hard. For

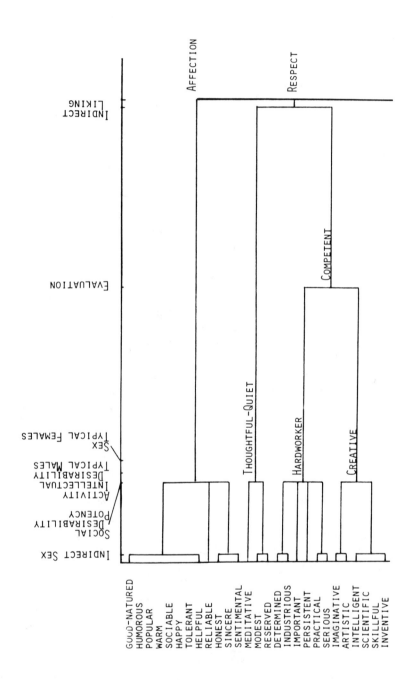

48

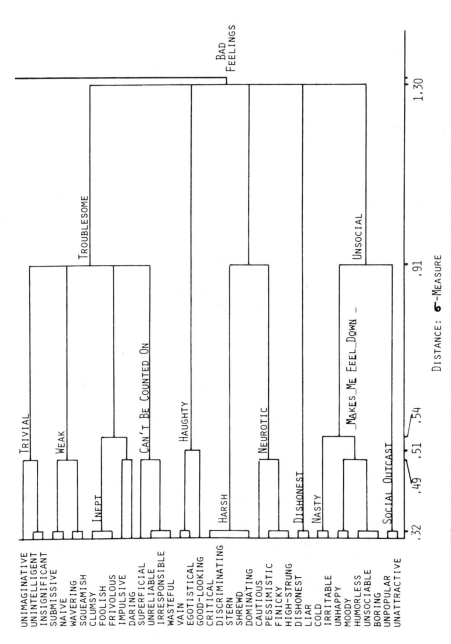

FIG. 2.2. Sorting Study: Tree diagram of six cluster levels of the 66 traits for female perceivers. (Each level represented is optimal with respect to a given property in distinguishing clusters.)

49

the tree diagrams generated by both female and male perceivers, the analyses of variance indicated that the social evaluation properties (i.e., Social Desirability, Indirect Liking, Evaluation) as well as Potency and Indirect Female–Male were highly successful in partitioning the traits. Thus, these properties were important in the typological as well as the dimensional representation of the relations among the traits. With respect to the second conclusion, the clusters of items used most often to describe male targets were also judged to be "hard," while female targets were assigned to "soft" clusters. When the Potency property reached its minimum p-value for female perceivers, the grouping with the most extreme "soft" rating ($M = 5.5$ on a 1 to 7 scale) comprised the items *submissive, naive, wavering,* and *squeamish,* whereas the two most "hard" clusters included *cold* and *irritable* ($M = 1.5$) and *critical, discriminating, stern, shrewd,* and *dominating* ($M = 2.2$). The extreme "soft" cluster, which was tentatively named "Weak," was subdivided into two groupings when Indirect Female–Male reached its minimum p-value, and these two clusters were among the most extreme in terms of being assigned to females ($M = .29$ for *submissive–naive*; $M = .18$ for *wavering–squeamish*). Likewise, the two "hard" clusters were used more often to describe male than female targets ($M = .65$ and .77, respectively). Male perceivers exhibited a similar pattern: Clusters that were extreme in terms of the hard–soft ratings tended to be assigned to male and female targets, respectively.

The scaling results were extended in two important ways—the demonstration of differences between female and male perceivers and the conceptual decomposition of the sex dimension into component content areas or "types." Sex of perceiver differences were manifested both in the local structuring of inferential relations (which will be discussed later) and in terms of the relative importance of the psychological properties. As noted in the foregoing, the clustering algorithm is called "hierarchical" because the groupings of items at a particular level are later merged to form more inclusive, higher-order clusters. Thus, it is possible to think of properties that reach their minimum p-values relatively late in the clustering process (i.e., where there are few clusters) as subsuming properties that are most successful in discriminating among the clusters at an earlier point. That is, the later in the clustering process a property reaches its maximum interpretability (i.e., minimum p-value) the more basic or central it is to the hierarchical structure underlying the perception of the traits (Jones & Ashmore, 1973). In the present study, there was a sex of perceiver difference in the hierarchical ordering of the properties: Sex-related properties were more central for males than for females. Of the 10 properties, Male–Female was most central for males and Indirect Female–Male was seventh, whereas for females these properties were tied for third and tenth, respectively.

Conceptual decomposition of the sex dimension was accomplished by partitioning the two clustering diagrams at the point where the Indirect Female–Male property reached its minimum p-value and then identifying those clusters with the highest (i.e., "male") and lowest (i.e., "female") mean ratings. These clusters are presented in Table 2.1. Females use four categories to describe women. The following tentative labels have been affixed to these groupings: "Weak," "Cautious," "Nurturant," and "Thoughtful–Quiet." Males have only two clusters, which we have designated as "Soft–Passive–Inept" and "Outgoing," that received low (i.e., "female") mean ratings on the Indirect Female–Male property. Females had four clusters to which they assigned males almost exclusively (i.e., "Important," "Harsh," "Daring," and "Scientific") and males had three such groupings (i.e., "Hardworker," "Problems-of-Having-Power," and "Can't-be-Counted-On").

Although we have no direct evidence, we believe that these groupings represent gender subcategories or types of women and men. Thus, within the broad social category *Woman*, the present results suggest that female college students

TABLE 2.1.

Sorting Study, Hierarchical Clustering: Types of Women and Men
Perceptually Discriminated by Females and Males

| Sex of Target | *Sex of Perceiver* | |
	Female	*Male*
Female	"Weak":	"Soft–Passive–Inept (Contempt)":
	"Dependent": *submissive, naive* (.29)	*sentimental, submissive, naive, frivolous, unintelligent, foolish, wasteful* (.34)
	"Indecisive": *wavering, squeamish* (.18)	"Outgoing": *humorous, sociable, popular, warm, good-natured, happy* (.34)
	"Cautious": *cautious* (.23)	
	"Nurturant": *honest, sincere, sentimental* (.26)	
	"Thoughtful–Quiet":	
	"Thoughtful": *meditative* (.29)	
	"Quiet": *modest, reserved*	
Male	"Important": *important* (.92)	"Hardworker": *practical, shrewd, determined, industrious, persistent, scientific, cautious, serious, stern* (.82)
	"Harsh": *critical, discriminating, stern, shrewd, dominating* (.77)	"Can't-Be-Counted-On": *unreliable, irresponsible, dishonest, liar* (.78)
	"Daring": *daring* (.77)	"Problems-Of-Having-Power": *important, dominating, critical, discriminating, egotistical, high-strung* (.75)
	"Scientific": *intelligent, scientific, skillful, inventive* (.72)	

Note. The number in parentheses following each cluster is the mean rating of the items comprised by the cluster on the Indirect Female–Male property.

identify a "Weak," a "Cautious," a "Nurturant," and a "Thoughtful-Quiet" type of woman. Males seem to have a simpler view of the fair sex, having just the "Soft-Passive-Inept" and "Outgoing" gender subcategories. In parallel fashion, the social category *Male* is partitioned into four types by females and three subcategories by males.

Table 2.1 reveals both subtle sex of perceiver differences and a suggestive pattern in the types of women and men distinguished by each. With regard to the former, the trait *sentimental* is seen by both sexes as a female quality, but females view it as part of a very positive type (what we have labeled "Nurturant"), while males cluster it with several negative traits to form what we term the "Soft-Passive-Inept" type. Also, female perceivers discriminate a "Thoughtful-Quiet" type, but in the male-generated tree diagram, the three traits comprised by this type appear in different clusters at the point where the traits are partitioned into three groups. Thus, for females *"Meditative-Modest-Reserved"* constitutes a coherent person type, whereas males appear to regard these traits as quite unrelated.

The labels given to some of the clusters in Fig. 2.2 and in Table 2.1 suggest the manner in which we interpret these findings. We speculate that the groupings of traits represent types of persons in that someone would be said to fit the type (or, to be a member of the gender subcategory for the types in Table 2.1) if her or his most central qualities matched the traits. At the present time, unfortunately, it is unclear how such "matching" might be done. The labels are considered important because it is assumed that type names, or "category concepts," are important in the encoding, storage, and retrieval of information about other people. Except for "Hardworker," the type labels we have assigned are close to the adjectives on which they are based. However, we speculate that noun type labels and "the _____ type" phrases may be very important in designating person types, including types of women and men. For example, in Table 2.1 it may be that the "Harsh" grouping is better thought of as "a bastard" or the "Nurturant" cluster best labeled "the motherly type." The question of type labels leads to an important point—the names used here are *our* words and intended primarily to facilitate discussion. Future work could fruitfully be directed at ascertaining whether respondents agree with these designations and, more generally, at assessing the type names that people spontaneously use to describe other people.

Impression Formation Study: A Trait Inference Approach to the Assessment of Sex Stereotypes

Del Boca and Ashmore (1980) used the second basic approach of implicit personality theory research, trait inference, to assess sex stereotypes. Two separate experiments were conducted in which the sex of target (among other things) was varied. The primary question was whether the inferences about the personality characteristics of women and men would parallel the results of the Sorting Study. That is, would female and male targets be distinguished primarily in terms of the trait distinction soft versus hard?

The Impression Formation Study also addressed two questions that might be raised about the interpretation of the results of the Sorting Study. It could be argued that subjects sorted the traits into piles on the basis of semantic similarity (D'Andrade, 1965; Shweder, 1975) rather than using the piles to describe specific women and men. A majority of subjects reported that they did the sorting in terms of specific people, but this does not rule out the semantic similarity argument. The second question is an extension of the first—Do the Indirect Female–Male property scores reflect sex-linked inferential relations or the judgment that a particular pile of traits logically implies one or the other sex? It is possible that subjects assigned the "female" or "male" label to each pile on the basis of the meaning of the traits rather than having sorted the traits together because they described a particular female or male. The subjects responded quite easily and quickly to the request to specify the sex of each pile, which suggests that the sorting piles corresponded to individuals. Again, however, this does not rule out the possibility that subjects inferred sex from the meaning of traits rather than ascribing traits on the basis of sex. The present study directly addressed both questions. Subjects were asked to respond to a specific target person rather than being allowed to "create"—or *not* "create"—a personality. The target person was described as either a man or woman, and subjects were asked to form an impression of the person. They were then requested to infer whether the target possessed a series of response traits. Thus, the direction of inference was clear: Because subjects were randomly assigned to either a female or male stimulus person, any resulting sex of target differences must be due to this manipulation.

Experiment 1.   The first experiment was an extended replication of Asch's (1946) classic *warm–cold* study. As in the original, subjects were presented with a target person who was said to be either *warm* or *cold*. Asch embedded these in a context of traits that Rosenberg et al. (1968) later demonstrated to be highly positive in Intellectual Desirability (e.g., *practical, intelligent*). In Experiment 1 a context of intellectually desirable traits was used, and an intellectually undesirable context was also created by selecting traits loading high at the negative end of the Intellectual Desirability fitted axis (in Rosenberg et al., 1968). Sex of target was manipulated simply by attributing the list of stimulus traits to either a "particular man" or a "particular woman." Thus, the experimental design was a fully crossed 2 (*warm–cold*) × 2 (positive–negative in Intellectual Desirability) × 2 (man–woman) factorial.

The major dependent measure was a set of bipolar scales designed to tap the following six dimensions of personality perception: Intellectual Desirability, Social Desirability, Potency, Activity, Agency, and Communion. The first four were drawn from the person perception literature. Agency and communion are

Bakan's (1966) fundamental modalities; as expressed by Block (1973), the former: "manifests itself in self-protection, self-assertion, and self-expansion . . . (whereas the latter) manifests itself in the sense of being at one with other organisms [p. 515]."

Inclusion of these six dimensions allowed the testing of predictions based on the results of the Sorting Study as well as others derived from the sex stereotype and sex-role identity literature. In a frequently cited paper on sex stereotypes, Broverman, Vogel, Broverman, Clarkson, and Rosenkrantz (1972) contend that the male stereotype comprises a "competency" cluster while the female stereotype denotes "warmth and expressiveness." Block (1973) found that males tended to describe their "idealized self" in terms of agency traits, whereas females used traits expressing communion. On the basis of this work it could be predicted that the male target would be rated relatively high on Intellectual Desirability (competency) and Agency while females would be judged higher in terms of Social Desirability (warmth and expressiveness) and Communion.

The results of the Sorting Study suggest a slightly different set of hypotheses. In the obtained multidimensional scaling configuration, the fitted axis for Indirect Female–Male was closest to Potency and was orthogonal to Social Desirability. Indirect Female–Male was somewhat related to Intellectual Desirability, which fell midway between Potency and Social Desirability. This pattern leads to the following prediction: The woman–man manipulation should have the largest influence on Potency, a moderate effect on Intellectual Desirability, and no impact on Social Desirability. (No predictions are possible regarding Agency and Communion since these dimensions were not included in the Sorting Study.)

The experimental manipulations and dependent measures were fully contained in a four-page booklet. Page one presented the three experimental inductions. Sex of target was conveyed in the first sentence, "Below are listed a number of characteristics that belong to a particular man (or woman)." The trait *warm* or *cold* and the Good Intellectual or Bad Intellectual context items were then listed. Page two offered the subjects (college students) an opportunity to describe in their own words their impression of the person presented on the first page. On the third page, adjective pairs were listed and subjects were instructed to indicate their impression of the stimulus person for each pair. The final page included questions regarding the physical and demographic characteristics of the target.

Summary scores were computed by summing a subject's response to the scales comprised by each of the six dimensions. The summary scores for each dimension and individual scales were subjected to a four-way univariate analysis of variance: Sex of Target, Social Desirability (*warm–cold*), Intellectual Desirability (trait context, positive–negative), and Sex of Perceiver. A large number of significant effects were obtained for the Social and Intellectual Desirability factors. The *warm–cold* main effect was significant for all the summary scales except Intellectual Desirability, and the main effect for the Intellectual Desirability manipulation was significant for all but the Communion summary scale.

Because the purpose here is to explore sex as a factor in implicit personality theory, the present discussion is restricted to Sex of Target main effects. (Significant, but unreported interactions do not change the interpretations advanced here.) The Sex of Target main effect was significant for the Intellectual Desirability summary scale and approached significance for the Communion index. The female target was rated lower in Intellectual Desirability but higher in Communion than the male stimulus person. In terms of specific items, the female target was rated as more *sympathetic* and *feminine* and as less *scientific, serious,* and *assertive* than the male.

Although these results tend to support the sex stereotype literature predictions more than those based on the Sorting Study, they must be regarded as quite tentative, inasmuch as the effect of target sex was quite weak in comparison with those of the other manipulated variables. While it may be that sex does not play a major role in the impression formation process, the design of Experiment 1 may have worked against demonstrating the role that it does play. The procedure focused the subjects' attention on the trait list: Subjects were told to form their impression on the basis of the traits, the traits were portrayed in a visually salient manner (i.e., as a list), subjects were told to read the list twice, and they were urged to take time to think about the person described by the traits. Sex of target, on the other hand, was communicated in a very indirect and nonsalient manner—the word ''man'' or ''woman'' was mentioned just once in the introductory paragraph. This situation certainly reduced the relative impact of the Sex of Target manipulation. Also, it seems to be much at variance with everyday social interaction where a person's sex generally is clearly conveyed whereas aspects of personality (i.e., trait information) often are not.

Experiment 2. The second Impression Formation Study experiment was designed to increase the salience of target sex relative to target personality. This was done in two ways. First, the traits said to describe the target were selected so as to convey less information, particularly evaluative information, about the person. Second, the target's sex was mentioned twice in the introductory paragraph.

One other major change was made. In addition to completing items assessing specific dimensions of personality perception, subjects were asked to describe the target using the sex stereotypic items of the Sex-Role Questionnaire (Broverman et al., 1972). This was done for two related reasons. First, it allowed assessing the inferential relations between the social categories ''female'' and ''male'' and a wider set of personal attributes than was used in the Sorting Study and the first Impression Formation Study experiment. Second, the added items have been found to be ''sex stereotypic'' (i.e., to be differentially characteristic of women and men) in previous research. The Sex-Role Questionnaire is an undisguised self-report measure and, as a consequence, is quite reactive. Since the manipulation of target sex in the present experiment was indirect, it was possible to compare (as was done in the Sorting Study) the results of relatively unobtrusive and relatively obtrusive methods of assessing sex stereotypes. That is, all 41 items from the Sex-Role Questionnaire had been found to differentiate the "average adult female" from the "average adult male." Would the female and male targets be rated differently on these scales?

As in Experiment 1, the materials were completely contained in one booklet. Target sex was manipulated in the opening sentence of page one and mentioned a second time toward the end of the introductory paragraph. The stimulus person was described as possessing one of the following two sets of traits: *talented, confident, emotional,* and *conservative; impulsive, daring, cautious,* and *reserved.* These items were chosen on the basis of their positioning in previous multidimensional scaling analyses of the structure of implicit personality theory (Rosenberg et al., 1968; Sedlak, 1971). The items have near-zero loadings on the Intellectual and Social Desirability dimensions and each list contains two slightly positive and two slightly negative traits.

Twelve scales were used to assess perception of the stimulus person in terms of the following four dimensions: Intellectual Desirability, Social Desirability, Potency, and Activity. In addition, the 41 sex stereotypic items of the Sex-Role Questionnaire were included. Four other items were added: *warm–cold* and *expressive–not expressive* (to assess the hypothesized "warmth-expressiveness" female stereotype), *competent–incompetent* (to index the hypothesized perception of males in terms of "competence"), and *masculine–feminine.*

Summary scores were computed for the four personality perception dimensions as in Experiment 1. Univariate analyses of variance—with Sex of Target, Trait Description, and Sex of Perceiver as factors—were computed for the summary indices, the scales included in these indices, and the sex stereotype items. The Sex of Target main effect was highly significant for the Intellectual Desirability summary scale and of borderline significance for the Potency index. The Intellectual Desirability effect can be traced primarily to the adjective pair *scientific–unscientific* and, to a lesser extent, *intelligent–unintelligent. Dominant–submissive* contributes most to the main effect for the Potency summary scale.

There was a very striking pattern of response to the sex stereotypic items: There were significant or near significant Sex of Target main effects for 12 of the 30 male-valued items but for only 2 of the 11 female-valued personal attributes. (Male-valued items are ones for which the pole seen as more typical of males than females is also judged to be more socially desirable for people in general [Rosenkrantz et al., 1968]). On the male-valued items the male target was seen as more *dominant, aggressive,* and *self-confident,* more likely to *hide emotions,* to *like math and science,* to be *skilled in business,* to *act as a leader,* to be *able to separate feelings from ideas,* and to *think men are superior to women;* the male target was judged as less *emotional,* and less likely to be *excitable in a minor crisis* or to *cry very easily.* There was also a strong Sex of Target main effect on the *competent–incompetent* pair, with the male stimulus rated as more *competent*. The only two female-valued items to show significant differences were *strong need for security* and *uses harsh language*. The female target was judged higher on the former, whereas the male was seen as more likely to *use harsh language*.

The results of the Impression Formation Study seem to be somewhat at variance with those of the Sorting Study. Intellectual Desirability was the only personality perception dimension to show a significant Sex of Target main effect in both experiments of this study. That is, only the personality trait distinction good in intellectual activities versus bad in intellectual activities was clearly shown to have a close inferential relation with the social categories male and female. Closer analysis of the results, however, suggests that it is not intelligence as fixed intellectual ability that respondents attributed differentially to the sexes. Rather, it appears that the subjects associated the social category male with a hard, rational style of thinking, feeling, and behaving, while the social category female was assumed to covary with a soft, emotional style. This difference can also be thought of in terms of controlling versus controlled. Subjects seem to infer that males control their thoughts and feelings (e.g., *able to separate feelings from ideas*) and are controlling or directive interpersonally (e.g., *dominant, acts as a leader*), whereas female targets are assumed to be controlled by thoughts and feelings (e.g., *excitable in a minor crisis*) and to be noncontrolling in interpersonal relations (e.g., *strong need for security*).

Although the Sex of Target effect for *intelligent–unintelligent* was significant in Experiment 2, it is the trait pair *scientific–unscientific* that seems to capture in both studies the subjects' implicit notions about males' alleged superiority in intellectual activities. Science is, at least in the minds of the lay public, an activity requiring disciplined thinking (in contrast with the stereotype of the "free spirited" and "spontaneous" artist) as well as the control of one's emotions (to prevent bias) and the manipulation of nature. In addition, the Potency index was near significant in Experiment 2 in differentiating the male and female targets. It is particularly significant in terms of the controlling versus controlled interpretation that *submissive–dominant,* which is probably one of the best indices of interpersonal control, contributed most to the main effect for the Potency summary scale.

The picture is less clear for inferential relations regarding the social category female. In fact, the present results—particularly the lack of significant Sex of Target main effects on the female-valued sex stereotypic items—suggest that the female stereotype may be less elaborated than the male stereotype. This conclusion is congruent with the results of the direct ratings for the property Typical of Females–Not Typical of Females in the Sorting Study. Both sexes rated most items (i.e., 36 of 66) as neither typical nor not typical of females. Further, only 3 items were rated as extremely nontypical (i.e., medians of 6). This was in marked contrast to the pattern of response to the Typical of Males property where the subjects were quite willing to rate items as both typical and not typical of males. Thus, two quite different methods provide converging evidence that college students' notions about the personal attributes of females are less clear or "set" than their parallel ideas regarding males.

Contrary to much of the extant sex stereotype literature, the social category female does not appear to be associated with being generally good in social activities. The Sex of Target main effect was not significant for the Social Desirability index in either experiment, and female targets were not perceived as more *warm* or *expressive* than male targets in Experiment 2. There was a hint, however, that females tended to be seen as softhearted and noncontrolling. In Experiment 1 the Communion main effect was almost wholly attributable to the pair, *sympathetic–unsympathetic*. The differences in Experiment 2 on *strong need for security* and *does not use harsh language* also suggest a "soft," submissive interpersonal style.

Sex Stereotypic Vocabulary Study: Personality Description Using the Language of Sex Stereotypes

The first two studies yield the same conclusion about sex stereotypes: The social category female is inferentially related to soft attributes of personality (particularly softheartedness) and a noncontrolling style, whereas the social category male is associated with hard traits (especially tough-mindedness) and a controlling style. However, an objection can be raised about the generality of this conclusion. The results obtained might be due to fortuitous selection of personality attributes. Except for the sex stereotypic items added to the response list in the second experiment of the Impression Formation Study, all the traits used in both studies were drawn from previous person-perception work. Researchers in this area may simply have built social evaluation and potency into the language they used for research.

The third study (Tumia & Ashmore, in preparation) was designed to address this potential problem. As in the Sorting Study, subjects were asked to describe other people by sorting attributes of personality into piles. Unlike the Sorting Study, however, the vocabulary used by respondents was not taken from person-perception research but from previous studies of sex stereotypes. Thus, in the present study the cognitive structure associated with the social categories female and male was explored using not the terms selected by person-perception researchers but the words and phrases found by sex stereotype researchers to be assigned differentially to the sexes.

Method.   As in the Sorting Study this investigation involved two groups of white college students of both sexes. The first group performed the sorting task. The second served as judges, providing ratings of the attributes of personality in terms of psychological property dimensions.

One hundred fifty-nine personal attributes were derived from studies by Sherriffs and McKee (1957) and Rosenkrantz and his associates (1968). The majority of the attributes were trait adjectives (e.g., *stable*), but there were some items that more directly described behavior (e.g., *does not use harsh language*), interests (e.g., *interested in own appearance*), and opinions or preferences (e.g., *likes art and literature*). The total vocabulary was divided into two separate lists of 80 personal attributes. (*Adventurous* was included on both lists.) The lists were equated as nearly as possible in terms of source of item (i.e., Sherriffs & McKee or Rosenkrantz et al.), sex linkage (i.e., whether the attribute had been judged to be characteristic of females or males), and, for the Sherriffs and McKee items, social desirability (i.e., whether the authors categorized the attribute as socially desirable or socially undesirable).

The procedure for the first group of subjects was the same as in the Sorting Study. Each subject was given 80 slips of paper with the personal attributes printed on them and was asked to sort the slips into piles in terms of their co-occurrence in the same person. Once the sorting was completed the subject indicated whether each pile described a female or a male, and a liked or disliked person. The disassociation measure and Indirect Female–Male and Indirect Dislike–Like indices were calculated as in the Sorting Study.

Each subject in the second sample rated the items on one of the following properties: Social Desirability, Intellectual Desirability, Potency, Activity, Male–Female, Typical of Females, Typical of Males. The mean rating of each item was calculated separately for female and male raters.

Results: Multidimensional Scaling. The data for female and male perceivers on the first and second lists were separately analyzed by means of Kruskal's (1967) MDSCAL computer program. As in the Sorting Study, a two-dimensional configuration was optimal in all four conditions.[3] Inspection and formal comparison indicated that the two-dimensional configurations for females and males were similar but far from identical for both lists of personal attributes. Thus, unlike in the Sorting Study the data were not collapsed across sex of sorter.

Although the locations of the points (i.e., attributes of personality) in the two-dimensional configurations were not identical, the overall structure of the four spaces was remarkably similar. Furthermore, this structure was quite similar to that obtained in our initial investigation. The social evaluation properties (i.e., Indirect Dislike–Like, Social Desirability) fit the configurations quite well (i.e., had high multiple R's), and the fitted axes for these properties were quite close in the four spaces (i.e., the largest angle separating them in the four spaces was only

---

[3] "Optimal" indicates the best when considering both how well the configuration represented the data (i.e., stress values) and how interpretable the solution is (i.e., multiple R's). The three-dimensional configurations for both sexes on List 1 are actually slightly better than the two-dimensional on both counts. However, the results of the two-dimensional configurations will be presented for ease of discussion. Also, the major conclusions would not be altered if the three-dimensional solutions were considered.

12°.) Roughly orthogonal to these properties was Indirect Female–Male, which fit the configurations only slightly less well than did Indirect Dislike–Like and Social Desirability. Further, Potency had high multiple R's in three of the four conditions (with a modest but acceptable .65 in the fourth) and was closely aligned with the Indirect Female–Male fitted axis. This basic structure is illustrated in Fig. 2.3, which depicts the two-dimensional configuration for female perceivers on List 2. In Fig. 2.3, the Social Desirability vector runs roughly from left to right with personal attributes such as *inhibited, foolish,* and *tactless* (from

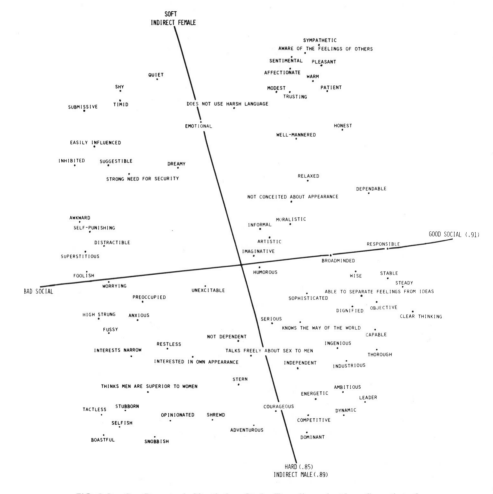

FIG. 2.3. Sex Stereotypic Vocabulary Study: Two-dimensional configuration of the 80 personal attributes for female perceivers on List 2 showing best-fitting axes of the Social Desirability, Potency, and Indirect Female–Male properties. (Each number in parentheses is the multiple correlation between projections on the axis and the property values.)

top to bottom) projecting onto the extreme bad social end of the axis and *sympathetic, responsible,* and *clear thinking* (again from top to bottom) being judged as qualities of a person who is extremely good in social activities. At an angle of 99° from Social Desirability is Indirect Female–Male. (Indirect Female–Male and Hard–Soft properties are depicted by one line in Fig. 2.3, inasmuch as they are separated by only 1°.) This vector, which runs roughly from the top to the bottom of the figure, indicates that traits such as *submissive, quiet,* and *sympathetic* (reading from left to right) are viewed as extremely "soft" and as being exhibited overwhelmingly by females, whereas *snobbish, dominant,* and *leader* are considered to be "hard" and "male" attributes.

Also as in the Sorting Study, the directly rated sex-related properties did not fit the configuration as well as the aforementioned properties. The present results for these properties, however, differed from the initial investigation in two primary ways. First, Typical of Males did not have a consistently better fit to the configurations as had been the case in the Sorting Study. Second, the quality of fit for the Sex (Male-Female), Typical of Males, and Typical of Females properties was highly variable across the four conditions. For example, the multiple R's for Sex ranged from .21 (males, List 2), which is very low, to a moderately high .73 (females, List 1). In light of these differences it may be necessary to qualify the conclusion reached at the end of the Sorting Study and simply note that direct ratings in terms of sex-related continua are not likely to be related in any clear and consistent way to structures for cognitively organizing impressions of others.

Results: Hierarchical Clustering. Again, the Johnson clustering program was used and the properties were fitted to the resulting clustering tree diagrams by means of a series of analyses of variance. In terms of the quality of fit, the results parallel those for the multidimensional scaling. Of the nine properties, the Indirect Dislike–Like property achieves the lowest p-value in all four conditions of sorting (i.e., female and male sorters on List 1 and List 2), with Social Desirability having the second lowest in three conditions and being fifth best for females on List 2. The social evaluation properties are clearly best at partitioning the 80 personal attributes into homogeneous groupings. Thus, social evaluation plays a central role in the typological as well as the dimensional representation of the cognitive structure underlying the perception of other people.

Indirect Female–Male and Potency are also significant in the categorical depiction of the implicit theories of personality of the members of the present sample. For the four conditions of sorting, the former is second, third, fourth, and fifth most discriminating, whereas Potency is third best twice, fourth best once, and falls to seventh position for males on List 1. As in the scaling, then, the unobtrusively derived sex property and the associated hard–soft trait distinction account quite well for parts of the cognitive structures assessed by means of the sorting task.

The remaining properties do less well in consistently relating to the hierarchical clustering tree diagrams. Activity and Intellectual Desirability do only slightly less well than Indirect Female–Male and Potency. The directly rated sex-related properties are consistently least discriminating among the clusters. Across the four conditions of sorting the best that these three properties can achieve is sixth most discriminating; in two conditions they are rank ordered seventh, eighth, ninth; in males on List 1 they are sixth, seventh, ninth; and for females on List 2 they are sixth, eighth, and ninth.

The fit of the Indirect Female–Male property to the clustering diagrams indicates the importance of the broad social categories female and male in structuring perceptions of other people. In addition, inspection of the content of the groupings of the personal attributes at the point where the property achieves its maximal differentiation is suggestive of types of women and men that the subjects perceptually distinguish. As was done for the Sorting Study, the clusters with the lowest (i.e., "most female") and highest (i.e., "most male") mean ratings have been abstracted from the tree diagrams and are listed in Table 2.2. Tentative labels have been suggested for the clusters. Again, these are the investigators' category names and are intended primarily to be illustrative.

The groupings listed in Table 2.2 contribute in three primary ways to the present line of inquiry. First, in all four conditions, the extreme female groupings also have extreme mean scores in the direction of "soft" and the "male clusters" have extreme mean scores in the direction of "hard" on the Potency property. The clustering results, then, further support the conclusion from the multidimensional scaling analysis that the social categories female and male are inferentially related to the trait distinction soft versus hard. This is, of course, consistent with findings of the Sorting Study and the Impression Formation Study.

Second, several of the sex-linked clusters seem quite similar to gender subcategories suggested by the clustering analysis of the Sorting Study data. On List 1 males group *sociable* and *cheerful* at the point where Indirect Female–Male is maximally discriminating and ascribe these traits more frequently to females than males. Although it is not as elaborated as the parallel cluster in the Sorting Study, we have labeled both groupings "Outgoing." It is significant that only males seem to distinguish such a subcategory of woman in either study. Also for males on List 1, a subcategory of man appears that seems to be, in abbreviated form, the "Hardworker" type. Again, female perceivers don't seem to make this categorization. On List 2 both female and male perceivers identify a "Nurturant" type of female as did females in the Sorting Study. Also, females have a cluster in the present data that is quite similar to the "Weak(Dependent-Indecisive)" subcategory found in the initial investigation.

Third, the present results suggest some possible additions to a developing taxonomy of gender subcategories. Of particular interest are the several groupings that concern emotionality. In all four conditions, at least one female and one male type involved emotions. While the male types are similar in conveying the impression that the target controls (perhaps overcontrols) his feelings rather than being directed in any sense by his affective experience, the different groupings suggest quite different types of people. Similarly, the woman subcategories are united by the suggestion that the target is influenced by her feelings, but the quality of this influence varies considerably. For example, the "Girlfriend" and "Neurotic" types discriminated by males on List 1 both appear to be influenced by emotions but in very different ways.

TABLE 2.2.
Sex Stereotypic Vocabulary Study, Hierarchical Clustering:
Types of Women and Men Perceptually Discriminated by Females and Males

Sex of Target	List 1	
	Female Perceivers	Male Perceivers
Female	"Nervous Nellie" (.27): weak, excitable, complaining, rattlebrained, moody, temperamental, neurotic, self-pitying, nervous, touchy, confused, fearful "Upper Class Young Woman" (.38): poised, idealistic, cautious, religious, likes art and literature, tactful	"Girlfriend" (.21): expresses tender feelings easily, sexy, sensitive "Neurotic" (.40): weird, neurotic, nervous, self-pitying, fearful, confused "Nurturant" (.43): gentle, softhearted, kind, understanding, lovable, "Outgoing" (.48): sociable, cheerful
Male	"Businessman" (.67): conservative, never cries, skilled in business, formal, unemotional "Knows What He Wants" (.65): determined, likes math and science, witty, sharpwitted, neat in habits, realistic, makes decisions easily, intelligent, reasonable, logical "Egotist" (.54): vain, reckless, mischevious, prejudiced, loud, frivolous, greedy	"Hardworker" (.95): determined, persistent, direct "Under Control" (.91): feelings not easily hurt, skilled in business, never cries, unemotional "Tough Guy" (.89): not uncomfortable about being aggressive, loud, forceful, aggressive "Outspoken" (.88): outspoken "Pain in the ass" (.86): complaining, greedy, prejudiced, argumentative, hard-headed

(continued)

TABLE 2.2. (Continued)

Sex of Target	List 2	
	Female Perceivers	Male Perceivers
Female	"Wallflower" (.13): *timid, does not use harsh* *language, quiet, shy* "Weak (Dependent-Indecisive)" (.16): *suggestible, strong need* *for security, inhibited,* *submissive, easily influenced* "Romantic Teenage Girl" (.22): *emotional, dreamy* "Nurturant" (.23): *trusting, patient, warm,* *well-mannered, honest,* *modest, aware of feelings* *of others, pleasant,* *affectionate, sentimental,* *sympathetic*	"Nurturant" (.27): *warm, sympathetic, aware of* *feelings of others, sentimental,* *affectionate* "Emotional" (.33): *emotional* "Submissive" (.34): *suggestible, distractible,* *submissive, easily influenced*
Male	"Male Chauvinist" (.82): *thinks men are superior to* *women, interests narrow* "Up Type" (.79): *energetic, restless, adven-* *turous, courageous* "Forbidding" (.72): *unexcitable, stern, serious* "Student Body President" (.67): *ingenious, dynamic,* *ambitious, leader, competitive,* *industrious, dominant*	"On the Way Up" (.84): *ingenious, ambitious,* *industrious, humorous,* *dominant, dynamic, com-* *petitive, shrewd, energetic,* *leader, independent,* *adventurous, courageous* "Cool, calm, collected" (.73): *responsible, able to separate* *feelings from ideas, capable,* *objective, clear thinking,* *thorough, wise, dependable* "Arrogant" (.72): *thinks men are superior to* *women, interested in own* *appearance, opinionated,* *selfish, tactless, interests* *narrow, boastful, snobbish*

Note. The number in parentheses following each cluster is the mean rating of the items comprised by the cluster on the Indirect Female-Male property.

IMPLICATIONS OF PRESENT FORMULATION

The proposed conceptual framework and the results of the research completed within this framework add to our understanding of three separate, yet related, topics: implicit personality theory, sex stereotypes, and stereotyping and intergroup behavior. The present approach also suggests possible directions for theory development and empirical research. In this concluding section, the implications of formulating sex stereotypes in terms of implicit personality theory are considered.

Implications for Implicit Personality Theory

At the base of the present formulation is the assumption that sex stereotypes are not aberrant cognitive structures and that progress in understanding how the sexes are perceived will be enhanced by relating sex stereotypes to research and theory on ''normal'' psychological, especially social psychological phenomena. It was proposed that the person-perception construct, ''implicit personality theory,'' provides a fruitful perspective for the study of beliefs about the sexes. This formulation also contributes to our understanding of implicit theories of personality. (Others have also linked stereotyping to trait attribution in general [Feldman, 1972; Feldman & Hilterman, 1975] and to implicit personality theory more specifically [Jones, 1977; Secord, 1958].)

The most obvious implication of the present formulation for ''implicit personality theory'' has already been noted—''social categories'' are important components of the cognitive structures that individuals use to organize their impressions of other people. The aforementioned studies clearly indicate that the social categories female and male are inferentially related in consistent ways to attributes of personality. Further, the clustering results suggest that respondents distinguish different types of women and men. These types are also social categories or subcategories. The present findings are complemented by recent research by Cantor and Mischel (1979). These investigators have shown in several different studies that people carve up the world of other people into a variety of types, that these types are described in consistent ways, and that they are part of an organized cognitive structure. Cantor and Mischel (1979) have focused their attention on person types (e.g., ''introvert,'' ''PR type'') that are quite different from the social categories female and male that we have used. That both lines of research point toward the important role of social categories in person perception suggests that such cognitive elements should be incorporated into implicit personality theory research and theory.

This line of reasoning has clear implications for future research directions. Most obviously, the present approach is not limited to perception of the sexes. We began with sex stereotypes because of an interest in the substantive issue of female–male relations. The guiding ideas, however, are relevant to any social category. Thus, it would be possible to use both personality description and trait inference methods to study ethnic stereotypes (e.g., views of Blacks, Russians, Jews) as well as occupational (e.g., doctors, politicians) and other (e.g., mentally retarded, elderly) stereotypes. In carrying out any extension of the present approach, it is important to note that individuals and members of subcultures may distinguish idiosyncratic groupings. First, an individual or a subculture might seem to ''see'' the same group of people, but the name attached to that group might indicate a set of rules for defining the social category that may not be culturally shared. Consider, for example, three social categories each with two alternative labels, "Blacks"–"niggers," "Italians"–"wops," and "homosexuals"–"faggots." Whether the coding of a social category by means of such alternative labels only reflects differences in the evaluation of the group or a different definition of the group is an important question for future research. Second, individuals and subgroups may partition the social environment in different ways. Wish, Deutsch, and Biener's (1970) study of nation perception provides a good example. They found that, in judging the similarity of pairs of nations, "doves" relied more on differences between nations in economic development (i.e., advanced nations versus underdeveloped countries), whereas "hawks" stressed the distinction between capitalism and communism. For some hawks, China, Russia, and Cuba were a single social category, "communist."

The present framework suggests a second "widening" of the construct, "implicit personality theory"—inclusion of attributes of personality other than trait adjectives. Content analyses of open-ended person descriptions reveal the wide variety of ways in which people describe—and presumably think about—other people (e.g., Beach & Wertheimer, 1961; Dornbusch, Hastorf, Richardson, Muzzy, & Vreeland, 1965; Fiske & Cox, 1979). Two types of "attributes of personality" seem to deserve particular attention in future research on stereotypes and implicit personality theory—feelings and expected action patterns (see Ashmore & Del Boca, 1979, for details). As will be developed later, Rosenberg (1977) has speculated that the feelings that others arouse in us may be the psychological encoding of success or failure in achieving interpersonal goals and may serve to mediate trait attributions and the organization of implicit theories of personality. Expected action patterns are specific sequences of behavior that a perceiver expects of a target in a particular setting. Expected action patterns may, in part, be important precisely because they are very specific, whereas traits are very general (i.e., the latter are person descriptions that "sum over" or summarize large numbers of expected action patterns). Also, expected action patterns, if they involve the perceiver as well as the target, are much closer to overt action and, as a consequence, are potentially significant shapers of that action. The notion of expected action sequences is quite similar to the construct of "script" as used by Schank and Abelson (1977), and their procedure and general approach might be used to explicate the proposed expected action pattern component of implicit theories of personality.

Having discussed social categories and attributes of personality separately, it is now appropriate to consider them jointly. The major question here is: Do the inferential relations among attributes of personality vary as a function of social category? Among person-perception researchers, this general question has been termed "meaning change." In the aforementioned research, this issue was not addressed. The structural representations in the Sorting and Sex Stereotypic Vocabulary studies were based on responses to targets of both sexes; the pattern of inferential relations was not assessed separately for female and male targets. This choice was made in order to be able to compare directly how the sexes are perceived. In the future, however, it seems appropriate to look at implicit personality theory structures separately for important social categories as well as for all targets regardless of category membership. This conclusion is based on accumulating evidence that the "meaning" of attributes of personality can vary systematically as a function of social category.

In the earliest study on this topic, Secord and Berscheid (1963) found that: "While some shift in mean ratings occurs because of categorization of a person as Negro, associations between cue-trait and judged trait remain markedly consistent whether the stimulus person is Negro or white or whether the judge is prejudiced or not [p. 75]." Several more recent studies, however, demonstrate meaning change as a function of perceived group membership of the target (see Schneider et al. 1979, pp. 184–188). Hanno and Jones (1973) found that intertrait associations were different when a "family doctor" was described than when a "national politician" was evaluated. Schneider and Blankmeyer (1978) obtained different patterns of trait inferences for an "introvert" versus an "extrovert."

Two investigations—both of non-American, nonstudent populations—provide the most pertinent evidence regarding change in inferential relations between attributes of personality as a function of social category. Kirk and Burton (1977) studied the implicit theories of personality held by members of the Maasai culture of Kenya. They asked respondents to judge the relative similarity of 13 personality descriptors. The judgments were done using eight separate instructional sets: one in which the descriptors were presented in isolation and seven in which the same descriptors were used as modifiers of a social identity term. In Maasai culture, an important set of social identities (in the present formulation, social categories) are defined by the combination of age and sex (e.g., "small boy," "adult female"), and it was these social identities that were used. The similarities data were analyzed by both multidimensional scaling and correlations. Although there were similarities in the structures obtained for all eight conditions (e.g., a consistent evaluative dimension) there was clear evidence that inferential relations varied systematically as a function of social identity.

This conclusion was also reached by White (1980) in his research among the A'ara inhabitants of Santa Isabel, Solomon Islands. Similarity judgments were obtained for pairs of 37 personality descriptors and a multidimensional scaling analysis done. A two-dimensional configuration was found to represent adequately the input data. This configuration was interpreted in terms of two orthogonal, bipolar properties—solidarity and dominance. A second sample of respondents was asked to identify, from the list of 37 traits, those that were most appropriate and most inappropriate for each of 10 different types of leaders (e.g., chief, priest, school teacher). A measure of similarity between pairs of traits was derived and used as input to a multidimensional scaling computer program. Again, a two-dimensional configuration was found to be the best representation of the similarities data. The overall pattern of this configuration was similar to that for the similarity judgments done without respect to any particular social category. There were, however, significant differences that indicated the way in which leadership status (or the various social categories of ''leader'') influenced the meaning of the trait terms. Of particular importance was the finding that traits appropriate to leadership (e.g., *strong*) are seen as higher in solidarity in the context of leadership than when not associated with this social category, and traits inappropriate to being a leader (e.g., *fearful*) are evaluated more negatively in a leader than when leader status is not specified. These findings and those cited previously suggest that future implicit personality theory research and theory will have to address the issue of meaning change. This need is particularly important for the present formulation, which seeks to incorporate social category within an implicit personality theory framework. As a general rule of thumb, it seems necessary, when possible, to obtain structural representations based on targets of a single social category as well as for targets of the various social categories of interest.

Implications for Sex Stereotypes

The present line of research contributes most directly to the sex stereotype literature. Four points are noteworthy in this respect. The first contribution to the area of sex stereotypes is in the form of a caution: The obtrusive nature of most sex stereotype assessment techniques may seriously impair their usefulness as indicators of how individuals personally view women and men. As noted in discussing the Sorting Study, 36 of 66 traits received ''neutral'' (i.e., 4 on a 1 to 7 scale) ratings by both female and male subjects on the scale, Not Typical of Females–Typical of Females. On the Male–Female rating scale, females produced 42 and males 31 items with median ratings of 4. Although there is no direct evidence, comments made by raters suggested that they did not like the idea that they were ''being asked to stereotype people.'' The relative success of the sex stereotype assessments based on the personality description and trait inference approaches used in the present line of research indicate that the subjects did have consistent beliefs about the personal attributes of women and men. This further suggests that the development and refinement of indirect assessments of sex stereotypes should be a high priority for researchers in this area.

The second contribution concerns the content of the cognitive structures associated with the social categories female and male. The Sorting and Sex Stereotypic Vocabulary Studies reported above clearly indicate that the social categories female and male are most closely associated with the personality trait distinction soft versus hard (Potency) and not generalized Evaluation (i.e., bad–

good). This is at variance with the conclusion reached in most sex stereotype studies, that the male stereotype is evaluated more positively than that of the female (e.g., Broverman et al., 1972). (The possible sources of this conflict will be discussed later.) The results of the Impression Formation Study suggest that sex stereotypes may vary not so much in terms of generalized Potency as in terms of the distinction between a hard, rational approach to thinking, feeling, and behaving and a soft-hearted interpersonal style, or the contrast between a controlling versus controlled type of person. This tough-minded versus softhearted distinction is similar to, though more general than, the tough-minded versus tender-minded dichotomy proposed by Eysenck (1954) with regard to social attitudes. The controlling versus controlled distinction is identical to White's (1980) "dominance/submission" dimension that denotes the cognitive structure representing the: "proclivity to influence or be influenced by another's goals or plans."

The third contribution to the sex stereotype literature is the notion of gender subcategories or types of women and men. As the multidimensional scaling results of the Sorting and Sex Stereotypic Vocabulary Studies indicate, there is an overall cognitive structure associated with the broad social categories female and male. This structure—whether it is thought of as soft versus hard, softhearted versus tough-minded, or submission–dominance—captures the "gist" of the general gender categories. It is likely, however, that subcategories are part of the cognitive apparatus of most perceivers and that these subcategories are used ". . . for molecular behavioral analysis and predictions of a person's concrete behavior in a highly specific situation" (Cantor and Mischel, 1979).

With the exception of one investigation by Clifton, McGrath, and Wick (1976), sex stereotype investigators have treated female and male as simple, homogeneous categories. The hierarchial clustering results of the Sorting and Sex Stereotypic Vocabulary Studies suggest that perceivers distinguish various types of women and men. The uncovering of perceived types of women and men seems a high-priority task. The use of the word "uncovering" is deliberate, and the reason for using it is best understood by comparing the approach of the aforementioned studies with that taken by Clifton and her collaborators. The Sorting and Sex Stereotypic Vocabulary Studies were designed to uncover types by identifying regularities in the way in which targets were described. Clifton et al. (1976), on the other hand, presented subjects with type names (e.g., "club woman," "female athlete") and assessed whether these type names elicited consistent patterns of response on bipolar adjective scales. That different patterns were obtained indicates that subjects *can* judge these types as distinctive. A premise of the approach advocated here, however, is that it is more fruitful to attempt to discover the types that people *do* use in structuring their cognitions regarding the social environment. If this view is taken, then the Clifton et al. procedure is part of the verification stage. That is, asking subjects to respond to type names should be preceded by a systematic process of finding the types that individuals use spontaneously. This process should, hopefully, be as free from investigator influence as possible.[4]

With respect to types of women and men, it is important to note that it is not being suggested that the specific labels attached in the foregoing to clusters of personal attributes (see Tables 2.1 and 2.2) are *the* kinds of women and men that perceivers distinguish. In fact, there is probably not one single category system for types of women or types of men. Consistent with the previous discussion of social category, it is most likely that there are types of women and men that are widely shared by members of American society (e.g., "macho," "Marian the Librarian"), other types that are recognized by members of particular subcultures (compare, for example, the meaning of the term "dude" as used by a cowboy in Wyoming and a black teenager in Newark), and still others that are completely idiosyncratic.

The final contribution involves a return to a point made at the outset of this chapter—the results of sex stereotype studies often seem to be contradictory or inconsistent. How does the present framework account for this state of affairs? First, it is here assumed that sex stereotypes are not long lists of specific words but rather are structured sets of inferential relations. Inasmuch as few studies have assessed the cognitive structures associated with the social categories female and male, it is difficult to know whether seemingly inconsistent findings are truly inconsistent or simply represent perturbations in the expression of the underlying cognitive structure due to methodological or other factors.

Second, it is possible that much of the confusion in the sex stereotype literature results from respondents describing different social categories. An extreme example is taken to illustrate this point. In the 1950s, Sherriffs and McKee (1957) asked college students to: "List 10 traits or characteristics of men and 10 traits or characteristics of women [p. 456]." There was considerable agreement that women and men differed on over 100 characteristics. In the mid-1970s Cowan and Stewart (1977) obtained open-ended descriptions in response to the following stimulus cue: "Imagine you are going to meet someone for the first time, and the only thing you know in advance is that he (she) is an adult [p. 207]." There was very little agreement about what this male (female) person would be like. It is tempting to account for the discrepancy in terms of change over time in the level of sex stereotyping. This is probably part of the picture. It is also tempting to account for the discrepancy in simple methodological terms. In the 1950s it was not socially undesirable to express beliefs about sex dif-

---

[4]In fairness to Clifton et al. (1976), it should be noted that they did elicit type names from subjects. However, the way in which they obtained and processed these responses is not clearly articulated in their article. Thus, it is not possible to judge how systematic and free of investigator influence this process was.

ferences, but today it is (particularly on college campuses). This, too, is probably part of the answer.

It is possible, however, that another factor is involved. When Sherriffs and McKee (1957) asked their respondents to list the characteristics of "women" and of "men" life was simpler (at least regarding sex roles) than it is today. The modal American adult female was a housewife and mother and the modal adult male was a husband who had a job. And, the media probably presented a sharpened view of these modal figures. As a consequence, most respondents probably thought in terms of the same two social categories—"typical female = housewife and mother" and "typical male = husband with job," particularly the idealized media version of these—when generating their attribute lists. Since the 1950s, of course, real change in the occupational and employment status of women has occurred, and a wider variety of women and men are depicted in the media. The lack of consensus revealed in the Cowan and Stewart (1977) data, then, might have resulted from subjects describing different social categories. That is, the subjects may have thought in terms of gender subcategories rather than simply "woman" or "man." For example, subjects asked to respond to the "female stimulus" may have described, among other types, a "housewife," "career woman," "female college student," "Bella Abzug type," and "middle-aged woman returning to college." This possibility was enhanced by the instructional set, which was quite nondirective. This allowed the respondents maximum freedom to imagine any one of a wide variety of people who happened to be female or male. In sum, much of the discrepancy in the results of sex stereotype research might be due to subjects' thinking in terms of different types of women and men when asked to provide their views of the sexes.

Implications for Impression Formation and Intergroup Behavior

The contribution of the present formulation to understanding impression formation and intergroup behavior is, at the same time, potentially very important and yet highly speculative. Because the possible yield is great, the temptation to speculate will not be avoided. Two basic questions are addressed in this section. First, how do stereotypes as part of implicit personality theory enter into the perception of, and behavior toward, specific individuals? In other words, how do the cognitive structures "stereotypes" influence what person-perception researchers call the "impression formation process?" Second, how does the proposed framework account for perception of and response to—especially evaluative response to—social categories? In short, what is the relation of stereotypes to prejudice and intergroup behavior?

The speculative answers to both questions are conditioned by two considerations. First, the present analysis is concerned only with stereotypes as individual-level phenomena (i.e., pictures in the heads of individuals). Thus, the attempt will be to lay out the role of stereotypes in the thoughts, feelings, and behavior of a single actor. Cultural stereotypes (except inasfar as they are part of an individual's cognitive repertoire) and collective intergroup behavior will not be discussed. Second, as was noted at the outset of this chapter, it is assumed that stereotypes serve two functions at the individual level: They summarize and organize knowledge regarding the social environment and they guide behavior. As discussed more fully elsewhere (Ashmore & Del Boca, 1979), we believe that stereotypes (as other cognitive categorizations such as schemata and prototypes) exist in a dynamic and mutually influencing relationship with the individual's behavior and "external reality."

Stereotypes, Impression Formation, and Interpersonal Behavior.   Although the present analysis is not intended to apply only to sex stereotypes, female–male relations are the focus in both this and the following section. The results of our research to date indicate that social evaluation and potency are the two major overall dimensions of implicit personality theory and that the distinction between the broad social categories female and male is closely related to the latter dimension. This configuration is, as was noted above, quite similar to that obtained by White (1980), and the first element of the present analysis is provided by his theoretical discussion of this general cognitive structure.

White (1980) reviews a wide range of studies in both psychology and anthropology and concludes that there is a universal two-dimensional structure of trait terms. He labels these "Solidarity versus Conflict" and "Dominance–Submission." As noted previously, these dimensions are quite similar to Evaluation and Potency, which Osgood and his colleagues have shown to have significant cross-cultural validity (cf. Osgood, May, & Miron, 1975). According to White (1980), however: "the conceptual significance of the orthogonal dimensions [of "Solidarity versus Conflict" and "Dominance versus Submission"] underlying personality descriptors] goes well beyond connotations of 'goodness' and 'strength'. Rather, these dimensions summarize common themes in presuppositions and inferences frequently associated with the use of trait terms to characterize personality." He further argues that the possibilities for agreement versus disagreement in interpersonal relations and for one actor in a dyad to have more influence than another are in a sense universal "facts of life." As such, they have become encoded in interpersonal language and the dimensions underlying that language.

White's analysis is important to the present argument for two reasons. First, he provides support for the general two-dimensional structure we have obtained. Second, and more importantly, he suggests how this cognitive structure might be related to impression formation and interpersonal behavior. If "Solidarity/Conflict" and "Dominance/Submission" reflect inferences about the way others will act and expectations about the likely course of interpersonal relations, then categorizing a new person into a social category associated with one of these dimensions should lead to a consistent set of inferences and expectations. White's (1980) comments on the Dominance/Submission distinction are particularly pertinent to the present findings regarding sex stereotypes: "the interpersonal significance of dominance might be that one actor (a) has the ability to influence, direct or control the actions of another, (b) is likely to attain his or her goals, and (c) will have a greater chance of achieving his or her aims in the case of goal conflict, etc.." The cognitive association of the social category female with the Submission pole and male with the Dominance pole of the Dominance/Submission dimension should lead to the initial impression not only that a female has "soft" personal attributes and a male "hard" traits but also to the expectation that the female will be more easily directed and less likely to "lead." And, if the perceiver acts on these cognitions, consistent behavioral differences should be elicited by female and male targets. Specifically, females should draw "dominating" (e.g., suggesting, directing) behavior to a greater extent than males.

The second contribution to the emerging model is provided by Rosenberg's (1977) speculation about how structural representations of implicit theories of personality might be related to social interaction and impression formation. Rosenberg finds that for individual perceivers Evaluation is the primary, probably the only major dimension of implicit personality theory.[5] (He notes, however, that individuals differ in the types of evaluation they emphasize, e.g., intelligence, maturity.) He suggests that this dimension might be related to social interaction as follows: (1) individuals are motivated to attain positive and avoid negative experiences; (2) in interpersonal relations this motivation is reflected in the tendency to approach certain people and avoid others; (3) this inclination to approach versus avoid is coded in one's implicit personality theory both in the form of traits attributed to others (e.g., *friendly* versus *hostile*) and in terms of the feelings they elicit in the perceiver (e.g., "makes me feel comfortable" versus "uneasy"); (4) in the course of forming an impression of a new

---

[5]Rosenberg and his associates find that Potency, Activity, and other dimensions are correlated with Evaluation when the implicit theories of personality of individuals are analyzed (see particularly Kim & Rosenberg, 1980). They argue that the semantic differential orthogonal dimensions of E, P, A (and, by extension, the present two-dimensional structure) are the result of investigator-supplied vocabularies and aggregating across respondents. Other research that does not involve aggregation, however, indicates that Potency is not always correlated with Evaluation (Kehoe & Reynolds, 1977). The position of the present author is that there is probably no single correct structure of implicit personality theory. The present "Solidarity/Conflict" and "Dominance/Submission" are regarded as distinctions that make sense to the modal subject in our research (see Funk et al., 1976, on this point). And White's (1980) analysis suggests that these distinctions are central to our language for describing others and are thus quite likely to be important for a broad range of perceivers. Wide individual differences, however, are expected, with some respondents fitting the structure favored by Rosenberg and others approximating the idealized configurations of two orthogonal dimensions found in our research.

person, positive or negative interpersonal events are experienced as positive or negative affects that shape both trait attributions and subsequent behavior; and (5) "getting to know" another person is basically a process of cognitively fitting that person to the most appropriate person cluster.

Two points in Rosenberg's analysis are important for the present speculation. The first is the central role given to affect in the impression formation process. We agree but would extend his argument. Specifically, it seems necessary, in order to have a feelings dimension analogous to the Dominance versus Submission trait continuum, to add a dimension of "Feel Superior" to "Feel Inferior" to Rosenberg's "Dislike" to "Like" dimension. Support for the existence of such a dimension of emotional expression (and hopefully emotional experience) is provided by Miller and Johnson-Laird (1976), who built on the earlier ideas of Krech and Crutchfield (1965). The extreme of "Feel Superior" is marked by terms such as "contempt" and "pity" (which are, at the same time, negative and positive feelings, respectively), whereas "resentment" and "admiration" represent extremes of "Feel Inferior" and "Dislike" and "Feel Inferior" and "Like," respectively. It is interesting to note that the "Feel Inferior" to "Feel Superior" dimension applies to feelings aroused by other people. When the structure of all emotions (rather than the subdomain of interpersonal feelings) is considered, this dimension is either weakly apparent (Russell, 1978) or does not appear at all (Russell, 1979).

The second point to be taken from Rosenberg (1977) is the idea that impression formation can be thought of as fitting a target to a person cluster. In Rosenberg's research, target persons as well as traits are clustered, and consistent groupings of individuals known to the perceiver are termed "person clusters." The concept of "person cluster" is analogous to what was previously described as a gender subcategory or type of woman or man. Thus, forming an impression of a particular target involves not only making general inferences about that person in terms of "Solidarity/Conflict" and "Dominance/Submission" but also identifying that person as a particular type of woman or man.

In order to relate this analysis to impression formation and interpersonal behavior, it is useful to think of a person's (the perceiver) interaction with another person (the target) as comprising the following steps: The perceiver notices the target, the perceiver attends to the target's appearance and behavior, the perceiver interprets the target's appearance and behavior, the perceiver behaves toward the target, the target responds, and the cycle begins again. (This scheme is, of course, too simple; the complications are temporarily postponed.) The association of the social categories of sex with "Dominance/Submission" suggests that this process of social interaction might be influenced systematically at each step. If the setting or target's behavior is ambiguous, the perceiver would be more likely to notice and attend to the dominating or directive activities of a male than of a female. If, however, the setting or the behavior itself forces recognition of female dominance or direct use of power, the perceiver may perceptually accentuate the action of influence or the meaning given to the action. For example, a woman's suggesting how to organize an agenda or spend an evening might be seen as "pushy" (and she categorized as a "pushy broad") or, in the extreme form, as "castrating" (and she coded as a "castrating bitch"). In terms of behavior and behavioral intentions, it would be predicted that the perceiver would expect to do more suggesting, directing, bossing, and so forth with respect to a female than a male target. As is suggested by research reported by Snyder (this volume), such behavior might cause the female target actually to behave in a more submissive manner than the male target. If so, this might reinforce the perceiver's tendency to associate the social category female with soft/weak/low power and the category male with hard/strong/high power.

In the preceding paragraphs the impression formation process is depicted as a simple step-by-step progression in which one person makes inferences about another in terms of an overall two-dimensional cognitive structure and a set of person clusters or gender subcategories. Three complications must now be noted. First, the perceiver is not simply motivated to make sense out of the social environment. Rather, she or he has other purposes and these can systematically influence how other people are perceived. For example, a politician who wants to get reelected is quite prone to categorizing others into "votes for me," "votes against me," or "nonvoters." Or, with respect to perceptions of the sexes, a 7-year-old boy, who doesn't want to play "girl games," is likely to cognitively structure females and males in ways quite different from the same boy 10 years later.

A second complication is apparent when it is recognized that in social interaction the perceiver is also a target and the target is also a perceiver. Thus far, only the perceiver has been given an active role in the impression formation process. It is the perceiver who is actively trying to make sense out of the world, who has goals, who interprets the appearance and behavior of others, and whose behavior can often serve to shape how the target behaves. This, of course, ignores the target, who is also trying to make sense out of his or her complex environment. As Goffman's (1959) work suggests, the target may be actively presenting a certain kind of self. In fact, it may be more accurate to think of the impression formation process as involving an attempt by both parties simultaneously to figure things out (which has been stressed here) and to present a particular self-image (as Goffman argues). Although the likelihood of impression management may complicate the scientific analysis of social interaction, it seems that such a complication is necessary.

A final complication arises when one considers the possibility that a particular target simply will not fit into an established person cluster or type of woman or man. With respect to the present formulation of sex stereotypes in terms of implicit personality theory, what happens when a perceiver is confronted with a target who does not fit into any existing female or male type? Our research to date has been concerned only with types of women and men that fit neatly within their respective higher-order social categories (e.g., the "Nurturant" woman accords well with the general association of women with "soft"). In other words, we have been explicating the subcategories of the two broader gender categories. It is tempting to argue that these are the only sex-related cognitive categories employed in social perception, that perceivers "force" (via selective interaction, perceptual distortion, and so on) all people whom they encounter into a particular gender category, with male subcategories being generally "hard" and female types generally "soft." This, however, is simply not the case. There are social categories for men that are not hard—e.g., the stereotype of the "swishy homosexual" or the "artistic type"—and, in parallel fashion, types of hard women—e.g., the "butch bull dyke" and the "tough lady."

According to the present line of reasoning, perceivers in everyday interaction will initially classify others as female or male and probably as a member of a more specific, congruent subcategory (e.g., "a hardworking guy," "a Thoughtful–Quiet woman"). (This scenario is still oversimplified; see Ashmore and Del Boca (1979) for more details regarding the categorization of persons in social interaction.) The perceiver then infers that the target possesses personality attributes associated with the assigned subcategory. If the target's behavior is congruent with the category assignment or at least ambiguous enough so as not be seen as incongruent, then the perceiver's certainty of the category assignment might be increased. If the target's behavior is clearly not in line with her or his category assignment, the perceiver is confronted with an instance of cognitive inconsistency. As will be discussed below, the present formulation does not include the assumption that there is an innate and strong need for cognitive consistency. It is true, however, that the "man (or woman) the scientist" analogy implies that the perceiver must somehow handle disagreements between cognitive constructions and observed reality. Certainly one answer would be to alter one's construct system or to hold that system more tentatively than before noting the inconsistency. However, as discussed more fully elsewhere (Ashmore & Del Boca, 1979), implicit theories of personality are often clung to quite tenaciously, and the naive personologist is not always rational when confronting evidence that is not consistent with her or his implicit notions about people. Another means of handling an inconsistency between one's expectation about how another should behave (based on his or her perceived social category membership) and that person's actual behavior is to alter their category assignment. Our findings suggest that certain recategorizations will be easier than others. If an individual perceived as a female must be acknowledged as a powerful person it would seem necessary that the person's membership in the social category female be revised or somehow made "special." (Sex stereotypes could also be maintained if, as Johnson (1976) has suggested, women are expected to, and in fact do, exert interpersonal power in a more indirect fashion than do men.)

The above discussion of the "change of meaning" phenomenon provides insight into such "special" categorizations. The present results suggest that females are assumed to be "soft" and "submissive" and males to be "hard" and "dominant." If it is assumed that sex stereotypes (as *inferences* based on sex) are associated with sex roles (as *prescriptions* based on sex) (Brown, 1965), then it is not only the case that males are expected to be controlling in interpersonal relations, but that they *should be* so. Females, on the other hand, should not demonstrate power. Given this state of affairs it may be that direct expressions of power and influence by a woman *mean something different* from the same action by a male. White's finding that Dominance traits were more positively evaluated in individuals who were leaders (and *should be* dominant) suggests that Dominance traits in males should be positively valued. Dominance in females, however, should be disvalued: "Standing up for one's rights" becomes "overreacting" and "making suggestions" becomes "nagging." And, by extension, special gender subcategories are created: "pushy broad" and, especially, "castrating bitch."

Stereotypes and Responses to Social Categories.   In addition to suggesting how stereotypes might be implicated in the impression formation process, the present formulation should be capable of accounting for how individuals respond to social categories. Because this important issue has not been directly addressed by our work to date, not a great deal can be said here. One point, however, seems worth discussing. The present conceptualization and empirical findings indicate that there is no overall tendency to approach (like) or avoid (dislike) either sex differentially inasmuch as the social categories female and male covary with Potency not Evaluation. Although this is congruent with common sense, it does not appear, as noted above, to jibe with the oft-reported conclusion that the male stereotype is more valued than the female stereotype. The inconsistency, however, may not be as great as it appears. The differential valuation of the stereotypes of the two sexes depends on how the value of each stereotype is calculated. If by "more valued" one means that the average value of the characteristics attributed to males is higher than that of those attributed to females, the differential evaluation conclusion is unwarranted. If, however, one simply counts the number of positively valued items ascribed to the sexes, males do get more. This suggests that the higher value of the male stereotype may reflect a wider range of alternative patterns of action (coded as traits) open to males. This seems quite likely given the traditional female "domestic" role versus the male "provider" role. Certainly the relative size of the areas in which the two roles are primarily acted out is congruent with the notion of males having a wider range of alternatives. Further, there are probably a wider variety of ways of successfully filling the provider than the domestic role.

But still, one has the feeling that the male sex is more highly valued than the female sex. Whether this is universal or not is much in dispute. Certainly in the United States it seems to this author that there is a general, though not open, tendency to value maleness over femaleness. If true, this seems to be contrary to the above finding that female–male is orthogonal to good–bad. I do not believe that there is an inconsistency. The structures we have obtained reflect how individual perceivers organize their impressions of specific other people. In this structure, there are good women and bad women, good men and bad men (though note that the sexes differ in *how* they are good or bad). In this structure men are perceived as dominant and hard, women are assumed to be submissive and soft. Although Solidarity/Conflict and Dominance/Submission are separate dimensions for perceiving others, it is my conjecture that American society generally regards power as good. If so, the higher evaluation of men in general or the male role may reflect this cultural tendency to place a positive value on power. At the level of the individual perceiver within our culture he or she would apply this differential evaluation to women and men *in general*. Whether this value influenced the perception of specific others is problematic. In meeting a person for the first time the perceiver would potentially have two inputs for evaluating the target: the cultural value placed on power (assuming he or she accepted and internalized that value) and the Solidarity/Conflict-Dominance/ Submission schema for perceiving others.

The suggestion here is that people are not highly consistent in their social cognition. Cognitive consistency theories notwithstanding, people apparently tolerate what would seem to an outsider to be illogical (cf. Bem, 1970, pp. 24–39). Students of public opinion have noted one common and pervasive form of cognitive inconsistency—acceptance of general principles of democracy (e.g., free speech) and rejection of a wide variety of specific instances of the principle (e.g., an atheist speaking at a public school). Certainly such rejection could be due to conflicting values (e.g., rejection of the atheist because of religious values). It is also possible, however, that most individuals do not store specific instances very tightly under general principles. If we apply this to views of the sexes we come to the possible conclusion that perception and evaluation of "women" and "men" (as generalized social stimuli) is not tightly constrained by the perceptions of the women and men one knows or can conceive of. Whatever the fate of this conjecture, it seems necessary to expand the present framework to address explicitly how "women as a group" and "men as a group" are cognitively represented. It is quite possible that it is these generalized cognitive elements that are more closely related to the making of important political decisions (e.g., voting for or against an avowed pro-ERA candidate) than are the cognitive structures associated with specific females and males. Any near-complete theory of female–male relations, or intergroup relations more generally, will need to address the question of how thoughts and feelings influence both interpersonal relations and intergroup behavior.

ACKNOWLEDGMENTS

The ideas in this chapter are, in part, the result of discussions with a number of my colleagues over the past few years. In particular, I wish to acknowledge the input of Frances K. Del Boca and Mary Lou Tumia. I thank Frances K. Del Boca, Susan T. Fiske,

David L. Hamilton, Shelley E. Taylor, and Geoffrey M. White for their helpful comments on an earlier draft of this chapter. Preparation of this manuscript was aided by National Institute of Mental Health Grant 27737 (Margaret K. Bacon and Richard D. Ashmore, Co-Principal Investigators) and by the following individuals: Carl Anderson, Victoria K. Burbank, Donna Geswaldo, LuAnn Herrod, and Jean Natereli.

REFERENCES

Asch, S. E. Forming impressions of personality. *Journal of Abnormal and Social Psychology*, 1946, *41*, 258–290.

Ashmore, R. D., & Del Boca, F. K. Sex stereotypes and implicit personality theory: Toward a cognitive–social psychological conceptualization. *Sex Roles*, 1979, *5*, 219–248.

Ashmore, R. D., & Tumia, M. *Sex stereotypes and implicit personality theory: III. Categories in the perception of women and men.* Unpublished manuscript, 1979.

Ashmore, R. D., & Tumia, M. Sex stereotypes and implicit personality theory: I. A personality description approach to the assessment of sex stereotypes. *Sex Roles*, 1980, *6*, 501–518.

Bakan, D. *The duality of human existence.* Chicago: Rand McNally, 1966.

Beach, L., & Wertheimer, M. A free-response approach to the study of person cognition. *Journal of Abnormal and Social Psychology*, 1961, *62*, 367–374.

Bem, D. J. *Beliefs, attitudes, and human affairs.* Belmont, Calif.: Brooks/Cole Publishing Co., 1970.

Block, J. H. Conceptions of sex-role: Some cross-cultural and longitudinal perspectives. *American Psychologist*, 1973, *28*, 512–526.

Broverman, I. K., Vogel, S. R., Broverman, D. M., Clarkson, F. E., & Rosenkrantz, P. S. Sex-role stereotypes: A current appraisal. *Journal of Social Issues*, 1972, *28*, 59–78.

Brown, R. *Social psychology.* New York: The Free Press, 1965.

Cantor, N., & Mischel, W. Prototypes in person perception. In L. Berkowitz (Ed.), *Advances in experimental social psychology* (Vol. 12). New York: Academic Press, 1979.

Cauthen, N. R., Robinson, I. E., & Krauss, H. H. Stereotypes: A review of the literature 1926–1965. *Journal of Social Psychology*, 1971, *84*, 103–125.

Clifton, A. K., McGrath, D., & Wick, B. Stereotypes of woman: A single category? *Sex Roles*, 1976, *2*, 135–148.

Cohen, G. *The psychology of cognition.* New York: Academic Press, 1977.

Cowan, M. L., & Stewart, B. J. A methodological study of sex stereotypes. *Sex Roles*, 1977, *3*, 205–216.

D'Andrade, R. G. Trait psychology and componential analysis. *American Anthropologist*, 1965, *67*, 215–220.

Del Boca, F. K., & Ashmore, R. D. Sex stereotypes and implicit personality theory: II. A trait-inference approach to the assessment of sex stereotypes. *Sex Roles*, 1980, *6*, 519–535.

Dornbusch, S. M., Hastorf, A. H., Richardson, S. A., Muzzy, R. E., & Vreeland, R. S. The perceiver and the perceived: Their relative influence on the categories of interpersonal cognition. *Journal of Personality and Social Psychology*, 1965, *1*, 434–440.

Eysenck, H. J. *The psychology of politics.* London: Routledge & Kegan Paul, 1954.

Feldman, J. M. Stimulus characteristics and subject prejudice as determinants of stereotype attribution. *Journal of Personality and Social Psychology*, 1972, *21*, 330–340.

Feldman, J. M., & Hilterman, R. J. Stereotype attribution revisited: The role of stimulus characteristics, racial attitude, and cognitive differentiation. *Journal of Personality and Social Psychology*, 1975, *31*, 1177–1188.

Fiske, S. T., & Cox, M. G. Person concepts: The effect of target familiarity and descriptive purpose on the process of describing others. *Journal of Personality*, 1979, *47*, 136–161.

Forgas, J. P. The perception of social episodes: Categorical and dimensional representations in two different social milieus. *Journal of Personality and Social Psychology,* 1976, *34,* 199–209.

Funk, S. G., Horowitz, A. D., Lipshitz, R., & Young, F. W. The perceived structure of American ethnic groups: The use of multidimensional scaling in stereotype research. *Sociometry,* 1976, *39,* 116–130.

Glass, A. L., Holyoak, K. J., & Santa, J. L. *Cognition.* Reading, Mass.: Addison–Wesley Publishing Co., 1979.

Goffman, E. *The presentation of self in everyday life.* Garden City, N.Y.: Doubleday–Anchor, 1959.

Gordon, C. Self-conceptions: Configurations of content. In C. Gordon & K. J. Gergen (Eds.), *The self in social interaction.* New York: Wiley, 1968.

Hanno, M. S., & Jones, L. E. Effects of a change in reference person on the multidimensional structure and evaluation of trait adjectives. *Journal of Personality and Social Psychology,* 1973, *28,* 368–375.

Hastorf, A. H., Schneider, D. J., & Polefka, J. *Person perception.* Reading, Mass.: Addison–Wesley, 1970.

Heider, F. *The psychology of interpersonal relations.* New York: Wiley, 1958.

Johnson, P. Women and power: Toward a theory of effectiveness. *Journal of Social Issues,* 1976, *32,* 99–110.

Johnson, S. C. Hierarchical clustering schemes. *Psychometrika,* 1967, *32,* 241–254.

Jones, R. A. *Self-fulfilling prophecies: Social, psychological, and physiological effects of expectancies.* Hillsdale, N.J.: Lawrence Erlbaum Associates, 1977.

Jones, R. A., & Ashmore, R. D. The structure of intergroup perception: Categories and dimensions in views of ethnic groups and adjectives used in stereotype research. *Journal of Personality and Social Psychology,* 1973, *25,* 428–438.

Kehoe, J., & Reynolds, T. J. Interactive multidimensional scaling of cognitive structure underlying person perception. *Applied Psychological Measurement,* 1977, *1,* 155–169.

Kelly, G. *The psychology of personal constructs.* New York: Norton, 1955.

Kim, M. P., & Rosenberg, S. Comparison of two structural models of implicit personality theory. *Journal of Personality and Social Psychology,* 1980, *38,* 375–389.

Kirk, L., & Burton, M. Meaning and context: A study of contextual shifts in meaning of Maasai personality descriptors. *American Ethnologist,* 1977, *4,* 734–761.

Krech, D., & Crutchfield, R. S. *Elements of psychology.* New York: Knopf, 1965.

Kruskal, J. B. Multidimensional scaling by optimizing goodness of fit to a nonmetric hypothesis. *Psychometrika,* 1964, *29,* 1–27. (a)

Kruskal, J. B. Nonmetric multidimensional scaling: A numerical method. *Psychometrika,* 1964, *29,* 115–129. (b)

Kruskal, J. B. *How to use MDSCAL, a multidimensional scaling program* (Version 3). Bell Telephone Laboratories, Murray Hill, N.J., May 1967.

Lippmann, W. *Public opinion.* New York: Harcourt, Brace, Jovanovitch, 1922.

Miller, G., & Johnson-Laird, P. N. *Language and perception.* Cambridge, Mass.: Harvard University Press, 1976.

Osgood, C. E., May, W. H., & Miron, M. S. *Cross-cultural universals of affective meaning.* Urbana, Ill.: University of Illinois Press, 1975.

Petro, C. S., & Putnam, B. A. Sex-role stereotypes: Issues of attitudinal change. *Sex Roles,* 1979, *5,* 29–40.

Rosenberg, S. New approaches to the analysis of personal constructs in person perception. *Nebraska Symposium on Motivation* (Vol. 24). Lincoln, Neb.: University of Nebraska Press, 1977.

Rosenberg, S., & Jones, R. A. A method for investigating and representing a person's implicit theory of personality: Theodore Dreiser's view of people. *Journal of Personality and Social Psychology,* 1972, *22,* 372–386. (a)

Rosenberg, S., & Jones, R. A. Ratings of personality trait words on nine semantic properties. *Journal Supplement Abstract Service,* 1972, *2,* 21–22. (b)

Rosenberg, S., Nelson, C., & Vivekananthan, P. S. A multidimensional approach to the structure of personality impressions. *Journal of Personality and Social Psychology,* 1968, *9,* 283–294.

Rosenberg, S., & Sedlak, A. Structural representations of implicit personality theory. In L. Berkowitz (Ed.), *Advances in experimental social psychology* (Vol. 6). New York: Academic Press, 1972.

Rosenkrantz, P., Vogel, S. R., Bee, H., Broverman, I. K., & Broverman, D. M. Sex-role stereotypes and self concepts in college students. *Journal of Consulting and Clinical Psychology,* 1968, *32,* 287–295.

Russell, J. A. Evidence of convergent validity on the dimensions of affect. *Journal of Personality and Social Psychology,* 1978, *36,* 1152–1168.

Russell, J. A. Affective space is bipolar. *Journal of Personality and Social Psychology,* 1979, *37,* 345–356.

Shank, R. C., & Abelson, R. P. *Scripts, plans, goals, and understanding: An inquiry into human knowledge structures.* Hillsdale, N.J.: Lawrence Erlbaum Associates, 1977.

Schneider, D. J., & Blankmeyer, B. *The effects of prototype salience on trait inferences.* Unpublished manuscript, University of Texas at San Antonio, 1978.

Schneider, D. J., Hastorf, A. H., & Ellsworth, P. *Person perception* (2nd ed.). Reading, Mass.: Addison–Wesley, 1979.

Secord, P. F. *The social stereotype and the concept of "implicit personality theory."* Paper presented at the American Psychological Association Convention, 1958.

Secord, P. F., & Berscheid, E. S. Stereotyping and the generality of implicit personality theory. *Journal of Personality,* 1963, *31,* 65–78.

Sedlak, A. *A multidimensional study of the structure of personality descriptions.* Unpublished master's thesis, Rutgers University, 1971.

Shepard, R. N., Romney, A. K., & Nerlove, S. B. (Eds.), *Multidimensional scaling: Theory and applications in the behavioral sciences.* Vol. 1: *Theory.* New York: Seminar Press, 1972.

Sherriffs, A. C., & McKee, J. P. Qualitative aspects of beliefs about men and women. *Journal of Personality,* 1957, *25,* 451–464.

Shweder, R. A. How relevant is an individual difference theory of personality? *Journal of Personality,* 1975, *43,* 455–484.

Tumia, M., & Ashmore, R. D. *The meaning of sex stereotypic terms.* Manuscript in preparation.

White, G. Ambiguity and ambivalence in A'ara personality descriptors. *American Ethnologist,* 1978, *5,* 334–360.

White, G. M. Conceptual universals in interpersonal language. *American Anthropologist,* 1980, *82,* 759–781.

Williams, J. E., & Bennett, S. M. The definition of sex stereotypes via the Adjective Check List. *Sex Roles,* 1975, *1,* 327–337.

Wish, M., Deutsch, M., & Biener, L. Differences in conceptual structures of nations: An exploratory study. *Journal of Personality and Social Psychology,* 1970, *3,* 361–373.

3 A Categorization Approach to Stereotyping

Shelley E. Taylor
Harvard University

Historically, work on stereotyping has focused around several issues: the content of stereotypes of particular groups (e.g., Katz & Braly, 1933); the functions that stereotypes serve for those who hold them (e.g., projection of unacceptable impulses); and the role that stereotypes play in maintaining the disadvantaged position of the stereotyped group (see, for example, Ashmore & Del Boca, this volume). An equally important but less explored issue is how and when stereotypes are applied in social interaction. That is, although it is important to know what stereotypes a person holds, what that person does with those stereotypes is ultimately of greater importance for understanding how stereotypes function to organize and shape social reality.

Fundamental to the process of stereotyping is the act of categorization. That is, we do not stereotype a person, we stereotype a person-as-a-member-of-a-group. For example, one person can be seen as a woman, an Italian, a bridge player, a mother, or a Catholic, and she becomes the object of a stereotype only after she has been placed into one or more of these categories. The focus of this chapter will be the causes and consequences of this categorization process.

Viewing stereotyping as a categorization process has a long, respectable tradition. Gordon Allport's (1954) classic volume on prejudice is surprisingly cognitive in its emphasis, arguing that stereotyping is the outgrowth of normal cognitive processes. Allport believed that, given the "separation of human groups" and the salience of particular social and physical cues (such as race or sex), people would use a "least effort" principle of organization and group apparently similar people into categories (see Pettigrew, 1979). That perceivers use discriminating cues as ways of organizing objects along lines of similarity is well established in the cognitive literature. Bruner (1956), for example, posited that the main function of categorization is to reduce the complex object world to a more simple and manageable structure. He suggested that the primary basis for categorization is perceived similarity–dissimilarity (e.g., objects are grouped on the basis of similarity of function or appearance) (see also Bousfield, 1953; Freedman & Loftus, 1971; Tulving & Pearlstone, 1966). It is not at all surprising, then, that people also are categorized along lines of similarity.

The leap from categorization to stereotyping, Allport argued, is a small one. Stereotypes, both benign and pernicious, evolve to describe categories of people, just as sunsets are characterized as colorful or balls as round. In this sense, the process of developing generalizations about social groups and imputing attributes to particular members of groups is not fundamentally different from that of developing generalizations and imputing attributes to groups of objects. Stereotypes are, in part, generalizations about social groups that are not necessarily any more or less inaccurate, biased, or logically faulty than are any other kinds of cognitive generalizations. Accordingly, many of the same factors that influence the imputation of attributes to other stimuli will influence the imputation of stereotypes to individuals or social groups.

Several impressive lines of theoretical inquiry and empirical investigation have drawn upon the stereotyping-as-categorization assumption. The ingroup–outgroup literature (see Wilder, in this volume) is one such endeavor. The findings of this research can be summarized, in part, as indicating that the act of categorization heightens the perception of similarities within categories and sharpens the perception of differences between categories (Campbell, 1956). Tajfel and Wilkes (1963), for example, demonstrated this phenomenon in the perception of lengths of lines. Subjects were shown four short lines labeled "A" and four long lines labeled "B" and asked to estimate the length of the lines. Subjects rated the short lines as more similar in length to each other and different from the long lines (which were seen as similar to each other), compared with the subjects shown the lines with no labels or random labels (Hensley & Duval, 1976; Tajfel, Sheikh, & Gardner, 1964).

A second finding of this literature is that once people are categorized into ingroup and outgroup, ingroup favoritism and outgroup discrimination often result (Allen & Wilder, 1975; Billig, 1973; Billig & Tajfel, 1973; Tajfel & Billig, 1974; Tajfel, Billig, Bundy, & Flament, 1971; Wilder & Allen, 1974). In these studies, subjects typically are brought into a laboratory, divided arbitrarily into groups on the basis of some minimal similarity (e.g., preferences for particular paintings), and then asked to evaluate their own group and the other group and allocate rewards between the groups. The results consistently demonstrate that outgroup members are evaluated less favorably and given fewer rewards than ingroup members, and this behavior holds even when the subject and the subject's group do not benefit from depriving or unfavorably evaluating the outgroup (see also Hamilton & Gifford, 1976). Apparently, then, people have a general stereotype of their own group as good and deserving and a general stereotype of outgroups as bad and undeserving that they employ descriptively and use as guidelines for behavior once an ingroup–outgroup categorization has been made (Brewer, 1979).

The effects observed in the ingroup–outgroup literature may be extended to predict perceptions of specific groups and the stereotypes held about them. Campbell (1956, 1967), for example,has argued that any salient physical or social cue may be a sufficient basis for categorizing others and that once this categorical judgment is made, perceptions of similarity within the group and differences from other groups are enhanced. Interpreting these effects from a learning theory standpoint, Campbell argues that these conditions will obtain as long as there is incomplete learning about the group. When one is processing large amounts of data about a great many members of a social group, a condition that is almost always met in the social world, complete learning is virtually impossible, and hence the exaggerated assimilation and contrast effects will remain. These effects will, in turn, be represented in stereotypes. Any distinctive difference between two groups is likely, according to Campbell, to be represented in the stereotype each group holds of the other. Thus, for example, if one of two groups is economically more privileged than the other, the advantaged group may attribute this fact to the stupidity of the disadvantaged group, whereas the disadvantaged group may stereotype the advantaged group as rapacious or exploitative (Tajfel, 1969, 1972). Thus, each group's stereotype about the other has a ''kernel of truth,'' though the significance attached to the kernel may differ strikingly between the groups.

However, a categorization theory of stereotyping must also explain why one categorical system is adopted over another. Because any individual may be subject to stereotyping on any of several dimensions, a good theory should be able to predict which attribute a perceiver will single out. A first factor may be the dimension of the individual that is made salient by the other people or objects available for classification. For example, an apple is less likely to be categorized as fruit if it is with the objects: beach ball, cube, cardboard box, and ball bearing than if it is with the objects: orange, carrot, beans, and pear. Likewise, a black woman may be more likely to be perceived as a black if she is in a group dominated by white people, but more likely to be seen as a woman in a group dominated by men. This line of reasoning suggests that minority or majority status will be one determinant of the salience of an attribute, a point that is supported by research on object perception. Research reported by Garner (1962), for example, clearly indicates that the fewer the number of items within a set, the better each item is discriminated. Continuing this line of reasoning, if the perceiver is categorizing an individual on the basis of a salient attribute, using a stereotype to interpret behavior and making within-category discriminations on the basis of category size, we should find that an individual will be stereotyped depending on the number of other members of his or her social group present. For example, an individual's race should be a more salient attribute when that person is the only one of his/her race in a group than when that person is with others of the same race, and, accordingly, people might be more inclined to interpret the person's behavior in racial (especially stereotyped racial) terms than when the person is in a racially mixed group.

A second factor that may influence the propensity to stereotype according to a particular attribute is the extent to which the perceiver has a well-developed concept for that attribute. An apple is not a piece of fruit if one has no concept of fruit. A Korean is simply Oriental, if one is unable to distinguish Koreans from other Asians. To pursue this point further, the ability to make within-category discriminations should also be influenced by one's familiarity with a group. For example, one might expect whites to be able to make discriminations within a group of whites better than within a group of blacks, because they have had more contact with whites. Furthermore, assuming membership in a category to be the epitome of familiarity with that category, we might expect females to be better at making discriminations within a group of females, and males within a group of males. Familiarity with the members of a category provides anchor points, either in the form of objective information about objects and their attributes or in terms of subjective opinions about them. Finally, the degree to which one has a well-articulated concept for a group should also depend on personal values. As Tajfel (1972) has noted, stereotypes represent not only some perceived group difference, but some value judgment regarding that difference. Individuals who differ in the degree to which they hold these values may also differ in the degree to which they will stereotype a given group.

Taken together, then, a categorical perspective on stereotyping requires considerably more than the mere assumption that people categorize people just as they categorize objects. The literature on object perception makes it clear that the perception and categorization of objects is a function of attributes of the objects themselves, the perceiver's categorical system, and the dimension(s) of the object made salient by the context in which they are perceived. Paralleling these points in the object literature, the stereotyping literature suggests that the extent to which any one individual (P) perceives another (O) in terms of the stereotype of a particular group (G) depends on at least three factors: O's actual behavior; P's personal attributes including stereotype(s) about G, their specific content and degree of differentiation; and contextual factors that make O's membership in some particular group (G) salient. More specifically, the following set of assumptions and hypotheses can be generated:

1. People use physical and social discriminators such as race and sex as a way of categorizing people and organizing information about them (e.g., incoming information is tagged as "male" or "female").

2. As a result of this categorization process, within-group differences become minimized and between-group differences become exaggerated (e.g., blacks are seen as similar to each other and different from whites).

3. As a result of the categorization process, within-group members' behavior comes to be interpreted in stereotyped terms. (For example, once you tag warm behavior as female, it may become "motherly," or once you tag an aggressive response as coming from a male, it may be seen as "macho.")

4. The social perceiver makes more discriminations within a subgroup, the fewer the members of the subgroup there are. For example, if one is looking at a group in which there are two blacks and four whites, one distinguishes (e.g., recalls, differentiates among) the blacks better and the whites less easily than if the group consists of four blacks and two whites.

5. Stereotyped attributes will be ascribed to any given individual in a social group as a function of the judgment that the person is a member of a (racial or sexual) subgroup and as a function of the number of other subgroup members there are in the group.

6. For a social perceiver to make categorical judgments, he or she must be familiar with the category. Furthermore, he or she should make more discriminations within a subgroup, the more familiar with the subgroup he or she is.

7. Categorization results from a learning process and as one becomes more familiar with a given social group, categories of subtypes will develop. This process will, in turn, lead to a more highly differentiated set of stereotypes for that social group. These stereotypes will reflect, in part, the discriminating cue (i.e., kernel of truth) that is used as the basis of (sub)categorization.

The research program we have conducted over the last 5 years draws on the previous seven assumptions and hypotheses.

CATEGORIZATION AND THE ORGANIZATION OF PERSON INFORMATION

Given a complex social environment, people must develop shortcuts for organizing incoming information, and one reasonable way of so doing might be to use salient social cues to categorize it. Our first studies drew on the assumption that people categorize others on the basis of salient physical and social cues and predicted that, as a result, information is actually encoded on the basis of such cues as race and sex. To test this hypothesis, we had subjects observe a group of interacting individuals that was racially or sexually mixed. After observing the discussion, the subjects' task was to recall who said what during the discussion. Our primary dependent measure was type of error. We reasoned that if subjects were indeed categorizing individuals on the basis of race (sex), they would make more intracategory than intercategory errors by virtue of perceived high similarity. That is, within each racial or sexual subgroup, members should be confused with each other, whereas differences between groups should be easier to recall.

In the first experiment (Taylor, Fiske, Etcoff, & Ruderman, 1978, Study 1), college student subjects listened to a tape of a small group discussion and simultaneously observed slides that purportedly pictured the group members.[1] This slide and tape presentation featured six men, three black and three white, discussing a publicity campaign for a play. After the discussion was over, subjects were given a list of all the suggestions that had been made and a set of pictures of all the participants and were told to indicate which speaker had made each suggestion. If race is used as a basis for encoding or retrieving information in the categorical sense just described, people should be able to recall *whether* a black or a white made a particular statement but not necessarily *which* black or which white made it. This should, in turn, produce a much higher within-race error rate than between-race error rate, indicating that people confuse black speakers with each other and white speakers with each other but make relatively few cross-racial errors. The data analysis confirmed this hypothesis. Within-race errors exceeded cross-race errors by a factor of three to two, and the effect was highly significant.

The second study (Taylor, Fiske, Etcoff, & Ruderman, 1978, Study 2) was a conceptual replication of the study just described that involved a slide and tape presentation of a group of three men and three women discussing a campaign to increase voter turnout in an off-year election. Each of the participants made a number of suggestions during the course of the group discussion. After observing the slide and tape discussion, subjects were again asked to match who said what. Again, high within-sex error rates compared with cross-sex error rates were found. Subjects often credited a male's comment to the wrong male, but rarely to a female; likewise, a female speaker's comment often was assigned to the wrong female, but rarely to a man. In short, people often can remember what sex made a particular suggestion, but not necessarily which member of that sex made the suggestion.

These data provide evidence that people organize the social environment into categories of males and females or blacks and whites and accordingly are able to discriminate quite well between the categories, but do not do as well discriminating within the categories. Members of racial or sex groups, to some extent, become difficult to distinguish from each other. However, these data go beyond the mere demonstration that people will use salient cues to categorize others. They suggest that this categorization process is dynamic, employed as a way of breaking down and organizing the flow of normal social intercourse. Thus, categorization is much more than a static mode of identifying others; it is an active mode of representing and reconstructing their behavior.

The fact that individuals are categorized according to basic physical or social discriminating cues has a number of important implications. One is that individu-

---

[1]In all the studies reported, the subjects have been predominantly white. The data of the few black subjects have always been examined separately, and in all cases to date, there have been no prominent differences between the races in the results their data provide.

als will be relatively distinctive as a function of the number of members of their category in the environment. That is, a black man is more distinctive when he is in an otherwise white environment and less so when he is in a black environment, because in the first case he is the only one in his category and in the latter case, he shares category membership with others. The next sections explore the implications of relative distinctiveness.

RELATIVE DISTINCTIVENESS IN THE SOCIAL ENVIRONMENT: THE EXAMPLE OF SOLO STATUS

Recent trends toward desegration have resulted in the creation of a situation uniquely suited to testing the implications of distinctiveness. This situation is solo status. Solo status is the case in which there is one member of a different race, sex, or ethnicity in a group that is otherwise homogeneous on that attribute. Frequently, when there is pressure to bring minority group members into a previously segregated organization, an intermediate step occurs prior to full integration. In this stage, a few members of a minority group (e.g., blacks or women) are brought into what was previously a white, male-dominated organization, thus creating instances of solo or token status. This kind of integration may come about for any of several reasons. The solo may be viewed as an example of how things will go if full integration does occur. He or she may be employed to accustom people to the idea of integration without the threat suggested by the influx of a larger number of minority group members. A solo may be hired simply to ward off affirmative action forces (token integration), or there may be a lack of other qualified applicants from the particular group. For whatever reason, the solo's behavior is usually considered to be some index of how well the group the solo "represents" will do in the organization.

However, field studies have suggested that solos are particularly subject to stereotyping. Kanter (1977) interviewed solo women middle-level managers in newly desegregated business companies and found high levels of dissatisfaction with their solo status. Likewise, Wolman and Frank (1975), who observed and interviewed solo women medical students in medical school work groups, reported that solos were much more isolated and unhappy than women in more sex-balanced work groups. Both investigations noted that solo women found themselves in stereotyped feminine roles vis-à-vis their male colleagues. The roles included:

1. *Mother*—a nurturant, consoler of men and solver of personal problems.
2. *Princess*—a role in which one man in a group pairs with the woman to protect her from other men.
3. *Seductress*—a role characterized by the use of overt sexual flirtation by the woman.
4. *Iron Maiden*—a cold, aloof, possibly dangerous woman.

5. *Pet*—a group mascot who applauds male achievements and gains acceptance by being a cute little person.
6. *Ms. Efficiency*—a glorified secretarial role of the super organizer; the person who keeps the group rolling.

In contrast, women in sex-integrated work situations were not as likely to fall into or be perceived as falling into sex stereotyped roles. This is a highly counterintuitive finding. Why would a solo woman be seen in *more* sex-stereotyped terms than a woman who is not a solo? Almost by definition the solo woman has some skill, training, or position that renders her atypical for her sex and more similar to the men with whom she is working, and so logically, she should be seen in less sex-stereotyped terms than a woman who is not a solo.

One explanation of this finding derives from the fact that a solo is a highly distinctive element in a social setting. The solo looks different from the other members of a work group, and the physical basis for the solo's distinctiveness (in this case, sex) is also a socially meaningful attribute. There are at least two psychologically important implications of a solo's salience. The first is based on a robust finding in the cognitive literature that attention is drawn to novel or distinctive stimuli; disproportionate attention to one person in a social environment to the relative exclusion of others leads to taking in more information about that person, attributing to him or her greater social influence and evaluating his or her attributes more extremely (Taylor & Fiske, 1978). Second, because it is a solo's sex or race that is the basis for his or her distinctiveness, that attribute will be highly available as an explanation for the solo's behavior (Taylor, 1981). Returning to the field studies of solo status, then, one can argue that the solo woman's sex is salient by virtue of her social environment, and so her behavior is interpreted in sex-stereotyped terms, despite factors that would argue that such stereotyping is inappropriate.

THE SOLO BLACK IN A WORK GROUP: AN EXPERIMENTAL DEMONSTRATION

To explore these hypotheses regarding solo status, we conducted a laboratory study to examine how people perceive a solo black in an otherwise white group (Taylor, Fiske, Close, Anderson, & Ruderman, 1975, Study 1). College student subjects listened to a tape of an all-male small group discussion. As the tape was playing, slides ostensibly picturing the group members were shown, such that as a person spoke, a slide purportedly picturing his face appeared on the screen. By playing one tape, but varying the content of the slides, it was possible to manipulate the perceived composition of the group. Racial composition of the group was manipulated by showing slides of either an all-white work group, a balanced work group of three blacks and three whites, or a group consisting of five whites and one black, the solo black condition. Given this methodology, any differential perceptions of the solo black are attributable to the inferences of the subjects, rather than to special qualities of the solo or the group of which he is a member. The taped group discussion consisted of planning a publicity campaign for a dramatic production. The six members of this leaderless group were of equal status, all six participants made suggestions of equivalent length, and the suggestions were pretested and equated for usefulness and creativity. Subjects listened to the tape and saw the slides, after which they were asked to evaluate the participants in the group.

How is a solo black perceived, and particularly, how is he perceived differently from a black in a balanced group? The solo black is distinctive by virtue of physical appearance and his distinctiveness is emphasized all the more by the fact that race is a socially meaningful category. Given a well-established finding in the cognitive literature that attention is drawn to distinctive stimuli, one can predict that more information will be retained about a solo than about a black in a balanced situation. In fact, these were our results. People remembered more of what the solo black said, suggesting that they were observing his behavior more closely than that of the blacks in the mixed group. Because perceptual prominence leads to attributions of power or influence (Taylor & Fiske, 1975, 1978), one would expect that the solo would also be perceived as more powerful or influential in the group than a black in a race-balanced situation. Supporting this prediction, subjects thought the solo had talked more and that he had been more influential than had the blacks in the balanced group. We had also predicted on the basis of previous work (Taylor & Fiske, 1978) that the solo would be evaluated more extremely than would a black in a mixed group. On evaluative dimensions, such as originality and warmth, the solo was rated more positively compared with the blacks in a balanced group, but there was no evidence of extreme negative evaluation.

Inasmuch as the field studies of solo status had found that a solo was commonly seen as playing a stereotyped role, our research also addressed this question. It may be that solos in fact do nothing different from other group members, but are simply perceived as playing stereotyped roles by virtue of being distinctive. That is, the perceiver may make an illusory correlation between distinctive appearance and distinctive behavior. To provide a basis for comparison with the field studies, subjects had been asked if the group members seemed to be playing special roles in the group, roles such as group leader, comedian, organizer, or deviant. In support of the prediction, the solo was far more likely to be seen as playing a special role in the group, compared with all other group members. Apparently, then, the solo need do nothing special to be cast into a special role; his distinctiveness is sufficient to create this impression. The content of those attributed roles was also analyzed, and the following pattern was found. A black, whether solo or not, was significantly less likely to be seen as the group leader; a black was more likely to be seen as the group comedian than a white; and a black was slightly more likely to be seen as the group deviant. The role that most clearly differentiated the solo black from a black in the balanced condition was that of group organizer. Subjects were more likely to report that the solo had played an organizational role compared with the blacks in the balanced group. This role is particularly revealing in that it seems to reconcile the facts that on the one hand, the solo is seen as prominent, but on the other hand, he is a minority group member and minority group members are not usually thought of as leaders. The group organizer role is a prominent role, but it is a backup, nonleadership position.

This study, then, provided some evidence that a solo black is perceived differently from a black in a racially balanced group situation. On the surface of it, however, the solo black seemed to fare quite well. Although there was some stereotyping of his behavior and some failure to credit him with leadership responsibility, evaluations of him tended to be quite positive, and he was seen as very prominent. However, there is reason to suspect these findings. Our college student subjects are very liberal, and they had been observing a highly positive, humor-filled interaction. Rather than leading to highly positive evaluations, what solo status may do instead is exaggerate the initial impression of an individual, whether positive or negative. There is some evidence that attending to a person or object polarizes one's reaction to it (see, for example, Taylor & Fiske, 1978; Tesser, 1978), and because the solo is attended to more than are other group members, perhaps his attributes are simply exaggerated more by virtue of this differential attention. Thus, a perceiver with a less positive view of blacks or a perceiver observing a less positive interaction might show more negative perceptions of a solo, compared with a perceiver observing the same individual in a fully integrated situation. A follow-up study shed some light on this issue.

PERCEPTIONS OF A SOLO MAN AND A SOLO WOMAN: EXPERIMENTAL EXTENSIONS

Our next study (Taylor et al., 1975 Study 2) examined perceptions of a solo woman in an otherwise male work group and a solo man in an otherwise female work group. As in the first study, subjects heard a tape of a group discussion and saw slides ostensibly picturing the group members. Because sex composition of a group cannot be manipulated solely by interchanging slides, voices were altered as well. To accomplish this, a male or female imitator mimicked each of the original female or male voices on the tape. Thus, armed with a male and female "version" of each speaker, groups varying in sex composition were created by splicing in and splicing out appropriate voices. Subjects watched the slide and tape presentation consisting of an informal conversation in an elementary school teachers' lounge in which conversation among six teachers drifted from gossip to

teacher unionization to problem children. At its close, subjects rated the participants on a number of attributes. Perceptions of the solo woman in an otherwise
male group, and the solo man in an otherwise female group could then be
compared with perceptions of those same individuals in a balanced group of three
men and three women.

The results showed that, first, as in the case of the solo black, both the male
and female solo were perceived as more prominent group members. The solo was
seen as talking more, as making a stronger impression, as having a stronger
personality, and as being more confident, assertive, and individualistic than was
the same individual in a mixed-sex group. The perceived prominence of a solo,
then, seems to be a fairly robust finding, and it did not vary depending on
whether the solo was a male or a female.

The results also addressed the question of whether or not perceptions of a solo
are exaggerated compared with perceptions of the same individual in a sex-
balanced group. In order to provide some generalizability of results and assurance that effects due to solo status were not peculiar to one particular individual,
two different speakers (henceforth called *A* and *B*) were designated target voices;
of the subjects who observed the solo condition, half saw *A* as a solo (male or
female) and half saw *B* as a solo (male or female). Quite by accident, *A* was
uniformly perceived quite favorably, whereas *B* was not. The more interesting
question was what happened to these perceptions when *A* and *B* were designated
as solos versus when they were in a sex-balanced group. Whereas *A* was perceived favorably in the mixed group, this impression was even stronger when *A*
was a solo. Whereas *B* was perceived negatively in the mixed group, this impression was even stronger in the solo condition. Thus, it appears that a solo's
behavior is evaluatively exaggerated in either a positive or a negative direction,
compared with the same behavior in a mixed sex group.

More important is the question of whether or not more sex stereotyping
occurred as a function of solo status. Subjects had been asked if each group
member had played a particular role in the group, and if so, what role. As was the
case with perceptions of the solo black, a special role was attributed to the solo
significantly more often than to the same person in a mixed group. The content of
these roles turned out to be highly sex stereotyped. Females were seen as
motherly types, secretary types, or bitches, whereas males were seen as father
figures, macho types, or cynics. This finding again confirms that the perception
of a solo's playing out a special role can be solely in the mind of the perceiver
and need not be a function of any special behavior exhibited by the solo.

However, the specific content of the attributed roles did vary according to
which speaker was rated. These differences were both qualitative and evaluative.
For example, Person *A* was usually perceived positively and, when he was male,
he was likely to be seen as a father figure; for those few subjects who disliked
Person *A*, the "fatherly" quality was retained but with the negative evaluation
"authoritarian." Similarly, Person *B* was usually disliked, and, when she was

female, she was usually called a "bitch"; however, the few people who liked her preserved the bitchy quality when they evaluated her, but they termed her a "cynic." Thus, although agreement regarding what role an individual was playing was by no means perfect, it was far from random. This observation suggests strongly that, although the fact of being perceived in a special role is facilitated by the contextual factor of solo status, the content of that role is sensitive to the individual's actual behavior.

Overall, our research has uncovered a pattern of responses to a solo that shows the following attributes: disproportionate attention to the solo, an overemphasis of the solo's prominence in the group, an exaggerated evaluation of the solo's attributes, and perception of the solo playing out special roles in the group, roles that are often highly stereotyped ones. In contrast, inferences about the same individual in a balanced group reveal that no more is recalled about him or her than about other group members; his or her influence is the same as that of other group members; his or her attributes are evaluated the same as those of other group members; and he or she is no more likely to be seen as playing out a special role in the group than are other group members. The evaluations of the solo, then, are more a function of solo status than of being a member of a particular social group. These differences appear to be mediated by the solo's distinctiveness in the group, but the content of those differences is dependent on both the attribute that makes that person salient and the behavior in which that person engages. The results of these studies, then, make a strong case for the importance of the perceiver's preconceptions, the target person's behavior, and the context in which the behavior occurs as bases for the imputation of stereotypes.

MINORITY–MAJORITY STATUS, DISTINCTIVENESS, AND STEREOTYPING

Though solo status is a particularly interesting context for examining hypotheses regarding distinctiveness, in a sense, it is merely one example of a much larger phenomenon. If people use physical and social discriminators such as race and sex as ways of categorizing people and organizing information about them, then they should do so not only for solos but for other groups and group members as well. The hypotheses regarding the impact of the solo status on perceptions and evaluations can be extended to perceptions of other group members by arguing that any person, whether male or female or black or white, is distinctive in inverse proportion to the number of other members of his or her race or sex present in the social context. A woman in a group with a few women is more distinctive than a woman in a group of all women, and a black man is more distinctive if there are one or two other blacks present than if there are five or six. Accordingly, individuals should also be evaluated on various dimensions, especially stereotyped ones, according to the number of other members of their race or sex present.

In our previous study in which we examined perceptions of a solo male and a solo female, we had constructed stimulus materials that made it possible to examine six-person groups that varied in other possible sex compositions. Specifically, because there were six speakers and a male and female version of each, it was possible to create all possible sex compositions of a six-person group, ranging from all male (6M), 5M–1F, 4M–2F, 3M–3F, 2M–4F, 1M–5F to all female (6F). In this study (Taylor, et al., 1978, Study 3), subjects observed one of these slide and tape presentations and then rated all the participants on a variety of attributes.[2] In order to examine the distinctiveness hypotheses, ratings of the two single-sex groups (all male, all female) were excluded from the data analysis. Each subject's average rating of the male group members and of the female group members was then computed and an analysis was conducted on subjects' averaged ratings of the male and female subgroups as a function of the sex composition of the group.

Because the stereotyping hypothesis under examination posits relative distinctiveness as a determinant of degree of stereotyping, the first question of interest is whether or not an individual is perceived as more prominent, the fewer the number of other members of his or her sex present in the group. On two items measuring prominence, the distinctiveness hypothesis was clearly supported. Both male and female group members were seen as more assertive and as having made a stronger impression, the fewer the number of other members of their sex were present in the group. Several variables measuring perceived warmth also showed the same effect. These results are clearly consistent with the distinctiveness hypothesis.

A second question is whether stereotyped attributes were imputed to the male and female subgroups at all. That is, it is not appropriate to ask the question, was an individual stereotyped in proportion to the number of other individuals of his or her sex present, unless there is overall evidence of stereotyping. Results showed that there were clear differences in perceptions of the subgroups as a function of their sex. Males were rated as more influential, less sensitive, more analytical, more confident, and more negative. They were also seen as somewhat more deserving of respect, less perceptive, and less warm than women. The qualities attributed to the two sex subgroups, then, are in a direction consistent with conventional sex stereotypes. These effects, of course, are pure stereotyping effects, unconfounded by stimulus-person behavior, inasmuch as there was a male and a female version of each stimulus person.

But the more important question, whether or not stereotyped attributes were imputed to individuals as a function of the number of their sex present, received only weak support. There was one marginally significant effect indicating that men were seen as less perceptive and women as more perceptive, the fewer the number of other members of their sex were present. However, on other trait

---

[2]The data analyzed in this study overlap somewhat with those in the previous study of the solo male and female.

measures of stereotyping, there was little support for a relationship between relative distinctiveness and degree of stereotyping. The exception to this overall weak pattern was on the item assessing number of roles imputed to group members. First, the content of the roles was coded for stereotypic content by a coder blind to experimental conditions. Eighty percent of the roles showed some stereotyped content. Males were typically cast as father figures, leaders, or macho types. Females were often cast as motherly, nurturant type, as bitches, or as the group secretary. The frequency of attributed stereotyped roles was then analyzed as a function of the numbers of men and women present in the group. The results indicated that a stereotypic role was more likely to be imputed to a group member, the fewer the number of other members of his or her sex present. In sum, although stereotyped trait attributes were generally not imputed to individuals as a function of the number of other members of their sex present, whether or not the individual was seen as playing out a sex-stereotyped role was sensitive to the group composition as predicted. Discussion of this pattern appears in a later section.

STEREOTYPING OF GROUPS AS A FUNCTION OF GROUP COMPOSITION

For the most part, stereotyping research has focused on stereotypes of homogenous groups (such as blacks or women) and on perceptions of individual members of those groups. However, adopting a categorization approach to stereotyping makes it possible to generate predictions regarding perceptions of social units that are mixed in their composition, for example, mixed-race or mixed-sex groups. Specifically, one can predict that mixed groups will be characterized on the basis of the proportion of different group members they hold. For example, one might predict that groups as a whole will be perceived as more masculine or feminine, the more males or females in the group, respectively, and hence the group might be stereotyped on sex-relevant lines according to group composition. If so, this would mean that the social perceiver is using categorical distinctions within a group not only to draw inferences about individual group members, but also to draw inferences about the group as a whole.

To provide a basis for testing this hypothesis, the sex stereotyping study just described had included not only items measuring perceptions of the individual group members, but also items examining perceptions of the attributes of the group as a whole. The question of interest in this context is, will a *group* come to be seen as reflecting male sex-typed or female sex-typed behavior in proportion to the number of males or females present in the group? The groups, identical in verbal conversation, had simply differed in sex composition. The members had been represented to subjects as a group of teachers chatting about school and possible teacher unionization. Accordingly, subjects were asked whether the group would work together effectively, unionize successfully, and the like. The analysis of the group ratings showed the following: The more females in the group, the more subjects believed that the group had trouble getting along, and that it would have trouble working together to unionize. The more females in the group, the more incompetent subjects regarded the group as being. Conversely, as the number of men in the group increased, ratings of the group's competence, ability to unionize, and congeniality also increased. Evaluations of groups as a whole, then, are sensitive to the dominance of some particular attribute in the group. In this case, the male-dominated groups were rated more favorably than were the female-dominated groups, and these differences reflected conventional sex-role stereotypes.

There is an apparent contradiction between the study just described and Rothbart's (this volume) study of perceptions of groups with extreme versus nonextreme members. In that study, subjects were exposed to hypothetical small groups, some members of which were extreme in height or in behavior. Rothbart found that ratings of the groups were determined by the highly salient attributes of the minority group members. However, in our study, group perceptions were a function of the dominant sex in the group (i.e., majority attributes). Both sets of data are consistent with an emphasis on the significance of social context in the imputation of stereotypes, but they obtain opposite data patterns. Accordingly, these discrepancies must be reconciled by specifying the conditions when the attributes of the majority are most salient and likely to influence group ratings and when the attributes of a distinctive minority are likely to influence group ratings. One possible reconciliation centers around memory load. Inasmuch as subjects rated only six stimulus persons in our sex-stereotyping study, it is possible that they were able to discriminate all six individuals from each other and also see the group as a separate unit altogether, rather than inferring group characteristics from salient individuals. This explanation is consistent with Rothbart's findings that group ratings were based on salient individuals' attributes only under conditions of high memory load, and not when the memory load was low. Thus, distinctive individuals may influence perceptions of groups in situations with lots of information and complexity, whereas majority attributes may influence perceptions of groups when the social environment is more manageable. A second possible explanation centers on the differences in informativeness of majority versus minority attributes between the two studies. Subjects may have regarded the sex of group members as a socially meaningful attribute that was informative regarding the group's attributes in our sex-stereotyping study, whereas in the Rothbart studies, the only socially meaningful information was the extreme attributes of the few members. Whether either of these explanations adequately addresses this controversy can ultimately be assessed only by future research. To summarize, then, categorization processes do seem to influence perceptions of groups that are mixed in their composition, but the circumstances under which minority versus majority attributes determine those perceptions have yet to be fully delineated.

THE PERCEIVER'S CONTRIBUTION TO STEREOTYPING

Thus far, we have considered the target person's behavior and the context in which it is enacted as two determinants of stereotyping. A third contribution is provided by the perceiver and his or her familiarity with, membership in, or values regarding particular social groups. In a sense, of course, this focus has been the traditional orientation of stereotyping research, because historically, efforts have been geared to identifying the individual differences in background and personality that lead one person to exhibit prejudice whereas another does not. However, a cognitive perspective on stereotyping leads the researcher to ask different questions regarding what perceiver predispositions contribute to stereotyping. Specifically, are there perceiver factors that influence the propensity to use race and sex as categorical systems; are there perceiver factors that influence the ability to make within-category discriminations; and will these factors further predict the extent to which an individual will stereotype another person?

First, given that stereotyping appears to be rooted in basic categorical processes, what are the individual differences that would influence the propensity to categorize or the ability to make within-category discriminations? One such factor may be familiarity with a particular category. Familiarity with a category provides reference points, based either on objective information about the category and its attributes or subjective opinions about it. Therefore, to the extent that a person is unfamiliar with grouped individuals or their attributes, the degree to which he or she perceives similarity among the objects should be greater. In terms of stereotyping, this hypothesis predicts that one will see members of a group with which one is not familiar as more similar to each other than one will regard members of groups with which one is familiar. This perception of "all X's (e.g., blacks, Jews) are alike" is commonly mentioned in accounts of prejudicial reactions (Malpass & Kravitz, 1969).

To examine this hypothesis, we (Taylor, et al., 1978, Study 1) reanalyzed data from our error-rate studies described earlier. If familiarity with a category facilitates the ability to make within-category distinctions, then white subjects would be more likely to confuse the black speakers with each other than white speakers with each other. However, an analysis of the intraracial errors found no evidence for this prediction. Assuming membership in a category to be the most extreme case of familiarity with that group leads to a revised hypothesis that one will regard members of another group (outgroup) as more similar to each other than one will regard members of one's own group (ingroup). Accordingly, we reanalyzed the data from the sex error-rate study (Taylor et al. 1978, Study 2) in an effort to examine the membership hypothesis, anticipating that male subjects would confuse female speakers with each other more than with male speakers and that the reverse might be true of female subjects. However, again, there was no effect of sex of subject on recall. Subjects were equally likely to confuse male or female speakers with each other, regardless of their own sex. Our previous studies provided a second basis for testing the hypothesis that membership in a category decreases the likelihood of stereotyping one's own group and increases the likelihood of stereotyping the other group. Specifically, we checked for sex of subject effects in stereotype ratings of the individual group members (Taylor et al., 1978, Study 3). There were no sex of subject effects, indicating that male and female subjects were equally likely to see male and female targets in sex-stereotyped terms.

To summarize, sex of subject and race of subject seem not to predict whether or not an individual will organize information by sex and race. Furthermore, individuals do not seem less prone to stereotyping members of their own versus another group. These results thus fail to confirm both the familiarity hypothesis and the membership hypothesis. It may be that familiarity only facilitates making discriminations within a group up to a point, and that once some basic level of familiarity with a group has been attained, increased familiarity, whether due to membership or experience, provides no extra advantage. If this is true, and our subjects had achieved this level of familiarity, these facts would explain the failure to find effects in the error-rate studies. However, it still would not explain why there were no sex differences in stereotyping of male and female target persons. On the basis of the ingroup–outgroup literature, one might expect males to evaluate males more favorably than females, and females to evaluate females more favorably than males. There may be unrecognized contextual or situational factors that promote ingroup–outgroup effects that were not present in this study; if so, identifying those factors would help provide the basis for further delineating the factors that make a particular cue salient as a basis for categorization. More is said about this point in a later section.

A third set of individual differences that may influence one's propensity to organize information along sex or race lines and stereotype accordingly are relevant attitudes and values. Tajfel (1972) and others have maintained that not only stereotyping, but the actual perception of differences among groups, can serve as an expression of an individual's values and attitudes. Sex role identification of the subject and feminist beliefs are two individual-difference variables that might influence the propensity to use sex as a categorical system and the propensity to stereotype by sex. Sex-role identification, as measured by the (BSRI) Bem Sex Role Inventory (1974), provides both a masculinity and a femininity score for each individual, and on the basis of the relative difference between the scores, an individual is said to be primarily Masculine, primarily

Feminine, or Androgynous (balanced masculinity and femininity scores). In previous studies (Bem & Lenney, 1976), sex-typed people have been found to use sex-related cues as a basis for their performance more than androgynous people who are equally responsive to masculine and feminine cues. The fact that sex-typed people make differential use of sex-typed cues, whereas androgynous people do not, leads to the hypothesis that sex-typed people may be more attuned to the sex of people and hence more likely to organize incoming information by sex and stereotype by sex. The Feminism (FEM) Scale (Smith, Ferree, & Miller, 1975) measures traditional versus liberal perceptions of the appropriateness of certain tasks and behaviors for women and therefore constitutes a measure of feminism. People low in feminism generally regard female tasks as different from male tasks, whereas people high in feminism generally consider it appropriate for men and women to perform the same tasks. Accordingly, because nonfeminists believe that sex should be a determinant of behavior, they might be more likely to use sex as a way of organizing person information and might stereotype more than feminists.

To test these hypotheses, we again used the six-person discussion of how to increase voter turnout, a discussion that involved three men and three women. Several weeks prior to participating in the study, subjects were given the BSRI (Bem, 1974) and the FEM Scale (Smith et al., 1975) to complete in an ostensibly unrelated context. Subjects were later recruited for a study on political behavior. They listened to the slide and tape presentation of the campaign to increase voter turnout, after which they were given two tasks. As in the previous study, they were asked to recall who said what. Unlike the previous study, they were also asked to evaluate all six participants in the group as to how politically savvy they were, how effective they would be in organizing a political campaign, how interesting their suggestions had been, how influential they had been in the group, and how comfortable they had seemed to feel in the group. These two sets of measures provide an assessment of the impact of sex-role identification and feminism on both the propensity to organize information by sex and the propensity to stereotype by sex.

The recall data indicated strongly that the propensity to organize incoming information by sex is by no means universal. Whereas highly sex-typed individuals (both masculine and feminine) clearly used sex as a categorical system for organizing information, androgynous people were far less likely to do so. Furthermore, the data indicated that androgynous people recalled an equivalent amount of information overall, suggesting that whatever categorical system they were using was serving them as efficiently as the sex-categorization system used by the sex-typed persons. Sex typing of the subject, then, clearly determined whether an individual employed sex as a strategy for organizing information. What these results suggest is that for sex-typed individuals, sex is a more salient cue for organizing social information than it is for androgynous people. This is consistent with Bem's underlying theoretical argument concerning the attributes of androgynous individuals. Specifically, these are people who see themselves as composed of roughly equal numbers of male and female attributes. Apparently, because sex typing is not considered by androgynous people to be self-descriptive, they do not regard it as an appropriate way of organizing information about others. Feminism, however, did not predict the extent to which an individual organized information by sex. High and low feminists were equally likely to use sex as a way of encoding information.

The stereotype–prejudice items revealed a very different picture. On four of the five items (political savvy, efficacy, interest value, and influence) male participants were rated much more favorably than female participants. What makes these results depressing is the fact that the suggestions participants made during the discussion had been equated for quality prior to the experiment, so the propensity to evaluate males more highly than females is a pure prejudice-stereotyping effect. In contrast to the results on organizing recall by sex, androgynous people were not less likely to show prejudice against women. The most favoritism toward male speakers was shown by the masculine sex-typed subjects followed by the androgynous subjects, with the least degree of male favoritism shown, not surprisingly, by the feminine sex-typed subjects. Feminism scores influenced prejudice in the expected direction. Subjects who scored higher on the FEM Scale showed less prejudice than did subjects low in feminism.

To summarize, sex-role identification influenced the propensity to organize information by sex but had less effect on degree of prejudice expressed. Feminism, on the other hand, had no impact on the organization of information by sex, but did predict degree of prejudice. These results suggest, first, that sex-role identification and feminism are measuring very different things. Sex-role identification seems to get at the salience of sex as a cue but does not necessarily predict sex-related attitudes; thus, it seems to be a measure of cognitive style, rather than a measure of general values. Feminism, on the other hand, predicts value expression, but not the salience of sex as a cue. The further more intriguing implication of these data is that organizing information by sex and stereotyping by sex may not necessarily work together. This result is consistent with an increasing body of evidence that shows that recall and impression measures often do not covary (see, for example, Anderson & Hubert, 1963; Dreben, Fiske, & Hastie, 1978). If so, this rules out a particular form of the cognitive explanation of stereotyping, specifically, one that maintains that stereotyping as a function of sex is dependent on the strategy of organizing information by sex. On a practical level, the apparent autonomy of the organization and stereotyping effects also has implications. It suggests that strategies designed to reduce the salience of sex as a variable for organizing information may not produce the expected results of reducing stereotyping.

AT WHAT LEVEL DOES STEREOTYPING OCCUR?

An issue that has received very little attention in the stereotyping literature is how stereotypes differentiate with experience. Perhaps because stereotypes have always been thought of as rigidly unresponsive to feedback (see Ashmore & Del Boca, this volume), researchers have been blind to the learning component in stereotyping. A stereotype is usually characterized as a set of trait adjectives that describes a social group. For example, women are said to be passive, dependent, social, warm, and sensitive. Men are described as aggressive, active, independent, analytic, and confident. Blacks are characterized as lazy, stupid, musical, athletic, and good dancers, and Jews are represented as smart, aggressive, grasping, and materialistic. However, increasing contact with any category of objects, be it tools, food items, or social groups, enables one to make finer and finer discriminations within the category. For example, although initial contact with a group (e.g., a football team) may lead to trait stereotyping (e.g., big, dumb), eventually contact with the group should facilitate the perception of subtypes (e.g., the playboy; the shy, sensitive boy who wouldn't hurt a fly except on the field; the arrogant hero type who grabs the media; the small town boy who can't handle the publicity and turns to drugs and alcohol). At some point, the diversity and volume of contact with any social group should be substantial enough that abstract trait conceptions of the group would no longer have any descriptive value. Rather, subtypes would emerge that would have more descriptive utility than the overall trait conceptions. What begins as a single category simply proliferates into subcategories, and categorization and stereotyping simply occur at this finer level, as they previously did at the more global level. Whereas, on the one hand, this observation may seem commonplace, on the other, it can help explain some riddles in our own and others' data. In our experiments our subjects rarely referred to general stereotypic trait conceptions when describing particular individuals. Although one could argue that these subjects were sufficiently sophisticated not to engage in such flagrant overgeneralization, the data belie this interpretation. The subjects showed no reluctance to stereotype; rather, their stereotypes were at a different level than that reflected in trait conceptions, a level one might term "role" or "persona" (Nisbett & Ross, 1979). For example, a woman was described as a bitch or a motherly type; a black, as an oreo cookie or a street-smart type; a man as a macho type or a father figure; or a Jew as a Jewish-American princess or a rabbi.

Our formal data analyses also provided a basis for distinguishing between trait stereotypes and role stereotypes. We had predicted that stereotyped attributes would be imputed to a member of a particular group (e.g., men, women, blacks) in inverse proportion to the number of other members of that race or sex present in the group. This hypothesis consistently received weak support. A man was not consistently seen as more aggressive, the fewer other men there were in the group, nor did perceptions of a woman's sensitivity differ as a function of the number of men or women present. In fact, only one of our stereotype *trait* measures showed any support for the hypothesis. In contrast, the item, "Did this person play a special role in the group?" did show the predicted effect. Subjects were more likely to report that an individual had played a special role in the group the fewer the other members of that person's race or sex were present in the group. Furthermore, recall the content of those attributed roles: mother, father, princess, bitch, etc.—in short, the persona level. Why might stereotyping occur at this role or "persona" level, rather than at the trait level? Referring to the earlier point about the role of learning in stereotyping, we would argue that our subjects had enough familiarity with each of the social groups they evaluated that role subtypes, rather than more global trait-level types, were their preferred level of description. Furthermore, the interface of role-level and trait-level stereotypes may not be very straightforward, and under some circumstances the two actually may be incompatible. An illustration may be provided by taking a sample stereotyped trait, "aggressive." Generally women are perceived as less aggressive than men. However, the "bitch" role or "pushy broad" role certainly has a strong aggressive component. Trait ratings of women seen as playing these roles, then, would not show the stereotypic perception of low aggression, but rather counterstereotypic high aggression ratings. Assuming that similar effects would occur for other trait measures as a function of the particular role involved, then all trait measures of stereotypes could fail to show stereotyping effects because the specific role stereotypes subsume implicit traits that would cancel out differences in overarching trait stereotypes. This is especially likely to be true in our own work because in our statistical analyses, male and female ratings were averaged across several men and several women who may have varied considerably on the trait in question as a function of the roles they were perceived as playing. In contrast, the role question assessed whether the group member played out *any* sex-stereotyped role, ranging from mother or father to "macho" or seductive to intellectual or intuitive. Thus, the role item may have shown effects because first, it tapped the level at which subjects were actually stereotyping and second, it permitted assessment of a wide diversity of role stereotypes.

This line of analysis raises a more basic issue in object and person categorization, namely, the question of levels of categorization. Rosch and her students (Rosch, Mervis, Gray, Johnson, & Boyes-Braem, 1976) have suggested that there is a basic level of objects in categories that "carries the most information, possesses the highest category cue validity, and is thus the most differentiated from one another [p. 382]." For example, within the category, "furniture," chair is a basic object category, whereas dining-room chair and kitchen chair are objects at a subordinate level of categorization. What makes "chair" basic is the high descriptiveness of the objects it includes coupled with its high degree of differentiation from other objects in the category, "furniture." Basic objects have been found to be, according to Rosch et al. (1976):

> the most inclusive categories whose members (a) possess significant numbers of attributes in common, (b) have motor programs which are similar to one another, (c) have similar shapes, and (d) can be identified from averaged shapes of members of the class.... Basic objects are shown to be the most inclusive categories for which a concrete image of the category as a whole can be formed, to be the first categorizations made during perception of the environment, to be the earliest categories sorted and earliest named by children, and to be the categories most codable, most coded, and most necessary in language [p. 382].

The obvious question this work raises is: Is there a basic level of person perception and if so, what level is it? To address this issue, Cantor and Mischel (1979) replicated a number of Rosch et al.'s experimental procedures using personality types, rather than objects, and found evidence for a basic level of person perception. Specifically, they presented subjects with taxonomies of person descriptions that included a superordinate trait level (e.g., committed, extrovert person) a middle level of the social role or persona (e.g., religious devotee, PR type), and a more specific level (e.g., Buddhist monk, door-to-door salesman). Groups of subjects were then asked to list attributes characteristic of and common to the people at one level of abstraction within a category. Lists of the commonly cited attributes (at each level within each category) were then coded for richness (number of attributes), differentiation (degree of category overlap), and concreteness (number of physical, social class, trait, and behavior statements cited). In a separate study, ease of imaging a person at each of the levels was assessed and coded for richness and consensus. Generally, the middle level of categorization, the role or persona level, (e.g., the PR type) maximized richness, differentiation, and vividness. That is, general categories of "extrovert" or "committed person" proved to have high differentiation from other types at the same level, but low descriptive value for the subtypes it contained. The very fine-grained level of "door-to-door salesman" or "Buddhist monk" proved to be highly descriptive but poorly differentiated from highly similar types such as "Hasidic Jew" or "campaign manager." The middle level proved to be both highly descriptive and highly differentiated, thus corresponding most closely to Rosch's concept of a "basic level."

In this context, our distinction between abstract trait stereotypic conceptions and stereotyped role conceptions becomes more meaningful, more comprehensible, and more important. If there is a basic level of person perception or description that people draw on in representing others and imputing attributes to them, and if this basic level involves personae or roles rather than more abstract traits, the conceptual and methodological implications for stereotyping are profound. We next discuss three obvious implications, but before doing so, one caveat is warranted.

We are not claiming that *no* stereotyping occurs at the trait level. In fact, our own data show that, overall, males and females were seen in fairly traditional sex-stereotyped terms as measured by trait ratings. What we are claiming is that the bulk of stereotyping of individuals in a social context, what we consider to be the most interesting, informative stereotyping, is occurring at the role or persona level, rather than at the trait level. However, people use abstract trait conceptions on some occasions or for some purposes. For example, developing expectations about someone when all one knows is the person's race or sex might be one instance, or imputing attributes to an individual about whom one has minimal information would be another. When we must characterize a social group as a whole (e.g., women, men, blacks) we may use the abstract trait level rather than individual role stereotypes. None of these points is inconsistent with the "basic levels" argument. Obviously, superordinate and subordinate categories have some utility, whether they apply to objects or social groups. We have "furniture" stores, not "chair" stores, and we have "tool" boxes, not "screwdriver" boxes. Likewise, our dining-room chairs are not placed in the den, and one uses a Phillips screwdriver, not just any screwdriver, for certain tasks. In a similar manner, we use different levels of person categories for different purposes.

However, we would argue that in describing individuals about whom we have at least a little information, role stereotypes will predominate. What are the implications of this point? First, by continuing to assess stereotyping through trait ratings, we may miss the level at which much stereotyping is occurring. The most substantively important consequence of this fact is that we may grossly underestimate how much stereotyping is actually going on. A specific example will illustrate this point. Suppose a researcher wants to see if sex integration reduces sex stereotyping in a business setting. An appropriate design would be to measure the male employees' stereotypes of women prior to integration, integrate the organization at all levels, and later reassess sex stereotypes. If a decrease in stereotyping ratings is found, one is tempted to conclude that sex integration reduces sex stereotyping. However, if stereotypes simply change their level in response to increased and/or diverse contact with the group, a different conclusion may be warranted. Consider the following specific case. If a man's co-workers include a few highly aggressive and competent women, it will be hard for him to maintain a stereotype of all women as helpless and passive. Trait ratings of this man's reactions to women on the dimensions of passivity and helplessness would probably suggest a decrease in his stereotyping. However, if this man believes that his female colleagues are obnoxious, pushy bitches who f_____d their way to the top, we might not want to claim that his stereotypes had abated (though our trait measures would suggest that they had).

A less hypothetical example of this problem may be found in the recent efforts to replicate the Katz and Braly (1933) stereotyping studies. In the original study subjects were given a list of trait adjectives and asked to characterize each of ten groups (e.g., Turks, Italians). Later replications (see, for example, Gilbert, 1951) found a decrease in trait attributions to groups, a finding that has optimistically been interpreted as evidence for a decline in stereotyping. This conclusion, we would argue, is premature, because it is impossible to detect a change in level of stereotyping using a Katz and Braly-like paradigm. Stereotypes of ethnic and national groups may be as alive and well as ever, but living in the form of role stereotypes. In short, we need to develop measures that will be sensitive to the role level of stereotyping in order to assess accurately the ways in which and the extent to which people are actually stereotyping in a given social context.

A second implication of assuming that stereotypes are imputed at the role level is that stereotypes will be extremely hard to disconfirm. The difficulty of disconfirming stereotypes has been noted for many years. Lippmann (1922), for example, included this point in his definition of stereotypes as factually incorrect products of illogical reasoning that are rigidly unresponsive to feedback. However, unresponsiveness to feedback has usually been explained as resulting from the intrapsychic needs of the perceiver (see Ashmore's, 1970, discussion of this point), rather than from cognitive factors. A cognitive explanation of this point begins with the assumption that increasing and diverse contact or experience with a group prompts an increasing number of role stereotypes that complement the overarching trait stereotype. For example, though a man may believe that women are basically passive, quiet, and none-too-bright, encountering an intelligent, aggressive, outgoing woman may lead him to develop a new stereotype such as "castrating female" or "career woman," a variant to his usual stereotype. If this process occurs, then the overarching stereotype will never be directly disconfirmed. Disconfirmations simply provide a basis for splitting off a new stereotype, not revising an old one. Accordingly, all of the stereotypes can persist and any new female encountered will fit at least one of them, without disconfirming the others.

To continue, a third point that is suggested by the idea of proliferating role stereotypes concerns the amount of behavior that can be "explained" by stereotypes. Returning to the male business person whose company has been recently sex desegregated, what will become of his stereotypes as a result of increasingly diverse contact with women? Eventually, as the number of stereotypes he has develops—mother, princess, bitch, castrating female, showgirl—any behavior a female performs can fit within at least one of those stereotypic conceptions. In theory, then, given enough role stereotypes, men and women could perform exactly the same behaviors and possess identical attributes, and there could still be a set of male-role stereotypes to explain the male behavior and attributes and a set of female-role stereotypes to explain the female behavior and attributes. Note, for example, that a trait abstraction of the "career woman" role consists of male traits: e.g., aggressiveness, competitiveness, activity, singlemindedness. The fact that the behaviors and attributes are male may not be noticed at the role level of stereotyping, and so male traits become components of a female stereotype. Our suspicion is that the sum total of all role stereotypes for either sex encompasses all the traits appropriate for both sexes combined (i.e., the range of attributes for all human behavior).

CONCLUSIONS AND FURTHER DIRECTIONS

Having examined the foundations of a categorical theory of stereotyping as expounded by Allport, Campbell, Tajfel, and others and having examined the results of recent research generated by a categorization approach, what can be said about the status of theory and research in this area? That stereotyping depends upon categorization is as clear as ever, having now been demonstrated by a large number of investigations using many different paradigms. However, our recent work makes it clear that categorizing others on the basis of salient cues is more than a simple process of identification and labeling; it is a dynamic process by which people extract information from the environment, organize it, and give it meaning.

The consequences of categorization for perceptions of social groups have also been filled out by recent research. As a result of the categorization process, within-group differences tend to be minimized, whereas between-group remain clearer. Following categorization, the behavior of members of a subgroup is interpreted in stereotyped terms. In our studies, for example, male stimulus persons were seen as more confident, less sensitive, more influential, more analytical, less warm, and somewhat more deserving of respect than women, despite the fact that the behavior in question was constant and only the sex designation varied. Further support for this hypothesis was found in the role data, in that when subjects ascribed roles to men in the group, these roles frequently had male sex-typed content, whereas the same behavior by a female was interpreted in female sex-typed terms.

A categorization approach to stereotyping also predicts that the social perceiver will make discriminations within a subgroup as a function of the number of other members of the subgroup present. This hypothesis also received some support. Both males and females were seen as more prominent (making a stronger impression, having a strong personality, and being more assertive, confident, and competent) in inverse proportion to the number of other members of the sex subgroup present. These results are consistent with a growing body of literature indicating that salience, by virtue of numerical distinctiveness, leads to exaggerated evaluations (Taylor & Fiske, 1978).

That size of category will in turn determine degree of stereotyping is also clear but with some important conceptual and methodological implications. The hypothesis that stereotyped attributes are imputed to a member of a particular subgroup in inverse proportion to the number of other members of the subgroup present received weak support and only in the role data. Males and females were seen as somewhat more likely to be playing a sex-stereotyped role, the fewer the number of other members of their sexual subgroup were present, but on the trait measures of stereotyping, there was virtually no support for this hypothesis. By way of resolution, it was suggested that, as people become more familiar with a social group, they develop role stereotypes that eventually replace their outmoded trait stereotypes. The implications of this observation are important. Unless a fairly broad measuring effort is employed, which taps roles in addition to traits, the relationship between categorization and stereotyping is likely to be obscured and the amount of stereotyping that occurs is likely to be underestimated. These conjectures also call into question the assumptions of "rigidity" and "unresponsiveness to feedback" that have until recently been considered the sine qua non of stereotyping. If stereotypes do indeed change their level as a function of experience and learning, then stereotypes begin to look like little more than a set of beliefs about the attributes of a social group (see Ashmore & Del Boca in this volume).

The hypothesis that social groups themselves are stereotyped as a function of their subgroup makeup received strong support. Groups were seen as less competent, as teaching a lower grade level, as less efficacious, and as less compatible, the more women were present in the group. These results indicate that people use distinctions or categories within a group to make inferences about the group as a whole.

Finally, the hypothesis that the discrimination process would be facilitated by familiarity with or membership in a category received no support. This was something of a surprise. It is a truism that whites cannot tell blacks apart or that females are seen by males as sharing many traits. It was suggested that all our subjects had reached a sufficient level of familiarity with all the groups evaluated that familiarity was no longer a basis for discriminating within categories. It may also be the case that membership in a category gives no special advantage in distinguishing one's own group members from other group members. However, it is something of a surprise that there were not even any ingroup–outgroup effects in these studies. That is, males and females did not evaluate their own group favorably and the other sex unfavorably.

Another curious finding is the apparent autonomy of degree of categorization and degree of stereotyping. That is, the degree to which one uses a variable like race or sex as a way of encoding person information seems not to predict degree of stereotyping using that same variable. This is not only surprising because categorization is assumed to mediate stereotyping, but because one would, at the very least, expect the two to be spuriously correlated. It is hard to know at this stage whether this surprise is antifactual due to improperly measuring either categorization (as error in recall) or stereotyping (as unfavorable attitudes) or whether it is an important clue regarding the interface of cognitive and motivational aspects of the stereotyping process.

Perhaps the most interesting conceptual development in categorical stereotyping work is the fact that theoretical developments in categorization research such as those uncovered by Rosch and her colleagues are finding their apparent analogues in stereotyping phenomena. There is some evidence, primarily from Cantor and Mischel (1979), for a basic level of person perception just as there is a basic level of object perception. The role level of generalization, rather than the trait level, appears to be basic in person perception, and the data in our own studies provide some fuel for this conjecture. However, there are also clear differences between a Rosch-ian formulation for objects and a role formulation for person perception. We have argued that the preferred level of stereotyping (trait versus role) changes as a function of experience with the group in question, a point that does not figure into the ''levels'' argument in the object literature (Rosch et al., 1976). Indeed, the implication of Rosch's work is that the ''basic''-ness of the basic object level is inherent in the features of the objects themselves and not solely in how they are construed by the perceiver. Assuming this differences between person perception and object perception is true, there are several possible reasons for it.

One is the fact that in the object world we share basic knowledge in a way that is not true in the world of people. Everyone, for example, knows what a chair is, but not everyone may know what an accountant is. Information about people is more ambiguous, less reliable, and more unstable than is information about objects, because people do not wear their personal attributes on their faces the way objects wear their color, shape, or size. Thus, personal attributes must be inferred rather than observed directly. Although objects maintain their attributes cross-situationally and over time, people's motives change from situation to situation, and goals and motives change over their lifetime. Intentions are a relevant way of inferring attributes, but not all intentions are directly stated. Given that most significant social actions can be committed for a variety of reasons and will produce a variety of consequences, the meaning of social action is fundamentally ambiguous.

The social world is stratified by sex, segregated by race and occupation, and isolated by roles. Different patterns of activity immerse an individual in one setting and completely segregate him or her from others. Thus, social knowledge, in contrast to object knowledge, may be more differentiated. Accordingly, there may be no one basic level of person perception. The trait level may be basic for groups with which one has little experience, the role level for groups with which one has more experience, and an even more finely grained level for groups with which one has a lot of experience. Alternatively, because the social world is organized by roles (e.g., occupational roles, family roles), rather than by traits, a feature analysis of social structure, analogous to Rosch's analysis of objects, might yield the finding that the structure is indeed "out there" in some objective sense. To summarize, whether there is a basic level of person perception remains to be seen; if there is, the best candidate for it is the role level.

Overall, two important features distinguish a categorization approach to stereotyping from other approaches. First, the approach maintains that processes that underlie person perception have much in common with those that underlie object perception. All of the hypotheses tested in our research were derived from the literature on categorization and not from what we normally think of as the stereotyping literature. Given that the hypotheses were generally supported, the results suggest that race and sex operate much as other categorical systems do. Race and sex are social categories that are used as means of organizing incoming person information. Stereotypes can be thought of as attributes that are tagged to category labels (e.g., race, sex) and imputed to individuals as a function of their being placed in that category, much as attributes of other categories are imputed to objects placed in those categories.

Second, a categorization approach implies that the process of stereotyping has a contextual basis. It is clearly not the case that the social perceiver has a stereotype about a social group that he or she evenhandedly attributes to every member of that group with whom he or she interacts. Rather, there appear to be contextual dimensions that facilitate or inhibit the imputation of stereotypes to individuals. Thus, although our categorical systems for organizing information about people may be highly structured, our ability to use them is remarkably fluid and dependent on the features of the context in which persons are observed.

Generally, we would argue that any factor that makes an individual's membership in a social group especially salient would engage the stereotype of the group. In our research, minority versus majority status had such an effect. An important task for future research should be identifying other contextual factors that will increase the salience of group membership. In other words, when *is* a person a woman, an Italian, a bridge player, a mother, or a Catholic? One factor may be participation in a group organized around a particular attribute. A person is never more of a woman than when she is at a women's convention. However, paradoxically, minority status or distinctiveness produces exactly the same effect. A woman is never more of a woman than when she is the only woman in a group of men. Thus, two contextual factors that promote the salience of a particular attribute are the nature of the group the person is in and his or her relative distinctiveness within that group. These two factors work, to some extent, in opposition. Other contextually significant factors may include the topic of conversation in a group situation. For example, a common experience in a group occurs when the topic of conversation shifts to a sensitive topic such as race, and suddenly everyone is acutely aware of who is black and who is white. Intergroup conflict or competition may also increase the salience of the attribute that is used as a basis for categorization, inasmuch as resources must be shared among groups of people. This is hardly an exhaustive list of contextual factors that lead to stereotyping, but it may provide some directions for empirical investigation.

The importance of examining contextual factors in stereotyping can also be seen clearly when we try to generalize the results of the laboratory studies of the ingroup–outgroup phenomenon. For example, in our work no ingroup–outgroup effects were found (i.e., males and females did not differentially evaluate their own and the other sex). Accordingly, there must be particular factors that make the fact of a group difference salient that promote an ingroup–outgroup effect. We would argue that the so-called minimal intergroup situation, far from delineating the minimum conditions necessary for an ingroup–outgroup distinction, in fact highlights categorization to an extreme rarely found in real-world settings. That is, precisely because so little occurs in this laboratory setting, the act of categorizing people into two groups achieves a very high degree of salience. Generalizing the ingroup–outgroup effect, then, requires defining conditions that might promote a comparable salience of group distinctions in naturalistic settings. Brewer's (1979) review of this literature suggests three possible contextual conditions that might promote ingroup–outgroup distinctions: competition among groups; high levels of perceived similarity within groups; and status differences among groups. To this list, Wilder (this volume) has added individual-difference variables such as focus of attention and cognitive set and, on the group level, contact with the ingroup, dissent within the outgroup, and the presence of other more extreme outgroups as relevant factors. Whether any of these is sufficient to produce an ingroup–outgroup effect in a natural setting remains to be seen. In sum, real-world analogues to the ingroup–outgroup manipulation must be found, for it is clearly not the case that merely knowing there are differences between groups will produce ingroup–outgroup effects.

A categorical approach to stereotyping leads to some blind spots, as well as illumination. Just as motivationally oriented researchers in stereotyping have often ignored the cognitive underpinnings of the stereotyping process, so cognitively oriented researchers in stereotyping tend to overlook the motivational side. Cognitively it may matter little whether a person categorizes a bright, successful female as a "career woman" or a "castrating bitch," but on both the practical level and the motivational side, it will matter a great deal. Taking a cognitive orientation, one is tempted to append motivational factors as an evaluative overlay on an otherwise cognitive process. That is, one can argue that the motivational component of stereotyping affects primarily the content of stereotypes and the evaluation of the target (positive or negative) but fails to have much impact on how the stereotyping process occurs in a social context and how stereotypes differentiate. Presumably, the content and evaluation derive from such factors as childhood socialization, long-term values, and short-term situations of threat. This separation of cognition and motivation is convenient and there is some basis for it in the literature, but it fails to ring true. Things must be more complex. There must be more points of intersection between the motivational and cognitive needs that are satisfied by stereotyping. It may be the case, for example, that when a person holds a stereotype about a particular group with great intensity, the threshold for seeing the relevant intergroup distinction is greatly lowered. Thus, a feminist sees male–female distinctions and issues in contexts where others do not.

Another possible point of intersection derives from the fact that, to a large extent, individuals create their reality and impose their own structures on the environment. Everyone knows of a person for whom a particular motivation (e.g., sex), is so salient that he introduces it into every situation. Thus, the male–female distinction is for him (as well as for those who interact regularly with him) a chronic mode of organizing the social environment, and hence that distinction, as well as its accompanying sex-role stereotypes, gets a lot of practice. His reality becomes a world of men and women, not people. The same is true for people who chronically organize along any group lines (e.g., race, ethnicity, wealth, or even personal interests or hobbies). (See Snyder in this volume for a discussion of some of these points.) To summarize, probably the most complex direction in which stereotyping research should move is in elucidating the nature of the cognition–motivation interface.

Turning briefly to a completely different issue, one can ask whether categorical approaches to stereotyping have led to any practical knowledge. Mapping out the policy implications of any research program is always risky, and it is complicated in stereotyping by the fact that the stakes are so high. One implication of a contextual emphasis in stereotyping is that certain structural conditions facilitate or inhibit extreme evaluations of racial or sexual groups and subgroup members and facilitate or inhibit stereotyping of them as well. Thus, for example, in an organizational setting, a situation of token integration is especially conducive to extreme evaluations and stereotyping of the minority group member. Kanter (1977) and Wolman and Frank (1975) have found precisely these effects in their field studies of token integration. Single-sex groups also seem to promote a high level of stereotyping, but at the group level rather than the individual level. Accordingly, social units such as particular occupations may come to be stereotyped as a function of the attributes of the people who customarily fill them. Groups that are more balanced in their composition may yield less impetus for stereotyping of both groups and individual members. Beyond these specific suggestions, the most useful outcome of this approach may be the development of a general strategy: structural and functional analyses of social settings to identify circumstances most conducive to stereotyping.

ACKNOWLEDGMENTS

The research presented in this paper and preparation of the paper was supported by National Institute of Mental Health Grants MH–25827 and MH–26460 and National Science Foundation Grant BNS 77–09922. I am grateful to David L. Hamilton for his comments on an earlier draft.

REFERENCES

Allen, V. L., & Wilder, D. A. Categorization, belief similarity, and intergroup discrimination. *Journal of Personality and Social Psychology*, 1975, *32*, 971–977.

Allport, G. W. *The nature of prejudice*. Cambridge, Mass.: Addison–Wesley, 1954.

Anderson, N. H., & Hubert, S. Effects of concomitant verbal recall on order effects in personality impression formation. *Journal of Verbal Learning and Verbal Behavior*, 1963, *2*, 379–391.

Ashmore, R. D. The problem of intergroup prejudice. In B. E. Collins *Social psychology*. Reading, Mass.: Addison–Wesley, 1970.

Bem, S. L. The measurement of psychological androgyny. *Journal of Consulting and Clinical Psychology*, 1974, *42*, 155–162.

Bem, S. L., & Lenney, E. Sex-typing and the avoidance of cross-sex behavior. *Journal of Personality and Social Psychology*, 1976, *33*, 48–54.

Billig, M. Normative communication in a minimal intergroup behavior. *European Journal of Social Psychology*, 1973, *3*, 339–343.

Billig, M., & Tajfel, H. Social categorization and similarity in intergroup behavior. *European Journal of Social Psychology*, 1973, *3*, 27–52.

Bousfield, W. A. The occurrence of clustering in the recall of randomly arranged associates. *Journal of Genetic Psychology*, 1953, *49*, 229–240.

Brewer, M. B. In-group bias in the minimal intergroup situation: A cognitive–motivational analysis. *Psychological Bulletin*, 1979, 307–323.

Bruner, E. M. Primary group experience and the process of acculturation. *American Anthropologist*, 1956, *58*, 605–623.

Campbell, D. T. Enhancement of contrast as a composite habit. *Journal of Abnormal and Social Psychology*, 1956, *53*, 350–355.

Campbell, D. T. Stereotypes and the perception of group differences. *American Psychologist*, 1967, *22*, 817–829.

Cantor, N., & Mischel, W. Prototypes in person perception. In L. Berkowitz (Ed.), *Advances in experimental social psychology* (Vol. 12). New York: Academic Press, 1979.

Dreben, E. K., Fiske, S. T., & Hastie, R. Impression and recall order effects in behavior-based impression formation. *Journal of Personality and Social Psychology*, 1979, 37, 1758–1768.

Freedman, J. L., & Loftus, E. F. Retrieval of words from long-term memory. *Journal of Verbal Learning and Verbal Behavior*, 1971, *10*, 107–115.

Garner, W. *Uncertainty and structure as psychological concepts*. New York: Wiley, 1962.

Gilbert, G. M. Stereotype persistence and change among college students. *Journal of Abnormal and Social Psychology*, 1951, *46*, 245–254.

Hamilton, D. L., & Gifford, R. K. Illusory correlation in interpersonal perception: A cognitive basis of stereotypic judgments. *Journal of Experimental Social Psychology*, 1976, *12*, 392–407.

Hensley, V., & Duval, S. Some perceptual determinants of perceived similarity, liking, and correctness. *Journal of Personality and Social Psychology*, 1976, *34*, 159–168.

Kanter, R. M. Some effects of proportions on group life: Skewed sex ratios and responses to token women. *American Journal of Sociology*, 1977, *82*, 965–990.

Katz, D., & Braly, K. Racial stereotypes of one hundred college students. *Journal of Abnormal and Social Psychology*, 1933, *28*, 280–290.

Lippmann, W. *Public opinion*. New York: Harcourt, Brace, 1922.

Malpass, R., & Kravitz, L. Recognition for faces of own and other race. *Journal of Personality and Social Psychology*, 1969, *13*, 330–334.

Nisbett, R. E., & Ross, L. *Human inference: Strategies and shortcomings in social judgment*. Englewood Cliffs, N.J.: Prentice-Hall, 1979.

Pettigrew, T. F. The ultimate attribution error: Extending Allport's cognitive analysis of prejudice. *Personality and Social Psychology Bulletin*, 1979, 5, 461–476.

Rosch, E., Mervis, C., Gray, W., Johnson, D., & Boyes-Braem, P. Basic objects in natural categories. *Cognitive Psychology*, 1976, *8*, 382–439.

Smith, E. R., Ferree, M. M., & Miller, F. D. A short scale of attitudes toward feminism. *Representative Research in Social Psychology*, 1975, *6*, 51–58.

Tajfel, H. Cognitive aspects of prejudice. *Journal of Social Issues*, 1969, *25*, 79–94.

Tajfel, H. Social categorization. In S. Moscovici (Ed.), *Introduction à la psychologie sociale*. Paris: Larousse, 1972.

Tajfel, H., & Billig, M. Familiarity and categorization in intergroup behavior. *Journal of Experimental Social Psychology*, 1974, *10*, 159–170.

Tajfel, H., Billig, M., Bundy, R. P., & Flament, C. Social categorization and intergroup behavior. *European Journal of Social Psychology*, 1971, *1*, 149–178.

Tajfel, H., Sheikh, A. A., & Gardner, R. C. Content of stereotypes and the inference of similarity between members of stereotyped groups. *Acta Psychologica*, 1964, *22*, 191–201.

Tajfel, H., & Wilkes, A. L. Classification and quantitative judgment. *British Journal of Psychology*, 1963, *54*, 101–114.

Taylor, S. E. The availability bias in social psychology. To appear in A. Tversky, D. Kahneman, & P. Slovic (Eds.), *Judgment under uncertainty: Heuristics and biases*. New York: Cambridge University Press, 1981.

Taylor, S. E., & Fiske, S. T. Point of view and perceptions of causality. *Journal of Personality and Social Psychology*, 1975, *32*, 439–445.

Taylor, S. E., & Fiske, S. T. Salience, attention, and attribution: Top of the head phenomena. In L. Berkowitz (Ed.), *Advances in experimental social psychology* (Vol. 11) New York: Academic Press, 1978.

Taylor, S. E., Fiske, S. T., Close, M., Anderson, C., & Ruderman, A. *Solo status as a psychological variable: The power of being distinctive*. Unpublished paper, Harvard University, 1975.

Taylor, S. E., Fiske, S. T., Etcoff, N., & Ruderman, A. The categorical and contextual bases of person memory and stereotyping. *Journal of Personality and Social Psychology*, 1978, *36*, 778–793.

Tesser, A. Self-generated attitude change. In L. Berkowitz (Ed.) *Advances in experimental social psychology* (Vol. 11). New York: Academic Press, 1978.

Tulving, E., & Pearlstone, Z. Availability versus accessibility of information in memory for words. *Journal of Verbal Learning and Verbal Behavior*, 1966, *5*, 381–391.

Wilder, D. A., & Allen, V. Effects of social categorization and belief similarity upon intergroup behavior. *Personality and Social Psychology Bulletin*, 1974, *1*, 281–283.

Wolman, C., & Frank, H. The solo woman in a professional peer group. *American Journal of Orthopsychiatry*, 1975, *45*, 164–171.

4 Illusory Correlation as a Basis for Stereotyping

David L. Hamilton
University of California, Santa Barbara

Much of the research comprising the extensive literature on stereotyping can be classified into two broad categories reflecting different foci of investigation. In the first of these categories the primary concern has been that of assessing the content of various widely shared stereotypes held by members of a particular culture. The stimulus entity in these studies is some racial, religious, sex, or national group, and the data obtained (e.g., trait ratings, adjective checklists) reflect the subjects' perceptions of the group as a whole. This research tradition began with the classic paper by Katz and Braly (1933), and studies of this nature have been prominent in the stereotyping literature ever since (Brigham, 1971; McCauley, Stitt, & Segal, 1980). In addition to determining the content and/or basic components of stereotypic conceptions of various groups, studies have investigated such issues as differences between groups in their stereotypes of another group, the relationship of the stereotype of a group to the self-stereotype held by members of that group, and the stability and change of stereotypes over time. The chapter by Ashmore in this volume represents a contemporary extension of this research tradition from a cognitive point of view.

A second major category of research on stereotyping has focused on the question of how a stereotype of a group affects one's reactions to an individual member of that group. Although historically this research tradition has not been as prominent as the first, a considerable amount of recent research reflects this approach. These studies investigate how one's judgments of or interactions with a member of a stereotyped group are influenced by one's stereotype of that group. A wide variety of such effects have been demonstrated. For example, stereotypes have been shown to influence how another's behavior is encoded by a perceiver (Duncan, 1976), what information about a person is retained (Cohen,

115

1977), the causal attributions one makes (Deaux, 1976), one's nonverbal behaviors (Word, Zanna, & Cooper, 1974), and the behaviors elicited in the other person (Snyder, Tanke, & Berscheid, 1977). Much of this work has been reviewed elsewhere (Hamilton, 1979). In the present volume the chapters by Taylor, by Snyder, and by Rose discuss research illustrating this approach.

The focus of interest in this chapter (as well as the following one, by Rothbart) is on a somewhat different problem. In our everyday experience we accumulate over time information about members of various groups by a number of means: interaction, observation, hearsay, etc. Each such experience can be thought of as an instance providing one (or more) items of information about a member of one or another social group. These items of information become encoded, organized, and stored in terms of our cognitive structures or stereotypes pertaining to these groups. It is this process of accumulating the available information and storing it in the form of a cognitive representation of a group that is the primary interest in this chapter. In particular, we examine the role of certain biasing factors that can potentially influence this process.

Our analysis focuses on two aspects of this process. The first concerns the case in which one has little or no prior knowledge of the groups to which the information to be acquired pertains. That is, in the absence of preexisting stereotypes of certain groups, how is information about members of those groups accumulated and represented as conceptions of the groups? Basically, this is the question of how stereotypes develop, and as such, is too broad a question to be considered fully here. We do, however, examine evidence of biases in this process. The second aspect of our analysis concerns the case in which the perceiver has well-developed stereotypic expectancies about members of certain groups. The question examined here is how information about members of those groups is processed as it is accumulated over time. The information itself might verify, or it might question, the validity of the perceiver's stereotypic conceptions. Again we examine evidence of biases in this process, in this case the biasing influence of preexisting stereotypes on how information about group members is processed.

In considering this issue, it is useful to think of a stereotypic statement about a social group as an expression of a correlational concept. That is, the statement expresses a relationship between group membership and some psychological attribute. Men are domineering. Blacks are lazy. Germans are serious. Each of these stereotypic beliefs implicitly states a relationship in which the group identified is characterized as possessing some attribute more than members of some other comparison group(s). Thus the statement ''Men are domineering'' reflects a perceived association between sex and dominance that implicitly includes not only the belief that men are likely to be domineering but also that women are not. Given this perspective, we can gain some understanding of stereotypic beliefs— their development and maintenance—by applying to this issue our knowledge of how people form and use concepts pertaining to the covariation between variables. Therefore we begin our analysis with a consideration of the research literature on how people develop and apply correlational concepts and the cognitive biases that have become evident in that research. We then discuss research that has pursued the implications of these findings for the development and maintenance of stereotypic beliefs.

CORRELATIONAL CONCEPTS: BASES AND BIASES

The simplest case for analyzing the formation of a correlational concept from an accumulation of relevant evidence is the case in which the two variables occur in dichotomous form. For example, each of two variables, say X and Y, either occurs or does not occur. The four types of information relevant to assessing the relationship between the two variables can then be represented in a 2×2 frequency table, as shown in Table 4.1. In studies of this kind, subjects typically are shown a series of statements, each one providing information that constitutes an instance of one of the four cells of the table. In Smedslund's (1963) study, for example, student nurses were given a deck of cards, each of which presumably provided information about a different patient. Each card indicated that a particular symptom (Variable X) was either present or absent and that the patient either did not have a certain disease (Variable Y). The number of items representing each cell of Table 4.1 can be varied, as can the actual degree of relationship between the two variables. In some studies, subjects have been asked directly to estimate the direction and strength of the relationship between the two variables. In other cases the subject's task has been to estimate the number of items of each of the four kinds that had occurred in the stimulus sequence. From these frequency estimates one can determine (by calculating a phi coefficient, for example) the subject's perceived relationship between the two variables, as well as the degree of accuracy achieved by the subject. In addition, by examining where the subject over- and underestimated the actual frequencies, the nature of the biases present can be determined.

TABLE 4.1.
Frequency Table of Information Relevant to Assessing Relationship Between Two Variables

		Variable Y	
		Present	Absent
Variable X	Present		
	Absent		

Correlational Concepts: An Intuitive Analysis

Many of the correlational concepts we develop are based on the accumulation of sequentially obtained evidence acquired over time in the course of our everyday experiences. Even in the simplified form represented in Table 4.1 the task of assessing the strength of relationship between two variables is not an easy one. Consider the demands that this task places on one's cognitive mechanisms. At the very least, accurately forming a correlational concept involves a complex sequence of steps that includes the accurate encoding of relevant information, the storage and retention of accumulated evidence over time, the retrieval of relevant instances at a later point in time, and an integration of this information into an accurate judgment as to the degree of relationship between the two variables. Each of these steps is briefly discussed in the following paragraphs.

1. *Encoding Relevant Information.*   Forming an accurate correlational concept requires that the observer accurately encode the relevant information. Events that are instances of variable X (or Y) must be encoded as instances of variable X (or Y); otherwise, pertinent data bearing on the relationship are lost. For the observer of human interaction, there are several reasons to suspect that accuracy in this process will be undermined.

One reason is that human behavior is often open to alternative interpretations. Any particular act can be encoded differently, depending on both contextual factors and perceiver expectancies. For example, the same behavior—one person giving a mild shove to another during a heated conversation—might be interpreted as a dramatic gesture if the shover is white, but might be encoded as an aggressive act if the shover is black (Duncan, 1976). If we consider the implications of this instance for the perceived relationship between an actor's race—black (X) or white (not X)—and a particular category of behavior—aggressive (Y) or not aggressive (not Y)—we see that the same behavior would be encoded into quite different cells of the 2×2 table shown in Table 4.1. The differential encoding in this case would bias the ''frequency table'' in the direction of a perceived relationship between race and aggression such that blacks would be seen as more likely than whites to engage in aggressive behavior.

A second reason is that the human observer is not (in fact, cannot be) equally attentive to all the information contained in the stimulus field. Perceivers are highly responsive to the salient features of the stimulus field, a fact that has been shown to have profound impact on social perception (McArthur, 1981); Taylor & Fiske, 1978). As Hamilton (1979) has pointed out, most stereotyped groups are easily identifiable by characteristics that are physically prominent (e.g., race, sex) and hence are salient to an observer. In addition, certain varieties of behavior are more attention demanding than others. These factors can contribute to a biased encoding of those aspects of the stimulus field that are highly salient.

A third reason to question the accuracy with which relevant information will be encoded is related to the preceding point. Consideration of Table 4.1 makes it clear that certain kinds of relevant information are particularly unlikely to be salient to the observer. Specifically, in most circumstances the *nonoccurrence* of an event class is hardly noticeable. For example, it seems unlikely that medical practitioners, such as those studied by Smedslund (1963), would encode the *absence* of a diagnostic sign in the presence of a particular disease as information bearing on the relationship between these two variables. Indeed, the results of several studies, discussed in the following section, indicate that subjects consider such information to be of little relevance to this question. In a similar vein, consider the stereotypic concept "Blacks are aggressive." In the framework of Table 4.1, instances of both aggressive (X present) and nonaggressive (X absent) behaviors by both blacks (Y present) and non-blacks (Y absent) are relevant to this concept. However, it seems unlikely that the human observer will consider a congenial interaction with a black, or the hostile behavior of a white, to be as pertinent to the concept that "Blacks are aggressive" as is the observation of an aggressive act by a black.

In sum, the potential for biased interpretation of behavior, the perceiver's responsiveness to salient components of the stimulus field, and the failure to recognize the relevance of the nonoccurrence of event classes can all impose limitations on the extent to which information relevant to a correlational concept will be encoded.

2. *Retention of Relevant Information.* Forming an accurate correlational concept requires that the encoded information be stored over some period of time. However, some of the evidence may be differentially susceptible to forgetting. For example, highly salient instances may be more likely to be retained than less salient, though equally relevant, information. To the extent that this occurs, the data base on which subsequent judgments are to be made will not be representative of the frequencies with which various kinds of information occurred in the observer's experience.

3. *Retrieval of Information.* Forming an accurate correlational concept requires retrieval from memory of the evidence relevant to assessing the relationship between the two variables. Ideally this would require that the perceiver generate from memory a 2×2 frequency table, such as that in Table 4.1, in which the relative frequencies of the various kinds of instances are represented in an unbiased manner. Although it seems unlikely that persons systematically engage in this activity, some effort to retrieve relevant instances probably occurs. However, each of the factors described earlier as potentially biasing the encoding process can result in retrieval distortions as well. For example, in searching one's memory one might reinterpret the relevance of certain instances to the issue at

hand (Snyder & Uranowitz, 1978). Similarly, the most salient aspects of the pertinent information may be most likely to be retrieved. And finally, instances reflecting the nonoccurrence of one or another of the variables may be less likely to be retrieved. Again, the consequence of these biases would be that the data base on which correlational judgments will be made—the intuitively generated frequency table—will be distorted. Whereas the encoding and storage biases discussed earlier can result in estimated frequencies that do not correspond to the actual pattern of stimulus instances, these retrieval biases can result in estimated frequencies that do not accurately reflect the relative frequencies of instances as stored in memory.

4. *Integration of Information.*   Forming an accurate correlational concept requires that the observer be able to make an accurate judgment from the available evidence as to the degree of association between the two variables. That is, even if the observer's perception of the relative frequency of co-occurrence of the two variables is accurate (e.g., the four cells of Table 4.1), that information must still be integrated into a judgment of the strength of relationship between those variables. In any statistical technique for assessing strength of association the various kinds of instances (X co-occurs with Y, X- co-occurs with not Y, etc.) are equally weighted. It seems plausible, however, that in performing this judgment task the human judge may deviate from this equal-weighting principle, with the consequence that certain types of evidence (e.g., instances that confirm prior expectations) will have differential impact on resulting judgments. Thus, it is likely that biases can occur at this stage of the process as well.

As this intuitive analysis indicates, the human observer faces a number of obstacles in using the available evidence to gain an accurate assessment of the degree of association between two variables. Given the variety of biases that can enter into this process, it would not be surprising to find that perceivers fail to achieve a high level of accuracy in this task.

Once a correlational concept regarding the association between two variables has been formed, additional biases can influence the processing of subsequent information pertinent to that relationship. The observer's expectancies based on this concept can influence one's selective attention to the behavior of others, may affect one's acceptance of the evidence provided in any given instance, and may even influence the manner in which evidence relevant to the relationship is sought (Snyder & Swann, 1978) and the behaviors elicited in others (Snyder, Tanke, & Berscheid, 1977). Thus, whereas subsequently obtained information may suggest that one's initial estimate was in error, the existence of a correlational concept itself may create biases such that new evidence is gathered and processed in a manner that confirms one's preexisting belief and avoids the recognition of the need for revision of that concept (see chapter by Snyder in this volume).

Correlational Concepts: Empirical Evidence

A number of experiments have investigated how people develop and utilize correlational concepts, although in view of the pervasiveness of this process the literature is not extensive. The findings from these studies are summarized briefly as a context for the author's research presented in subsequent sections of this chapter. Comprehensive reviews of this literature are provided by Abramson and Alloy (1980) and Crocker (1980).

Several experiments have sought to determine subjects' ability to detect accurately the degree of contingency or relationship between two binary variables, as in the example in Table 4.1. Despite their formal similarity, quite different tasks have been employed in these studies. Smedslund (1963) presented nursing students with a series of cards, each of which presumably provided information about a different patient. Letters presented on the card indicated the presence or absence of a certain symptom in a patient who had or had not been diagnosed as having a particular disease, and the subject's task was to determine whether or not there was a relationship between symptom and diagnosis. Jenkins and Ward (1965) had subjects judge the extent to which their responses controlled outcomes in a two-response, two-outcome task. On a series of trials, subjects pushed one of two buttons and attempted to make one of two lights come on. Ward and Jenkins (1965) presented subjects with a series of items, each of which indicated that clouds had or had not been seeded and that subsequently it had or had not rained. The subject's task was to judge the degree of control that seeding of clouds exerts over the occurrence of rain. Despite these varying tasks, the results of these three studies were highly similar, and can be summarized in two points. (1) Subjects' ability to judge accurately the degree of contingency or relationship between two variables was quite low. In fact, Smedslund (1963) was led to conclude that "normal adults with no training in statistics do not have a cognitive structure isomorphic with the concept of correlation [p. 172]," a conclusion with which Jenkins and Ward (1965) agreed. (2) Subjects' judgments of the degree of association between variables were primarily a function of the absolute frequency of instances in one of the four cells of Table 4.1, namely, the cell representing the joint occurrence of the two events whose relationship was being considered. Thus, in Smedslund's (1963) study, subjects' judgments of diagnosticity was largely determined by the absolute number of cases in which both symptom and disease were present. In Jenkins and Ward's (1965) research, the degree of control subjects felt over the outcomes was a function simply of the number of successes they had had. And in Ward and Jenkins' (1965) experiment, judgments of the extent to which cloud seeding influences the occurrence of rain was strongly related to the frequency of the seeding–rain combination in the stimulus series. In all three studies the other three types of information relevant to determining degree of association—the frequency of co-occurrence of X and not

Y, of not X and Y, and of not X and not Y—had little impact on subjects' judgments. These findings indicate a rather selective use of information by subjects in performing these tasks: Subjects' correlational concepts were based on the frequency of joint occurrences.

One other finding from these studies is of interest. Ward and Jenkins (1965) varied the manner in which the stimulus information was presented to the subjects. Some subjects received a serial presentation, with items occurring one after another. For a second group of subjects this sequential presentation was followed by a table summarizing the various frequencies of co-occurrence, similar to Table 4.1. A third group of subjects received only the tabular summary of the stimulus information. This manipulation had a substantial influence on the way subjects utilized the available information. Subjects in the first group (sequential presentation) were particularly prone to rely on the number of joint occurrences of the two variables in making their judgments. In contrast, judgments of subjects in the third group, who received only an organized summary of the stimulus data, reflected a use of all four kinds of relevant information and a comparison of relative frequencies. However, availability of a tabular summary is not, in and of itself, sufficient to overcome a reliance on confirming cases. This was evidenced in the fact that judgments of subjects who received the summary table following sequential presentation did not differ significantly from those in the first group (sequential presentation only), but did differ significantly from those in the third group (summary table only). Thus the biasing effect appears to occur during the instance-by-instance sequential accumulation of information. This finding has implications for social perception because most of our correlational concepts pertaining to persons and groups probably emerge from and are subsequently tested against the gradual accumulation of evidence over the course of our everyday experiences with others.

All the studies discussed in the preceding paragraphs examined perceived relationships between two variables, each of which was defined dichotomously. Although reduction of each variable to two levels creates the simplest case for investigating correlational concepts, it may be that this constitutes a special case in which subjects are at some disadvantage. There are, after all, relatively few variables that we encounter in our social world in dichotomous form (although it may well be that we encode information in that manner anyway). There have been a few studies of subjects' ability to estimate direction and strength of correlation from information about co-occurrence of continuous variables (Beach & Scopp, 1966; Erlick, 1966). Unfortunately, these studies are few in number, their findings are not entirely consistent, and hence it is difficult to draw any firm conclusions from them.

Perhaps the best known of the research on correlational concepts is the series of papers by the Chapmans (Chapman, 1967; Chapman & Chapman, 1967, 1969) on illusory correlation. The term *illusory correlation* was proposed by Chapman (1967) to refer to an erroneous report by an observer regarding the degree of association between two variables or classes of events. In a laboratory demonstration of an illusory correlation, Chapman (1967) visually presented subjects with pairs of stimulus words, the stimulus pairs being constructed from two lists such as those shown in Table 4.2. Each word from List X was paired an equal number of times with each word from List Y, meaning that "events" in "Class X" were unrelated to (uncorrelated with) "events" in "Class Y." However, the lists were constructed in a manner that incorporated certain properties in the stimulus sequence. First, for two of the 12 word pairs (hat–head; knife–fork) the List Y word was a strong associate of the List X word. Second, one of the word pairs (building–magazine) consisted of two words, each of which was longer than the other words in their respective lists, a feature that made these words (and hence their co-occurrence) distinctive within the context of the stimulus sequence. Each of the 12 word-pairs was presented a number of times, each pair occurring equally often.

After viewing the stimulus sequence, subjects were given a questionnaire on which they were asked to estimate, for each word in List X, the percentage of times it had been paired with each of the items in List Y. The correct answer in each case was 33⅓%. Subjects' judgments, however, were systematically biased such that they significantly overestimated the frequency of occurrence of word pairs that either: (1) were high in associative strength; or (2) were distinctive because they contained two atypically long words. On the basis of these findings Chapman (1967) concluded that both associative connections between stimulus events and the co-occurrence of distinctive stimulus events can produce illusory correlations.

Before such a general conclusion can be accepted, evidence for the generalizability of these results is needed. Fortunately, fairly good evidence to this effect is available. Within the context of Chapman's paradigm, the results were quite robust. The word lists shown in Table 4.2 comprise one of three stimulus sets used in this study, and all three sets produced highly comparable results. Also, varying the overall length of the stimulus series (each of the 12 pairs occurred 4, 10, or 20 times) had little effect on these outcomes. In addition, several studies have reported results substantiating Chapman's findings in a variety of experimental contexts (Chapman & Chapman, 1967, 1969; Golding &

TABLE 4.2.
Sample of Stimulus Lists Used in
Chapman's (1967) Study

List X	List Y
hat	head
knife	fork
building	magazine
door	

Rorer, 1972; Hamilton & Gifford, 1976; Hamilton & Rose, 1980; Hartsough, 1975; Starr & Katkin, 1969; Tversky & Kahneman, 1973). Thus, Chapman's (1967) findings appear to be rather reliable.

The present author's research has extended this line of investigation to the study of stereotyping and has pursued its implications for both the development and maintenance of stereotypic beliefs. Our discussion of this research, presented in the next two sections, is organized in terms of the two bases for illusory correlations demonstrated in Chapman's (1967) study. Thus, the first section focuses on the tendency of observers to overestimate the frequency with which distinctive events have co-occurred as a basis for the formation of a new correlational concept, and explores its implications for the development of beliefs about members of social groups. In the second section we consider the effect of an observer's prior associative beliefs about the relationship between two categories of information on subsequent processing of evidence relevant to that belief, again focusing on its implications for stereotyping.

ILLUSORY CORRELATION AND THE DEVELOPMENT OF STEREOTYPIC BELIEFS

One of Chapman's (1967) intriguing findings was that subjects consistently overestimated the frequency of co-occurrence of items that were distinctive within the context of their respective stimulus lists. Although several studies of illusory correlation were published following Chapman's original paper, it is surprising that none of them was concerned with this basis for an illusory correlation.

We have, however, come across one interesting instance in which such a mechanism has been offered to account for the formation of an erroneous belief. On August 13, 1978, the Santa Barbara area was rocked by a moderately strong earthquake. As commonly occurs in the days following a significant tremor, there was a considerable amount of talk about how the quake might have been anticipated. One popular theory is that animals, responding to as-yet-unknown cues, frequently will engage in unusual behavior patterns prior to an earthquake, and that animal behavior might therefore signal in advance the occurrence of a tremor. Although this theory does not yet enjoy a scientifically sound evidentiary basis, its folk popularity did prompt a reporter from the local newspaper to inquire into its validity. The reporter (Bolton, 1978) interviewed Dr. Adrian Wenner, a professor of natural history at UCSB, who offered his views on how such beliefs come about:

> Wenner said such notions usually start after a quake, when people start trying to remember what happened before. "People tend to remember only the unusual

things,'' he said. ''Suppose you have 100 people who are all watching a different animal's behavior and then there's a quake. At any given moment one of those animals is likely to be behaving ''unusually,'' but the other 99 might be acting normally. . . . That one guy, though, might decide, after the fact, that the animal's behavior was actually a signal that the quake was coming. [p. B-1].''

This analysis, along with the conclusion that ''coincidence seems to be the most likely explanation for an apparent correlation between animal behavior and tremors,'' represents a fairly clear statement of an illusory correlation based on the co-occurrence of distinctive stimuli.

Our research on the illusory basis of stereotypic beliefs began with the following intuition. It is typically the case that members of majority groups have relatively little interaction with members of minority groups. For the majority group person, then, interaction with a minority group member is a statistically infrequent occurrence, and hence in the context of one's everyday experiences can be considered a distinctive event. It is also true that certain categories of behaviors, such as undesirable behaviors, occur infrequently and hence also can be considered distinctive events. Therefore, when a minority group member performs some undesirable behavior, it constitutes the co-occurrence of two distinctive stimulus events for a majority group observer. If Chapman's finding generalizes to the social-perception situation just described, it suggests that the typical observer would overestimate the frequency with which members of the minority groups commit undesirable acts. If so, then a cognitive bias in the way perceivers process information would lay the foundation for the differential perception of majority and minority groups.

Hamilton and Gifford (1976, Experiment 1) have provided evidence in support of this contention. Subjects in this experiment read a series of 39 sentences. Each sentence described a different person, identified by first name and membership in one of two groups, as having performed some behavior. In order to assure that subjects would have no preexisting beliefs about the stimulus groups, the two groups were simply identified as Group A and Group B. Majority and minority groups were created by having 26 of the 39 sentences describe persons belonging to Group A, whereas 13 of the sentences described members of Group B. Similarly, a majority of the sentences (27) described desirable behaviors, with undesirable behavior occurring in 12 instances. Thus, both membership in Group B and undesirable behavior were made distinctive by their relative infrequency within the context of the total stimulus set. However, there was absolutely no relationship between group membership and the desirability of the behaviors describing the group members. The frequency of desirable and undesirable behaviors performed by members of Group A was exactly double that for Group B (Group A—18 desirable, 8 undesirable; Group B—9 desirable, 4 undesirable). The four instances of undesirable behavior performed by members of Group B represent the co-occurrence of distinctive events. Based on Chapman's (1967) results, we expected that subjects would overestimate the frequency with which these descriptions occurred in the stimulus set.

To test this hypothesis, we gave subjects a list of the behavior descriptions they had read in the stimulus sentences and asked them to identify for each one the group membership of the person who had performed that behavior. For each subject a 2 × 2 frequency table was constructed in which the desirable and undesirable behaviors were classified according to the group membership assigned by the subject. From these data, a phi coefficient was determined for each subject. Because there was no relationship between behavior desirability and group membership in the stimulus sentences, a phi coefficient based on the stimulus information would be zero. However, the average phi coefficient based on the subjects' data was significantly greater than zero, indicating the presence of an illusory correlation in which subjects perceived a relationship that did not exist.

Our hypothesis stated that such an illusory correlation would be due to the subjects' overestimation of the frequency of co-occurrence of the distinctive stimulus events (i.e., undesirable behaviors performed by members of Group B). Two additional aspects of these data lend support to this interpretation. First, the evidence indicated that in attributing behaviors to groups, subjects' bias was in the assignment of undesirable behaviors. In the stimulus sentences, one third of both the desirable and the undesirable behaviors described members of Group B. On the average, subjects' attributions of desirable behaviors to groups reflected this distribution quite well, assigning 35% to Group B. In contrast, over half (52%) of the undesirable behaviors were attributed to members of Group B. Clearly, then, subjects overestimated the frequency of co-occurrence of the distinctive stimulus events. Second, if observers are particularly attentive to distinctive stimuli (Langer, Taylor, Fiske, & Chanowitz, 1976; McArthur, 1981; Taylor & Fiske, 1978), then we might expect that subjects would have encoded this category of information more effectively than others. To examine this possibility, we determined the number of correct group membership assignments made by the subjects for the four categories of sentences. These data indicated that subjects' accuracy exceeded chance level by the greatest amount in the case of sentences describing undesirable behaviors performed by members of Group B. In sum, these two analyses substantiate our contention that the observed illusory correlations were based on subjects' differential responsiveness to the infrequently co-occurring stimuli.

To determine whether these illusory correlations influenced subjects' perceptions of the two groups, subjects were asked to rate Groups A and B on a series of 20 trait scales. In developing the stimulus materials, the sentences describing the two groups were equated in terms of desirability (based on pretest norms). Subjects' ratings of the groups, however, indicated that members of Group A were rated more favorably than members of Group B, a finding that would naturally follow from their overestimation of the frequency of undesirable behaviors committed by the latter group.

Thus, an illusory correlation based on a cognitive bias in perceivers' processing of co-occurrence information has resulted in the differential perception of two groups of stimulus persons. Inasmuch as differential perceptions of groups (regardless of their origins) can constitute the basis for social stereotyping, the results of this experiment demonstrate a mechanism by which stereotypic beliefs can have a purely cognitive foundation.

Although these findings were entirely consistent with our hypotheses, alternative interpretations remained viable. One possibility is that the results may reflect "mere exposure" effects. Zajonc (1968) has shown that repeated exposure to a stimulus enhances the observer's evaluation of it. Because subjects in this experiment were exposed to members of Group A twice as often as they were exposed to members of Group B, it is possible that the more favorable ratings of Group A were due to this differential frequency of exposure. A second possibility is that subjects may have assumed that Group B, being the smaller group, must be a minority group, and their lower evaluations of this group may have reflected their preconceptions about minority group members. Although both of these alternative explanations would have difficulty accounting for all of the obtained results, their contribution to these findings was unknown.

Fortunately, a means of differentiating these interpretations from the bias due to co-occurring distinctive stimulus events was available, inasmuch as both of these alternative explanations are linked to evaluation in a way that the illusory correlation explanation is not. A mere exposure effect would always be evidenced in heightened evaluations of the more frequently occurring stimulus group. Similarly, a bias against minority groups would always produce less favorable ratings of the smaller stimulus group. In contrast, if *desirable* behaviors occurred less frequently than undesirable behaviors, then an illusory correlation based on the co-occurrence of distinctive (infrequent) stimulus events should result in more *favorable* evaluations of the smaller group. Hamilton and Gifford (1976, Experiment 2) conducted an experiment to test this hypothesis.

As in the first experiment, subjects in this study read a series of sentences describing a person who belonged to either Group A or Group B as having performed a behavior that was either desirable or undesirable in evaluation. Again, there were twice as many members of Group A as of Group B (24 versus 12), and there was no relationship between group membership and behavior desirability. In contrast to the previous study, however, desirable behaviors were relatively infrequent (12) in comparison to undesirable acts (24). Thus, instances of a member of Group B performing a desirable behavior represented the co-occurrence of distinctive stimulus events. We expected that subjects would overestimate the frequency with which this type of sentence occurred in the stimulus sequence.

The dependent measures and data analyses were the same as those employed in the first experiment. Subjects were given a list of the behaviors presented in the stimulus sentences and for each one were asked to identify the group membership of the person it had described. Each subject's responses were classified in a 2 (desirable versus undesirable behavior) × 2 (group membership assigned by subject) frequency table, and a phi coefficient was calculated to determine the degree of relationship between group membership and behavior desirability manifested in the subject's responses. Whereas a phi coefficient based on the actual stimulus information was zero, the average of the subjects' coefficients was again significantly greater than zero. Thus, an illusory correlation was again evident in the subjects' responses. The mean number of desirable and undesirable statements attributed to each group was then examined to determine the basis for this illusory correlation. Again, as predicted, subjects overestimated the frequency with which members of Group B had performed the infrequently occurring category of behavior—in this case, desirable behavior. As in the first experiment, one third of both the desirable and the undesirable stimulus sentences had described members of Group B. For the frequently occurring category of behavior (undesirable), subjects' responses again corresponded closely to this differentiation, attributing 35% of these behaviors to Group B. However, in support of our hypothesis, over half of the desirable behaviors were attributed to this group. In addition, subjects' accuracy in assigning group membership exceeded chance performance by the greatest amount in the case of desirable behaviors performed by members of Group B. These findings support our interpretation that the illusory correlation was based on subjects' differential sensitivity to infreqeuntly co-occuring stimulus events.

To determine the influence of this illusory correlation on subjects' perceptions of the groups, subjects again rated the two groups on a series of trait scales. In contrast to the first experiment but in support of our hypothesis, members of Group B received significantly more favorable ratings than did members of Group A.

Together, these two experiments indicate that illusory correlations of the kind reported by Chapman (1967) can occur in social information processing and can have important consequences for the perception of social groups. Biases in the processing of information about co-occurring variables resulted in distorted retrieval of that information, such that subjects' attributions of behaviors to groups reflected a correlation between group membership and behavior desirability that was not present in the stimulus sentences they read. The consequence was that the two groups were evaluated quite differently on a variety of trait rating scales.

Implications for Stereotyping

These findings would seem to have important implications for stereotype formation. As noted earlier, majority group members typically have infrequent contact with members of minority groups, and certain forms of behavior, including nonnormative behaviors, occur infrequently. Hamilton and Gifford's (1976) results demonstrate that, even though the infrequent behavior may be no more representative of one group than the other, observer biases can lead to the disproportionate attribution of these behaviors to the minority group, with the consequence that the groups are differentially perceived. The specific content of those differential perceptions will depend on the nature of the infrequent behaviors salient at the time. Once established, these differential perceptions can provide the foundation for stereotyping.

Given that a cognitive bias that could be the basis for stereotyping has been demonstrated, the question naturally arises as to its actual importance for understanding the development of present-day stereotypes. When we think about the predominant stereotypes in our society—stereotypes of blacks and whites, of women and men, of Jews, Catholics and Protestants, of young persons and old persons—the role of socialization and acculturation processes in shaping our beliefs about these groups would seem to be of overwhelming importance. As Ehrlich (1973) has said: "No person can grow up in a society without having learned the stereotypes assigned to the major ethnic groups [p. 35]." What, then, can we say about the role of illusory correlation in the formation of real-world stereotypes? The question is difficult to answer because any actual stereotype about a social group is probably multiply determined, reflecting the contribution of several processes to both its development and maintenance. (Thus, for example, it was necessary to use the artificial Groups A and B in the Hamilton and Gifford (1976) studies to demonstrate a cognitive bias in the absence of the previously formed beliefs that would be associated with any actual social groups.) We can, however, offer speculations on two issues raised by this question: first, conditions under which distinctiveness-based illusory correlations might result in stereotype formation; and second, the interplay between this cognitive basis and other processes on which stereotyping might be based.

To argue that a particular stereotype is based solely on a perceiver's overresponsiveness to the co-occurrence of distinctive stimulus events, it would have to develop under conditions in which the perceiver had few, if any, preexisting beliefs regarding the nature of the stimulus group in question. Under what conditions would such a requirement be met? For mature adults, these conditions probably are few in number, although it isn't difficult to generate examples (e.g., most Americans have few well-established preconceptions about Latvians). There is, however, a context in which these conditions are more pervasive. Young children often live in ethnically homogeneous surroundings, and only gradually (e.g., when they begin school) do they begin to accumulate experiences in which they are exposed to members of other groups. A child's initial response to such a person is frequently a "pure" response to stimulus distinctiveness; that is, their reaction is virtually content-free, and simply a behavioral manifestation of his or her perceptual recognition of the "differentness" (based on physical appearance, such as race) of the person. If that "different" person also performs some normatively infrequent (but not differentially characteristic of the minority person's group) behavior, it would constitute an instance of a distinctive stimulus person performing a distinctive behavior, distinctiveness in both cases being defined by relative infrequency in the young perceiver's experience. As the child encounters such experiences from time to time, the conditions of the illusory correlation paradigm described earlier would be fulfilled. Based on Hamilton and Gifford's (1976) findings, one might expect that the child would come to view those distinctive behaviors as being more representative of the minority group than of his or her own. Thus, it seems plausible that young children's conceptions of social groups are to some extent based on the processes discussed in this section.

Now let us depart from an analysis based solely on cognitive bias and consider how distinctiveness-based illusory correlations might interact with other processes potentially underlying stereotypes. First of all, suppose there were some "kernel of truth" on which differential perceptions of two groups were made. To pursue the example discussed in the preceding paragraph, suppose some distinctive behavior were in fact somewhat more characteristic of minority than of majority group persons. In that case, there would be some modest correlation between group membership and performance of that type of behavior. Observers are not particularly astute at detecting correlational relationships, especially when the degree of contingency is not strong (Crocker, 1980). The child's overresponsiveness to the co-occurrence of distinctive stimuli, however, would facilitate recognition of this relationship, and if the relationship is in fact weak (as most stereotypic relationships almost certainly are), this overresponsiveness may lead to an overestimate of the extent to which the infrequent type of behavior is representative of the minority group. In this case, then, the processes on which the illusory correlations described above were based would lead to overgeneralization of a contingent relationship for which there was some weak evidentiary base.

There is a second way that distinctiveness-based illusory correlations may contribute to stereotyping. Suppose, for example, that a white child learns (through parental instruction, acculturation within a white society, etc.) that blacks have certain undesirable characteristics. Possessing this "knowledge," the child would not want to interact with blacks and may actively avoid such experiences. In that case, interaction with blacks and the undesirable behaviors they are believed likely to perform would both be infrequent occurrences, and hence the child's experiences would conform to the pattern represented in the stimulus sentences in Hamilton and Gifford's (1976) first experiment. The biased processing of those experiences (i.e., overrepresentation of the co-occurrence of distinctive events in memory) would constitute an illusory correlation of the kind described above, but in this case one that both emanates from and reinforces preexisting beliefs acquired through other processes.

By way of summary, in this section we have discussed two experiments demonstrating that the differential perception of groups can result from cognitive biases in the way information about stimulus co-occurrences is processed. In considering the implications of these findings for stereotyping we have suggested that such distinctiveness-based illusory correlations: (1) can themselves provide the basis for stereotypic beliefs, especially in a child's early experiences with members of minority groups; (2) may contribute to the overgeneralization of the perception of intergroup differences for which there is some "kernel of truth"; and (3) may reinforce stereotypic beliefs acquired through social learning processes.

ILLUSORY CORRELATION AND THE MAINTENANCE OF STEREOTYPIC BELIEFS

Of the two bases for an illusory correlation demonstrated in Chapman's (1967) study, subsequent research on this topic has been concerned almost exclusively with the effect of prior associative connections between event pairs on the observer's assessment of covariation. Much of this work has been in the clinical domain, focusing on illusory correlations in clinicians' use of diagnostic tests. Because the findings of these studies are informative, we summarize them briefly before proceeding to an analysis of their implications for stereotyping.

The rationale behind this work is well illustrated in a series of studies by Chapman and Chapman (1967). The problem they noted was the persistence in clinicians' belief in the usefulness of certain diagnostic signs, such as those obtained from projective tests, in spite of an accumulation of empirical evidence indicating that those signs have no validity. They hypothesized that when there is an associative relationship between a test indicator and a symptom, clinicians' belief in the diagnostic value of the indicator for that symptom will be maintained due to an illusory correlation based on the associative relationship. To test this hypothesis they utilized the Draw-A-Person Test, a widely used projective technique around which a considerable amount of clinical folklore has developed. In particular, there are several features of human figure drawings that clinicians believe reflect psychological problem areas, even though the research evidence indicates that these test signs are of little or no diagnostic value. Chapman and Chapman's (1967) strategy was to show that undergraduate college students who had no familiarity with this test "rediscovered" the same relationships between figure-drawing characteristics and psychological symptoms that clinicians report from their clinical experience, even though no such relationships existed in the materials judged by the students. Specifically, subjects were given a set of human figure drawings, each one accompanied by two statements presumably indicating emotional problems of the person who drew the figure (e.g., "is suspicious of other people"; "is worried about how manly he is"). Six symptom statements were used, and in the total set of materials each symptom was paired with each drawing once. Thus in the stimulus materials there were no actual relationships between symptoms and characteristics of the drawings. Following presentation of these materials subjects were given a six-item questionnaire, one item for each of the symptoms. The item identified a particular symptom (''Some of the pictures were drawn by men who are suspicious of other people'') and asked subjects to indicate the characteristics of the pictures drawn by these men. A similar questionnaire asking the frequent characteristics of figure drawings by patients with each of the six symptoms was sent to a number of experienced clinicians. The results showed that the undergraduate students reported the same pattern of observations as the clinical psychologists. For example, both groups reported that persons suspicious of others tend to draw figures with atypical eyes; that men who are worried about their masculinity tend to draw muscular figures with broad shoulders; and so forth. Because it is known (1) that these characteristics of figure drawings are not valid indicators of emotional problems; and (2) that the reported relationships were not contained in the materials judged by the students, it is likely that both sets of responses reflect illusory correlations based on high associative correspondence between body parts and problem areas indicated in the symptom statements.

Subsequent studies have demonstrated similar illusory correlation effects for other clinical instruments, such as the Rorschach (Chapman & Chapman, 1969; Golding & Rorer, 1972) and the Incomplete Sentences Blank (Starr & Katkin, 1969). The power of these illusory correlations is evidenced in the findings from various conditions of these experiments in which manipulations designed to reduce the illusory correlations were included. These studies have shown that the illusory correlation persisted: (1) when subjects were given repeated exposures to the stimulus materials (Chapman & Chapman, 1967); (2) when the actual correlation between the illusory sign and the symptom was varied, including the case in which this relationship was negative (Chapman & Chapman, 1967; Golding & Rorer, 1972); (3) when other cues that validity predict the symptom were present (Chapman & Chapman, 1969; Golding & Rorer, 1972); (4) when subjects were offered monetary incentives to achieve a high degree of accuracy (Chapman & Chapman, 1967); and (5) when subjects were given prediction feedback and encouraged to formulate a rule for making accurate diagnoses (Golding & Rorer, 1972). In sum, these associatively based illusory correlations were highly resistant to change.

A stereotypic belief states an expectancy that some psychological attribute is associated with membership in a particular social group (Tajfel, 1969). The illusory correlation research summarized in the preceding paragraphs indicates that such associative beliefs can influence the processing of co-occurrence information. If perceivers' processing of social information is similarly biased, then their stereotypic expectancies may influence their judgments in the same way. That is, information (traits, behaviors) stereotypically associated with group members may be judged as occurring more frequently than other information equally characteristic of the group but not stereotypically associated with the group. If this were so, then such an illusory correlation would serve to maintain the stereotypic belief.

Hamilton and Rose (1980) have conducted a series of experiments testing this line of reasoning. Subjects in these experiments read a series of statements, each of which described a stimulus person by first name, occupation, and two trait-descriptive adjectives (e.g., "Mark, a salesman, is talkative and wealthy."). In the first study, stimulus persons belonged to one of three occupational groups, for example, accountants, doctors, and salesmen. Within a set of 24 stimulus sentences there were eight members of each occupational group. Eight trait adjectives were used in constructing these sentences. Based on preratings, two of these traits were known to be stereotypic of accountants, two were stereotypic of doctors, two were stereotypic of salesmen, and the final two were not stereotypically related to any of the three groups. For example, in the sample sentence given earlier, the trait "talkative" is stereotypic of salesmen, whereas "wealthy" is not, the latter being stereotypic of doctors. The sentences were constructed such that each of the eight adjectives was associated with each occupational group twice. In other words, in the 24 sentences each trait occurred six times, twice in sentences describing accountants, twice describing doctors, and twice describing salesmen. Thus, each adjective characterized each group with equal frequency. The hypothesis tested was that subjects' judgments would reflect a belief that attributes stereotypically associated with a particular group had described that group more often than had other attributes unrelated to the group stereotype.

After they had read the set of stimulus sentences, subjects were asked to estimate how often each of the eight traits had described a member of each of the three groups. Analyses of these frequency estimates provided strong support for the hypothesis. For example, subjects estimated that attributes stereotypically associated with accountants (timid, perfectionistic) had described accountants more frequently than had the other six trait characteristics. This estimate also significantly exceeded their judgment of how often those same two words had described members of the other two occupational groups. This pattern of findings was obtained for all three occupational groups (and was replicated in a second, totally independent stimulus set) despite the fact that all traits described each group with equal frequency. The results, then, demonstrate an illusory correlation in which subjects' judgments were biased in the direction of expectancy–confirming relationships.

In this experiment, because each attribute described each occupational group equally often, the stimulus information contained no relationships between group membership and trait characteristics. The obtained pattern of results is quite consistent with the findings of other studies demonstrating similar effects of prior expectations on judgments of co-occurrence under conditions of complete independence between variables (Chapman, 1967; Rothbart, Evans, & Fulero, 1979; Tversky & Kahneman, 1973). This is somewhat of a special condition, however, in that we do not live in a world in which variables are totally unrelated to each other. More specifically, in the context of social perception of interest in this chapter, certain attributes *are* more characteristic of some groups than of others. Doctors, for example, generally are in fact wealthier than accountants and salesmen. The question then becomes whether or not our stereotypic expectancies bias our processing of information about and judgments of the relationship between variables, even when those variables are associated with each other. Previous research suggests that expectancies will have such an effect. Berman and Kenny (1976), for example, found that although subjects were able to detect differences in actual correlation between pairs of traits, their implicit expectations regarding the relationship between two variables influenced their judgments of the strength of association manifested in the stimulus evidence.

Hamilton and Rose (1980) conducted a second experiment to investigate whether or not such a bias would influence processing of information relevant to group stereotypes. As in their first experiment, subjects read a series of sentences, each of which provided information about a stimulus person's occupation and two trait characteristics. In this case, stimulus persons belonged to one of two occupational groups, and among the trait attributes used, some were stereotypic of one (but not the other) group, whereas some were stereotypically neutral for both groups. In contrast to the previous study, the traits did not describe the two groups with equal frequency. Rather, each trait described one group more often than the other, thereby incorporating empirical relationships between trait characteristics and group membership in the stimulus information. These relationships, however, were the same for both kinds of traits—that is, traits stereotypic of a group and stereotypically neutral traits were both positively and equally correlated with membership in that group. For example, in the stimulus sentences, both the trait "responsible," which is stereotypic of doctors (but neutral for salesmen), and the trait "humorous," which is neutral for both of these groups, described doctors more frequently than they described salesmen; both traits, then, were correlated with group membership, and to an equal extent. (Each trait occurred six times in the stimulus sentences. On the average, each one described one group five times and the other group once.) Because the interest of this study was in biased processing of information that *confirms* stereotypic expectancies, the stereotypic traits always described their associated group with greater frequency.

After reading through the set of stimulus items, subjects again estimated how frequently each attribute had described each occupational group. Our hypothesis was that, although subjects ought to recognize the attribute–occupation correlations for both stereotypic and neutral traits, those correlations would be judged as stronger in the case of stereotype-confirming relationships.

The results of this study provided strong support for the hypothesis. Not surprisingly, subjects appropriately gave higher frequency estimates for those attributes that had in fact described a group with high frequency. That is, subjects apparently were aware of the empirical relationships we had built into the stimulus materials. The theoretically more important question is whether their judgments differed for the stereotypic and neutral traits. As predicted, traits stereotypic of a particular group (as, for example, "responsible" is for doctors) were judged to have described that group more frequently than did stereotypically neutral attributes (for example, "humorous") that actually had described the group equally often.

Taken together, these two experiments demonstrate the consistent influence of stereotypic expectancies on subjects' differential processing of information that is congruent with or unrelated to those expectancies. The first study showed that subjects will perceive an attribute–group membership relationship if it confirms a stereotype, even if the information presented contains no evidence in support of such a relationship. The second study showed that when attribute–group membership relationships do exist in the information available, subjects will perceive that relationship as being stronger if it is congruent with stereotypic expectations.

The final experiment reported by Hamilton and Rose (1980) was concerned with how stereotypic conceptions of groups influence the processing of information *incongruent* with one's prior expectancies. As in the two previous studies, subjects read a series of sentences in which each stimulus person was described by occupation and two trait characteristics. Again, half of those attributes were neutral or unrelated to the stereotypes of the occupational groups described, but in this case the other half were counterstereotypic for one or the other of the stimulus groups. If judgments of frequency of co-occurrence are influenced by associative expectations, as demonstrated in the preceding studies, then we might expect subjects to estimate that descriptions incongruent with those expectations had occurred less often than equally frequent neutral descriptions.

This hypothesis was tested under two conditions in this experiment. In one, the No-Correlation condition, stimulus sentences were constructed such that there were no actual relationships between trait characteristics and group membership in the information presented, as in Hamilton and Rose's first experiment. Specifically, trait adjectives were selected that were either (1) incongruent with the stereotype of one group (e.g., "quiet" for salesmen) but neutral for the other group, or (2) unrelated to the stereotype of both groups. In the stimulus sentences each attribute described a member of each group the same number of times. When subjects were later asked to estimate how often each of these traits had described members of each group, it was found that their estimates for incongruent pairings (quiet salesman) were significantly lower than their estimates for how often that same trait had described the other group, as well as how often neutral attributes had described the same group. Thus, the relative frequency of incongruent descriptions was underrepresented in subjects' estimates; information that would disconfirm one's stereotypic belief did not have proportionate impact on subjects' judgments.

In the Correlation condition, similar to Hamilton and Rose's second study, the set of stimulus sentences contained strong group membership–trait attribute relationships. However, in contrast to the earlier study in which some of those relationships were congruent with stereotypic expectancies, in this case group–attribute associations that were incongruent with those expectancies were built into the stimulus set. In the series of 24 sentences that subjects read, each trait adjective occurred a total of six times, describing members of one group five times and the other group once. Half of these traits were selected because they were neutral with regard to the stereotype of both groups. The other half of the attributes were selected because they were incongruent with the stereotype of the group they described five of the six times they occurred. In other words, the stimulus information contained cases of strong positive correlations between group membership and counterstereotypic characteristics, as well as equally strong correlations between group membership and traits unrelated to stereotypic conceptions of the groups. Subjects again were asked to estimate how often each attribute had described members of each group. In this case the stereotypic association of a trait did not differentially influence subjects' estimates. For both counterstereotypic and neutral traits subjects' judgments reflected a recognition of the correlation between these attributes and group memberships contained in the stimulus sentences, and this was neither more nor less true for the incongruent as compared to the neutral traits.

Thus, somewhat different patterns of findings were obtained in the No-Correlation and the Correlation conditions of this experiment. When the trait descriptors were empirically unrelated to group membership in the stimulus sentences, counterstereotypic information was recalled as having described the group for which it was incongruent less frequently than neutral information that had been equally descriptive of the group. This bias was not manifested when both counterstereotypic and neutral attributes were strongly correlated with group membership. Exactly why this bias was not observed in the Correlation condition is at present unclear. We can, however, speculate that the information presented in this condition may have been so strongly counterstereotypic that it in effect neutralized the typical influence of subjects' biases. For example, five of the six times the attribute ''quiet'' occurred, it described a salesman; put another way, of the 12 salesmen described in the stimulus set, five of them were characterized as being ''quiet.'' The stimulus information, then, contradicted stereotypic expectancies to a degree rarely encountered in one's everyday experience, and it did so in the absence of any stereotype-confirming evidence. Under such conditions the fact that the attributes were in fact correlated with group membership, though in a counterstereotypic manner, may have been made inescapably apparent to the subject.

The results obtained in the No-Correlation condition converge with those of Hamilton and Rose's first two experiments in demonstrating a consistent influence of preexisting stereotypic expectations on the processing of co-occurrence information. The nature of this influence was such that the pattern of evidence reflected in subjects' judgments was more congruent with stereotypic beliefs than was the pattern of evidence actually presented. Due to this biased processing of the information, then, subjects in these experiments obtained subjective "confirmation" of their stereotypic expectancies in the absence of validating evidence.

There is an old adage that states "I wouldn't have believed it if I hadn't seen it." The predominant pattern of findings in these experiments suggests that the reverse of that adage may also be true—"I wouldn't have seen it if I hadn't believed it." The consequence, of course, is that the bias manifested in these data contributes to the maintenance and the persistence of stereotypic beliefs and hence makes them resistant to change.

EXPLAINING ILLUSORY CORRELATIONS

The series of experiments described in the two preceding sections extends previous research on the naive human observer's development of and utilization of beliefs about the relationship between variables. Biases demonstrated in prior studies on illusory correlation (Chapman, 1967; Chapman & Chapman, 1967, 1969) have been shown to produce similar distortions in the way subjects processed information about members of social groups. Although the primary concern of this chapter is with the implications of these biases for stereotyping, it is nevertheless worthwhile to consider briefly, in more specific terms, the processes by which these biases in judgment might be produced.

The fact that subjects' estimates of correlational relationships are often erroneous, given the available evidence, has been known for over a decade (Chapman, 1967; Chapman & Chapman, 1967, 1969; Jenkins & Ward, 1965; Smedslund, 1963; Ward & Jenkins, 1965). There has, however, been surprisingly little theoretical effort to explain how these errors come about. In this section we discuss two conceptual frameworks that might be useful for understanding these findings.

Availability Heuristic

Tversky and Kahneman (1973) have proposed that, in estimating the frequency with which some event has occurred, persons often engage in a process of retrieving instances of the event class from memory. The ease with which such instances can be retrieved is said to influence the judged frequency of the event. If an event class actually has occurred with high frequency, then a large number of its instances would presumably be available in memory. Use of the availability heuristic reflects a judge's intuitive assumption that the reverse also will be true: If instances can easily be retrieved from memory, the event class must have occurred frequently. Because frequency of occurrence often will result in a large number of instances being available in memory, use of this heuristic will produce valid judgments in many circumstances. However, other variables unrelated to actual frequency also can influence the availability of information in memory. When this is true, use of the availability heuristic can lead to errors in judgment.

Tversky and Kahneman (1973) have made use of this concept in explaining Chapman's (1967) original illusory correlation findings. They argued that the greater the associative bond between two stimulus words, the greater would be their availability in memory. Thus, item pairs with high associative relationships (as, for example, knife–fork in Chapman's study) would be more available, would thus be more easily retrieved from memory, and hence would be judged to have co-occurred more frequently than item pairs low in associative value. The same mechanism can be used to explain the findings obtained by Hamilton and Rose (1980). Compared to neutral traits, traits stereotypic of an occupation would have strong associative values for that occupation, whereas incongruent traits would be low in associative value for that occupation. If availability reflects the strength of such associative connections, then use of the availability heuristic would produce judgments of higher frequency of co-occurrence for the stereotypic traits and judgments of lower frequency of co-occurrence for the incongruent traits, compared to those for the neutral traits. The predominant pattern of results obtained in Hamilton and Rose's (1980) experiments is consistent with these expectations.

In their application of the availability heuristic to the findings of illusory correlation studies, Tversky and Kahneman (1973) did not address Chapman's (1967) finding that the co-occurrence of distinctive stimulus items also resulted in high frequency estimates. However, their explanation can easily be extended to account for this case and hence provide a basis for understanding Hamilton and Gifford's (1976) results, which were also based on the co-occurrence of distinctive stimuli. As noted earlier, a number of factors (in addition to actual frequency of occurrence) can influence the availability of information in memory. One such factor—the associative bond between stimuli—was used in the preceding paragraph to explain certain kinds of illusory correlation. Another variable that presumably would influence the availability of information is its salience or distinctiveness. If the co-occurrence of stimuli that are distinctive by their relative infrequency makes them particularly salient to the observer (as Hamilton and Gifford's results suggest), then these stimulus pairs would be highly available in memory. If subjects subsequently used the availability heuristic in making judgments, the relative ease of retrievability of this information would result in subjects overestimating the frequency of co-occurrence of these stimulus pairs.

Thus the same cognitive mechanism—a bias in the retrieval of information from memory, based on its availability—can be used to provide an account for most of the results reported in the two preceding sections, as well as other findings on biased judgments of relationships between variables. The versatility of Tversky and Kahneman's (1973) availability heuristic as an explanatory concept is demonstrated in its ability to account for illusory correlations of the two kinds we have discussed, that is, illusory correlations based on the co-occurrence of distinctiveness information and those based on preexisting associative relationships. The problem is that there are any number of factors that will affect the ease with which information can be retrieved from memory, a fact that can result in some interpretive ambiguities. For example, in discussing Hamilton and Rose's (1980) findings we suggested that the associative connection between incongruent occupation–trait pairs would be weak, making these items unavailable in memory, and hence be underrepresented in subjects' frequency judgments. An alternative possibility is that such incongruency would make certain item pairs salient because they violate expectations. In this case these items would be highly available in memory and hence should be overrepresented in subjects' frequency judgments. Use of the availability heuristic in making frequency judgments can thus result in erroneous estimates due to a number of variables that potentially can make information differentially available. The argument can be made, then, that an explanation in terms of the availability heuristic is only a partial explanation, for although it accounts for judgment errors in terms of retrieval biases, it ignores the issue of what it is that makes certain kinds of information differentially available.

Schema-Driven Processing

A second approach to understanding the origin of the biases reflected in illusory correlations emphasizes the role of schemata in information processing. Schemata are cognitive structures that contain a person's knowledge and beliefs pertaining to some domain of content and have been shown to play a role in the encoding, organization, and retrieval of information (Rumelhart & Ortony, 1977; Taylor & Crocker, 1981). Hamilton (1979) has suggested that stereotypes can be viewed as schemalike concepts in that (1) they represent the perceiver's knowledge, beliefs, and expectations regarding members of some social group, and (2) they perform many of the same functions in processing information that are attributed to schema structures. That is, knowledge of a person's membership in some stereotyped group can influence the perceiver's encoding, interpretation, retention, and retrieval of information about that person (cf. Hamilton, 1979, for a review of relevant literature).

According to this approach, when information is relevant to a schema it is more likely to be attended to, comprehended, and represented in memory than when it is not. If stereotypes act as schemata then one might expect that information congruent with stereotypic expectations would be more likely to be attended to, comprehended, and represented in memory than would information unrelated to the stereotype. The results of Hamilton and Rose's (1980) first two experiments are consistent with this prediction: Subjects judged stereotype-confirming descriptions as having occurred more often than had equally frequent but stereotypically neutral descriptions.

As was the case with the availability heuristic, the schema approach encounters some difficulty in accounting for Hamilton and Rose's third experiment, in which stereotypically incongruent information was included in the person descriptions. The difficulty arises in part from the fact that schema theories are ambiguous regarding how schema-inconsistent information is processed. One possibility is that such items, due to their inconsistency with schematic expectations, receive differential attention during encoding, with the consequence that they are effectively represented in memory. When the schema (for example, for an occupation) is subsequently activated during a retrieval task, this information should be easily recalled and disproportionately represented in frequency estimates. Although some findings consistent with this contention have been reported (Hastie & Kumar, 1979), no support for it was obtained in Hamilton and Rose's study. Another possibility is that schema-inconsistent items, because they do not "fit" the cognitive structure employed in processing the incoming information, will be processed inefficiently and/or will not be stored as a part of the schema in question and hence will be underrepresented in subsequent judgments. The results of Hamilton and Rose's No-Correlation condition are consistent with this view, but those obtained in the Correlation condition are not. The general issue of how schema-inconsistent information is processed remains an important but unresolved question that schema theorists will need to address (Hastie, 1981).

Most schema research has investigated the influence of preexisting schematic conceptions on subsequent information processing. In contrast, the Hamilton and Gifford (1976) experiments were concerned with conditions under which the perception of intergroup differences can develop in the absence of prior stereotypic expectancies regarding the target groups involved. That is, the stimulus sentences used in their studies described persons as belonging to one of two groups identified only by a letter code. This was done specifically so that illusory correlations based on the co-occurrence of distinctive information, in the absence of preexisting associations, could be investigated in the context of social perception. Thus, notions about "schema-driven" processing would appear irrelevant to an understanding of Hamilton and Gifford's findings. However, their research may be viewed as having other implications for schema theory. Subjects in these experiments ended up with divergent perceptions of the two groups (as reflected in differential evaluative trait ratings), despite the fact that the information describing these groups was evaluatively comparable. Hamilton and Gifford thus concluded that an illusory correlation based on the co-occurrence of distinctive information can constitute a basis for the development of stereotypic beliefs. If, as was suggested earlier, stereotypes are schema-like cognitive structures, then Hamilton and Gifford's research can be viewed as demonstrating a mechanism (though certainly not the only one) by which schematic conceptions can initially develop.

SUMMARY AND CONCLUSIONS

We began this chapter with a recognition of two points regarding stereotypic judgments about members of ethnic groups. First, we noted that in the course of our everyday experiences we acquire, piece by piece, items of information about members of social groups. This sequential accumulation of information obtained from our observations of, interactions with, or learning about different members of a group is an important process that has not been represented in the paradigms traditionally used in the study of stereotypes. Its significance for stereotyping can be seen in two ways. First, the initial development of our beliefs about a group will be influenced by the way in which information acquired over time is processed and represented in memory. Second, preexisting stereotypic conceptions of a group can affect what and how information about members of that group will be processed and hence can influence the consequences that that information will have for the persistence or change of stereotypic beliefs. Thus the question of how sequentially acquired information about individual members of a group affects one's stereotypic conception of the group as a whole is of considerable importance to an understanding of stereotyping.

The second point made at the outset was that a stereotypic judgment can be viewed as an expression of a belief in a correlational relationship between group membership and some psychological attribute. Based on this premise, the existing research literature on the development and utilization of correlational concepts was examined. This research has shown that errors in the judgment of correlational relationships are common and that certain systematic biases in the way co-occurrence information is processed produce consistent, replicable distortions in such judgments. Viewing stereotypic beliefs as correlational concepts, the research reported in this chapter has pursued the implications of these biases for the development and maintenance of stereotypes.

Our research first investigated a means by which biased processing of information can create an illusory perception of intergroup differences. When exposure to members of two groups occurs with differential frequency, and when one category of behavior occurs less often than another, observers tend to overestimate the frequency with which members of the smaller group performed the infrequent class of behavior. Hamilton and Gifford (1976) have shown that this bias can produce an erroneous perception of a relationship between group membership and the type of behavior characteristic of those groups. The consequence was that the two groups were perceived quite differently, in the absence of any informational basis for such differential perceptions. The implication of these findings is that a bias in the processing of co-occurrence information can constitute the initial basis for differential conceptions of social groups.

Our second series of studies investigated the effect of existing stereotypic conceptions on the processing of co-occurrence information. Previous research had shown that an associative relationship between two stimulus events can result in inflated estimates of their frequency of co-occurrence. Given that stereotypic beliefs represent associative expectations regarding the relationship between group memberships and psychological attributes, one might anticipate comparable effects on judgments in this domain. In line with this view, experiments by Hamilton and Rose (1980) have shown that information congruent with stereotypic expectations is overrepresented in subjects' judgments, relative to equally descriptive but stereotypically neutral information. Subjects were more likely to "see" or remember information that fit with their stereotypic beliefs than information unrelated to those beliefs. Such a bias would have the consequence of perpetuating a person's stereotypic conceptions in the absence of confirming evidence.

Thus we have seen that cognitive biases in the way we process sequentially obtained information about members of social groups can result in erroneous perceptions of intergroup differences and can serve to maintain preexisting beliefs about those groups. These findings are important for several reasons. First, they demonstrate that stereotyping can occur and can persist solely as a result of characteristics of the perceiver as an information processor. This means that explanations of phenomena related to stereotyping need not *necessarily* include reference to the perceiver's learned prejudicial attitudes or to the motivational functions served by stereotypic beliefs (Hamilton, 1976). Second, the nature of the cognitive biases discussed in this chapter and several others in this volume tend to lead to the same end, in that their consequence is that perceptions of intergroup differences are maintained. When one recognizes that the social learning and motivational processes that contribute to stereotyping typically have the same effect, it becomes clear that stereotypes are overdetermined in that several processes can contribute to the same outcome. Viewed from this perspective, one can understand why stereotypic beliefs have proven to be so resilient. Finally, it is clear that efforts to change stereotypes not only will have to be directed at the learned bases and motivational functions of these beliefs but also will have to recognize the cognitive foundations on which these conceptions of groups are based.

ACKNOWLEDGMENTS

Preparation of this chapter was supported in part by NIMH Grant 29418. The author is grateful to Marilynn Brewer and Terry Rose for their valuable comments on an earlier version of this chapter.

REFERENCES

Abramson, L. Y., & Alloy, L. B. Judgment of contingency: Errors and their implications. In A. Baum & J. E. Singer (Eds.), *Advances in environmental psychology* (Vol. 2): *Applications of personal control.* Hillsdale, N.J.: Lawrence Erlbaum Associates, 1980.

Beach, L. R., & Scopp, T. S. Inferences about correlations. *Psychonomic Science,* 1966, *6,* 253–254.

Berman, J. S., & Kenny, D. A. Correlational bias in observer ratings. *Journal of Personality and Social Psychology,* 1976, *34,* 263–273.

Bolton, T. Caller's quake question is one for the crickets. *Santa Barbara News-Press,* August 16, 1978, p. B-1.

Brigham, J. C. Ethnic stereotypes. *Psychological Bulletin,* 1971, *76,* 15–38.

Chapman, L. J. Illusory correlation in observational report. *Journal of Verbal Learning and Verbal Behavior,* 1967, *6,* 151–155.

Chapman, L. J., & Chapman, J. P. Genesis of popular but erroneous psychodiagnostic observations. *Journal of Abnormal Psychology,* 1967, *72,* 193–204.

Chapman, L. J., & Chapman, J. P. Illusory correlation as an obstacle to the use of valid psychodiagnostic signs. *Journal of Abnormal Psychology,* 1969, *74,* 271–280.

Cohen, C. *Cognitive basis of stereotyping.* Paper presented at the meeting of the American Psychological Association, San Francisco, August 1977.

Crocker, J. *Judgment of covariation by social perceivers.* Unpublished manuscript, Northwestern University, 1980.

Deaux, K. Sex: A perspective on the attribution process. In J. H. Harvey, W. J. Ickes, & R. F. Kidd (Eds.), *New directions in attribution research* (Vol. 1). Hillsdale, N.J.: Lawrence Erlbaum Associates, 1976.

Duncan, B. L. Differential social perception and attribution of intergroup violence: Testing the lower limits of stereotyping of blacks. *Journal of Personality and Social Psychology,* 1976, *34,* 590–598.

Ehrlich, H. J. *The social psychology of prejudice.* New York: Wiley, 1973.

Erlick, D. E. Human estimates of statistical relatedness. *Psychonomic Science,* 1966, *5,* 365–366.

Golding, S. L., & Rorer, L. G. Illusory correlation and subjective judgment. *Journal of Abnormal Psychology,* 1972, *80,* 249–260.

Hamilton, D. L. Cognitive biases in the perception of social groups. In J. S. Carroll & J. W. Payne (Eds.), *Cognition and social behavior.* Hillsdale, N.J.: Lawrence Erlbaum Associates, 1976.

Hamilton, D. L. A cognitive–attributional analysis of stereotyping. In L. Berkowitz (Ed.), *Advances in experimental social psychology* (Vol. 12). New York: Academic Press, 1979.

Hamilton, D. L., & Gifford, R. K. Illusory correlation in interpersonal perception: A cognitive basis of stereotypic judgments. *Journal of Experimental Social Psychology,* 1976, *12,* 392–407.

Hamilton, D. L., & Rose, T. Illusory correlation and the maintenance of stereotypic beliefs. *Journal of Personality and Social Psychology,* 1980, *39,* 832–845.

Hartsough, W. R. Illusory correlation and mediated association: A finding. *Canadian Journal of Behavioral Science,* 1975, *7,* 151–154.

Hastie, R. Schematic principles in human memory. In E. T. Higgins, C. P. Herman, & M. P. Zanna (Eds.), *Social cognition: The Ontario Symposium.* Hillsdale, N.J.: Lawrence Erlbaum Associates, 1981.

Hastie, R., & Kumar, P. A. Person memory: Personality traits as organizing principles in memory for behaviors. *Journal of Personality and Social Psychology,* 1979, *37,* 25–38.

Jenkins, H. M., & Ward, W. C. Judgment of contingency between responses and outcomes. *Psychological Monographs,* 1965, *79* (1, Whole No. 594).

Katz, D., & Braly, K. Racial stereotypes of one hundred college students. *Journal of Abnormal and Social Psychology,* 1933, *28,* 280–290.

Langer, E. J., Taylor, S. E., Fiske, S., & Chanowitz, B. Stigma, staring, and discomfort: A novel-stimulus hypothesis. *Journal of Experimental Social Psychology,* 1976, *12,* 451–463.

McArthur, L. Z. What grabs you? The role of attention in impression formation and causal attribution. In E. T. Higgins, C. P. Herman, & M. P. Zanna (Eds.), *Social cognition: The Ontario Symposium on Personality and Social Psychology.* Hillsdale, N.J.: Lawrence Erlbaum Associates, 1981.

McCauley, C., Stitt, C. L., & Segal, M. Stereotyping: From prejudice to prediction. *Psychological Bulletin*, 1980, *87*, 195–208.

Rothbart, M., Evans, M., & Fulero, S. Recall for confirming events: Memory processes and the maintenance of social stereotypes. *Journal of Experimental Social Psychology*, 1979, *15*, 343–355.

Rumelhart, D. E., & Ortony, A. The representation of knowledge in memory. In R. C. Anderson, R. J. Spiro, & W. E. Montague (Eds.), *Schooling and the acquisition of knowledge*. Hillsdale, N.J.: Lawrence Erlbaum Associates, 1977.

Smedslund, J. The concept of correlation in adults. *Scandinavian Journal of Psychology*, 1963, *4*, 165–173.

Snyder, M., & Swann, W. B., Jr. Hypothesis-testing processes in social interaction. *Journal of Personality and Social Psychology*, 1978, *36*, 1202–1212.

Snyder, M., Tanke, E. D., & Berscheid, E. Social perception and interpersonal behavior: On the self-fulfilling nature of social stereotypes. *Journal of Personality and Social Psychology*, 1977, *35*, 656–666.

Snyder, M., & Uranowitz, S. Reconstructing the past: Some cognitive consequences of person perception. *Journal of Personality and Social Psychology*, 1978, *36*, 941–950.

Starr, B. J., & Katkin, E. S. The clinician as an aberrant actuary: Illusory correlation and the incomplete sentences blank. *Journal of Abnormal Psychology*, 1969, *74*, 670–675.

Tajfel, H. Cognitive aspects of prejudice. *Journal of Social Issues*, 1969, *25* (4), 79–97.

Taylor, S. E., & Crocker, J. Schematic bases of social information processing. In E. T. Higgins, C. P. Herman, & M. P. Zanna (Eds.), *Social cognition: The Ontario Symposium on Personality and Social Psychology*. Hillsdale, N.J.: Lawrence Erlbaum Associates, 1981.

Taylor, S. E., & Fiske, S. T. Salience, attention, and attribution: Top of the head phenomena. In L. Berkowitz (Ed.) *Advances in experimental social psychology* (Vol. 10). New York: Academic Press, 1978.

Tversky, A., & Kahneman, D. Availability: A heuristic for judging frequency and probability. *Cognitive Psychology*, 1973, *5*, 207–232.

Ward, W. C., & Jenkins, H. M. The display of information and the judgment of contingency. *Canadian Journal of Psychology*, 1965, *19*, 231–241.

Word, C. O., Zanna, M. P., & Cooper, J. The nonverbal mediation of self-fulfilling prophecies in interracial interaction. *Journal of Experimental Social Psychology*, 1974, *10*, 109–120.

Zajonc, R. B. Attitudinal effect of mere exposure. *Journal of Personality and Social Psychology*, 1968, *9* (2, Pt. 2).

5 Memory Processes and Social Beliefs

Myron Rothbart
University of Oregon

When people make statements of the form "Women are bad drivers," "Jews are aggressive," or "Blacks are devious," they are expressing a belief about events in the social world that in principle can be empirically verified or disconfirmed. Although beliefs referring to the attributes of groups have, through common usage, been called "stereotypes," there is no reason to believe that stereotypic beliefs behave in ways significantly different from other potentially verifiable propositions.

By treating stereotypes as beliefs that are potentially vulnerable to evidence and therefore distinguishable from beliefs that are true by definition (e.g., "The area of a rectangle is equal to its width multiplied by its length") or not subject to empirical verification (e.g., "Equality is more important than freedom"), we may be able to gain some insight into the more general way in which relevant evidence influences, or fails to influence, our internal representation of the external world.

When we are functioning well as scientists and wish to determine whether our representation (or theory) of the external world is correct, we are able to rely on an elaborate set of rules that enable us to determine whether the implications of our theories are corroborated through systematic (i.e., unbiased) observation of the outside world. By then determining which theories are consistent or inconsistent with the data, we allow the structure of reality to determine the form of our models.

When we are functioning well as people, however, without the advantage (or disadvantage?) of scientific rigor, our representations not only are structured by, but act to structure information received from the external world. Thus the relationships between reality and our representation of reality is not unidirectional but bidirectional and mutually interdependent. I argue that this mutual interdependence holds enormous importance for understanding the longevity of social beliefs and for understanding the unique advantages and disadvantages of unaided human thought.

In order to develop this argument further, I have organized the chapter into two sections. The first section attempts to elaborate on the implications of mutual interdependence by comparing the differences between systematic and nonsystematic hypothesis testing in the context of a stereotypic belief. Comparisons made in the first section of the Chapter are then used to develop, in the second section, a general psychological model of belief formation and maintainence. And finally, I discuss briefly some of the benefits that accrue from having an information-processing system that organizes and structures external input.

SYSTEMATIC AND NONSYSTEMATIC HYPOTHESIS TESTING

It is hardly novel to suggest that the way in which we implicitly assess the validity of our beliefs about social objects in natural settings differs from the way in which such beliefs would be tested if we were to follow traditional methods of scientific inference. What is probably less apparent, however, is that deviations that occur from a rational or scientific hypothesis-testing procedure are systematic and specifiable.

The comparison between scientific and casual hypothesis testing will be illustrated with the stereotypic belief of women as bad drivers. This example is chosen, not to heap further calumny upon women, but because it is a stereotype that is readily subject to test (e.g., by reference to accident rates) and persists despite a notable lack of corroborating evidence.

In the following section I attempt to delineate the various steps associated with systematic hypothesis testing and to contrast prescriptive behavior with the actual behavior of people in natural settings. My purpose is not to compare invidiously the sophisticated scientist with the inept layperson (inasmuch as both images tend to be caricatures), but to compare two different strategies of thought, each with its own advantages and disadvantages. I illustrate some common violations of systematic hypothesis testing, with the intention of arguing later that these violations are a necessary consequence of psychological processes that are otherwise highly adaptive. What I am not arguing is that scientists think in a way superior to that of laypersons. Scientific thinking is idealized in these pages, and the behavior of living and breathing scientists frequently deviates from the ideal; certainly there is an abundance of evidence indicating that scientists are highly susceptible to common biases and illusions in thought (Chapman & Chapman, 1967; Tversky & Kahneman, 1971, 1974).

One of the first requirements of scientific inference is a strict separation between the formation and verification of hypotheses. Although students first exposed to the scientific method find such a distinction obvious and trivial, it is a distinction of cardinal importance. Hans Reichenbach (1951) makes such a distinction by differentiating the "context of discovery" from the "context of proof" (which we now refer to as Stage I and Stage II, respectively). In Stage I, the context of discovery, the observer forms tentative beliefs or hypotheses about interrelationships among events. Although the process leading to the discovery of a relationship may be of interest to students of the creative process, it has no relevance for assessing the validity of the hypothesis. It is only in Stage II, the context of proof, that evidence is collected to affirm or falsify the hypothesis. The distinction between the two stages is exemplified well by the discoveries of William Harvey, whose religious and philosophical beliefs of a circulating cosmos inspired his hypothesis about circulation of the blood. The merit of Harvey's ideas is assessed not by judging the validity of his religious beliefs, but by examining the strength of his laboratory experiments.

Stage I: Context of Discovery

In Stage I there would be two discernible steps, corresponding to the discovery and explicit formulation of the hypothesis.

1. *Sample and Observe the Environment.*   If we accept Reichenbach's argument, the origins of a belief or hypothesis are irrelevant for assessing its validity. Because a hypothesis can be arrived at legitimately by systematic or haphazard observations, from mystical experiences as well as from directed, purposive reasoning, there is no reason to conclude that one mode of hypothesis formation is more appropriate than another. For argument's sake, let us suppose that after observing other drivers, we have hypothesized, for whatever reason, that "women are bad drivers."

2. *Formulate Hypotheses in an Explicit Manner.*   When hypotheses are tested in a systematic way, it is necessary that the data bear directly and appropriately on the hypothesis being tested. In order for this to occur the hypothesis must be stated explicitly enough to define the data that are relevant to the hypothesis. Although this second step seems obvious, important consequences may result when a hypothesis remains *implicit* rather than *explicit*. Later in this chapter I argue that the explicitness or salience of an expectancy may be important in determining whether information is coded as confirmatory or not. But of greater importance, however, is that in the process of transforming an implicit stereotypic expectancy into one explicit enough for verification or disconfirmation, we reduce the imprecision and ambiguity of normal linguistic usage. When people assert that "women are bad drivers," exactly which hypothesis is being proposed and what data would be necessary to assess its validity? Casual asser-

tions put forth in ordinary language are frequently vague and are subject to differing interpretations; depending on which hypothesis is being proposed, the criteria for disconfirmation vary. Is the statement, ''women are bad drivers'': (1) a diagnostic judgment that the incidence of bad driving is higher among women drivers than among the appropriate comparison group, men drivers (i.e., p(bad driving/women drivers) $>$ p(bad driving/men drivers); (2) a magnitude estimation that the majority of women are bad drivers (i.e., p(bad driving/women drivers) $>$ .50); or (3) the trivially uninformative observation that *some* women are bad drivers (i.e., p(bad driving/women drivers) $>$ 0)?

Although most people would interpret the statement ''women are bad drivers'' to mean a greater prevalence of bad driving among women than among men drivers (interpretation (1)), as this is what is commonly implied by a stereotype (McCauley & Stitt, 1978), there is good evidence to suggest that people are insensitive to comparative differences and focus instead on the frequency (or proportion) of confirming instances (i.e., p(bad driving/women drivers), or interpretation (3)). Research by Schweder (1977), Smedslund (1963), Jenkins and Ward (1965), and Chapman and Chapman (1969) suggests that subjects do not respond to the magnitude of the contingency or correlation between sets of events (e.g., the diagnostic power of anal signs on the Rorschach to discriminate homosexuals from nonhomosexuals), but to the frequency of co-occurrence of particular events (e.g., the co-occurence of anal signs with homosexuality). Thus when people casually remark that ''women are bad drivers,'' they may implicitly be making a comparative judgement that bad driving is more prevalent among women than among men, but they may actually be testing a far weaker interpretation of this statement: There exist women who are bad drivers (i.e., p(bad driving/women) $>$ 0).

By failing to state the hypothesis explicitly, people are using an incomplete data set from a very weak hypothesis (bad women drivers exist) as evidence for a far stronger hypothesis (there are sex differences in quality of driving). The virtue of explicitly stating the hypothesis, as would be true (at least, ideally) of scientific hypothesis testing, is that it is more likely to ensure an appropriate fit between data and hypothesis.

After the hypothesis is stated explicitly, the hypothesis-testing procedure moves into the second stage. The hypothesis to be tested is that the incidence of bad driving is higher among women than men.

Stage II: Context of Proof

1. *Define the Appropriate Sampling Domains.*   Clearly, the appropriate *groups* to be sampled are women drivers and men drivers, and the behaviors to be sampled include all driving behaviors that can then be categorized as either good or bad (for simplicity's sake, let us assume that all driving instances can be categorized into one of two mutually exclusive and exhaustive categories: good

driving and bad driving). To put this another way, we have a 2 × 2 table in which we enter the frequencies of good and bad driving instances for women and for men. The *sequence* of events in placing entries into the table is to *first* define the population of drivers (men versus women) and *second* note whether a delineated segment of that person's driving is good or bad. The consequence of reversing the sequence, noting first the quality of the driving and then the sex of the drivers, allows for the possibility of systematic error if there are biases in sampling particular rows or columns in the fourfold table.

Consider for example, the hypothetical set of data depicted in Table 5.1. If subjects sampled all four cells (Table 5.1a) they would find no correlation between sex of driver and quality of driving. Although a systematic analysis would require sampling from all four cells, there is good reason to believe that for a variety of reasons people do not sample equally from all cells in ordinary settings. One reason for inappropriate sampling has already been discussed; that is, an inadequate or vague statement of the hypothesis may lead to inadequate sampling. There are numerous other reasons for inappropriate sampling in

TABLE 5.1.
Frequency Data on the Relationship
Between Sex of Driver and Quality of Driving When:
(a) All Data in Fourfold Table are Sampled;
(b) Sampling is biased Toward Bad Driving; and
(c) Sampling is Biased Toward Women Drivers

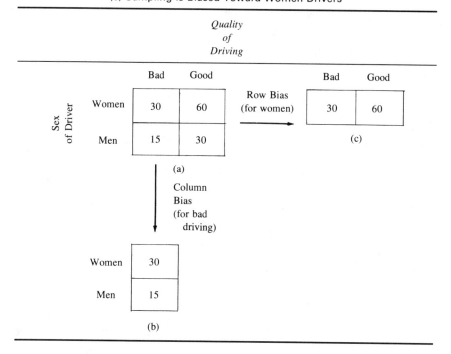

natural settings, not the least of which is the importance or significance of events. A strong argument can be made, for example, for disproportionately sampling negative events (cf. Kanouse & Hanson, 1971, to be discussed later in this chapter). If, for example, subjects implicitly and erroneously defined bad driving as the sample domain, and noted the frequency of women and men within this domain, they would record more instances of bad driving among women than among men (Table 5.1b). The effect of sampling disproportionately from one column is to leave the data uncorrected for differences in the base rates of men and women and to lead to the erroneous conclusion that women are more likely to be bad drivers than are men. Given the distribution of frequencies in Table 5.1a, the p(bad driving/women) $\neq p$ (women/bad driving).

Similarly, if subjects showed a bias for one row over another, as would be the case if they sampled only women drivers, the disproportionate sampling from one row would leave the data uncorrected for differences in the frequency of good and bad driving and could lead to a third (and erroneous) conclusion that women are better drivers than men (Table 5.1c).

An additional source of inappropriate sampling occurs as a natural consequence of decision making. Einhorn and Hogarth (1978) have emphasized that when we *act* on the basis of our beliefs, we often eliminate or restrict our access to control data, which leads to predominantly confirming information and overconfidence in the validity in our beliefs. For example, when we insist that our graduate students have high math GREs and then observe that the students we selected have been successful, we conclude that the selection criterion is a good one even though we do now know: (1) how well the rejected applicants would have done in our program; and (2) whether the selected applicants' success is due to the benefits of being selected and being in the program rather than their high math GRE's.

Another important source of inappropriate sampling *in vivo* is attributable to the power of social roles to structure information, a phenomenon that can be illustrated by trying to understand the prevalence of racist attitudes among white police who work in black communities. White police who patrol black areas sample almost exclusively negative behaviors from blacks, inasmuch as the job of the police (at least as defined in this country) is to deal with criminal behavior. Because the sample of white behavior is predominantly favorable (whites' behaviors are sampled from within their own comparatively safe neighborhoods), police are sampling almost entirely from the cells containing unfavorable black behavior and favorable white behavior and have few entries of favorable black and unfavorable white behaviors. Under these conditions, it is not surprising to find white police who hold a disparaging view of blacks, and the problem is unlikely to be corrected unless data are sampled from unrepresented cells, either by changing the definition of the job or by choosing police who are more likely to sample unrepresented behaviors (e.g., black policemen). The important point is that an understanding of people's beliefs must be based on what Einhorn and

Hogarth (1978) have called "task structure." In the police example, this means an understanding of the inappropriate sampling created by situational demands.

2. *Sample Representatively from the Appropriate Domains.* Because systematic hypothesis testing requires that we sample in a representative way from the defined population, our comparison of women and men drivers obviously requires that we sample from those two groups in a way that is *equally* representative. Obviously we do not want to compare the quality of driving of male racing-car drivers with women who are going for their first driving test. Although equally representative samples are required for a comparison, there is an abundance of evidence to suggest that our social preferences and social roles almost preclude the possibility of representative sampling in natural settings. The predilection for psychotherapists to believe in the pathological origins of homosexuality may be due in part to the fact that they sample only those homosexuals who are disturbed and seek out psychotherapy; therapists are, as a logical consequence of their role, less likely to come into contact with nondisturbed homosexuals[1].

Freud observed, at a more subtle level, that our unconscious preferences may lead us to structure our sampling of events in an unrepresentative way. For example, we may conclude that members of the opposite sex often turn out to be cold and exploitative. This conclusion may not be unreasonable, however, if the only opposite-sex persons we were originally attracted to were the "challenging" ones who were disinterested and aloof rather than the ones who showed an interest in us. Kelley and Stahelski (1970) found that competitive players in a game setting tended, by their own competitive behavior, to turn initially cooperative players competitive, thus providing them with a plethora of evidence for others' defections and validating their view of the world as one that requires a competitive orientation.

3. *Code Behaviors into Categories in a Way That is Equivalent for Both Groups.* Once we have defined our sample, we are in a position to observe the driving behavior of the two groups and code the ongoing behaviors into categories relevant to the hypothesis. To test our original hypothesis, we are going to have to translate or code the ongoing sequence of driving "events" into segments that can then be assessed as "good driving" or "bad driving." As students of observational method, we know that the interjudge agreement in

---

[1]It is interesting to ask why therapists do not conclude that heterosexuality is associated with pathology, inasmuch as most of their patients are both heterosexual and disturbed. Although there is evidence that therapists tend to overstate the incidence of pathology in the general population, obviously this pathology is not associated with heterosexuality. Our answer to this question concerns what we later call the "level of encoding" and concerns the label with which events are stored in memory.

coding good and bad driving is going to be far from perfect, and although we can tolerate an imperfect measure, we cannot tolerate a biased measure. That is, because the process of translating an ongoing stream of events into judgmental categories involves either an implicit or explicit set of rules for transferring one set of events into another, we have to be certain that the *criteria* used for establishing a good or bad driving instance are the *same* for women and men.

Probably the most well-established finding in social psychology is that the criteria for judging behaviors, attributes, products, or events vary with context and that a given physical stimulus does not invariably lead to one and only one psychological response. Lorge (1936) demonstrated very early that the same revolutionary statement is found less acceptable when ascribed to Karl Marx than to Samuel Adams, and there is abundant evidence as to the effects of prior attitude on the judgment of personality (Asch, 1946; Kelley, 1950), facial features (Rothbart & Birrell, 1977), social behaviors (Allport & Postman, 1947) and groups (Peabody, 1968).

Research on the criterion problem involving group impressions is particularly interesting in light of the problem being discussed here. Peabody (1968) asked Chinese and Japanese subjects living in the Philippines to ascribe traits to each of the two groups. Using quartets of traits representing both favorable and unfavorable ways of labeling bipolar forms of behaviors, Peabody found that both groups were likely to agree on the descriptive component of a trait in describing their own or the other group (i.e., Chinese and Japanese both show a ''tendency not to spend money''), but they did not agree on the evaluative terms ascribed to the group (i.e., ''we are thrifty, they are stingy'').

The question of how a complex ongoing sequence of behaviors is coded into linguistic descriptors (with whatever combination of descriptive and evaluative components) is an enormously complicated question and one that we do not wish to address at any length in this chapter. There are several points that should be made, however.

First, the common words we use to ''describe'' behavior (such as adjective traits), in fact summarize a complex stream of behavior and contain a mixture of descriptive information, causal ascription, and evaluative judgments. Despite the inferential and evaluative nature of trait descriptions, we nontheless succumb to what Campbell (1967) has called ''phenomenal absolutism,'' the tendency to view our attributions (e.g., laziness, intelligence, stinginess) as qualities that exist within the stimulus object rather than as judgments about the stimulus object.

Second, to the degree that judgment is used in translating a sequence of events into a behavior code, the judgment will reflect prior attitudes and expectancies about the stimulus object. Duncan (1976) found, for example, that whites coding an ambiguously ''angry'' interaction between two persons (either of whom could be white or black) were more likely to interpret a white person's behavior as "aggressive," whereas a black's behavior was more likely encoded as "violent."

A third point is that to the extent that the inferential judgment of behaviors is evaluative rather than descriptive, the empirical referents for validating or disconfirming the belief are unspecified. To the extent that the difference between being stingy and thrify represents an evaluative judgment rather than any describable difference in behavior, there will be no way to distinguish empirically between the two constructs. Thus, one of the central assumptions underlying this chapter, that stereotypic judgments are beliefs with empirical referents, is called into question when the constructs become evaluative in nature. This problem is examined later in this chapter.

4. *Compute Measure of Contingency Between Behavior and Group.* Once behaviors are appropriately coded, and the prevalence of particular kinds of behaviors compared *between* groups, systematic hypothesis testing requires an assessment of whether the differences between groups are large enough to be taken seriously or whether they can reasonably be attributed to sampling error. There are several problems with assessing the magnitude of a contingency. As we have already indicated, there is evidence that subjects are insensitive to diagnostic or contingency data and respond instead to the frequency of co-occurrence of associated events. Certainly the question of how well subjects can learn to perceive contingencies is far from solved, but at present there is reason to believe that subjects are insufficiently attentive to contingencies or comparative information (Jenkins & Ward, 1965).

In addition to the fact that people seem unlikely to attend to comparative differences between samples, there is additional evidence that even when people are forced to make comparisons their judgments may reflect frequencies rather than proportions. Estes (1976) presented subjects with sequences of outcomes in which candidate A defeated candidate B on 75 out of 100 occasions, and D defeated C on 100 out of 200 occasions. When asked whether A would defeat C, which would be expected if subjects were predicting on the basis of proportions rather than frequency of wins, subjects instead predicted C would defeat A.

If information is not encoded as proportions but as frequencies, as Estes' data would suggest, it has important implications for people's ability to draw meaningful conclusions from the sort of data presented in Table 5.1. It suggests that the "fullest" cell, uncorrected for base rates or marginal frequencies, may dominate subjects' judgments of the relatedness of the variables.

One additional question that occurs is how large differences between groups have to be before they are taken seriously or judged to be "significant." Morlock (1967) has shown that the size of a sample that subjects deem adequate for inferring a population characteristic from a sample value depends on the desirability of the population having that characteristic.

To return to our example, subjects who believed (or wished) women to be inferior drivers might accept smaller differences between men and women in quality of driving as evidence for the hypothesis than would subjects who did not hold such a belief. Although Bayesian decision making recognizes the rationality of using prior expectancies in making probabilistic inferences, it nonetheless implies that the criterion for accepting a group difference as meaningful varies inversely with the strength of one's belief that differences ought to exist.

5. *Retain or Discard Original Belief.*   The last step in the sequence is to decide, on the basis of the outcome in Step 4, whether or not the belief should be discarded. Whether or not subjects actually change their beliefs on the basis of new information has been a central preoccupation in social psychology for the last half century, and it would be impossible for me to do justice to the literature on this topic. Although the topic of responsivity to disconfirming information is examined later, one observation is in order.

There is no single or simple set of rules to predict how a given bit of information is used as a basis for forming or modifying beliefs. At one extreme, it appears that subjects are willing to adopt the beliefs of a credible communicator when the subject has no prior attitudes about the belief object (as was the case, for example, in Hovland and Weiss' research (1952) involving attitudes toward antihistamines). At the other extreme, there is intense resistance to change when the target beliefs are important and centrally implicated in a variety of other beliefs. The most colorful anecdote illustrating this point concerns the clinical case often used to illustrate the limitations of rationalistic psychotherapy. In an attempt to alter the beliefs of a psychiatric patient who thought she was dead, the therapist explored with the patient some of the necessary implications of being dead. After extracting from the patient the implication that dead people do not bleed, the therapist pricked the patient's finger and demonstrated to her that she was bleeding. Rather than discard her original belief, however, she concluded instead that "dead people *do* bleed!"

It should now become apparent to the reader that a fundamental difference between the prescribed scientific method and the manner in which people actually behave in testing their beliefs resides in the relationship between Stage I (discovery/hypothesis) and Stage II (justification/proof): Whereas scientific investigation requires strict independence between Stage I and Stage II, such independence appears absent in most settings where people are likely to test their beliefs.

All the departures from appropriate scientific procedure occur as a result of an intrusion of expectancies, hypotheses, or beliefs on the processes of data collection and analysis. Historically, of course, the scientific method evolved to minimize the sort of error in human perception and judgment that occurred as a result of an observer's implicit (or explicit) expectancies. Although it reasonably can be asked (and is asked later in this chapter) what advantages accrue as a result of having an interdependence between hypothesis and proof, the point to be made now is that the lack of independence between Stage I and Stage II creates at least two fundamental problems in generating an accurate internal representation of the external world:

1. Expectancies formed in Stage I influence the data collection and analysis in Stage II.
2. Expectancies formed in Stage I alter the nature of the social world from which the data is collected.

Although it may sound as though these two statements are saying the same thing, they are not. The first states that the data obtained from the external world (and judgments derived therefrom) are biased by one's beliefs, whereas the second asserts that the nature of the world itself is altered by one's expectancies. Because research and theory on this second problem—the self-fulfilling nature of expectancies—is discussed by Mark Snyder elsewhere in this volume, I will continue to focus only on the first problem.

A GENERAL OUTLINE OF THE ROLE OF MEMORY IN SOCIAL BELIEFS

In the first section of this chapter I noted the lack of independence between discovery and verification or hypothesis and proof. In the second part of this chapter, I wish to explore some of the possible psychological mechanisms that may be responsible for this nonindependence. The model that is proposed assumes that one major source of evidence for our beliefs comes from relevant instances drawn from memory. It is assumed further that the effects of memory are manifest through three discrete but interrelated processes: encoding, retrieval, and judgment. Encoding refers to the selective manner in which events are summarized and stored in memory, and judgment refers to the processes by which the retrieved events are integrated into a relatively simple decision that can serve as the basis for action (verbal or otherwise). For purposes of explication, I will treat the three processes in the order listed. However, it will shortly become apparent that each process can influence the others, and the order in which they are discussed should not be interpreted as the unique causal sequence by which these processes operate.

Encoding

It is apparent that information about a person or group can occur in a variety of forms. We can observe the behaviors/attributes of a person/group either on the basis of firsthand observation or learn of them through a secondary source;

moreover, the information may be first-order observations based on observance of actual behavior (e.g., seeing a specific man or woman run a red light) or may be higher order observations in which inferences are already drawn (e.g., reading an article on the comparative accident rates of women and men). In any event, the unit of analysis is some pairing between either a group or constituent member of a group on the one hand, and an action, set of actions, or attributes on the other. For convenience, let us label these the agent and behavior, respectively.

Levels of Encoding and Salient Attributes of the Agent.   If we directly observe Jim, a thin Rosicrucian, spanking his child, we are confronted immediately with the question of how this complex event is going to be summarized for storage into memory. Let us focus first on the question of how the agent is encoded.

In Jean-Paul Sartre's book *Anti-Semite and Jew* (1948), Sartre briefly cites the example of a women who dislikes Jews because of her "most horrible experiences with all (Jewish) furriers." Sartre asks: "But why did she choose to hate Jews rather than furriers? Why Jews or furriers rather than such and such a Jew or such and such a furrier? [p. 120]." Sartre is asking a fundamental question about the *level* of encoding the agent. Given all the available information about a person, all the possible classificatory dimensions that can be used to categorize him or her, why are some dimensions more likely to be chosen than others? Going back to our example, we may use the most specific levels of encodings such as "Jim spanked his child," or even more specific yet, "Jim, in an irritable mood, spanked his child." But we may also choose more general levels of coding, such as "A thin person spanked his child," or "A Rosicrucian spanked his child," or we may go to one of the most general levels and code the event as "A man spanked his child."

Readers who are familiar with contemporary issues in semantic memory will realize that the question of how attributes are coded (or inferred) in memory is a controversial area, and one that is well beyond the scope of this chapter. The only point I wish to make here is that some bases for classification are more probable than others and that the chosen level of encoding ultimately affects the retrieval of information about, and the judgments concerning particular social groups. Obviously, Sartre's example is one in which aversive experiences were paired not with specific persons, or even with the occupation (furriers) but with the category "Jews." Had the choice of classification been otherwise, there is a possibility that her group impressions may also have been otherwise.

There is, however, one fundamentally important question that arises from this analysis: What determines which dimensions of classification are most salient and likely to be used? There can be no single or simple answer to this question, but there are two factors that obviously contribute substantially to this phenomenon. The first involves what Rosch (1977) has called basic-level concepts, which concerns the segmentation of events in such a way that maximizes commonality among elements within the category and maximizes differences between categories. Jim is not going to be categorized as a human being because that does not distinguish him from other people; categorization as a man at least distinguishes him from one half the population, but categorization by sex is not highly discriminating. Presumably we are going to settle on a level of categorization that is less broad, but still allows us to predict something useful.

If utility or predictive value is one of the criteria for categorization then obviously one determinant of real or imagined predictability is the subject's prior expectancies. Inasmuch as Sartre's acquaintance expected Jews to be the source of negative events, it is not unlikely that the category "Jew" was highly salient to her and likely to be invoked when appropriate. This is the reasoning behind the early research of Allport and Kramer (1946), who expected anti-Semites to be highly sensitive to and accurate in spotting Jewish faces; the salience of Jewish attributes was expected to be higher among those prejudiced against Jews.

Although we stated earlier that it was useful to distinguish between encoding, retrieval, and judgment processes, it is clear that in reference to social beliefs, the three processes affect one another. The categories used during the encoding process are to a large degree going to be influenced by our prior expectancies and judgments, as well as by context. Because racial characteristics, for a variety of historical reasons, are clearly associated in people's minds with discernible behaviors, and because issues of race are salient in contemporary America, it is not at all surprising that categorizing by race is likely to occur, even when other dimensions are readily available.

This line of argument leads to an interesting prediction about the ways in which we may encode and store information about ingroups and outgroups and is a prediction we are currently attempting to test. There is a common argument that we perceive ingroups as more heterogeneous and differentiated than outgroups. One way we can think about the psychological meaning of differentiation (or lack of differentiation) is in the level of encoding that we use when storing information about ingroup and outgroup members. Consider the following two sentences: (1) "Jim, a white construction worker, rescued a child from a burning building"; and (2) "Jim, a black construction worker, rescued a child from a burning building." In the first sentence, Jim, like myself, is white, and because the ingroup lable "white" is to me meaninglessly large (in Rosch's terms, the commonality among elements within the category is too small), I am going to look for a lower level, or subordinate category to store information about Jim. Using the subordinate category related to occupation, I may at a later date only remember that Jim, a construction worker, rescued a child from a burning building. Whereas to me the category "white" may be meaningless, and therefore not used to encode behavior, I may perceive "blacks" as a meaningful category (according to the outgroup homogeneity bias) and use the superordinate category "black" rather than the subordinate category "construction worker" when storing the behavior. In sum, I use the lower-order category to encode ingroup behavior and the higher-order category to encode outgroup behavior. It is expected that a black person would behave similarly and would use the superordinate category for whites and the subordinate category for blacks. We are currently conducting experiments using reaction time and memory errors to see if such differential encoding occurs for ingroups and outgroups.

Encoding of Behaviors.   Thus far, we have discussed two factors, utility and past experiences, that influence the level at which the *agent* is encoded. But *behaviors* also are encoded in memory, and it is at this point that we can begin to discuss some of the ways in which expectancies and labels structure the encoding and retrieval of relevant behavioral information.

In an attempt to see how prior expectancies structure the recall of behavioral exemplars, Rothbart, Evans, and Fulero (1979) presented subjects with 50 behavior descriptions, where each behavior was associated with one member of a group of 50 men. The 50 items consisted of 17 intelligent, 17 friendly, 3 nonintelligent, 3 unfriendly, and 10 unrelated behaviors. One half the subjects were led to believe the group was intellectual, and one half that the group was friendly. In addition, to assess whether superior memory for confirming or disconfirming events could be localized in the retrieval or encoding process, approximately one

TABLE 5.2.
Frequency Estimates and Recall for the Five Categories of Behavior
as a Function of Type of Expectancy and Time of Expectancy[a]

	Confirming Behaviors		Disconfirming Behaviors		Unrelated Behaviors
	Intelligent	Friendly	Nonintelligent	Unfriendly	
A. Actual number of items presented	17	17	3	3	10
B. Frequency estimates					
Expectancy before items					
Intelligent expectancy	14.16	11.58	6.74	4.90	8.74
Friendly expectancy	11.17	14.39	5.63	5.37	6.73
Expectancy after items					
Intelligent expectancy	12.13	11.03	5.00	4.49	6.38
Friendly expectancy	14.67	14.41	5.51	5.15	6.38
C. Recall					
Expectancy before items					
Intelligent expectancy	4.83	4.05	1.33	1.21	2.83
Friendly expectancy	4.02	4.74	1.42	1.19	2.49
Expectancy after items					
Intelligent expectancy	3.18	3.64	0.87	0.95	1.46
Friendly expectancy	3.38	3.49	1.03	1.08	2.00

[a] Reprinted from Rothbart, Evans, and Fulero, 1979.

TABLE 5.3.
Recall for Four Categories of Behavior as a Function of Type of Expectancy

	Confirming Behaviors		Disconfirming Behaviors	
	Intelligent	Friendly	Nonintelligent	Unfriendly
A. Actual number of items presented	17	17	8	8
B. Recall				
Intelligent expectancy	4.17	3.86	3.00	2.63
Friendly expectancy	3.97	4.65	3.30	2.32

half of the subjects were given the expectancy prior to presentation of the behaviors, whereas the other half received the expectancy afterward. After presentation of the behaviors, subjects estimated the frequency of the five classes of behaviors and recalled the specific items within each category. These results are presented in Table 5.2.

Inasmuch as the results for frequency estimates and recall parallel each other exactly, we will discuss only the data for recall. It is apparent that memory for instances of behavior is better when subjects expect those behaviors than when they do not. Thus, when subjects held an expectancy *prior* to presentation of the items, they recalled behaviors significantly better when those behaviors were confirming ($M = 4.79$) than when those same behavioral items were not relevant to the expectancy ($M = 4.04$). There were no such effects when the expectancies were given *after* the presentation of the items. Recall for items was no better when there were disconfirming ($M = 1.26$) than when they were irrelevant ($M = 1.32$).

Because it is possible that the failure to find heightened recall for disconfirming items could be due to the very small number of disconfirming items ($N = 3$ in each category), a second experiment was conducted in which the number of disconfirming items was increased to eight in each category, and the unrelated items were deleted from the list (Rothbart & Evans, 1980). Recall of these items is presented in Table 5.3.

Although the effect is somewhat reduced, there is again significantly greater recall for items when they are confirming ($M = 4.41$) than when they are irrelevant ($M = 3.92$), but again recall is not better for items when they are disconfirming ($M = 2.66$) than when they are irrelevant ($M = 2.97$). In fact, in both experiments there is a very slight tendency to remember a given set of items *less* well when they disconfirm an expectancy than when they are irrelevant to the expectancy.

Because the experiments tend to show strong evidence of superior memory for *confirming* events (with no evidence of heightened recall for disconfirming events), and because superior memory for confirming events is specific to the conditions where the expectancy is prior to rather than subsequent to the presentation of the items, the data were interpreted as being congruent with the idea of encoding specificity (Tulving & Thompson, 1973). As we interpret the applicability of this idea, an expectancy may act to establish or activate a category label (e.g., "intelligence"), so that subsequent confirming events (e.g., "straight-A student"), are encoded as category instances; that is, specific exemplars are "tagged" with the category label when stored in memory. When a subject is later asked to recall specific events, the category label can be used as an efficient retrieval cue for category instances. Items not encoded with a common tag or label would be stored in a more diffuse manner, ultimately making retrieval more difficult.

It should be noted, however, that Hastie and Kumar (1979) have found that when subjects are given an *equal* number of confirming and disconfirming instances (in their case, in relation to an expectancy about a single person), there was evidence for slightly greater recall of disconfirming items. Although there are several possible reasons for the discrepant results, there is one explanation that is of particular theoretical interest.

Consider the encoding specificity hypothesis described above, in which an activated category label stores relevant items in a functionally localized area and later serves as a retrieval cue. If it is true that the activation of a superordinate category label facilitates recall of category instances, it is important to ask how such a category label becomes activated. In the present research, categories were activated by the experimenter's instructions. But subjects obviously are extremely good at abstracting common properties from clusters of similar items (Posner & Keele, 1968, 1970) and are able to recognize (and generate labels for) clusters in a list (it probably did not take subjects in our friendly expectancy condition very long to realize there was also a set of items related to "intelligence"). The likelihood that a given category label will be activated, then, will certainly depend on the relative and absolute number of category instances and the salience of a given cluster in relation to other clusters in the list. Thus, subjects in the Hastie and Kumar experiments would be far more likely to form a category for disconfirming items, due to both the relatively large number of items in that cluster and the fact that there were only one or two other categories of items in their experiments. In our experiments, subjects would have been less likely to form a category for disconfirming items, because they were so few in number and there were four other categories of items present in the list. If this analysis is correct, it suggests that future research should pay careful attention to the context in which confirming and disconfirming items are embedded, inasmuch as it is unrealistic to assume that superior recall for confirming over disconfirming events (or vice versa) will be independent of those events' relative and absolute frequencies in the list, the number of categories or clusters in the list, and the experimental context.

The important point to be drawn from this work, however, is that activation of a category label, whether by direct instruction or context, structures *both* encoding and retrieval. Moreover, subjects' *judgments* about category frequency in turn appeared to be a function of category instances retrieved from memory (in accord with an availability heuristic). The processes of encoding, retrieval, and judgment thus appear to be closely interrelated, and it seems reasonable to expect that in natural settings the judgments that are made at one time may well structure the encoding and retrieval categories that are activated in comparable settings at later times. Thus judgment can structure, as well as be structured by, the categories used to encode behavior.

In an attempt to apply this analysis toward an understanding of intergroup perception and conflict, Howard and Rothbart (1980) argued that the widespread perception of ingroup superiority (discussed more fully in Chapter 7 by Wilder) may be attributable to the fact that ingroup–outgroup categorizations implicitly activate the expectancy that "we" are better than "they," and subjects selectively learn or remember ingroup and outgroup behaviors consistent with that expectancy. To test the hypothesis that ingroup–outgroup dichotomies are associated with the expectation of ingroup superiority, we used a procedure developed by Tajfel (1970) to create social categories in a minimal group situation. Subjects were categorized as under-or overestimators of dots and then asked to sort favorable and unfavorable behavior statements into the group that was most likely to have engaged in that behavior. According to prediction, subjects assigned more favorable than unfavorable behaviors to the ingroup. In a second experiment, different subjects were categorized as under-or overestimators of dots and then presented with favorable and unfavorable information (in a 2:1 ratio) associated with ingroup and outgroup members and later tested for recognition memory. Although there was no difference in the memory for favorable behaviors when paired with ingroup or outgroup, subjects remembered significantly more unfavorable outgroup behaviors than unfavorable ingroup behaviors. The research thus supported the hypothesis that implicit biases aroused by social categorization can transform information indicating equality between ingroup and outgroup into a "psychological" data base in which unfavorable outgroup behaviors are disproportionately represented.

Encoding of Behavior and the Generality of Labels.   One aspect of the previous expectancy experiments that warrants elaboration is the relationship between the trait labels and the behavioral exemplars. In the Rothbart, et al. (1979) research we chose two trait labels, intelligent and friendly, because we felt they had several useful properties: (1) it was possible to generate good confirming instances (e.g., "getting straight A's" or "inviting friends over for dinner''), as well as good disconfirming instances (''flunked out of school,'' ''avoided talking to his neighbors''); and (2) the behavioral domains that were delineated by these traits were reasonably circumscribed; that is, one could generate behavioral instances that were relevant to, say, intelligence, but irrelevant to friendliness. In other words, the traits we used had reasonably limited domains with fairly clear confirming and disconfirming referents.

But it would have been possible to pick other traits, for example, "devious" or "messy," in which both the size of the reference domain and the prevalence of disconfirming instances differed dramatically. Messiness refers to quite a limited domain of events but readily allows for potential disconfirmability. If I expect person X to be messy, and I repeatedly find his or her office and home to be neat and orderly, I eventually will decide that the label is incorrect. Contrast this trait with the trait "devious," which can refer to virtually every aspect of a person's social behavior and for which there may be no clearly disconfirmatory behaviors. Acts of apparent generosity, caring, or spontaneity on the part of X may serve only to confirm my impression of her or him as a devious and manipulative person. Indeed, in this case what behaviors can cause the label to be disconfirmed or repudiated?

In Rosenhan's (1973) study of the psychiatric staff's reactions to pseudopatients (normals who had been admitted to mental hospitals under false pretext), he notes the power of the labels "mentally ill" or "schizophrenic" to incorporate virtually any behavior, however normal the subjects may otherwise appear. In fact, when the pseudopatients were discharged, the original diagnostic label (schizophrenic) was not modified, but only temporarily suspended (schizophrenia, in remission). It is worth considering what kind of behaviors would negate some of the labels that are often applied to people who engage in deviant behavior, such as, schizophrenic, crazy, homicidal, or psychopathic. Although the behaviors that exemplify these labels are quite clear (hallucination, nonlogical thought and language, violent assaults, etc.), these labels have two interesting characteristics: (1) the confirming instances are usually infrequent in occurrence, as a consequence of which the *lack* of confirming behaviors does not negate the label; and (2) there are no actions that clearly *dis*confirm the label. Given these two characteristics, it is indeed easy to see why such labels, once attached, become very difficult to remove.

Trait labels are concepts and, as with other concepts, vary in their properties. We have suggested that trait concepts vary in at least three important ways: (1) their degree of generality (the number of events they refer to); (2) their "absorbing power" (the degree to which a variety of relevant instances can be assimilated into the label); and (3) temporal structure (the frequency with which relevant behaviors are expected to occur). Because traits vary dramatically on these attributes, it would be an error to assume that all traits can be treated as if they were equally disconfirmable. Clearly a great deal of further thought and research is needed on this problem.

Attention and Encoding.   Thus far we have been discussing the way in which information about an agent or behavior is encoded into memory. Inasmuch as there are numerous possible ways to categorize such information, there is *selectivity* occurring in the choice of categories. But there is also selectivity occurring at a more global level that affects the type of agents or behavior to which a person attends. In Taylor's experiments, reported elsewhere in this volume, she argues that the unique individual in a group, whether a single woman among men, or a single black among whites, is going to receive a disproportionate amount of attention, which in turn implies better memory for the solo's behavior as well as a more polarized view of the person's attributes.

There are undoubtedly many factors that determine which persons or behaviors are most attended to, not the least of which is the goal of the observer. But one factor that has attracted particular attention is the evaluative significance of the information. In a highly original analysis, Kanouse and Hanson (1971) speculated that the disproportionate influence of *negative* information in impression formation could be attributed to at least two different causes. The first can be called *motivational* in that there may be greater motivation to avoid negative consequences than to enhance positive consequences. The greater motivational power of negative events would then result in greater attention to, and learning of negative information (as suggested earlier in the bias to sample only bad driving). The second explanation can be called *informational,* and indicates that the power of negative events derives from their relative infrequency and hence their greater informational value.

Although there is no necessary relationship between negativity and infrequency, it has been observed that for many kinds of social stimuli (e.g., bipolar adjective pairs) negative events are less frequent than positive events (Zajonc, 1968). To attempt to assess the independent effects of desirability and frequency, Fulero and Rothbart (1980) selected personality traits previously scaled on social desirability (Anderson, 1968; Goldberg, 1974) and had them rated by college students as to their prevalence in the population (i.e., Of 100, 18- to 40-year-old men, how many would have this trait?''). Plotting social desirability against frequency, we found a correlation of +.51, confirming previous findings that negative events are seen as low frequency and positive events as high frequency. Eight target traits were then chosen from each of the four quadrants (low frequency–negative, low frequency–positive, high frequency–negative and high frequency–positive).

Each target trait, with 15 other traits, was then presented to subjects, and the entire set of traits was described as illustrating the attributes of a group of men. Subjects were later asked to judge how well each trait in the group could be used to describe the group as a whole.

The results were quite clear. Over a range of different *frequencies of presentation,* the undesirable target traits, quite irrespective of their base rates in the population, were more likely to be used to describe the group than were desirable target traits. The frequency of the traits in the population had no independent effect on subject's stereotypic judgments. Although much more work needs to be done on the question of frequency and negativity, these data clearly lend support to the motivational interpretation cited earlier.

Retrieval and Judgments

Memory Organization, Retrieval, and Judgment. Probably the clearest example of how the organization of information in memory influences retrieval is illustrated in the study by Anderson and Hastie (1974), in which an identity between two agents (e.g., John; a lawyer) is created either before or after information about the agents is learned. That is, if I learn that John engaged in acts A_1, A_2, and A_3, and a lawyer engaged in acts A_4, A_5, and A_6, and I then learn that John is a lawyer, the information is stored differently than if I learned at the outset that John is a lawyer, and then am presented with the acts $A_1 \ldots A_6$. Using reaction time to verify propositions (e.g., John did A_6) they found that a single node was created for John and lawyer when the identity was established prior to the information, whereas two nodes were generated when the identity was established afterward. Even when the identity was established afterward, it appeared that the acts associated with one agent (e.g., lawyers) do not automatically transfer to the other (John).

If information stored in memory is to be used in forming impressions of a group, that information must be retrieved, and it is possible that information organized in one way may be difficult to retrieve in another. Consider an example relevant to our earlier discussion of superordinate and subordinate categories. If information about a teenage women was stored only under the label "women," and we later tried to retrieve information associated with teenagers, it is likely that the information would be less available when searching for information associated with "teenagers." Thus the mode of storage may well be an important determinant of what information is available to memory and, obviously, the judgments that emanate from that information.

In a series of experiments by Rothbart, Fulero, Jensen, Howard, and Birrell (1978) it was argued that the information learned about individual group members may be organized in memory in different ways, and judgments about the characteristics of the group may vary according to that particular form of organization. For example, subjects who have repeated experiences with particular members of a group may organize their perceptions around individual group members or around the group as a whole. To see the implications of these two forms of organization, assume that a subject has contact with four Dallonians— Joe, Bill, Frank, and Jim—each of whom has a different trait. However, suppose Joe and Bill, who are described by negative traits, are observed twice, whereas Frank and Jim, who have positive traits, are observed only once. The two

ORGANIZATION BY INDIVIDUAL GROUP MEMBERS

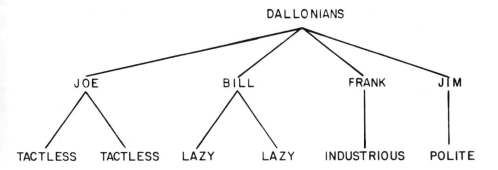

ORGANIZATION BY GROUP

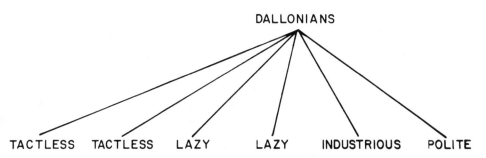

FIG. 5.1.   Two possible ways to organize trait information about four Dallonians, where two group members appear twice as often as the others (Reprinted from Rothbart, Fulero, Jensen, Howard, and Birrell, 1978).

possible types of organization resulting from these experiences are shown in Fig. 5.1. Note that the proportion of individual group members with undesirable traits is .50, whereas the proportion of times an undesirable trait appears (irrespective of whom it is paired with) is .67. Thus, if subjects organize this information around the group as a whole, ignoring which person goes with which trait, they subsequently will be unable to differentiate the repeated appearance of a trait in the same individual from the repeated appearance of that same trait in different individuals. Subjects would, in effect, be treating each occurrence of a trait as if it were an independent event and would form a more negative impression of Dallonians than would subjects who organized their perceptions around individual group members, who would be more likely to treat each *group member* as an independent event.

When subjects attempt to retrieve from memory information about the group, subjects who organized information around individuals will retrieve individual group members with their associated traits, whereas subjects who organized information around the group as a whole will retrieve only traits (without the associated persons).

Once events are retrieved from memory, subjects must use this information to estimate the predominant characteristics in the group. Tversky and Kahneman (1973) have argued that when subjects make frequency or probability judgments about a class of events, they use the availability of instances (from the class) as a cue to judging class frequency. The frequency with which an item is presented clearly influences its availability, and Tversky and Kahneman argue that subjects act as if the reverse were also true—that the availability of an item in memory is taken as an index of its frequency.

To return to the example illustrated in Fig. 5.1, this implies that for subjects who organize information around individual group members, Joe and Bill (both of whom have undesirable traits) will be more available than Frank and Jim (who possess desirable traits); for subjects who store only the traits, the attributes "tactless" and "lazy" are more available than the attributes "industrious" and "polite." When subjects are then asked to estimate the preponderance of undesirable *persons* in the group, subjects who organize information around the group can use only the relatively high availability of negative traits to conclude that undesirable persons predominate among Dallonians. However, subjects who organize information around individual group members have knowledge of both the traits and the persons who possess them. Thus, even though the two undesirable Dallonians (Joe and Bill) are most available to memory and therefore should be judged most frequently (if subjects are relying heavily on an availability heuristic), subjects may recall that some group members were presented more frequently than others and may be able to correct for this disproportionate sampling in their judgments about the group. Obviously, to the degree that subjects are able to make this adjustment or correction, they are able to modify, or at least attenuate, the effects of availability on frequency judgments.

Probably one of the strongest determinants of mnemonic organization is the demand on memory during the learning process. Clearly there are more demands on memory in learning which persons in a group possess a given trait than in learning which traits exist within the group (given an equal number of different traits in both conditions). It is expected that when there is a low demand on memory, subjects will be able to organize their perceptions of a group around its individual members and their attributes. Under high memory load, however, subjects may be more apt to organize their perceptions around the group as a whole (ignoring the origins of the traits). To test these hypotheses, subjects were presented with identical trait information about group members in a single- or multiple-exposure condition (see Fig. 5.2) and under a low memory load (16 trait presentations) or under a high memory load (64 trait presentations) condition.

In the *single*-exposure condition, each presentation of a trait was paired with a different stimulus person, and each stimulus person was presented only once. In the *multiple*-exposure condition, a given trait (e.g., "lazy") was paired with one and only one stimulus person, who was then presented a multiple number of times. As indicated in Fig. 5.2, the configuration of traits (content and frequency) was identical in both conditions.

The relative frequency of presentation of desirable and undesirable traits was also varied, holding constant the number of different desirable and undesirable traits. That is, in all conditions of the experiment, the *number* of desirable traits was always equal to the number of undesirable traits. However, desirable traits were presented either one third as often, or three times as often as undesirable traits. (For illustration, Fig. 5.2 shows two desirable and two undesirable traits, with the former presented less frequently than the latter.)

The extent to which subjects organize their perceptions around individuals or around the entire group could be inferred from their judgments of the *proportion of desirable* stimulus persons in the group. In the single-exposure condition, the proportion of desirable stimulus persons is identical to the relative frequency of presentation of desirable traits; in the multiple-exposure condition, however, the proportion of desirable stimulus persons remains constant across the three frequency conditions. Thus, if subjects organize their perceptions around group members, their judgments of the proportion of desirable stimulus persons should, in the multiple-exposure condition, be relatively constant as the relative frequency of presentation of desirable traits is increased, but should, in the single-exposure condition, increase with the relative frequency of presentation of desirable traits. However, if subjects are organizing their perceptions around the number of traits (rather than around group members), their judgments of the proportion of desirable stimulus persons should increase under *both* single- and multiple-exposure conditions as the relative frequency of presentation of desirable traits increases. Subjects' recall of desirable traits and their ratings of group attractiveness should parallel their estimates of the proportion of desirable stimulus persons (as would be predicted by the use of an availability heuristic).

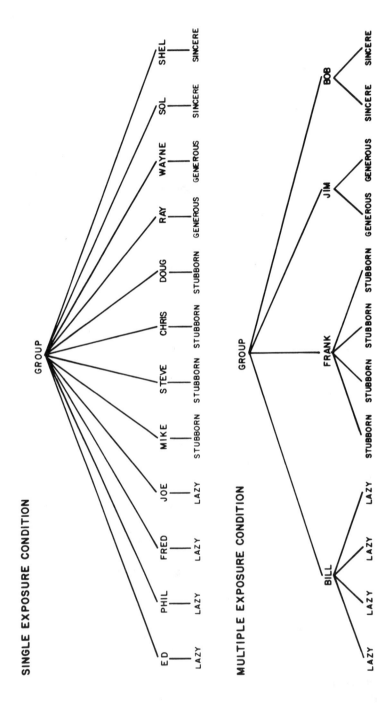

FIG. 5.2. Schematic description of name–trait pairings, where either each presentation of a trait corresponds to a different stimulus person (single-exposure condition), or a given trait is repeatedly paired with the same stimulus person (multiple-exposure condition). Reprinted from Rothbart, Fulero, Jensen, Howard, and Birrell, 1978.

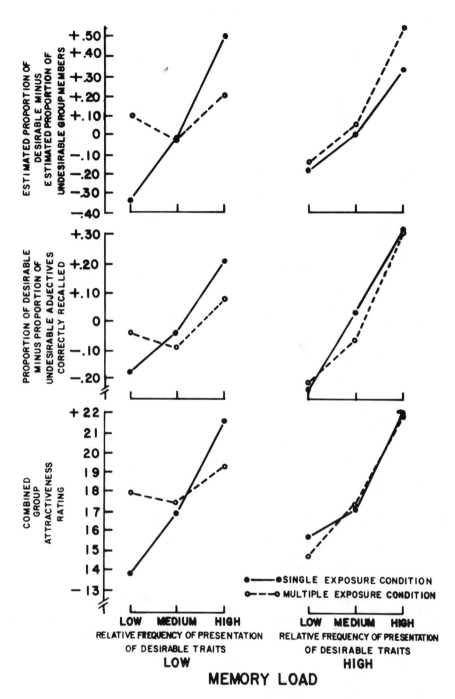

FIG. 5.3. Frequency estimates, recall, and judged attractiveness as a function of memory load, relative frequency of presentation of desirable traits, and number of exposures of stimulus persons (Reprinted from Rothbart, Fulero, Jensen, Howard, and Birrell, 1978).

Fig. 5.3 shows subjects' estimates of the proportion of desirable and undesirable stimulus persons, recall for desirable and undesirable traits, and their judged attractiveness of the group. As is apparent from this figure, under high memory load, where subjects are expected to organize traits in a way that is undifferentiated with respect to specific group members, they do not differentiate between a condition in which a given trait (e.g., lazy) appears only once but with several different persons (the single-exposure condition) from a condition in which the trait appears with only one person, but that person is presented several times (the multiple-exposure condition).

Under conditions of low memory load, where subjects are expected to organize traits around the individual group members, they clearly distinguish between a condition in which a person with a given trait appears several times (multiple exposure), and a condition in which several different persons have the same trait (single exposure).

These results suggest that the tendency to infer the characteristics of the group from the availability of particular traits to memory depends in part on how the information is organized in memory. Under conditions of overload, where there is dissociation between the agent and the trait, subjects seem to rely on the most available trait (irrespective of whether it was originally associated with a single person repeatedly presented or several persons presented only once) in forming judgments about the group. However, under minimal load conditions, the availability of the trait is clearly not the only determinant of how subjects use the information from memory in forming a judgment about the group.

Under real life conditions, when the number of encounters with members of a group is high and/or the encounters have occurred under conditions in which there are other significant demands on memory, the setting most approximates that of our high memory load condition. Under these circumstances we would expect peoples' impressions of a group to be influenced by the most available (most memorable) traits or behaviors, uncorrected for correlated occurrences (multiple presentations of the same individual[s]). Under high load, repeated experiences with a subgroup of, say, noxious individuals may disproportionately influence the perception of the entire group, whereas under a low load, these experiences would be correctly assigned to those members and not necessarily attributed to the group as a whole.

We conducted two other experiments to test further the idea that the attributes of a group are disproportionately influenced by its most memorable constituents. If it is true that the most memorable instances are disproportionately weighted in our impressions of a group, then the obvious question is, "What factors influence the memorability of social behaviors or attributes?" There is reason to believe that extreme instances, by virtue of their novelty, dramatic quality, or importance should be particularly memorable and influential in our impressions of groups. If this is true, it may clarify an important source of error in our perceptions of groups, inasmuch as people would be inclined to view infrequent and extreme individuals as typical or representative of the group.

Previous research on the effects of extreme instances in impression formation has demonstrated that highly evaluatively polarized events carry more weight in impression formation than do events that are less evaluatively extreme (Leon, Oden, & Anderson, 1973; Manis, Gleason, & Dawes, 1966). There is no evidence, however, that the frequency of extreme events is perceived to be greater than that of mild events. Moreover, past research, by using stimulus materials that have clear evaluative significance, has confounded extremity with hedonic relevance.

We designed an experiment to see whether subjects would estimate the frequency of individuals with extreme *physical* attributes to be greater than the frequency of equal numbers of individuals with less extreme physical attributes (Rothbart et al., 1978).

Subjects were presented with the height, in feet and inches, of each person in a group of 50 men. For all subjects, the frequency distribution for height had a mean of 5 ft 10 in., and 20% of the group were over 6 ft in height. For half of the subjects the stimulus persons over 6 ft were only slightly over 6 ft (mild condition), whereas for the other subjects, the stimulus persons were considerably over 6 ft (extreme condition). After being presented with the heights of 50 men in succession, subjects were asked to estimate the number (or proportion) of stimulus persons over 6 ft in height.

In accord with the prediction, subjects in the extreme group gave significantly higher estimates of the number of stimulus persons over 6 ft $(\bar{X}_{mild} = 10.53, \bar{X}_{extreme} = 14.95; F(1, 73) = 13.12, p < .001)$.

Another experiment was conducted to determine whether we could obtain the same overestimation of extreme instances using social rather than physical stimuli (Rothbart et al., 1978). Moreover, although the data from the previous experiment are consistent with the availability hypothesis, it was not meaningful to obtain recall measures for the different heights to determine whether recall and frequency data covaried. In this experiment it was possible to obtain both frequency estimates and recall data.

Using a direct analogue of the previous experimental paradigm, subjects were presented with 50 statements, each depicting a behavior engaged in by a different man. For all subjects, 40 of the statements depicted either mildly favorable, neutral, or mildly unfavorable behaviors. The remaining 10 behaviors depicted an act considered by pilot subjects to be criminal. The criminal acts shown to half the experimental subjects were relatively nonserious (shoplifting, vandalism), whereas those shown to the other half were quite serious (murder, rape). After being presented with the series of 50 behaviors, subjects were asked to estimate the frequency of criminal acts and to recall as many of the acts as they could.

After each behavior was presented, subjects were asked how many of these men "engaged in a criminal behavior" and then to recall the criminal activities.

In accord with the prediction, estimates of the number of people who engaged in criminal activity were greater for the extreme than for the mild condition $(\bar{X}_{mild} = 12.37, \bar{X}_{extreme} = 15.43, F(1, 153) = 9.71, p < .002)$. The recall data (coded by a rater ignorant of the hypothesis) also showed the predicted effect ($\overline{X}_{\text{mild}}$ = 5.62, X_{extreme} = 6.43, $F(1, 153)$ = 8.35, $p < .01$).

Both experiments strongly suggest that individuals with extreme characteristics were more memorable and, due to their availability in memory, were estimated as more frequent than corresponding numbers of "mild" individuals. More generally, these experiments indicate that our impressions of groups may be disproportionately influenced by the characteristics of the group's most memorable constituents.

The findings of these experiments have particular relevance for understanding the effects of the mass media on stereotype formation. Because much of our information about minority groups is filtered through the news media, and because the information usually defined as newsworthy represents extreme forms of behavior, repeated exposure of extreme individuals will lead to an overrepresentation of extreme behaviors in our images of these groups. Further, the overestimation of extreme instances may interact with ingroup or outgroup status, inasmuch as extreme instances of ingroup behavior may be counterbalanced by all the other information we have about our ingroup, whereas our relative ignorance and less differentiated view of the outgroup may lead us to accept extreme instances of outgroup behaviors as highly representative.

The experiments may also shed some light on the predominance of *unfavorable* group stereotypes. Kanouse and Hanson (1971) have suggested that because the most prevalent life outcomes are moderately favorable, favorable outcomes are comparatively less extreme than unfavorable outcomes (by virtue of favorable outcomes being closer to our normative experiences); thus it is the deviant negative behaviors rather than the deviant positive behaviors that are likely to be overrepresented in the stereotype.

It remains to be solved whether the superior memory for extreme events is attributable to hedonic value or infrequency, although the Fulero and Rothbart (1980) experiment cited earlier lends support to the hedonic interpretation.

Marginal Frequencies, Availability, and Illusory Correlation.   As indicated in the chapter by Hamilton, our perception of a group's attributes may be a consequence of illusory correlation; that is, an overestimation of the co-occurrence of particular pairs of events. In the original studies by Chapman and Chapman (1967) on illusory correlation, the co-occurrence of anal signs and homosexuality on the Rorshach were consistently overestimated, presumably because they were, as Tversky and Kahneman (1973) have since argued, more "available" as a pair than: (1) anal signs with other symptoms; or (2) the symptom of homosexuality with other signs.

In one of the first studies of the effects of cognitive processes on intergroup perception, Hamilton and Gifford (1976) argued that one dimension along which events could be paired is that of infrequency; that is, two events sharing the same attributes of infrequency could be erroneously perceived as "going together" (co-occurring). In attempting to account for the negative perceptions of minority groups, Hamilton and Gifford reasoned that this may be an instance where an infrequent class of individuals (minority group members) is paired with an infrequent class of behaviors (socially undesirable behavior), and the co-occurrence of these two classes of events is then overestimated. Hamilton and Gifford then presented subjects with contrived pairs of events in which either a desirable or undesirable behavior was associated with a person from a large (*A*) or a small (*B*) group. There were always twice as many *A*'s as *B*'s and the ratio of favorable to unfavorable behaviors was 9:4 (or 4:9). In two experiments, subjects overestimated the co-occurrence of the smaller group (*B*) with the less frequent behavior (whether undesirable or desirable); moreover, subjects' judgments about the attributes of the smaller group were consistent with their overestimates (i.e., when negative behaviors were overestimated, the group was judged more negatively, and when positive behaviors were overestimated, the group was judged more positively).

It is clear that their subjects perceived an illusory correlation between a group· and a set of attributes. The explanation offered by Hamilton and Gifford for this illusory correlation is that the least frequent events are going to be most distinctive and therefore better learned than the less distinctive events. In other words, the cell in the fourfold table associated with the less frequent behaviors for the smaller group is going to be the most distinctive, better learned, and most available in forming group impressions.

An alternative interpretation, based on an availability heuristic, is also consistent with Hamilton and Gifford's findings and may provide a general explanation for the prevalence of illusory correlation when both marginal frequencies are highly skewed.

Consider again the fourfold table contrived by Hamilton and Gifford in Table 5.4 (where the cells are drawn proportional to their size).

TABLE 5.4.
Contrived Frequencies in the Hamilton and Gifford Experiments
(Cell Size Drawn Proportional to Frequencies)

	Dominant Group (A)	Minority Group (B)	
Frequent behaviors (e.g., positive)	18	9	27
Infrequent behaviors (e.g., negative)	8	4	12
	26	13	39

TABLE 5.5.

Hypothetical Data Relating Ingroup and Outgroup Membership to
Favorability of Behavior, in Which Ingroup Members Are More
Frequent Than Outgroup Members, and Good Behaviors Are More
Frequent Than Bad Behaviors
(Cell Size Drawn Proportional to Frequencies)

		Ingroup	Outgroup	
	Good	72	8	80
Behaviors	Bad	18	2	20
		90	10	100

If we ask which pairs of instances are going to be most available to memory, we can reasonably assert that it would be the most frequent category; in this instance it would be the cell containing positive behaviors associated with members of the *A* group. In fact, inasmuch as fully 46% of all pairings occur in this category, it is not unreasonable to assume that these instances are most available and that subjects would judge *A* to be comparatively more favorable than *B*—exactly the findings obtained by Hamilton and Gifford.[2] Note that this alternative interpretation does not question the finding of an illusory correlation but does raise the possibility of another interpretation of that finding. I mention this interpretation because the Hamilton and Gifford study, in addition to being extraordinarily interesting in its own right, is the only study I know of where subjects provide frequency estimates of a contingency table in which: (1) both marginals are skewed; and (2) there is no correlation between the two variables.

What I would like to argue now is that one of the classic problems in the area of judgment, the perception of contingencies in the absence of true correlation, may be understood as a case in which an imbalance in the marginal frequency leads to a preponderance of instances in particular cells and to a corresponding availability of those instances to memory.

Attempts to account for illusory correlation, or the overestimation of co-occurring events, have relied on such principles as strength of association between events (Chapman, 1967), the availability of associations (Tversky & Kahneman 1973), or the similarity of events along some physical or semantic dimension (Hamilton & Gifford, 1976; Schweder, 1977). But it is also possible

[2]The differences between this interpretation and the one offered by Hamilton and Gifford is that they would predict superior memory in the smallest cell whereas this explanation would predict superior memory in the largest cell—both predictions that are readily testable.

that the structure of the data itself can lead to the perception of a correlation in the absence of a real contingency.

Consider the problem of ethnocentrism, or the perception of ingroup superiority, in which we have come to associate favorable behaviors with the ingroup. Let us assume that we are nine times as likely to interact with ingroup members as with outgroup members (a not unreasonable assumption, given the definition of ingroups and outgroups) and that we experience favorable interactions four times as often as unfavorable interactions (also a reasonable assumption, given that we actively structure our world to achieve positive experiences). Consider now the data presented in Table 5.5, and see how difficult it is *not* to perceive a correlation between group status and favorability of behavior. Of course, the likelihood of good behavior is no greater for the ingroup than for the outgroup, but fully 72% of *all* instances are examples of good behaviors associated with the ingroup. Given the imbalance in the marginal frequencies, the resulting inequality in cell size, and the use of an availability heuristic in estimating quantity, it is not surprising that people will infer a relationship in the absence of differences in conditional probabilities.

EXPECTANCIES, POSITIVE FEEDBACK, AND CHANGE IN BELIEFS

In the first section of this chapter, I made a comparison between what people ought to do and what they normally do in testing their social beliefs, and I have argued that a central difference between the two modes of thought resides in the separation of discovery and proof. Whereas hypothesis and verification must be independent in scientific thought, there is a continual and pervasive interplay among people's expectancies and the "data" that pertain to those expectancies. As Walter Lippmann (1922) has stated in the context of stereotypes: "(It) stamps itself upon the evidence in the very act of securing that evidence [p. 99]."

The effect of this nonindependence is a self-confirmatory system that, through its inertia, creates stability (more than actually exists) and a lack of responsiveness to disconfirming information. Until now, I have probably given the impression that the lack of independence between hypothesis and verification, and the resulting self-confirmatory bias, represents an inferior mode of thought. However, consider what the world would be like if prior expectancies did not structure new information. The amount of cognitive effort that would be required to treat every new stimulus as unique would lead us to be overwhelmed by events and would render us virtually immobile in a world that requires action.

Given the bias toward self-confirmation, a centrally important question now arises as to how beliefs can be altered. We have already discussed the possibility that different beliefs or expectancies have different degrees of "absorbing power''; that is, some beliefs may be able to absorb diverse and numerous instances as confirming, whereas other beliefs may have a limited domain and also be specific enough to define clear disconfirming instances. Attributions of homicidal, schizophrenic, or crazy refer to *potential* behaviors that may be extremely infrequent (an act of homicide may have to occur only once over a lifetime in order to justify the label ''homicidal''), and therefore the absence of the relevant behavior over even a long period of time does not constitute disconfirming evidence for the label. It is not surprising that some constellations of beliefs, such as paranoia, are virtually impossible to modify by evidentiary assault (Colby, 1975), inasmuch as there is very little evidence that *could* be disconfirming.

On the other hand, there are concepts that are amenable to disconfirmation, and the research by Hamilton and Bishop (1976), discussed in the chapter by Rose, constitutes an important field research on this problem. They found that whites' attitudes toward a new black family in the neighborhood became more positive over time even though there was no contact with the family, presumably because the *absence* of socially undesirable behaviors disconfirmed the expectancy that the black family was going to cause trouble for their white neighbors. This is one instance in which the *absence* of a behavior was apparently sufficient to change people's attitudes.

Although an understanding of how beliefs can be disconfirmed is fundamental for the development of an adequate theory of beliefs, we know very little about this problem. I would like to offer two ideas that may be useful in thinking about the disconfirmation process. The first idea relates to people's use of confirming and disconfirming instances in modifying their beliefs. Consider two possible theoretical models, one deliberate, methodical, and predictable in nature (the ''bookkeeping'' model), and the other somewhat erratic, impulsive, and unpredictable in character (the ''converson'' model). The bookkeeping model would suggest that people implicitly monitor the number of confirming and disconfirming instances, periodically comparing the difference, ratio, or proportion of these two types of events and, on the basis of this discrepancy, retain or reject the belief in question. It assumes that there is continual awareness of and monitoring of the status of the belief and implies, I believe, that the slow accrual of (roughly) equally weighted disconfirming instances eventually can overwhelm the confirming instances and lead to a repudiation of the belief.

In contrast, the ''conversion'' view implies instead that change is more catastrophic than gradual and that a few highly salient, critical instances play a dominant role in the disconfirmation process. Although I know of no data at present that would support one view rather than the other, I tend to favor the conversion model, viewing it as an extension of the reasoning we have used to explain the discrepancy between the Hastie and Kumar (1979) experiments and our own. Recall that our interpretation of the Hastie and Kumar experiments was that subjects became clearly aware of the disconfirming instances and could tag the specific instances with the disconfirming label, allowing efficient retrieval at a later time. This was in contrast to our own research, where the disconfirming instances were less salient to subjects and may have failed to activate a label or tag for disconfirming instances.

The argument I wish to make is that disconfirming instances may be particularly potent when people are aware of a powerful discrepancy between what they expect and what they obtain. This discrepancy view implies that the power of a particular instance to disconfirm a belief does not reside solely in the characteristics of the disconfirming instance but exists as well in the conscious expectancies (or lack of them) when confronting that instance. The critical assumption of this view is the subject's awareness of the discrepancy; if, for one reason or another, the subject is not aware that he or she holds a particular expectancy, the disconfirming instance will have little effect. Although this hypothesis appears trivial, I don't think it is. It is not unlike the psychoanalytic assumption that unconscious expectancies are difficult to disconfirm as long as they are unconscious; events that are potentially capable of disconfirming the expectancies are not perceived as disconfirming and thus do not alter the belief. Certainly the history of science is replete with examples of events that are perceived as unimportant or irrelevant until someone is able to articulate explicitly the discrepancy between the event and contemporary beliefs. One implication of this model is that heightened awareness of an expectancy will increase the power of disconfirming events, and this is an idea we are currently attempting to test.

The second general idea about disconfirmation is related to the view of Rosch (1977), who has argued that the categories we use to segment the natural world are *not* arbitrary but have utility in grouping together stimuli with common attributes. Clearly this view implies that as the nature of the world changes, the categories also will change. If 20 years ago I expected women to be housewives, I would not have had many disconfirming examples and "housewife" may have been a predictable attribute associated with the category "women." Although the change is not as great as desired, there clearly are more examples of doctors, lawyers, and teachers among women to cause the category "women" to become much less homogeneous with respect to associated behaviors and less useful as a category label. As I argued earlier, categories have utility, and when they lose their utility they would, with some degree of inertia to be sure, be expected to change.

It is important to add, however, that the categories would be expected to change in response to changes in the external world, and it is less reasonable to expect them to change solely as a result of moral admonition. For this reason, it can be argued that if we wish to change our stereotypes of female and black inferiority, we would do well to change *first* their inferior social and economic status.

CONCLUDING COMMENT

At the beginning of this chapter, I emphasized an important distinction in science between discovery and proof or between hypothesis and verification—distinctions that I labeled Stage I and Stage II—and I then proceeded to argue that the mind, in its efforts to develop internal structures that represent the external world, blurs that distinction. Whereas science insists that hypothesis and proof be independent, the mind integrates the two processes.

A psychological model of belief formation and maintenance was proposed, based on five hypotheses: (1) evidence pertaining to a particular belief is drawn from relevant instances in memory; (2) biases in the relevant instances are a natural consequence of biases in the encoding and/or retrieval processes; (3) although encoding, retrieval, and judgment are discrete processes, each of which critically influences the nature of social beliefs, the three processes interact in a dynamic way to influence one another; (4) this interaction creates a self-confirming system in which there is considerable inertia in response to discrepant information; and (5) despite the bias toward self-confirmation, disconfirming information may significantly alter existing beliefs under highly specified conditions.

In attempting to answer the question as to why the mind does not clearly separate hypothesis and verification, I have suggested that there are clear advantages to a system that is biased toward constancy; it allows for efficiency in not having to treat each new piece of information as unique. But there is an additional point to be made that is in some way the converse of the argument made by Einhorn and Hogarth (1978). They have argued that action biases the available information in the direction of confirmation. I would argue that the need for action demands that we choose one response alternative over another, and that demand often requires the use of data that may be quantitatively and qualitatively deficient. No rational person would choose a spouse solely on the basis of his or her first name (Wilde's play notwithstanding), but if we had no other information about a potential spouse *except* a first name, wouldn't there be agreement that Eric and Samantha are more exciting than Bill and Jane?

The exigencies of living often require decisions when there is inadequate information, and although we may utilize all conceivably relevant information in making a decision under uncertainty, the dangers inherent in this process are clear: We may generate expedient categories and groupings that simplify events for the purposes of reaching an immediate decision, but those expectancies then may be validated by the self-confirming processes we have already described.

Despite their self-perpetuating nature, however, beliefs occasionally do appear to change in response to external events, and the important question that remains is whether the inertia in modifying human beliefs is so great as to allow major misrepresentations of the world to be retained indefinitely. Walter Lippman (1922) said it best:

For the real environment is altogether too big, too complex, and too fleeting for direct acquaintance. We are not equipped to deal with so much subtlety, so much variety, so many permutations and combinations. And although we have to act in that environment, we have to reconstruct it on a simpler model before we can manage with it. To traverse the world, men must have maps of the world. Their persistent difficulty is to secure maps on which their own need, or someone else's need, has not sketched on the coast of Bohemia [p. 16].

ACKNOWLEDGMENTS

This research was supported by grant number SOC 75–16133 from the National Science Foundation. I am indebted to Sheldon Cohen, Ray Hyman, and Mary Rothbart for their comments and am particularly grateful to Robyn Dawes, Hillel Einhorn, and Dave Hamilton for their careful, critical assessment of an earlier draft of this chapter.

REFERENCES

Allport, G. W., & Kramer, B. M. Some roots of prejudice. *Journal of Psychology,* 1946, *22,* 9–39.
Allport, G. W., & Postman, L. *The psychology of rumor.* New York: H. Holt & Co., 1947.
Anderson, J., & Hastie, R. Individuation and reference in memory: Proper names and definite descriptions. *Cognitive Psychology,* 1974, *6,* 495–514.
Anderson, N. H. Likableness ratings of 555 personality-trait words. *Journal of Personality and Social Psychology,* 1968, *9,* 272–279.
Asch, S. E. Forming impressions of personality. *Journal of Abnormal and Social Psychology,* 1946, *41,* 258–290.
Campbell, D. Stereotypes and the perception of group differences. *American Psychologist,* 1967, *22,* 817–829.
Chapman, L. J. Illusory correlation in observational report. *Journal of Verbal Learning & Verbal Behavior.* 1967, *6,* 151–155.
Chapman, L. J., & Chapman, J. P. Genesis of popular but erroneous psychodiagnostic observations. *Journal of Abnormal Psychology,* 1967, *72,* 193–204.
Chapman, L. J., & Chapman, J. P. Illusory correlation as an obstacle to the use of valid psychodiagnostic signs. *Journal of Abnormal Psychology,* 1969, *74,* 271–280.
Colby, K. M. *Artificial paranoia: A computer simulation of paranoid processes.* New York: Pergamon Press, 1975.
Duncan, B. L. Differential social perception and attribution of intergroup violence: Testing the lower limits of stereotyping of blacks. *Journal of Personality and Social Psychology,* 1976, *34,* 590–598.
Einhorn, H. J., & Hogarth, R. M. Confidence in judgment: Persistence of the illusion of validity. *Psychological Review,* 1978, *85,* 395–416.
Estes, W. K. The cognitive side of probability learning. *Psychological Review,* 1976, *83,* 37–64.
Fulero, S., & Rothbart, M. *Encoding individual traits into group stereotypes: The effects of frequency and desirability of trait descriptors.* Manuscript in preparation, 1980.
Goldberg, L. R. *Toward a taxonomy of personality trait terms: Round V.* Unpublished manuscript. Oregon Research Institute, 1974.
Hamilton, D. L., & Bishop, G. D. Attitudinal and behavioral effects of initial integration of white suburban neighborhoods. *Journal of Social Issues,* 1976, *32,* 47–67.

Hamilton, D. L., & Gifford, R. K. Illusory correlation in interpersonal perception: A cognitive basis of stereotypic judgments. *Journal of Experimental Social Psychology*, 1976, *12*, 392–407.

Hastie, R., & Kumar, P. A. Person memory: Personality traits as organizing principles in memory for behaviors. *Journal of Personality and Social Psychology*, 1979, *37*, 25–38.

Hovland, C. I., & Weiss, W. The influence of source credibility on communication effectiveness. *Public Opinion Quarterly*, 1952, *15*, 635–650.

Howard, J., & Rothbart, M. Social categorization and memory for ingroup and outgroup behavior. *Journal of Personality and Social Psychology*, 1980, *38*, 301–310.

Jenkins, H. M., & Ward, W. C. Judgment of contingency between responses and outcomes. *Psychological Monographs: General and Applied*, 1965, *79*, 1–17.

Kanouse, D. E., & Hanson, L. R. Negativity in evaluations. In E. E. Jones, D. E. Kanouse, H. H. Kelley, R. E. Nisbett, S. Valins, & B. Weiner, (Eds.), *Attribution: Perceiving the causes of behavior.* Morristown, N.J.: General Learning Press, 1971

Kelley, H. H. The warm–cold variable in first impressions of persons. *Journal of Personality*, 1950, *18*, 431–439.

Kelley, H. H., & Stahelski, A. J. Social interaction basis of cooperators' and competitors' beliefs about others. *Journal of Personality and Social Psychology*, 1970, *16*, 66–91.

Leon, M., Oden, G. C., & Anderson, N. H. Functional measurement of social values. *Journal of Personality and Social Psychology*, 1973, *27*, 301–310.

Lippmann, W. *Public opinion.* New York: The Macmillan Co., 1922 (Reprinted 1961).

Lorge, I. Prestige, suggestion, and attitudes. *Journal of Social Psychology*, 1936, *7*, 386–402.

Manis, M., Gleason, T. C., & Dawes, R. M. The evaluation of complex social stimuli. *Journal of Personality and Social Psychology*, 1966, *3*, 404–419.

McCauley, C., & Stitt, C. L. An individual and quantitative measure of stereotypes. *Journal of Personality and Social Psychology*, 1978, *36*, 929–940.

Morlock, H. The effect of outcome desirability on information required for decisions. *Behavioral Science*, 1967, *12*, 296–300.

Peabody, D. Group judgments in the Philippines: Evaluative and descriptive aspects. *Journal of Personality and Social Psychology*, 1968 *10*, 290–300.

Posner, M. I., & Keele, S. W. Retention of abstract ideas. *Journal of Experimental Psychology*, 1970, *83*, 304–308.

Posner, M. I., & Keele, S. W. On the genesis of abstract ideas. *Journal of Experimental Psychology*, 1968, *77*, 353–363.

Reichenbach, H. *The rise of scientific philosophy*, Berkeley, Calif.: University of California Press, 1951.

Rosch, E. Human categorization. In N. Warren (Ed.), *Advances in crosscultural psychology* (Vol 1). London: Academic Press, 1977.

Rosenhan, D. L. On being sane in insane places. *Science*, 1973, *179*, 250–258.

Rothbart, M., & Birrell, P. Attitude and the perception of faces. *Journal of Research in Personality*, 1977, *11*, 209–215.

Rothbart, M., & Evans, M. Replication of "Recall for Confirming Events." Unpublished manuscript: University of Oregon, 1980.

Rothbart, M., Evans, M., & Fulero, S. Recall for confirming events: Memory processes and the maintenance of social stereotypes. *Journal of Experimental Social Psychology*, 1979, *15*, 343–355.

Rothbart, M., Fulero, S., Jensen, C., Howard, J., & Birrell, P. From individual to group impressions: Availability heuristics in stereotype formation. *Journal of Experimental Social Psychology*, 1978, *14*, 237–255.

Sartre, J. P. *Anti-Semite and Jew.* New York: Schocken Press, 1948.

Schweder, R. A. Likeness and likelihood in everyday thought: Magical thinking in judgments about personality. *Current Anthropology*, 1977, *18*, 637–658.

Smedslund, J. The concept of correlation in adults. *Scandinavian Journal of Psychology*, 1963, *4*, 165–173.

Tajfel, H. Experiments in Intergroup Discrimination. *Scientific American*, 1970, *223*, 96–102.

Tulving, E., & Thomson, D. M. Encoding specificity and retrieval processes in episodic memory. *Psychological Review*, 1973, 80, 352–373.

Tversky, A., & Kahneman, D. Belief in the law of small numbers. *Psychological Bulletin*, 1971, *76*, 105–110.

Tversky, A., & Kahneman, D. Judgment under uncertainty: Heuristics and biases: *Science*, 1974, *185*, 1124–1131.

Tversky, A., & Kahneman, D. Availability: A heuristic for judging frequency and probability. *Cognitive Psychology*, 1973, *5*, 207–232.

Zajonc, R. B. Attitudinal effects of mere exposure. *Journal of Personality and Social Psychology Monograph*, 1968, *9*, 1–27.

6

On the Self-Perpetuating
Nature of Social Stereotypes

Mark Snyder
University of Minnesota

It is a basic fact of social life that we form impressions of other individuals whom we encounter in our day-to-day lives. In our relationships with others, we seem to want to know not only what they do but why they do what they do. To the extent that we think we understand the global attributes that underlie the specific actions of other people, we may feel better able to understand their actions and to predict their future behavior. Moreover, we may use these beliefs to guide our behavioral interactions with them.

Almost without exception, students of the processes of person perception and social cognition have endorsed the view that these perceptual and cognitive activities serve to stabilize, make predictable, and make manageable the individual's view of the social world. One consequence of this quest to see others as stable and predictable creatures is the creation of social stereotypes. In stereotyping, the individual: (1) categorizes other individuals, usually on the basis of highly visible characteristics such as sex or race; (2) attributes a set of characteristics to all members of that category; and (3) attributes that set of characteristics to any individual member of that category. Stereotypes are usually simple, overgeneralized, and widely accepted.

There is no denying the existence of social stereotypes. For examples, there exist stereotypes about sex, age, race, ethnicity, national origin, bodily appearance, religion, sexual orientation, occupation, political affiliation, and social class. But, stereotypes are often highly inaccurate. It is simply not true that all Germans are hardworking and industrious, that all women are dependent and conforming, that all physically attractive people have good personalities, that all lesbians have "masculine" personalities, that all Jews are materialistic, or that all professors are liberals. However, as we shall see, even erroneous stereotypes may profoundly affect the course of social interaction and interpersonal relationships.

This chapter is concerned with the processes by which one individual's initially erroneous stereotyped beliefs about another person (a "target") can and do exert powerful channeling influences on subsequent thought and social interaction. Specifically, this chapter is concerned with two sets of processes: (1) those by which current stereotyped beliefs influence the individual's attempts to remember and interpret previously learned information about the target; and (2) those by which current stereotyped beliefs influence the dynamics and the outcomes of subsequent social interaction between the individual and the target. The series of empirical investigations to be reviewed in this chapter converge on the following assertions. An individual, having adopted stereotyped beliefs about a target, will: (1) remember and interpret past events in the target's life history in ways that bolster and support these current stereotyped beliefs; and (2) will act upon these current stereotyped beliefs in ways that cause the actual behavior of the target to confirm and validate the individual's stereotyped beliefs about the target.

As consequences of these processes, even those stereotypes that are erroneous in the general case may perpetuate themselves by defining and creating their own social reality in the context of specific interpersonal relationships. By virtue of their involvement in *reconstructing the past* and *constructing the future,* stereotypes may generate for themselves both *cognitive bolstering* and *behavioral confirmation.* To some extent, it will be argued, these processes may help us to understand why so many widely held but clearly erroneous social and cultural stereotypes are so stubbornly resistant to change.

RECONSTRUCTING THE PAST: COGNITIVE BOLSTERING OF SOCIAL STEREOTYPES

Can and do stereotyped beliefs influence attempts to remember and interpret previously learned factual events in another person's life history? At least two sources of evidence suggest an affirmative answer to this question. The first source is case histories in the sociology of deviance; the second source, basic research on the process of remembering.

Labeling and Remembering

Sociologists concerned with the social labeling of deviance have provided observational and case history evidence for a process of retrospective interpretation by which the past may be used as a source of evidence with which to bolster, rationalize, and justify current labels of deviance (for a review, see Schur, 1971). For example, Kitsuse (1962) interviewed 75 people who claimed that they knew a homosexual individual (one can only infer from Kitsuse's writings that these people actually regarded their homosexual acquaintances as "deviants"). From these interviews, Kitsuse (1962) pieced together the following account of the interpretive processes stimulated by assigning one's friend or acquaintance to the stereotyped category "homosexual":

> this imputation of homosexuality is documented by *retrospective interpretations* of the deviant's behavior, a process by which the subject reinterprets the individual's past behavior in the light of the new information concerning his [or her] sexual deviance. . . . The subjects indicate that they reviewed their past interactions with the individual in question, searching for subtle cues and nuances of behavior which might give further evidence of the alleged deviance. This retrospective reading generally provided the subjects with just such evidence to support the conclusion that "this is what was going on all the time [p. 253]."

According to proposals by other labeling theorists, this process of retrospective reinterpretation is thought to focus on identifying special events in the deviant's past that specifically explain current deviant labels. According to Lofland (1966):

> We see most clearly the social need of others to render actors as consistent objects . . . there must be a *special* history that *specifically* explains current imputed identity. Relative to deviance, the *present evil* of current character must be related to *past evil* that can be discovered in biography [p. 150].

Moreover, according to this viewpoint, in the words of Garfinkel (1956):

> It is not that the new attributes are added to the old "nucleus". He [or she] is not changed, he [or she] is reconstituted. The former identity, at best, receives the accent of mere appearance . . . the former identity stands as accidental, the new identity is the "basic reality". What he [or she] is now is what, "after all", he [or she] was all along [p. 422].

As compelling as the descriptive prose of the sociological labeling theorists may be, it hardly constitutes empirical documentation of the proposed role of stereotypes in reconstructing the past. Fortunately, basic research on memory suggests the processes by which stereotypes may influence attempts to remember and interpret events in the past history of stereotyped individuals. Memory researchers long have emphasized the role of active constructive processes in remembering (Bartlett, 1932; Bower, 1976; Bransford, Barclay, & Franks, 1972; Gauld & Stephenson, 1967; Loftus, 1975; Mandler & Johnson, 1977; Spiro, 1976). According to this viewpoint, individuals do not remember an event by activating or replaying some fixed memory trace. Rather, they construct a schematic representation of their past experience by piecing together remembered bits and pieces and augmenting them with new facts that they (knowingly or unknowingly) supply to flesh out or augment their emerging knowledge of the past. In particular, much attention has focused on the role of thematic information in memory for stories and narratives. However, researchers have tended to focus their efforts on demonstrating the role of themes presented at a narrative's outset in encoding and organizational processes. There has been relatively less attention devoted to uncovering the role of thematic information presented after narratives in the proposed retrospective reconstructive processes. Nonetheless, what evidence does exist (Bransford & Johnson, 1972; Dooling & Christiaansen, 1977; Thorndyke, 1977) certainly enhances the plausibility of proposing the existence of reconstructive consequences of social stereotypes.

Social Stereotypes, Social Relationships, and Reconstruction

In continuing and long-term social relationships, individuals may accumulate extensive stores of historical information about those with whom they have had extended interaction. There may come times in such relationships when events force an individual to adopt a new interpretation of the other person's characteristic nature. This new information then may precipitate a review of the individual's past interactions with the other person in search of events that bolster and augment the current interpretation. The individual may *reconstruct* the past in various ways that make it maximally supportive of current beliefs about the other person.

The proposed reconstructive processes may take at least two forms: (1) preferential remembering of information that is consistent with current interpretations of the target; and/or (2) selective reinterpretation of past events to give them meanings consistent with current interpretations of the target. For example, guided by my current interpretation of you as a generous person (perhaps generated by my just now learning that you are a member of a category of individuals [e.g., philanthropists] who are stereotypically thought to be generous beyond all belief), I might be particularly likely to remember all the generous actions you have committed, explain these generous actions in terms of the generous disposition shared by you and all those of your type, and explain away any stingy acts on your part in terms of transitory situational pressures. If so, my memory search and retrieval processes, as well as my interpretations of what these activities may uncover, would have been guided by my stereotype-based anticipations of what I would find in memory and the meanings to be attached to the discovery of consistent and inconsistent information. Empirical research has examined the contribution of both preferential remembering and selective interpretation to reconstructive processes.

Social Stereotypes and Reconstruction: Empirical Investigations

Experimental investigations of reconstructive processes have sought to model life situations in which an individual might have extensive knowledge of a target's past actions before learning new information that induces stereotyped interpretations of that person. Accordingly, these investigations represent attempts to document the influences of stereotypes on the remembering and reinterpretation of previously learned events in a target's life uncontaminated by any influences of stereotypes on the learning and interpretation of new information about a target. Typically, in these investigations, individuals have read identical life histories that were *later* followed by information that induced different stereotyped interpretations of the main character's nature. The extent to which individuals remembered factual information of the life history in ways that confirmed and supported their current stereotyped beliefs about the main character then have been assessed.

In the initial investigation of reconstruction precipitated by current stereotyped beliefs about another individual, Snyder and Uranowitz (1978c) had participants read identical narratives about the life history of a woman named Betty K. One week later, these individuals acquired information that induced different interpretations of Betty K. Some participants learned that Betty K was currently living a lesbian life-style. Other participants learned that she was currently living a heterosexual life-style. Still others learned nothing about her current life-style.

The extensive chronicle of the events of Betty K's life followed her from her birth, through her childhood, her education, and her choice of profession. It provided information about the climate of her early home life, her relationship with her parents, her social life in high school and in college, etc. The life and times of Betty K were constructed to "fit" either the lesbian or the heterosexual outcome. Research on the content of stereotyped conceptions of female sexuality yielded the following stereotyped images of lesbian and heterosexual women. For example, according to the stereotyped image of the lesbian woman, she had an abusive father, never had a steady boyfriend, never dated men, and was rather unattractive. By contrast, the stereotyped image of the heterosexual woman dictated that she had a tranquil childhood, often dated men, had a steady friend, and was rather attractive. In accord with these stereotyped conceptions, Betty K was provided with a background rich in events that potentially could provide confirmation for either stereotype. For example, although she never had a steady boyfriend in high school, she did go out on dates.

The effects of the new knowledge about Betty K's sexual life-style on recognition memory for the previously learned factual information about her life were then assessed. These recognition memory measures were obtained from answers to a series of multiple-choice questions that dealt with factual information in the case history. In particular, some of the questions concerned Betty K's attitudes toward males and females, her dating habits in high school and college, and her relationship with her parents. These items probed memory for factual information within domains relevant to stereotyped conceptions of sexual orientation.

The participants' new knowledge about Betty K's sexual life-style exerted considerable influence on their answers to factual questions about the actual events of Betty K's life. Participants reconstructed the events of this woman's life in ways that supported and bolstered their current stereotyped interpretations of her sexual orientation. Participants who learned that Betty K was living a lesbian life-style reconstructed the events of her life in a manner that reflected stereotyped beliefs about lesbians. Participants who learned that Betty K was living a heterosexual life-style reconstructed the events of her life in a manner that reflected stereotyped beliefs about heterosexuals.

Finer grained analyses of these outcomes suggested that separate processes of "differential accuracy" and "differential error" contributed to reconstruction. That is, there is evidence that participants were better able to identify accurately those facts of Betty K's life that confirmed their stereotyped beliefs about her sexuality. Moreover, when participants erred in answering questions about Betty K's life, their errors reflected their newly acquired stereotyped beliefs about her sexuality. Furthermore, additional evidence suggested that these results are best characterized as the product of an interaction between stereotypic conceptions of female sexuality and genuine memory for factual events (for details, see Snyder & Uranowitz, 1978c).

Several replications of this demonstration have sought to assess its generalizability across diverse methods of assessing reconstruction. Thus, one such replication assessed remembering of the facts of Betty K's life with a free-recall measure (Snyder & Uranowitz, 1978a). In this investigation, individuals read the history of Betty K's life (the same narrative constructed for the initial demonstration of reconstructive processes) and later learned either that she was living a heterosexual life-style, or that she was living a lesbian life-style, or nothing about her current life-style. They then were asked to write an essay that included as many facts from the life history that they could recall. Rater judges then read the essays and classified them according to their best estimate of the writer's beliefs about Betty K's sexual life-style (all direct references to Betty K's sexual life-style [e.g., Betty K lived with her husband, Betty K lived with a woman, etc.] had been deleted from the essays). These rater judges could correctly classify essays written by participants who believed that Betty K was living a lesbian life-style at a rate substantially and reliably better than chance. Rater judges, however, could not classify "heterosexual" or "no-information" essays any better than chance. Evidently, there was something about the way biographers of a lesbian Betty K chronicled her history that communicated their beliefs about her sexual life-style to readers of their essays. Yet, whatever it was about these essays that made them "lesbian" biographies was not to be found in the factual information recorded about the influences of Betty K's father, her relationships with men, her relationships with women, her attitudes toward men, the importance to her of her career, and her overall adjustment. Ratings of the essays on these six dimensions failed to reveal any measureable differences in the actual content of the essays. Yet, somehow, and for reasons as yet unknown, readers could detect with considerable accuracy those essays written by individuals who believed that Betty K was living a lesbian life-style.

The first two investigations focused on the role of preferential remembering in the reconstructive process. The next investigation directed its attention to the role of *interpretive* and reinterpretive activities in the reconstructive process (Snyder & Uranowitz, 1978b). Once again, participants read the narrative account of Betty K's life, and one week later learned information about her current sexual life-style. They then answered a series of questions about factual events in Betty K's background (e.g., What do you know about Betty K's dating history in high school?''). Moreover, for each of their answers, they provided *interpretations* of what meaning those events (as they remembered them) had for understanding Betty K. These interpretations reflected, to a considerable degree, the participants' current beliefs about Betty K's sexual life-style. Participants who believed that Betty K was living a lesbian life-style were particularly likely to offer "lesbian" interpretations of the events that they remembered; by contrast, those who believed that Betty K was living a heterosexual life-style were particularly likely to offer "heterosexual" interpretations of her past. The participants' skill in interpreting events in ways that bolstered their current beliefs was evident not only in interpretations of remembered events that fit with current beliefs (e.g., a participant who accurately remembered that a purportedly lesbian Betty K never had a steady boyfriend in high school might see that occurrence as an early manifestation of lack of interest in men), but also in interpretations of remembered events that did not fit with current beliefs (e.g., a participant who accurately remembered that a purportedly lesbian Betty K did go out on dates in high school might see that occurrence as a sign of Betty K's early attempts to cover her lesbian tendencies and "pass" as heterosexual). In general, participants were remarkably adept at interpreting whatever they (accurately or inaccurately) remembered about Betty K's past as manifestations and reflections of her emerging sexual orientation.

Another investigation of reconstruction examined the role of stereotyped conceptions of targets on the reconstruction of aspects of their expressive behavior and self-presentational style (Uranowitz, Skrypnek, & Snyder, 1978). In this investigation, individuals observed one of two videotaped conversations between a man and a woman. These conversations had been staged to provide no firm impressions of the two characters. For example, they discussed college courses they had taken, work experiences, leisure activities, and other bland topics of conversation in a manner that was neither particularly warm and friendly nor particularly cool and aloof. After viewing the videotape, some participants read Personal Information Questionnaires describing each participant that they had observed; other participants learned nothing more about the two characters. Those who read the Personal Information Questionnaires learned (by reading the responses to one of the items in the questionnaire) of the characters' sexual preferences. All the participants learned that the man was heterosexual. Half of the participants learned that the woman was heterosexual; half, that she was lesbian. All participants then reported their retrospective estimates of the impressions they had formed of the two characters while watching the videotape. Compared with participants who learned that the woman claimed to be heterosexual, participants who learned that the woman was living a lesbian life-style "remembered" and/or inferred that she had seemed to them to be less secure, less sexually warm, less sociable, and less happy. These participants also were less likely to want her as a friend, less favorable in their overall impressions, and saw themselves as less similar to her. Moreover, when the female character had been labeled after the fact as lesbian, participants "remembered" and/or inferred that she had rarely smiled at the man, hardly flirted with him at all, acted coolly toward him. All in all, participants seemed to have reconstructed the impressions that they formed of the target woman during the conversation as if they actually had seen on the videotapes all the expressive and self-presentational attributes implied by their current stereotyped interpretations of her sexual orientation.

Reconstruction: A Theoretical Account

This series of experimental investigations suggests one role that stereotypes play in defining and creating reality: Stereotypes influence and guide the remembering and interpretation of the past in ways that support and bolster current stereotyped interpretations of other people. Of course, the empirical investigations reported in this chapter represent rather "pure" cases of reconstructive processes in action. Participants acquired considerable amounts of information about Betty K before they learned anything about her current sexual life-style. Of course, individuals frequently have long histories of interaction with other people before learning their sexual and affectional preferences. By contrast, rarely do individuals accumulate considerable knowledge of other people before learning their gender, their race, or other attributes that have stereotypes associated with them. Nonetheless, individuals may have considerable opportunity to interact with other people before such attributes and their associated stereotypes become centrally relevant to their understanding of them. Thus, for example, it may be only when my longtime friend announces his entry in the "Mr. Macho" contest that his gender identity becomes central to my understanding of him. I may then, for the first time, try to remember his past behaviors that reflect stereotyped conceptions of masculinity. Similarly, reconstructive processes may be initiated whenever events make familiar attributes and their associated stereotypes newly relevant and particularly central to understanding other people.

How might such reconstructive processes operate? Presumably, new information about the target (for example, the knowledge about an individual's sexual life-style) may bring to mind preexisting and well-defined beliefs (e.g., stereotyped conceptions about sexual and affectional preference). This preconceived knowledge then may initiate and guide the processes of remembering. First of all, the individual may search preferentially for stereotype-confirming factual evidence. Accordingly, the individual may invest more cognitive time and/or effort in trying to remember those factual events of the target's life that are implied by the current stereotyped beliefs. Such a preferential search for stereotype-confirming evidence may make it easier to remember accurately those events that fit with current stereotyped beliefs. Second, when the individual is in some doubt about specific events in the target's past, these same stereotypes may provide convenient sources of clues for augmenting or filling in the gaps in his or her knowledge with evidence that further bolsters and supports current stereotyped beliefs. Third, stereotypes and their associated preconceived knowledge bases may provide guidelines for interpreting remembered events in ways that enhance their congruence with current stereotyped beliefs about the target.

From this perspective, stereotypes function as "theories" that not only contain within them anticipations of what facts ought to be found in one's memory but also initiate and guide the processes of remembering and interpretation in ways that provide the individual with stereotype-confirming evidence more readily than stereotype-disconfirming evidence. According to this viewpoint, reconstructive processes are the product of (explicit or implicit) guiding assumptions about the nature of social reality: that the present ought to be meaningfully reflected in the past, that contemporary effects ought to be traceable clearly to historical causes, and that the events of a target individual's life ought to unfold in compelling and understandable form. In a loose and partial sense, the assumption of an orderly, consistent, stable, and predictable world provides the impetus (or, if you will, the motivation) for the processes of reconstruction.

Furthermore, according to this viewpoint, reconstruction occurs because knowledge and understanding of the origins of personal attributes is represented in terms of "this leads to that" historical propositions. When one is faced with an outcome to be understood (e.g., someone leads a heterosexual life-style), one's search for the origins of that outcome is guided by preconceived and stereotyped hypotheses about what ought to have happened in an orderly and a consistent world (e.g., the stereotyped hypothesis that heterosexuals ought to have had steady dates in high school).

As consequences of this dynamic character of people's intuitive understanding of human nature, the processes of remembering and interpretation of the past may be channeled in the direction of providing stereotype-confirming evidence more readily than stereotype-disconfirming evidence. In the face of current stereotyped interpretations, people both remember and "write" all the history that fits and reinterpret and "rewrite" all the history that seems not to fit. Accordingly, the processes of reconstructing the past may create cognitively, for the individual, a world in which even erroneous stereotyped inferences about other people may perpetuate themselves.

Reconstruction as a Cognitive Bolstering Process

Reconstruction is but one member of a larger family of cognitive bolstering processes. Even in the absence of a history to rewrite, current stereotype-based beliefs may guide the search for and the interpretation of new information about another person. In addition to remembering retrospectively "all the history that fits," we may notice prospectively "all the news that fits." Indeed, there exists considerable evidence that stereotypes can and do influence information processing such that new evidence that confirms these stereotypes is more easily noticed, more easily stored in memory, and more easily brought to mind than is disconfirming evidence (Berman & Kenny, 1976; Cantor & Mischel, 1977; Chapman & Chapman, 1969; Cohen, 1977; Hamilton, 1977; Rothbart, 1977; Zadny & Gerard, 1974).

Thus, cognitive bolstering processes may be prospective and exert "before-the-facts" influences on the acquisition and interpretation of later learned information about the target. Or, they may be retrospective and exert "after-the-facts" influences on the remembering and reinterpretation of previously learned information about the target. For many stereotypes, prospective and retrospective cognitive bolstering processes may operate hand in hand. Thus, in the early stages of his relationship with Mary, John may be particularly likely to notice and learn information that confirms his stereotyped conceptions of women; later on, this preferential learning of stereotype-confirming information may make it all the easier for John to reconstruct the past history of their relationship in accord with these same stereotyped conceptions of women.

Cognitive bolstering processes (whether of the prospective or the retrospective form) together may endow stereotyped beliefs about specific individuals with a cognitive reality that is independent of the general stereotypes from which these specific beliefs were derived. This occurrence suggests that even if one were to challenge successfully the general validity of a social stereotype, an individual nevertheless might cling tenaciously to stereotyped beliefs about a specific target person because these beliefs may have gained their own unique set of justifications as a result of the operation of cognitive bolstering processes (Ross, Lepper, & Hubbard, 1975; Valins, 1974; Walster, Berscheid, Abrahams, & Aronson, 1967).

CONSTRUCTING THE FUTURE: BEHAVIORAL
CONFIRMATION OF SOCIAL STEREOTYPES

Cognitive bolstering processes may provide the individual with an evidence base that gives compelling cognitive reality to any beliefs that he or she may have formed about a specific target on the basis of general stereotypes. This reality is, of course, a subjective one: It exists in the eye and the mind of the beholder. However, it is a reality with potentially profound consequences. For, stereotyped beliefs may serve as grounds for predictions about the target's future behavior and may guide and influence the individual's subsequent social interaction with the target. This process in turn may generate behaviors on the part of the target that confirm the predictions and validate the stereotyped beliefs of the individual. How others treat us is, in large measure, a reflection of our treatment of them (Bandura, 1977; Snyder, 1979; Wachtel, 1973). Thus, when individuals use their stereotyped beliefs as guides for regulating their interactions with others, they may constrain the others' behavioral options in ways that produce actual *behavioral confirmation* for these stereotyped beliefs of the target.

Empirical investigations have sought to demonstrate that social stereotypes may create their own social reality by channeling social interaction in ways that cause the stereotyped individual to confirm the stereotype behaviorally. These investigations of behavioral confirmation in social interaction have focused on the earliest stages of the development of social relationships—first encounters between strangers. When individuals first meet others, they cannot help but notice certain highly visible and distinctive characteristics; for example, their sex, age, race, and bodily appearance. Try as they may to avoid it, their first impressions often are molded by these pieces of information. And these pieces of information, which are among the first to be gathered in social interaction, tend to have stereotyped conceptions associated with them. Accordingly, these pieces of information and their associated stereotypes may gain high priority for channeling initial acquaintance processes and the unfolding dynamics of social interaction. Empirical investigations have demonstrated the behavioral confirmation of the stereotypes associated with three of these characteristics: physical appearance, race, and sex.

Social Stereotypes and Behavioral Confirmation:
Experimental Demonstrations

One of the first things that people notice about others is their physical appearance. A widely held stereotype in this culture suggests that physically attractive people are assumed to possess more socially desirable personalities and are expected to lead better personal, social, and occupational lives than their unattractive counterparts (Berscheid & Walster, 1974). In short, the widespread stereotyped conception of the links between physical attractiveness and personality dictates that beautiful people are good people.

What of the validity of the physical attractiveness stereotype? As it happens, there is remarkably little evidence that physically attractive people actually are, in general, more likable, friendly, sensitive, and confident than unattractive people (Berscheid & Walster, 1974). Nevertheless, independently of the general validity (or invalidity) of the stereotype, it may channel interaction so as to confirm itself behaviorally in *specific* dyadic interaction contexts. Individuals may have different patterns and styles of interaction for those whom they perceive to be physically attractive and those whom they consider unattractive. These differences in self-presentation and interaction style may, in turn, elicit and nurture behaviors from the target person that are in accord with the stereotype. That is, individuals thought to be physically attractive may actually come to behave in a friendly, likable, sociable manner because the behavior of others who regard them as attractive may elicit and maintain behaviors taken to be manifestations of such dispositions.

A series of investigations (Snyder, Tanke, & Berscheid, 1977; Tanke, 1976), has documented the impact of stereotyped beliefs about physical attractiveness on the unfolding dynamics of social interaction and acquaintance processes in dyadic relationships. These investigations have sought to demonstrate behavioral confirmation in social contexts designed to mirror as faithfully as possible the spontaneous generation of stereotyped beliefs in everyday life and the subsequent channeling influences of these stereotyped impressions on subsequent social interaction. Pairs of previously unacquainted individuals have interacted in a getting-acquainted situation that had been specifically constructed to allow control of the information that one member of the dyad (the perceiver) received about the physical attractiveness of the other person (the target).

In the initial investigation of this series (Snyder, et al., 1977), male perceivers interacted with female targets in a getting-acquainted situation in which they could hear but not see each other (a telephone conversation). Before initiating the conversation, the male member of each dyad received a Polaroid snapshot of his female interaction partner. These photographs, which had been prepared in advance and assigned randomly to dyads, identified the target woman as either physically attractive or physically unattractive. To measure the extent to which each target woman's self-presentation provided behavioral confirmation of her male perceiver's stereotype about physical attractiveness, listener judges (who had no knowledge of the actual or perceived physical attractiveness of either participant) listened to separate tape recordings of the conversational behavior of each member of the dyad and evaluated their behavior.

In anticipation of the forthcoming interaction, perceivers fashioned "erroneous" images of their specific conversation partners that reflected general stereotypes about physical attractiveness. Perceivers who anticipated physically attractive partners expected interaction with comparatively sociable, poised, humorous, and socially adept persons. By contrast, perceivers faced with the prospect of getting acquainted with relatively unattractive partners fashioned images of rather unsociable, awkward, serious, and socially inept creatures.

Moreover, perceivers had very different patterns and styles of interaction for targets whom they perceived to be physically attractive or unattractive. These differences in self-presentation and interaction style, in turn, were accompanied by behaviors in the *targets* that were consistent with and provided actual behavioral confirmation for the perceivers' initial stereotypes. Targets who were perceived (unbeknownst to them) to be physically attractive actually came to behave in a friendly, likable, and sociable manner. This behavioral confirmation was discernible even by outside listener judges who knew nothing of the actual or perceived physical attractiveness of the targets.

In this demonstration of behavioral confirmation in social interaction, the perceivers' stereotype-based beliefs had initiated a chain of events that had produced actual behavioral confirmation of these beliefs. The initially erroneous impressions of the perceivers had, in a sense, become real. The "beautiful people" had become "good people" not necessarily because they possessed the socially valued dispositions that had been attributed to them, but because the actions of the perceivers based on their stereotyped beliefs had erroneously confirmed and validated these beliefs.

Might not other important and widespread social stereotypes (such as those concerning sex, race, social class, and ethnicity) also channel social interaction so as to create their own social reality within the context of individual relationships? Empirical research has examined the behavioral confirmation of stereotypes associated with race and sex. Consider, first, two investigations of Word, Zanna, and Cooper (1974) on behavioral confirmation in interracial interaction. In the first investigation, white Princeton undergraduates interviewed both white and black job applicants. The job applicants were, in actuality, confederates who had been trained to respond similarly in relatively constant fashion from interview to interview. Unbeknownst to the interviewers, the researchers made careful measurements of their verbal and nonverbal behaviors during the interview. These measurements revealed substantial differences between the treatment accorded black and white job applicants by the same interviewers. Black applicants were treated to less immediacy, higher rates of speech errors, and shorter amounts of interview time. In the second investigation, white confederates were trained to approximate the immediate and nonimmediate interview styles identified in the first investigation as they interviewed naive white job applicants. A panel of judges who evaluated videotape recordings of these interviews agreed that applicants subjected to the nonimmediate interview styles experienced by blacks in the first investigation performed less adequately and were more nervous than job applicants treated to the immediate interview styles experienced by whites in the first investigation. Considered together, these two investigations suggest that, in interracial interaction, racial stereotypes may channel and constrain the behavior of the interactants in ways that generate behavioral confirmation for those stereotypes.

Other examinations of behavioral confirmation in social interaction have probed the consequences of stereotyped conceptions of men and women. Here, the fundamental question is: Will the common stereotype that women are more conforming and less independent than men (Broverman, Vogel, Broverman, Clarkson, & Rosenkrantz, 1972) influence interaction so that targets believed to be female actually will conform more, be more dependent, and be more success-fully manipulated than interaction partners believed to be male? At least two empirical investigations of self-presentational processes have pointed to the pos-sible self-perpetuating nature of sex-role stereotypes. Zanna and Pack (1975) had female undergraduates describe themselves to a male partner. He was either desirable (a 6'1" tall, 21-year-old Princeton senior, with no girlfriend) or rather undesirable (a 5'1" tall, 18-year-old non-Princeton freshman with a girlfriend, and no interest in meeting other women). Furthermore, the male's stereotype of the ideal woman either conformed to the traditional female stereotype (that is, the ideal woman should be very emotional, deferent to her husband, home oriented, passive) or its opposite (that is, the ideal woman should be very independent, very competitive, very ambitious, very dominant). This information about the hypothetical partner and his beliefs affected the women's self-presentation. When the partner was described as desirable, the women presented themselves (on a paper-and-pencil self-presentation measure) as extremely conventional when his ideology was conventional. However, when the desirable male partner expressed a nontraditional ideology, the women described themselves in much more nontraditional terms. When the partner was generally undesirable, his viewpoints had little impact on the images conveyed by the women.

In a related investigation of self-presentation, vonBaeyer, Sherk, and Zanna (1978) scheduled female job applicants to be interviewed by male interviewers. Once again, the women learned (by reading a questionnaire purportedly com-pleted by the interviewer) that the male interviewers' stereotype of the ideal female job applicant either conformed to the traditional female stereotype or to its opposite. Of major concern to the researchers was the appearance (e.g., clothing, accessories, makeup) of the women when they arrived for their interviews. Indeed, the women in this experiment dressed to meet the stereotyped expecta-tions of their interviewers. Women who anticipated a traditional interviewer looked more feminine (both in appearance and in their use of makeup and accessories) than did women who anticipated nontraditional interviewers. During the actual interview, women who encountered (supposedly) traditional inter-viewers also offered traditionally feminine answers to the question "Do you have plans to include children and marriage with your career plans?".

Clearly, in the investigations of Zanna and Pack (1975), and vonBaeyer, Sherk, and Zanna (1978), expectations shaped self-presentations. In these exper-iments, the women read clear and unambiguous statements of the males' viewpoints about their "ideal women" and then engaged in various verbal and nonverbal self-presentational activities. Accordingly, it is not altogether clear from these investigations whether, in actual ongoing social interaction and social relationships, one individual's views about sex roles can initiate a chain of events that cause another person to behave in accord with these preconceived convictions about the nature of the sexes. To provide a compelling demonstration of these processes would require an interaction structured along these lines: Pairs of unacquainted individuals are allowed to interact in a situation that permits the investigators to control the information that each receives about the apparent sex of the other individual. Skrypnek and Snyder (1980) have conducted just such an investigation.

This investigation of the behavioral confirmation of sex-role stereotypes employed a "division of labor" task in which two previously unacquainted individuals (located in separate rooms) communicated by means of a signaling system (to eliminate the need for verbal communication) to divide up a series of pairs of worklike tasks that differed in their sex-role connotations (Bem & Lenney, 1976). The tasks were simple activities that varied along the dimensions of masculinity and feminity (e.g., sharpen a hunting knife—masculine; polish a pair of shoes—neutral; iron a shirt—feminine). In two of the experimental conditions, one member of the dyad (the perceiver) was led to believe that the other member of the dyad (the target) was either male or female, respectively. These dyads then negotiated (communicating by means of the signaling system) their division of labor of the worklike tasks. The pattern of choices provided clear evidence of behavioral confirmation. The perceivers' beliefs about the sex of their targets influenced the outcomes of the division of labor tasks. Targets came to choose tasks "appropriate" to the "sex" to which they had been assigned by the experimental manipulation of the perceivers' beliefs. Targets believed by their perceivers to be male came to choose relatively many stereotypically masculine tasks. By contrast, targets regarded by their perceivers as female came to choose relatively many stereotypically feminine tasks. Moreover, a fine-grained scrutiny of this outcome revealed that, although this behavioral confirmation effect was initially elicited as reactions to overtures made by the perceivers, it persevered so that eventually targets began actually to initiate behaviors "appropriate" to the sex with which they had been labeled by their perceivers.

The implications of this demonstration of the behavioral confirmation of sex-role stereotypes, as well as the earlier ones by Zanna and Pack (1975) and by vonBaeyer, Sherk, and Zanna (1978), are considerable. According to this view, many apparent sex differences may not be so much the product of inherent biological or temperamental differences between women and men, but rather the result of differences in the images that people project in their attempts to act out stereotyped sex-role images defined by other individuals. As these stereotypes shift, so too may sex-role behaviors. In fact, autobiographical statements by individuals who have undergone surgical sex reassignments have pointed to the power of such processes in their adjustment to their new lives as individuals of the other sex. Thus, writer Jan Morris (1974), in her autobiographical chronicle of her transition from James to Jan, observed: "The more I was treated as a woman, the more woman I became [p. 165]."

Behavioral Confirmation: Internalization and Perseveration

Thus far, investigations of the behavioral confirmation of social stereotypes have demonstrated the ways that stereotypes (as diverse as those concerning physical attractiveness, race, and sex roles) may channel subsequent interaction between perceiver and target in ways that cause the target's behavior to confirm these stereotypes. But how stable and enduring are the effects of the behavioral confirmation process? Once a target displays behaviors that confirm the perceiver's stereotypes, for how long will the target continue to do so? Will behavioral confirmation be limited to the confines of the specific interaction between perceiver and target? Or, will it persevere to new interaction contexts with new perceivers? If behavioral confirmation were limited to the specific interaction between perceiver and target, behavioral confirmation would be a rather transitory and ephemeral consequence of social stereotypes. If so, one hardly would want to regard behavioral confirmation as a fundamental process by which stereotypes create and construct their own behavioral and social reality.

The search for answers to these questions has involved theoretical and empirical attempts to understand the perseveration of behavioral confirmation beyond the bounds of the original confirmation context. At the theoretical level, the following account of perseveration may be offered. If the "new" behaviors displayed by the target as a result of behavioral confirmation are not overly discrepant from his or her own self-image, then these new behaviors may be internalized and incorporated into the target's self-conception. If internalization occurs (and there are good reasons to believe that the latitude of acceptance for internalization or accomodations of self-conceptions to new behaviors may be rather wide; see Secord and Backman, 1965; Snyder and Swann, 1978a), then both the target and the perceiver will share stereotyped conceptions of the target. The target then may be prepared to act on his or ner new stereotyped self-conception in contexts beyond those that include the original perceiver who first initiated the behavioral confirmation process. Then, the target may provide other perceivers with behavioral evidence consistent with the original perceiver's stereotyped beliefs.

Empirical research has suggested that internalization and perseveration are fostered and promoted when behavioral confirmation first occurs in environments that encourage targets to regard their new behaviors as representative reflections of their underlying stable traits and enduring dispositions. To chart this process empirically, Snyder and Swann (1978a) observed successive interactions between one target and two perceivers. In the first interaction, perceivers were led to label erroneously (as a result of an experimental manipulation) targets as hostile or nonhostile persons. During the first interaction, the perceivers' initially false conceptions of their targets evoked new behaviors that made their originally false conceptions come true. They treated their targets as hostile or nonhostile persons and, indeed, these targets responded in kind and began to behave in hostile or nonhostile fashion. However, some of these targets were induced to regard (once again, as a result of an experimental manipulation) their actions as a reflection of corresponding personal dispositions; that is, to believe that actually they were of hostile or nonhostile character. For these targets, the process of behavioral confirmation extended and persevered beyond the bounds of the original confirmation interaction. They behaved in a hostile manner not only for the perceivers who first had labeled themselves as hostile, but also for new and different perceivers in new and different contexts. They had become truly hostile persons whose behaviors reflected the cross-situational consistency and temporal stability that are the calling cards of personality traits and dispositions. Apparently, the processes of behavioral confirmation, internalization, and perseveration had succeeded in socializing, within the confines of the laboratory, a "trait" of hostility in individuals who once were labeled falsely as hostile individuals.

Although this investigation of perseveration of behavioral confirmation does not deal directly with social stereotypes, its relevance to the consequences of stereotypes is considerable. The choice to induce perceivers to label targets as hostile or nonhostile individuals was a purposeful one, inasmuch as so many potent stereotypes involve the ascription of hostility to targets of those stereotypes (e.g., stereotyped conceptions of the mentally ill, ex-mental patients, former prisoners, some racial minorities, disadvantaged youths). An individual, having been tagged as inherently hostile because all members of his or her category are stereotypically thought to be hostile, may find his or her behavioral options constrained in ways that actually force him or her to become a hostile person. In such fashion, ex-mental patients or former prisoners may be provoked by the stereotype-based prejudicial treatment of others into angry reactions that then may be interpreted as manifestations of their disturbances. These reactions, in turn, may justify treating these individuals as hostile and dangerous deviants. In this way stigmatized individuals may fall victim to cultural stereotypes and expectations (Goffman, 1963; Scott, 1969; Szasz, 1961).

More generally, some sociologists have implicated such processes of social labeling in theoretical accounts of the origins of crime and delinquency. According to Tannenbaum (1938):

> The process of making the criminal, therefore, is a process of tagging, defining, identifying . . . ; it becomes a way of stimulating . . . and evoking the very traits that are complained of. . . . The person becomes the thing he [or she] is described as

being. . . . The community expects him [or her] to live up to his [or her] reputation, and will not credit him [or her] if he [or she] does not live up to it [pp. 19–20 and 477].

The application of this labeling perspective at the societal level is made more justifiable and more plausible by research on behavioral confirmation and its perseveration.

Behavioral Confirmation: A Theoretical Account

What are the psychological processes that might underlie and generate the behavioral confirmation of social stereotypes? Behavioral confirmation may be viewed in terms of those activities by which individuals formulate strategies of action. Consider the perspective of a perceiver in the investigation of the behavioral confirmation of stereotypes concerning physical attractiveness. In anticipation of the getting-acquainted conversation with the stranger in the other room, he may imagine possible scenarios of the events and outcomes of their forthcoming interaction. In so doing, his stereotyped conceptions about the general relationship between physical attractiveness and personality may provide a "theory" that permits him to predict whether that specific person will be friendly or unfriendly, sociable or unsociable, warm or cold, likable or unlikable, poised or awkward, humorous or serious, socially adept or socially inept. These stereotype-generated anticipations of the target's likely behavior provide a ready source of guidelines for the perceiver's strategy of initiating and guiding their conversation. Of course, to the extent that the perceiver acts on these anticipations, social interaction may be channeled and constrained in ways that will provide actual behavioral confirmation for the perceiver's stereotyped beliefs about the target.

At the core of this analysis are these propositions: (1) perceivers anticipate their forthcoming interactions with targets in the light of available stereotypes; (2) these stereotypes guide the formation of scenario-like anticipations of what events are to appear as the interaction unfolds; (3) in these scenarios targets are imagined to behave in accord with stereotype-based inferences and predictions about their attributes and behavior; (4) these scenarios actively guide the perceiver's interactional strategy. From this perspective, behavioral confirmation is the consequence of the individual perceiver's active use of general stereotypes in the planning and regulation of social interaction with specific targets of those stereotypes. The content of those general stereotypes provide perceivers with guidelines for formulating strategies for coping with specific targets. These interactional strategies generate the behavioral evidence that appears to confirm those stereotypes.

THE PERPETUATION OF SOCIAL STEREOTYPES

Of what consequence are the processes of reconstruction and behavioral confirmation? Empirical investigations suggest that these processes together conspire to turn social stereotypes into self-perpetuating stereotypes. By reconstructing the past and constructing the future, these processes create an evidence base that provides all the support that one needs to retain one's stereotyped beliefs. In the investigations of reconstructive processes, participants remembered the facts of a target's life in ways that confirmed their current stereotyped interpretations of the target's nature. In the investigations of behavioral confirmation processes in social interaction, perceivers treated the targets of stereotypes in ways that caused them to confirm behaviorally the perceiver's stereotypes. As consequences of these processes, neither one's remembering of past events nor one's experience with future events may provide any compelling indication that stereotypes may be inaccurate. The "facts" of any individual target's behavior (as one remembers them and as one sees them in actual interaction) seem to confirm, bolster, and support one's general stereotypes.

From this perspective, it becomes easier to understand why so many widely held stereotypes that essentially are inaccurate in *the general case* are so stubbornly resistant to change. Individuals never see and experience "the general case." Instead, what they do see and experience is *the individual case*. And, in the individual case, cognitive bolstering and behavioral confirmation processes help manufacture an evidence base that makes the individual case appear to confirm general stereotypes. In the face of this wealth of manufactured stereotype-confirming evidence that individuals experience in their relationships with specific targets of their stereotypes, individuals seldom (or never) may encounter reasons to doubt the accuracy of these stereotypes. Accordingly, the operation of the processes of reconstruction and behavioral confirmation may serve to perpetuate essentially inaccurate stereotypes.

The cognitive and behavioral processes that perpetuate stereotypes notwithstanding, attempts often are made to alter erroneous stereotypes. Central to all social movements for civil and human rights are attempts to alter widely held and generally unfavorable stereotypes about the groups involved. In the last several decades, we have experienced (and continue to experience) large scale educational campaigns to erase demeaning stereotypes about blacks, women, gays, and lesbians. Accordingly, it is both theoretically and socially appropriate to ask "How can individuals be helped to discover which of their stereotyped conceptions about human nature are inaccurate?". More specifically, one may ask "If reconstruction and behavioral confirmation tend to perpetuate inaccurate stereotypes, how can the stereotype-perpetuating consequences of these processes be inhibited, overcome, and/or counteracted?". At least two approaches suggest themselves. The first approach involves an *after-the-fact* undoing or reversal of the consequences of reconstruction and behavioral confirmation. The second approach involves a *before-the-fact* short-circuiting or inhibiting of reconstruction and behavioral confirmation.

Consider, first, the possibility of retroactively undoing the consequences of reconstruction and behavioral confirmation. Consider this hypothetical turn of events in the life of one participant (christened "Joe") in the initial investigation of reconstructive processes. One week ago, Joe learned all about the life and times of a woman named Betty K. Now, one week later, he learns that this same Betty K is living a lesbian life-style. Based upon his stereotyped intuitions about female sexuality, Joe now proceeds to reconstruct the events of Betty K's life history to bolster and support his current knowledge about her sexual life-style. What if, in an attempt to rid Joe of his general stereotype, one subsequently informed him that it is simply not true (as he and his peers believe) that all lesbian women had abusive fathers, never had steady boyfriends, never dated men, and are rather unattractive? One could bolster this educational attempt with appropriate references to the writings of eminent researchers in the field of human sexuality (Gagnon & Simon, 1973; Katchadourian & Lunde, 1975; Klaich, 1974; Martin & Lyon, 1972; Money & Ehrhardt, 1972; Riess, Safer, & Yotive, 1974), all of whom agree that there is no basis in fact for any and all of the stereotyped beliefs about sexuality that Joe and his peers endorse. One could inform him, as graphically as possible, that, as Money and Erhardt (1972) have concluded: "The state of knowledge as of the present does not permit any hypotheses (many psychodynamic claims to the contrary) that will predict with certainty which biographical conditions will ensure that an anatomically normal boy or girl will become erotically homosexual, bisexual, or heterosexual [p. 235]."

Much as Joe might want to defer to the authority of this statistical and scientific evidence, he would still be faced with the "knowledge" (generated by the reconstructive process) that Betty K (who just may be the one and only lesbian he knows) indeed did have an abusive father, never did have a steady boyfriend, never dated men, and actually was rather unattractive. At least, that's the way that Joe remembers those "facts" of her life history. Given the choice between abstract secondhand statistics about other nameless women whom he had never met and concrete firsthand experience with Betty K, there are reasons to suspect (and one may draw on empirical evidence offered by Nisbett, Borgida, Crandall, and Reed [1976] to bolster and support this suspicion) that Joe will regard his knowledge of Betty K as more informative than any statistical evidence and thus cling tenaciously to his initial stereotypes about female sexuality. After all, the immediate case of Betty K so perfectly exemplifies and proves (at least in his mind) what he has known all along.

Consider another illustrative scenario. This time, enter the world of Frank, a hypothetical participant in the initial investigation of behavioral confirmation in social interaction. Frank has just spent fifteen minutes on the telephone getting acquainted with a young woman who has turned out to be just as sociable, friendly, outgoing, and warm as he anticipated (based upon her rather attractive picture and his "knowledge" that good-looking people have good personalities) that she would be. Now, one tells Frank the true facts. One lets him know that, despite widespread acceptance of the stereotype that links physical attractiveness and personality, there is virtually no evidence for its general validity (for a review of the evidence for the general validity of the physical attractiveness stereotype, see Snyder et al., 1977). Does Frank go with this summary of the research evidence, or with his recent experience and, presumably, his preferential remembering of all the beautiful people he has known who have had wonderful personalities? Once again, there are reasons to suspect that immediate experience will win out over remote data (Nisbett et al., 1976).

Perhaps, one needs to do more than just provide data on the general validity of erroneous stereotypes to those who endorse them. Based on available evidence on the relative potency of concrete firsthand experience and abstract secondhand data (Nisbett et al., 1976) and on the ineffectiveness of after-the-fact debriefing procedures (Ross et al., 1975), it seems unlikely that one can effectively counteract or reverse the outcomes of reconstruction and behavioral confirmation once they have occurred. An alternate, and perhaps more promising, strategy might involve procedures that *short-circuit* or *inhibit* the processes of reconstruction and behavioral confirmation *before* they can exert their reality-constructing effects. How might one prevent stereotypes from guiding attempts to remember the past? Similarly, how might one prevent stereotypes from guiding the course of subsequent social interaction?

One possibility is to induce individuals to adopt procedures designed to assess the accuracy of their stereotyped interpretations of their targets. For example, participants in a reconstruction experiment could be asked to review the life and times of Betty K to determine whether, based on their remembering of the facts, they think that Betty K currently is living a lesbian life-style. Of, in an investigation of behavioral confirmation, participants could be asked to use their getting-acquainted conversations to determine whether their partners actually were physically attractive or unattractive or whether they actually had the sociable or unsociable personalities implied by their appearance. Were one to rewrite the scenarios of the reconstruction and behavioral confirmation experiments along these lines, these revised scenarios essentially would provide participants with "hypotheses" about their targets and ask them to test these hypotheses. In the former case, they would test their hypotheses by searching for relevant previously learned information. In the latter case, they would use their forthcoming interactions as testing grounds actually to collect new "data" relevant to testing their hypotheses. Perhaps, when individuals actively attempt to determine whether or not the attributes of specific targets match those of general stereotypes, they may encounter evidence (either remembered from past experience with the target, or observed in subsequent interaction with the target) that will encourage them to question the accuracy of some of their erroneous general stereotypes.

As it happens, a series of investigations has examined the processes of hypothesis testing, both in the cognitive domain and in the behavioral domain. Most of these investigations have examined the testing of hypotheses involving stereotypes about personality types; in particular, stereotypes about the categories "extravert" and "introvert." Research on people's naive theories of personality indicate that people share well-defined stereotypes about the personal attributes that are typical of members of particular personality types (Cantor & Mischel, 1977). For example, most people's conception of the prototypic extravert dictates that such a person have the following attributes: outgoing, sociable, talkative, bold, self-assured, enthusiastic, etc. Moreover, as is the case with so many of the stereotypes employed in research on the cognitive and behavioral consequences of stereotyping, these stereotypes about personality types have remarkably little basis in fact. The data of human social behavior reflect substantially less consistency than the data of stereotyped conceptions of personality types (Mischel, 1968). Accordingly stereotypes about personality types are ideally suited for the present purposes; they are widely held, widely accepted, and without general validity.

Cognitive Tests of Hypotheses Involving Stereotypes

To examine hypothesis testing in the case where people can use previously learned information to test cognitively hypotheses about others, Snyder and Cantor (1979) had individuals (in two separate investigations) read identical accounts of events in one week of the life of a woman named Jane. This knowledge provided them with an archival store of historical information about Jane's actions in different situations and with different people over a period of time. For purposes of this investigation, this knowledge was able to "stand in" for that store of knowledge that one might accumulate in one's history of interaction with another person, that store of knowledge to which one might turn in search of evidence that would permit one to test hypotheses about that person's personal attributes.

Two days later, they were asked to use this historical knowledge to test hypotheses about Jane's suitability to apply for one of two jobs: either the rather extraverted job of real estate salesperson, or the rather introverted job of research librarian. Jane's history was constructed to provide considerable support for either hypothesis: In different situations and at different times Jane was as likely to behave in extraverted and introverted fashion. In their hypothesis-testing activities, participants were required first to report those facts about Jane they previously had learned that they regarded as relevant to deciding Jane's suitability to apply for the job under consideration and then to report their judgments about her suitability for that job. This information permitted examination of both the processes and outcomes of hypothesis testing.

The results of these investigations indicated that the hypothesis being tested constrained not only the gathering of evidence with which to test that hypothesis, but also the ultimate fate of the hypothesis itself. To test their hypotheses, participants preferentially reported as relevant factual information that would *confirm* their hypotheses. To test the hypothesis about Jane's suitability for the job of real estate salesperson, participants were particularly likely to report instances of Jane behaving in accord with their construct of the prototypic extravert. To test the hypothesis about Jane's suitability for the job of research librarian, participants were particularly likely to report instances of Jane behaving in accord with their construct of the prototypic introvert.

Moreover, to the extent that they preferentially remembered hypothesis-confirming factual information they had learned about Jane's background, participants were particularly likely to accept their hypotheses. In fact, having tested a hypothesis about Jane's suitability for one job, participants judged her to be better suited to apply for that job than for the other job. As a consequence of basing their judgments about Jane's personal attributes on the outcome of confirmatory hypothesis-testing activities, what was once only a hypothesis for these individuals had become, in their minds at least, a reality. Little did these individuals know that had they been assigned the task of testing precisely the opposite hypothesis about Jane, they would have as readily generated substantial and convincing (to them) amounts of evidence in support of that hypothesis.

Behavioral Tests of Hypotheses Involving Stereotypes

Of course, people do not always have access to sufficient historical knowledge of a person's actions in diverse situations and over extended periods of time to test hypotheses by bringing to mind previously learned information. Or, they may find that they have not accumulated sufficient information to permit a convincing test of the hypothesis under consideration. In such situations, people may test their hypotheses by using their subsequent interactions as opportunities to collect behavioral evidence relevant to testing their hypotheses. A series of empirical investigations has attempted to chart the unfolding dynamics of hypothesis-testing processes in social interaction (Snyder, 1981). Some of these investigations have examined the strategies that individuals formulate to test hypotheses about others with whom they anticipate social interaction; others, the extent to which these hypothesis-testing strategies channel and influence social interaction in ways that actually cause the target to provide behavioral confirmation for the hypothesis being tested.

Typically, in investigations of the formulation of hypothesis-testing strategies individuals have been provided with hypotheses about the personal attributes of other people (targets). These individuals then prepared to test these hypotheses (e.g., that their targets were extraverts, or that their targets were introverts) by planning a series of questions to ask of their targets in (what they believed to be) forthcoming interviews (for procedural details of the basic experimental paradigm, see Snyder & Swann, 1978b). Specifically, the experimenter informed participants that they would be taking part in an investigation of how people come to know and understand each other. The experimenter explained that one way to learn about other people is to ask them questions about their likes and dislikes, their favorite activities, their life experiences, and their feelings about themselves. Each participant would attempt to find out what another person (supposedly waiting in another room) was like by asking questions designed to determine whether or not that person was the type whose personality was outlined on a card provided by the experimenter.

These personality profiles provided the participants with hypotheses about the other individual. The personality profile was one of two that had been prepared in advance. Some participants learned that it would be their task to assess the extent to which the target's behavior and life experiences matched those of a prototypic extravert (e.g., outgoing, sociable, energetic, confident, talkative, and enthusiastic); other participants, that their target's behavior and experiences matched those of a prototypic introvert (e.g., shy, timid, reserved, quiet, and retiring). Participants then chose 12 questions that they believed would best help them find out whether or not the target's specific beliefs, attitudes, and actions in life situations matched the general characteristics described in the profile.

Time and again, in this series of investigations, participants planned to test their hypotheses by treating their targets as if they were the type of person they were hypothesized to be: They planned to search preferentially for behavioral evidence that would *confirm* their hypotheses. To test the hypothesis that their targets were extraverted individuals, participants were particularly likely to choose to ask precisely those questions that one typically asks of individuals already known to be extraverts (e.g., "What would you do if you wanted to liven things up at a party?"). To test the hypothesis that their targets were introverted individuals, participants were particularly likely to choose to ask precisely those questions that one typically asks of individuals already known to be introverts (e.g., "What factors make it hard for you to really open up to people?").

Moreover, the commitment to confirmatory hypothesis-testing strategies appears to be a pervasive one. It seemed to matter not at all to participants in this series of investigations where their hypotheses originated, how likely it was that their hypotheses would prove accurate or inaccurate, whether the hypothesis explicitly defined both confirming and disconfirming attributes, or even whether the hypothesis was defined exclusively in terms of disconfirming attributes (for a fuller exposition of these attempts to induce individuals to eschew confirmatory hypothesis-testing strategies, see Snyder, 1981). Participants in these investigations appear to have accorded all hypotheses equal status when preparing a strategy to solicit information with which to test these hypotheses. In each case, they planned to solicit preferentially (by means of the questions they chose to ask of their targets) behavioral evidence that would tend to confirm their hypotheses.

Of what consequence are the enactment of these confirmatory hypothesis-testing strategies in social interaction? So far, hypothesis testers in these investigations never had the opportunity to interrogate their targets. What would happen if one were to allow hypothesis testers the opportunity to interview their targets and "collect the data" that their confirmatory strategies would provide them? Would these confirmatory evidence-gathering procedures generate behaviors that would erroneously confirm their hypotheses? Would targets who are being "tested" for extraversion actually come to behave in relatively sociable and outgoing fashion? Would targets who are being "tested" for introversion actually come to behave in relatively shy and reserved fashion? After all, the more often one inquires about the target's extraversion or introversion, the more often the target will have opportunities to provide instances of extraverted or introverted behaviors. Indeed, the enactment of confirmatory hypothesis-testing strategies in social interaction can and does constrain targets to behave in ways that provide actual behavioral evidence that appears to confirm the hypothesis under scrutiny.

In an experimental investigation of hypothesis testing in action, hypothesis testers first formulated their hypothesis-testing strategies and then carried out these strategies by actually interviewing their targets. Once again, hypothesis testers attempted to evaluate the accuracy of their hypothesis about their targets by preferentially soliciting evidence that would confirm their hypotheses. Moreover, during the interview the targets came to provide precisely the behavioral evidence that would appear to confirm the hypotheses being tested by the hypothesis testers. Naive judges who listened to tape recordings of the targets' contributions of the interviews provided clear evidence that targets hypothesized to be extraverts actually presented themselves in more extraverted fashion than did targets hypothesized to be introverts. Evidently, the targets' answers to the hypothesis testers' questions did provide actual behavioral confirmation for the hypotheses being tested by the hypothesis testers.

The Consequences of Confirmatory Hypothesis Testing

As a result of these investigations of hypothesis testing, it becomes all the more understandable why so many popular beliefs about other people (in particular, clearly erroneous social and cultural stereotypes) are so stubbornly resistant to change. Even if one were to develop sufficient doubt about the accuracy of these stereotypes that one might proceed to test them, one nevertheless would be likely to find all the evidence that one needs to confirm and retain these beliefs.

For example, if one ever were to question the validity of the stereotype that "what is beautiful is good," one would be likely to adopt one of two strategies to evaluate and assess its accuracy. One might think back over one's history of interactions with particularly beautiful people. If so, most likely one would preferentially think of instances of those people behaving in friendly and sociable fashion. Alternately, one might decide to use forthcoming interactions with beautiful people to test the hypothesis that beautiful people have friendly and sociable personalities. If so, one probably would treat those beautiful people as if they were friendly and sociable and, sure enough, they would come to behave as if they actually were friendly and sociable. In either case, one would conclude that the stereotype had been confirmed by the evidence provided by one's hypothesis-testing activities. And, in the end, one may be left with the secure (but totally unwarranted) feeling that these stereotyped beliefs must be correct because they have survived (what may seem to the individual) perfectly appropriate and even rigorous procedures for assessing their accuracy (for a fuller treatment of the consequences of confirmatory hypothesis testing, see Snyder, in press).

CONCLUSIONS

In the light of the outcomes of these investigations of the cognitive and behavioral consequences of stereotyping, what may be said about the nature of social stereotypes? Clearly, social stereotypes play an active and initiatory role in channeling the processes of thought and social interaction. These investigations have documented the ways in which social stereotypes guide and influence: (1) the remembering and the interpretation of previously learned information about the target; (2) the course and the outcome of social interaction between perceiver and target; and (3) the evaluation of the accuracy of stereotype-based beliefs about targets.

It is as if stereotypes contain within them anticipations or "theories" of what information about stereotyped targets is to be found stored in memory and anticipations or "theories" of what events are to appear as interaction between perceiver and stereotyped targets unfolds. To the extent that these anticipations or "theories" guide subsequent thought about the target and subsequent social interaction with the target, the perpetuation of social stereotypes through reconstruction and behavioral confirmation are likely, if not inevitable, consequences of the active and initiatory nature of social stereotypes.

Such may be the power of social stereotypes. Whether individuals regard them as facts or hypotheses, they channel the remembering of past interactions and unfolding of future interactions in ways that provide both cognitive bolstering and behavioral confirmation for even erroneous social stereotypes. But, clearly, social stereotypes can and do change. Once widespread and negative stereotypes about black people have shifted over the years (Smedley & Bayton, 1978) but have not disappeared altogether (Alfert, 1972). Stereotyped conceptions of sex roles are also in transition (Oppenheim-Mason, Czajka, & Arber,

1976). Stereotypes about religious affiliation have faded considerably over the years (Allport, 1954). One little-noticed manifestation of this trend has been the steady increase in willingness to vote for a woman or a black person for president. For example, in the two decades from the late 1950s to the late 1970s, the percentages of Americans who say that they would be willing to vote for a woman or a black for president have risen from 52% and 38%, respectively, to 76% and 77%, respectively (Gallup, 1978).

The fact that some stereotypes do change over time is all the more impressive when one considers the powerful cognitive and behavioral forces, including the processes of cognitive bolstering and behavioral confirmation, that work to perpetuate stereotypes. Often, changes in stereotypes appear to have been accompanied by (and, perhaps, precipitated by) organized social movements to mobilize members of stereotyped groups to ameliorate their circumstances and, at the same time, to dispel negative stereotypes about those groups. The emergence of organized social movements (e.g., the women's movement, the gay/lesbian movement) may be critical to induce changes in general stereotypes. Recall the suggestion that stereotypes that are inaccurate in the general case may resist change because individuals don't encounter "the general case" in their day-to-day interactions with specific members of stereotyped categories. Rather, it was suggested, that individuals encounter "the individual case" where cognitive bolstering and behavioral confirmation together cause individual cases to appear to confirm the general stereotype. Perhaps the emergence of organized social movements increases the visibility of "the general case" and provides the stereotype-altering information that the individual case tends not to provide.

Moreover, investigations of the reality-constructing consequences of social stereotypes make clear just what it is that is inherently and fundamentally *social* about social stereotypes. That is, these investigations sensitize us to the links between social stereotypes and social reality. Social stereotypes can and do create their own social reality. The very events of the social world (in particular, the behaviors of the targets of social stereotypes, both as they appear in memory and in social interaction) may be reflections and products of preconceptions about the social world (in particular, stereotyped beliefs and hypotheses about the characteristic nature of particular types of people). Social stereotypes are *social* stereotypes precisely because of their intimate involvement in the construction and the reconstruction of social reality in ongoing and continuing social relationships. Social stereotypes are *social* stereotypes precisely because of the links they create between the domain of thought and the domain of action.

It is because of these links between thought and action that stereotyped beliefs about the social attributes of people are fundamentally and inherently different from stereotyped beliefs about the physical attributes of objects. No matter how firmly convinced I may be that all Swedish cars are built like tanks and handle like sports cars, my interactions with my Swedish car will not generate actual confirming evidence for my stereotype unless that stereotype happens to be true.

However, if I believe that all Swedish men are friendly and sociable, my interactions with my Swedish friend may generate actual confirming evidence for my stereotype even if that stereotype lacks general validity. Acting on stereotyped beliefs about objects and physical events does not influence the reality of those objects and events. Acting on stereotyped beliefs about people and social events does influence the reality of those people and their behavior. For, when it comes to stereotyped conceptions of other people, individuals may construct for themselves a world in which beliefs create reality.

ACKNOWLEDGMENTS

This research and the preparation of this chapter have been supported in part by National Science Foundation Grants SOC 75-13872, "Cognition and Behavior: When Belief Creates Reality," and BNS 77-11346, "From Belief to Reality: Cognitive, Behavioral, and Interpersonal Consequences of Social Perception," to Mark Snyder. For their comments on the manuscript, my thanks to Anne Locksley, Eugene Borgida, and David L. Hamilton.

REFERENCES

Alfert E. Are social stereotypes vanishing: A study of a non-college population. *Journal of Social Issues*, 1972, *28*, 89–99.

Allport, G. W. *The nature of prejudice*. Reading, Mass.: Addison–Wesley, 1954.

vonBaeyer, C. L., Sherk, D. L., & Zanna, M. P. *Impression management in the job interview: When the female applicant meets the male (chauvinist) interviewer*. Unpublished manuscript, University of Waterloo, 1978.

Bandura, A. *Social learning theory*. Englewood Cliffs, N.J.: Prentice–Hall, 1977.

Bartlett, F. C. *Remembering: A study in experimental and social psychology*. Cambridge: University Press, 1932.

Bem, S. L., & Lenney, E. Sex typing and the avoidance of cross-sex behavior. *Journal of Personality and Social Psychology*, 1976, *33*, 48–54.

Berman, J. S., & Kenny, D. A. Correlational bias in observer ratings. *Journal of Personality and Social Psychology*, 1976, *34*, 263–273.

Berscheid, E., & Walster, E. Physical attractiveness. In L. Berkowitz (Ed.), *Advances in experimental social psychology* (Vol. 7). New York: Academic Press, 1974.

Bower, G. Experiments on story understanding and recall. *Quarterly Journal of Experimental Psychology*, 1976, *28*, 511–534.

Bransford, J. D., Barclay, J. R., & Franks, J. J. Sentence memory: A constructive versus interpretive approach. *Cognitive Psychology*, 1972, *3*, 193–209.

Bransford, J. D., & Johnson, M. K. Contextual prerequisites for understanding: Some investigations of comprehension and recall. *Journal of Verbal Learning and Verbal Behavior*, 1972, *11*, 717–726.

Broverman, I. K., Vogel, S. R., Broverman, D. M., Clarkson, F. E., & Rosenkrantz, P. S. Sex-role stereotypes: A current appraisal. *Journal of Social Issues*, 1972, *28*, 59–78.

Cantor, N., & Mischel, W. Traits as prototypes: Effects on recognition memory. *Journal of Personality and Social Psychology*, 1977, *35*, 38–48.

Chapman, L. J., & Chapman, J. P. Illusory correlations as an obstacle to the use of valid psycho-diagnostic signs. *Journal of Abnormal Psychology*, 1969, *74*, 271–280.

Cohen, C. *Cognitive basis of stereotyping*. Paper presented at the meeting of The American Psychological Association, San Francisco, August, 1977.

Dooling, D. J., & Christiaansen, R. E. Episodic and semantic aspects of memory for prose. *Journal of Experimental Psychology: Human Learning and Memory*, 1977, *3*, 428–436.

Gagnon, J. H., & Simon, W. *Sexual conduct: The social sources of human sexuality*. Chicago: Aldine, 1973.

Gallup, G. Prejudice declines in U.S. presidential races. *American Institute of Public Opinion*, 1978. (Reported in Minneapolis Tribune, September 21, 1978)

Garfinkel, H. Conditions of successful degradation ceremonies. *American Journal of Sociology*, 1956, *61*, 420–424.

Gauld, A., & Stephenson, G. M. Some experiments relating to Bartlett's theory of remembering. *British Journal of Psychology*, 1967, *58*, 39–49.

Goffman, E. *Stigma: Notes on the management of spoiled identity*. Englewood Cliffs, N.J.: Prentice-Hall, 1963.

Hamilton, D. L. *Illusory correlation as a basis for social stereotypes*. Paper presented at the meeting of The American Psychological Association, San Francisco, August, 1977.

Katchadourian, H. A., & Lunde, D. T. *Fundamentals of human sexuality* (2nd ed.). New York: Holt, Rinehart & Winston, 1975.

Kitsuse, J. I. Societal reactions to deviant behavior: Problems of theory and method. *Social Problems*, 1962, *9*, 247–256.

Klaich, D. *Woman & woman: Attitudes toward lesbianism*. New York: Simon & Schuster, 1974.

Lofland, J. *Deviance and identity*. Englewood Cliffs, N.J.: Prentice-Hall, 1966.

Loftus, E. F. Leading questions and the eyewitness report. *Cognitive Psychology*, 1975, *7*, 560–572.

Mandler, J. M., & Johnson, N. S. Remembrance of things parsed: Story structure and recall. *Cognitive Psychology*, 1977, *9*, 111–151.

Martin, D., & Lyon, P. *Lesbian/woman*. San Francisco: Glide, 1972.

Mischel, W. *Personality and assessment*. New York: Wiley, 1968.

Money, J., & Ehrhardt, A. A. *Man & woman: Boy & girl*. Baltimore: Johns Hopkins University Press, 1972.

Morris, J. *Conundrum*. New York: Signet, 1974.

Nisbett, R. E., Borgida, E., Crandall, R., & Reed, H. Popular induction: Information is not always informative. In J. Carroll & J. Payne (Eds.), *Cognition and social behavior*. Potomac, Md.: Lawrence Erlbaum Associates, 1976.

Oppenheim-Mason, K., Czajka, J. L., & Arber, S. Change in U.S. women's sex-role attitudes, 1964–1974. *American Sociological Review*, 1976, *41*, 573–596.

Riess, B. F., Safer, J., & Yotive, W. Psychological test data on female sexuality: A review of the literature. *Journal of Homosexuality*, 1974, *1*, 71–85.

Ross, L., Lepper, M. R., & Hubbard, M. Perseverance in self-perception and social perception: Biased attributional processes in the debriefing paradigm. *Journal of Personality and Social Psychology*, 1975, *32*, 880–892.

Rothbart, M. *Stereotype formation and maintenance*. Paper presented at the meeting of The American Psychological Association, San Francisco, August, 1977.

Schur, E. M. *Labeling deviant behavior: Its sociological implications*. New York: Harper & Row, 1971.

Scott, R. A. *The making of blind men*. New York: Russell Sage, 1969.

Secord, P. F., & Backman, C. W. An interpersonal approach to personality. In B. Maher (Ed.), *Progress in experimental personality research* (Vol. 2). New York: Academic Press, 1965.

Skrypnek, B. J., & Snyder, M. *On the self-perpetuating nature of stereotypes about women and men*. Unpublished manuscript, University of Minnesota, 1980.

Smedley, J. W., & Bayton, J. A. Evaluative race–class stereotypes by race and perceived class of subjects. *Journal of Personality and Social Psychology*, 1978, *36*, 511–520.

Snyder, M. Self-monitoring processes. In L. Berkowitz (Ed.), *Advances in experimental social psychology* (Vol. 12). New York: Academic Press, 1979

Snyder, M. Seek, and ye shall find: Testing hypotheses about other people. In E. T. Higgins, C. P. Herman, & M. P. Zanna (Eds.), *Social cognition: The Ontario Symposium on Personality and Social Psychology.* Hillsdale, N.J.: Lawrence Erlbaum Associates, 1981.

Snyder, M., & Cantor, N. Testing hypotheses about other people: The use of historical knowledge. *Journal of Experimental Social Psychology*, 1979, *15*, 330–342.

Snyder, M., & Swann, W. B., Jr. Behavioral confirmation in social interaction: From social perception to social reality. *Journal of Experimental Social Psychology*, 1978, *14*, 148–162. (a)

Snyder, M., & Swann, W. B., Jr. Hypothesis-testing processes in social interaction. *Journal of Personality and Social Psychology*, 1978, *36*, 1202–1212. (b)

Snyder, M., Tanke, E. D., & Berscheid, E. Social perception and interpersonal behavior: On the self-fulfilling nature of social stereotypes. *Journal of Personality and Social Psychology*, 1977, *35*, 656–666.

Snyder, M., & Uranowitz, S. W. *Reconstructing the past: An investigation of interpersonal biography.* Unpublished research, University of Minnesota, 1978. (a)

Snyder, M., & Uranowitz, S. W. *Reconstructing the past: The role of interpretive processes in reconstruction.* Unpublished research, University of Minnesota, 1978. (b)

Snyder, M., & Uranowitz, S. W. Reconstructing the past: Some cognitive consequences of person perception. *Journal of Personality and Social Psychology*, 1978, *36*, 941–950. (c)

Spiro, R. J. Remembering information from text: Theoretical and empirical issues concerning the state of schema reconstruction hypothesis. In R. C. Anderson, R. J. Spiro, & W. E. Montague (Eds.), *Schooling and the acquisition of knowledge.* Hillsdale, N.J.: Lawrence Erlbaum Associates, 1976.

Szasz, T. S. *The myth of mental illness.* New York: Dell, 1961.

Tanke, E. D. *Anticipated future interaction and the self-fulfilling prophecy effects of the physical attractiveness stereotype.* Doctoral dissertation, University of Minnesota, 1976.

Tannenbaum, F. *Crime and the community.* Boston: Ginn, 1938.

Thorndyke, P. W. Cognitive structures in comprehension and memory of narrative discourse. *Cognitive Psychology*, 1977, *9*, 77–110.

Uranowitz, S. W., Skrypnek, B. J., & Snyder, M. *Reconstructing the past: The role of stereotypes in remembering observed social interaction.* Unpublished research, University of Minnesota, 1978.

Valins, S. Persistent effects of information about internal reactions: Ineffectiveness of debriefing. In H. London & R. E. Nisbett (Eds.), *Thought and feeling: Cognitive modification of emotions and motives.* Chicago: Aldine, 1974.

Wachtel, P. Psychodynamics, behavior therapy, and the implacable experimenter: An inquiry into the consistency of personality. *Journal of Abnormal Psychology*, 1973, *82*, 324–334.

Walster, E., Berscheid, E., Abrahams, D., & Aronson, E. Effectiveness of debriefing following deception experiments. *Journal of Personality and Social Psychology*, 1967, *6*, 371–380.

Word, C. O., Zanna, M. P., & Cooper, J. The nonverbal mediation of self-fulfilling prophecies in interracial interaction. *Journal of Experimental Social Psychology*, 1974, *10*, 109–120.

Zadny, J., & Gerard, H. B. Attributed intentions and informational selectivity. *Journal of Experimental Social Psychology*, 1974, *10*, 34–52.

Zanna, M. P., & Pack, S. J. On the self-fulfilling nature of apparent sex differences in behavior. *Journal of Experimental Social Psychology*, 1975, *11*, 583–591.

7 Perceiving Persons as a Group: Categorization and Intergroup Relations

David A. Wilder
Rutgers-The State University

A recurring theme in social psychology is that persons seek to understand or make sense of their environment (Asch, 1951; Carroll & Payne, 1976; Heider, 1958). In most social situations we are bombarded with a multitude of stimulation. Because we cannot possibly analyze and respond to all of this information, we must narrow our focus to some subset of the field. That subset may be further reduced as we identify and categorize the selected stimuli.

Categorization has long been acknowledged to be a pervasive cognitive process (Bruner, 1958; Rosch & Lloyd, 1978). Moreover, categorization serves several useful functions for us. Most obviously, we can simplify our environment by categorizing objects. Second, categorization enables us to generate expectations about the properties of those objects. These expectations, in turn, guide our behavior toward the objects. A third consequence of categorization is that it permits us to consider a greater amount of information at any one time. For example, when we categorize a person as a member of a particular group, we may assume he or she possesses a variety of characteristics that we believe members of that category have. We may, therefore, not need to monitor her or his behavior too closely to discover that information inasmuch as we already have inferred its existence. But if we have any doubts about her or his membership in the group, we may monitor those characteristics critical to group membership all the more closely to determine whether our categorization is accurate.

Categorization is an active process in which stimuli may be altered by the act of categorization itself as well as by the specific category to which the stimuli are assigned (see the chapters by Taylor and Rothbart). For instance, on the most fundamental level, the manner in which persons "chunk" information can affect later recall of that information (Miller, 1956). Similarly, persons may chunk or

213

categorize others into social groups. Inasmuch as a group is a category, we would expect to observe the same cognitive processes in the handling of information about members of a group as with elements in a category. Furthermore, we might expect the likelihood of organizing persons into a group or of perceiving a given individual as a group member to be dependent on which cues are salient in the situation. Thus, if cues are salient that emphasize persons' similarity to one another, we would expect them to be categorized as a group. In the same manner, if cues are available that indicate a person's similarity to some existing group category, we are likely to perceive her or him as a member of that category (Taylor & Fiske, 1978).

This chapter focuses on the group as a category. In discussing the group as a category, one may consider: (1) the manner in which groups are created in the perceiver's mind; (2) the choice of which group of those possible a person will be perceived to be in; (3) consequences of categorizing a person into a group for one's conception of that group; and (4) consequences of categorization for behavior toward the person. I focus primarily upon this last topic. First, I consider the behavioral consequences of merely organizing persons into groups versus perceiving them as an aggregate of relatively independent individuals. In addition, where possible, implications are drawn from this research to the nature of the categorization process itself. In this way bridges may be constructed between this chapter, which focuses on behavioral implications of categorization, and some of the other chapters that focus more on the molecular dynamics of the categorization process (e.g., chapters by Rothbart and Taylor). Second, I address more complex issues of intergroup relations—situations in which not only do persons perceive others to be members of a group but also consider themselves to be members of a different group. Primary attention is given to intergroup bias resulting from the creation of mutually exclusive groups in situations where no prior history of group interaction exists. Third, I consider strategies to alter the categorization process so that simple ingroup/outgroup categorizations have less impact on one's behavior. Finally, several of the findings from the research reviewed in the chapter are extended to a few accepted principles in the area of intergroup relations.

CATEGORIZATION OF PERSONS INTO A GROUP

In this section the social group is explored as a category for the organization and interpretation of others' behavior. The research reviewed here has demonstrated that the categorization of persons into groups affects responses to those persons in a manner consistent with, although not necessarily identical to research on object categorization. As a point of departure, it is necessary to define a group and to distinguish a group from a mere collection or aggregate of individuals. Then a series of studies is summarized that have examined differences in responses to persons categorized as a group as compared to persons perceived as independent individuals. In particular, attention is focused on the following topics: assumptions of a person's belief and behavioral similarity to others present in the situation; recall of information about the person; information value of the person's behavior; attributions of causality for the person's behavior; and the persuasive impact of the person's behavior. These topics were chosen because they represent a graduated progression from simple to more complex cognitive inferences on the part of the perceiver.

On the most basic level, before even observing a person's behavior, one might ask whether categorization of the person into a group affects assumptions about the person's probable beliefs and behaviors. Later, when actually observing the person, the match between her or his behavior and one's expectations should affect the amount of information the person's behavior conveys about her or him. Furthermore, the correspondence between a person's behavior and one's expectations should affect attributions of causality for the behavior. Finally, effects of categorization on attributions of behavioral causality should, in turn, influence judgments of the persuasiveness of the person's behavior. Several experiments are reviewed that test this chain of inferences.

Definition of a Group

Attempts to define a psychological group have been numerous and less than unanimous (Cartwright & Zander, 1968). In a review of the group lexicon, DeLamater(1974) reported several similarities among definitions of a group. Some authors have focused on ''interaction'' as a defining property (Bales, 1953; Homans, 1950; Merton, 1957; Newcomb, 1963), on the perception of a ''relationship'' (Bales, 1953; Krech & Crutchfield, 1948; Lewin, 1948), or on the ''interdependence'' of group members (Cartwright & Zander, 1968; Cattell, 1951; Newcomb, 1963).

Although there is no generally agreed upon definition of a group, clearly we frequently organize others into group categories, and we use group labels in describing others and in anticipating their behaviors. To begin with, then, one might consider the cues persons use to categorize others into groups. Campbell (1958) has drawn some interesting parallels between principles of perceptual organization and the organization of persons into groups.[1] He notes that all

---

[1]One might be tempted to argue that organizing persons into groups is similar to categorizing any set of stimuli. The group, though, is a special kind of category in that its elements are not static. In most situations group members interact and, consequently, have the capacity to change one another. Thus, the group is reflexive; it acts upon itself (Billig, 1976). Compare this with categories where the elements do not affect one another directly as a consequence of their membership in the same category. Research presented in this chapter has not made use of this reflexive property of groups. I mention this issue only as a caution to the reader not to assume that social groups are identical to object categories.

groups possess boundaries that separate members from nonmembers (Homans, 1950).[2] Boundaries are created through cognitive organization of persons in an analogous manner to that used in the organization of physical objects. Persons characterized by common fate, similarity, or proximity are organized into a unit (group) separated from others by a psychological boundary. There is some evidence to suggest that these principles borrowed from object perception possess some validity. Research has indicated that persons who have shared a common fate (Zander, Stotland, & Wolfe, 1960), possessed similar beliefs (Stotland, Zander, & Natsoulas, 1961), or interacted frequently (Stotland, Cottrell, & Laing, 1960) and in close proximity (Knowles & Bassett, 1976) have exhibited the greatest degree of unity. Taylor, Fiske, Etcoff, and Ruderman (1978) also have argued that persons employ physical cues to categorize others. Subjects in their research used such apparent characteristics as race and sex in organizing information about a collection of persons.

For purposes of this chapter, a group is defined as a collection of persons who share (or are thought to share) some set of characteristics and who may (but not necessarily will) interact with one another. Note that the focus here is on a perceiver's categorization of others as a group. Whether the others consider themselves to be a group or not is irrelevant unless communicated to the perceiver. Moreover, in a topological sense a group may be distinguished from an aggregate by the existence of a boundary such that some interactions among group members are not available to nonmembers.

Perceptual cues such as those suggested by Campbell (1958) may satisfactorily predict group categorization when only one set of cues is present or dominant. But suppose, as is often the case, that multiple cues are present. For example, suppose that one interacts with a collection of persons where sex, race, occupation, and physical proximity are all potential cues for organization. Which cue(s) will be used? This is obviously a complex question, and one that I beg in this chapter. Some of the work described by Taylor and Rothbart in their chapters addresses this question.

Experimental Paradigm

The following paragraphs review briefly a series of experiments that have examined the consequences of categorizing persons into groups on the perception and interpretation of their behavior. Essentially the same paradigm was employed in

---

[2]Without question, a group is delimited by a boundary. That a group may not exist cognitively without a boundary is a stronger statement. In perception a figure does not exist without a ground (Köhler, 1967). Similarly a group may have no meaning unless there are regions or persons excluded from the group.. For instance, Mead (1937) reported that the mountain Arapesh had no name for themselves. Dwelling in mountainous terrain, they had little contact with outsiders. Consequently, there was no need to demarcate the group's boundary with a tribal name.

each of these experiments. Subjects were informed that they would be asked to give their reactions to a videotape of one or more persons who would be stating their opinions on a legal case. Subjects then read a summary of the mock civil suit. After familiarizing themselves with the case, they viewed a videotape in which: (1) the persons (confederates) were presented as members of the same discussion group (group condition); (2) half of the persons belonged to one discussion group and half belonged to a different group (two-groups condition); or (3) the persons were described as independent individuals whose presence together was coincidental (aggregate condition). In both the group and two-groups conditions, several visual cues were inserted on the videotapes to emphasize the group manipulation (e.g., they all sat at a common table and wore group identification tags). The same confederates appeared in all versions of the videotape and gave the same opinions about the civil suit. Subjects were informed that the confederates had formed their opinions independently before presenting them on the tape. Following exposure to one of these tapes, subjects completed a set of dependent measures. Minor variations in this method are mentioned in the following discussion of these studies. It was hypothesized that persons categorized into a group (group and two-groups conditions) would be reacted to differently from persons viewed as a collection of independent individuals (aggregate condition).

Expectations About Beliefs and Behaviors

Some research indicates that persons overestimate similarities among elements of a category and overestimate differences between elements of different categories (Tajfel, 1969; Tajfel & Wilkes, 1963). To illustrate this point Tajfel and Wilkes (1963) asked subjects to estimate the lengths of a series of lines. Lengths of adjacent lines varied by a constant amount. In one condition the first half of the lines were labeled A, and the second half were labeled B. In making judgments, subjects estimated larger differences between a line in group A and an adjacent one in group B than between adjacent lines in either group A or B. Thus, elements within a category were moved together (assimilation), whereas elements from different categories were spread farther apart (contrast). On the basis of this and other relevant research (Campbell, 1956), one would expect members of a group to be perceived as relatively more similar to one another than members of different groups or persons in an aggregate.

Results from a field experiment by Tajfel, Sheikh, and Gardner (1964) supported these predictions. In their study two Indians were interviewed in front of a class of Canadians. The Indians were queried about their tastes in books, films, etc. (The experimenters had elicited the general stereotypes Canadians had about Indians from another group of subjects.) The Indians were judged to be more alike on characteristics that were part of the general stereotype (e.g., submissive, religious, family-oriented) than on those characteristics not part of the stereotype (e.g., sociable, optimistic). Given the uncontrolled field setting of this study, it does not provide an unambiguous test of the hypothesis that distortions were due to categorization. It is possible that the Indians were, in fact, more alike on characteristics relevant to the stereotype.

To provide such a test, Wilder (1978a) designed an experiment in which stimulus persons were assigned to a single group, assigned to two mutually exclusive groups, or not categorized into groups at all. Subjects observed the behavior of one stimulus person and were asked to predict the beliefs and behaviors of another person. It was hypothesized that the assumed similarity of two persons would be greater when both were members of the same group than when they were members of different groups or when they were not members of groups at all. Subjects read a summary of a legal dispute. They then listened to the opinion of a person who was either an independent individual among an aggregate of others, a member of a single group, or a member of one of two groups. Subjects predicted the beliefs of another person in the aggregate (aggregate condition), another member of the group (group condition), or a member of the other group (two-groups condition). A control condition was included in which subjects predicted the opinion of a person without having heard anyone's opinion. As expected, subjects in the group condition assumed the most similarity between the person they had heard and the person they were asked about. On the other hand, subjects in the aggregate and two-groups conditions assumed little similarity between the two persons. In the latter conditions the two persons were not members of the same social category; they were either unrelated individuals (aggregate condition) or members of different groups (two-groups condition). This pattern of findings was obtained on both measures of belief similarity and predictions of future behavior. Results of this experiment indicated that categorization of a person into a group establishes expectations about the person; expectations that are formed before actually seeing the person's behavior.

Recall of Information

If perceivers have definite expectations about the similarity of group members, then one might expect to see evidence of such expectations in the recall of information about group members. Specifically, distortions in recall of information about group members should be consistent with the expectations or schemas persons hold about the group (Srull & Wyer, 1980). Such errors should, of course, be less probable when the persons are not perceived to be group members.

There is ample evidence that recall of stimuli is affected by the category of which they are members. Consider, for example, two classic studies that illustrate this point. Carmichael, Hogan, and Walter (1932) presented subjects with several ambiguous figures. The objects were identified and, later, subjects were asked to reproduce them. The investigators reported systematic distortions in the drawings. The distortions were in the direction of the categories to which the objects had been assigned when initially viewed. In Allport and Postman's (1947) study of rumor transmission, subjects were asked to transmit a description of a picture to the person sitting next to them who, in turn, described the contents to the next person, and so forth. Errors in the transmission of information were largely in the direction of prevailing stereotypes.

These findings are also consistent with those reported elsewhere in this book (see the chapter by Taylor). Taylor et al. (1978) found that subjects had less difficulty making between-category discriminations in recall of information than making within-category discriminations. In one study subjects observed stimulus persons, half of whom were black and half of whom were white. In another study half of the persons were males and half were females. Subjects were required to identify which persons had made various statements during the discussion. Subjects were more accurate in remembering which category the stimulus person was a member of (race or sex) than in remembering which individual within the category made the statement.

Cantor and Mischel (1977) have argued that persons organize information about others into an integrated structure—a prototype. When presented with information about others, subjects were better able to recall information that was consistent with the prototype they held. Moreover, when given the opportunity to recognize information that may have been presented, subjects made more false recognitions of items relevant to the prototype than of items unrelated to the prototype.

An experiment by Cohen (1977) illustrates this process. As part of her research, Cohen ascertained the characteristics persons think are typical of members of two categories—waitress and librarian. From these lists of characteristics she constructed a prototype of a librarian and a waitress. She then made videotapes of a person performing behaviors, some of which were typical or atypical of a waitress and a librarian. Before viewing the tape, subjects were told that the stimulus person was either a waitress or a librarian. Later, subjects were given a list of items and were instructed to identify all those that were present on the tape. Subjects were more accurate in the recognition of information that was consistent with their prototype of the stimulus person.

Information Conveyed by a Group

If we expect group members to behave similarly to one another, then when they do behave alike we gain information about them only in the sense that they have confirmed our expectations. We may, as a consequence, be all the more certain of the justifiability and accuracy of our categorization of the persons. But the similar behavior of the group members does not provide us with unambiguous information about their individual qualities or dispositions. It may be difficult to discern under such circumstances whether their similar behavior reflects common dispositions (e.g., similar beliefs, likes and dislikes, personality traits) or conformity to actual or implied group norms. On the other hand, when persons are not perceived to be members of a group, similar behavior is less expected. It is relatively less predictable and, therefore, should convey more information about the persons (Jones & Davis, 1965). Thus, common behavior by persons in a group should be viewed as more ambiguous and less informative about them than the same behavior performed by persons perceived to be independent of one another. This hypothesis was tested in an experiment in which subjects were asked to partition a stimulus person's behavior into meaningful units of action (Wilder, 1979).

The methodology employed in this experiment was developed by Newtson (1973, 1976). Newtson and others (Barker, 1963) have argued that observers organize an actor's behavior into units from which inferences are made about the actor. For example, consider the behavior of a person who leaves a house and walks to a nearby store. An observer who perceives the behavior as one act (e.g., going to the store) may infer that the person intends to shop. On the other hand, an observer who perceives several discrete acts (e.g., leaving the house, walking several blocks, looking at the store, entering the store) may infer that the person is out for a stroll and just happens to stop at the store. In a series of studies Newtson (1976) found that subjects who divided the actor's behavior into many units made more extreme inferences about the actor with greater confidence than subjects who divided the actor's behavior into few units of action.

Based on the foregoing arguments, it was hypothesized that similar behavior among persons would be judged less meaningful about a given person when that person and the others were members of a common group than when they were unrelated. Subjects were assigned to one of three conditions in which they viewed the behavior of a group of four confederates, an aggregate of four, or a lone confederate. Subjects were asked to segment the behavior of one confederate into meaningful units. If behavior by the person in an aggregate is more informative about him, the actor's behavior should be partitioned into more units and should elicit a more extreme attribution in the aggregate than in the group condition. (The alone condition, where subjects viewed the behavior of only one person, was included to test for the effect of having others present on the videotapes in the aggregate and group conditions.)

Subjects viewed two tapes of the confederate(s) and signaled each meaningful act they observed by pressing a button attached to an event recorder. Included in the postexperimental questionnaire was an item asking subjects to locate the primary cause of the actor's behavior. They were required to check one alternative indicating that the primary cause rested either with the actor's disposition or with the situation. As hypothesized, the actor's behavior was segmented into more meaningful units when the actor was among an aggregate than when either a group member or alone. Parallel findings emerged in the attribution data. Subjects were more likely to make a dispositional attribution (85%) when the actor was among an aggregate than when a member of a group (58%) or when alone (50%). As hypothesized, the actor's relationship to the others affected both the perceived informativness of her or his behavior and the causal attributions for the behavior.

In this study the stimulus persons behaved similarly whether group members or individuals. If one or more members of the group behaves differently from the others, the information value of her or his behavior should increase and attributions of causality should change as well. Specifically, a dissenter's behavior should be judged to be more dispositionally caused. This point is discussed more fully in the following experiment dealing specifically with attributions of causality.

Attributions of Causality

In observing another, we frequently press beyond the apparent actions and infer possible causes of the behavior (Heider, 1958; Jones & Davis, 1965; Kelley, 1967). An issue of concern to attribution theories is the delineation of circumstances under which persons attribute the cause of an actor's behavior to internal (dispositional) properties as opposed to external (situational) forces. We assume that observers utilize some subset of the cues available to them in the person's behavior and in the broader situation to arrive at some causal inference. One such cue is the behavior of others who are in the same situation as the actor. Kelley (1967) has proposed that common behavior among persons (consensus) encourages an attribution to situational causes, whereas unique behavior is attributed to properties of the agent performing the behavior. Tests of the consensus prediction have not yielded uniform results, with several investigators reporting varying degrees of support for Kelley's prediction (Feldman, Higgins, Karlovak, & Ruble, 1976; Hansen & Lowe, 1976; Harvey, Arkin, Gleason, & Johnston, 1974; Orvis, Cunningham, & Kelley, 1975; Ruble & Feldman, 1976; Wells & Harvey, 1977, 1978), and others finding little or no support (McArthur, 1972; Nisbett & Borgida, 1975).

When observing the behavior of an actor who is among others, attributions of causality may be made either to the actor's disposition or to elements of the situation—the task and the presence of the other persons. The importance of this last agent (presence of others) should be affected by the perceived relationship of the actor to the others. Previously cited research (Taylor et al., 1978; Wilder, 1978b) has shown that persons assume group members behave relatively similarly in the presence of one another. Because persons expect group members to behave similarly, unique behavior by a group member is unanticipated and should evoke a relatively internal attribution (Jones & Davis, 1965; Jones & McGillis, 1976).

Common behavior among group members can reasonably be attributed to common properties (dispositions) of the persons or to common social influences as a result of belonging to the same group and presumably experiencing the same environment (situation). Thus, common behavior among group members may reflect similar dispositions, similar task requirements, or expectations of consensus in a group. No such expectations of agreement exist with an aggregate, so that external cause is not available to explain common behavior among an aggregate. Consequently, having more plausible external causes for their behavior, common behavior among group members should evoke a more situational attribution than common behavior in an aggregate. This hypothesis was examined in the following experiment (Wilder, 1978b).

Subjects were assigned to one of six conditions and observed the behavior of an actor who gave either a common opinion (agreed with the others) or a unique opinion (disagreed with the others) in a single group, in one of two groups, or among an aggregate of others. (The two-groups conditions were included to see if findings from the one-group conditions generalized to situations involving multiple groups.) In addition, in two control conditions an actor gave either the "common" or "unique" opinion alone. Subjects were then asked to make attributions about the cause of the actor's behavior. Using bipolar scales, they indicated the extent to which the actor's behavior was due to dispositional versus situational causes, to personality, to ability, to task characteristics, and to the presence of the others. Overall, attribution data from the questionnaire supported the hypothesis. When a member of a group (one-group and two-groups conditions), the actor was perceived to be more influenced by the situation, by the nature of the task, and by the presence of the other group members when he or she agreed than when he or she dissented. But the actor's agreement or disagreement with the others did not affect attributions when the actor was perceived to be one of an aggregate of persons. In support of the second prediction, agreement with others was attributed more to situational factors in the group conditions than in the aggregate conditions. The agreeing group member was judged to have been more influenced by the presence of the others than was the agreeing individual in an aggregate.

If causal attributions can be affected by the mere categorization of persons into groups, then behaviors dependent on these attributions should be affected in an analogous manner. For instance, the credibility imputed to a person depends, in part, on attributions made about the cause of his or her behavior (Ross, Bierbrauer, & Hoffman, 1976). In the next section a series of studies are reviewed that have examined effects of categorization on a person's persuasiveness.

Persuasiveness of a Group

That the behavior of a person categorized into a group is viewed as somewhat influenced by the others suggests that her or his behavior is not perceived to be independent of the others. Consequently, group members should be viewed as less credible and should have less persuasive impact than persons not categorized into a group. This hypothesis was tested in four experiments in which subjects viewed a videotape of several confederates who attempted to influence the subjects' opinions (Wilder, 1977, 1978a).

In the first experiment (Wilder, 1977), instructions were manipulated so that subjects perceived four persons on a videotape as a single group of four, as two separate groups of two persons each, or as four independent persons. The confederates expressed unanimous opinions about the responsibility of the parties involved in a legal dispute. Their opinions were strongly opposed to those held by most subjects (as determined from pilot data). After viewing the tape, subjects were given the opportunity to express their own opinions about the case. As hypothesized, influence in the direction advocated by the confederates was greater when the actors were perceived as separate individuals than when organized into either two groups or a single group. Furthermore, when categorized into two separate groups, the confederates were more persuasive than when they were all perceived to be members of the same group.

Two subsequent experiments replicated and extended these findings (Wilder, 1977, 1978a). Using the same procedure, subjects viewed a tape of six persons who were organized into a single group of six, two groups of three each, three groups of two, or an aggregate of six individuals. Social influence was found to vary linearly with the number of groups in opposition, even though the number of communicators did not vary. Thus, the influence of a collection of persons was shown to decrease as they were organized into fewer social units. Furthermore, those subjects who were influenced attributed greater independence to the confederates and were better able to recall the opinions of the individual confederates (Wilder, 1978a).

In a final experiment in this series, subjects received social support from one confederate, whereas three others disagreed with the subjects' position (Wilder, 1977). As in the preceding two experiments, the confederates had been categorized into a single group, two separate groups of two persons each, or not categorized into a group at all. Consistent with previous research (Allen, 1975), social support effectively reduced opinion changes in the direction of the communicators in all conditions. Of greater interest was the finding that social support was more effective in reducing conformity when the opposition had been categorized into a group than when the opposition was perceived to be an independent collection of individuals. Again, the majority persons had greater impact on the subject's opinions when they were viewed as relatively unrelated individuals than when they were perceived to be a group.

Summary

Research reported in the preceding sections has focused on effects of categorizing a collection of persons into a group. These studies have shown that persons organize and interpret the behavior of a group member differently from the behavior of an individual not categorized into a group. Specifically the group member's behavior was viewed as less informative than the individual's behavior. Attributions about the cause of the group member's behavior were more situational or external than those made about the individual. (This occurred when the stimulus persons behaved the same as the others. Differential effects of categorization on attributions diminished when the stimulus person did not behave like the others.) The stimulus person was assumed to possess more similar beliefs and was thought to behave more similarly to the others when a member of a group than when independent of the others. Recall of information about group members was distorted in the direction of prevailing stereotypes about the group. Finally, stimulus persons were less persuasive when they were categorized as members of a common group than when they were perceived to be an aggregate of persons. The pervasiveness of these group/aggregate differences across several levels of cognition (from organization of behavior to attributions to attitude change) suggests that differences arise early in person perception and exert significant effects upon higher-order responses.

Thus far, attention has been focused solely on the perceiver's categorization of stimulus persons into a group. The next section expands the domain to include the perceiver's self-categorization into a group, and how such group membership may affect interpretations of and responses to the behavior of a target person. Emphasis is placed on situations where the perceiver and target persons are members of different and mutually exclusive groups.

CATEGORIZATION INTO INGROUPS AND OUTGROUPS

The perceivers (subjects) in the research discussed in the preceding section did not interact with those they observed and had no relationship to them. In the experiments reviewed in this section, the perceivers as well as the actors were categorized into explicit groups. Moreover, the perceivers' group (ingroup) was distinct from the actors' group (outgroup), such that membership in one group precluded membership in the other group. Topics considered include the following: expectations of similarity and homogeneity of ingroup and outgroup members, recall of information, preference for information about the groups, and bias in the distribution of rewards between the groups. Following a review of the ingroup/outgroup literature, several current explanations are presented that attempt to account for these findings.

Assumption of Similarity

Membership in a category is contingent on the possession of specified similarities to other elements of the category and differences from elements not in the category (Bruner, 1958; Tversky & Gati, 1978). To the extent that persons perceive groups as categories, they should assume that group members possess characteristics that are relatively similar to one another and dissimilar from nonmembers. To test this hypothesis, an experiment was designed to show that members of a group perceive themselves to be similar to one another and different from members of other groups (Allen & Wilder, 1979).

Subjects were divided into two mutually exclusive groups on the basis of a relatively trivial task (Brewer, 1979; Tajfel, Billig, Bundy, & Flament, 1971). Subjects privately expressed their preferences among pairs of paintings by two artists (Klee and Kandinsky). The experimenter collected their responses and supposedly tabulated their preferences while they completed a questionnaire. On the questionnaire subjects expressed their beliefs and opinions on a variety of topics, some pertaining to art and some irrelevant to the painting judgment task (e.g., political beliefs). When they had finished the opinion survey, the experimenter informed each subject privately of his or her group assignment (either Klee group or Kandinsky group). In reality, group assignment was random. Then subjects were asked to complete the belief survey, but this time they were to answer the questions in the manner they thought another ingroup (or an outgroup) member would respond to the items. Subjects assumed a fellow ingroup member possessed more beliefs similar to their own than did a member of the outgroup. This finding held both for items relevant to art and for items less relevant to the criterion on which the intergroup boundary was drawn.

Assumption of Homogeneity

A subsequent experiment (Wilder, 1980a) examined assumptions about the variance or homegeneity of beliefs among ingroup and outgroup members. Assuming that we generally interact more with ingroup members than with outgroup members, we should encounter a greater variety of persons and have a greater variety of experiences with ingroup members than with outgroup members. We may, therefore, expect ingroup categories to be more differentiated than outgroup categories. When asked to estimate the beliefs of members of an ingroup and an outgroup, subjects should assume a greater range of beliefs for members of the ingroup than for members of the outgroup.

Following the method of the preceding experiment (Allen & Wilder, 1979), subjects were divided into two groups on the basis of their painting preferences. In a control condition subjects were not divided into explicit groups; otherwise, they completed the same set of dependent measures. Items on the inventory assessed subjects' beliefs and attitudes toward a legal dispute, several political issues, and preferences in art (e.g., styles of paintings, such as impressionist). Following an unrelated filler task, subjects estimated the range of opinions among members of both groups. Measures were constructed in the following manner. Subjects were presented with a range of possible positions or beliefs on each topic—artistic preferences (from primitive to abstract), political beliefs (from reactionary to radical), and opinions about the legal case (from favorable to unfavorable reactions to the defendants). Some subjects predicted the positions they thought members of the ingroup were likely to endorse, whereas others estimated the positions of members of the outgroup. As hypothesized, ingroup members were assumed to have a wider range of beliefs than outgroup members. Relative to the ingroup, the outgroup was thought to be more homogeneous on items (art and politics) related to the criterion for categorization. Subjects in the control condition did not differ in their estimate of the range of beliefs among others in the session. Half of the subjects in each condition did not complete the dependent measures at the end of the experiment. These subjects returned one week later and responded to the same dependent measures that the other subjects answered immediately following their session. The delay subjects displayed the same pattern of responses one week after the initial categorization as subjects who had completed the measures immediately. More interestingly, assumptions of homogeneity within the outgroup were somewhat, thought not significantly, enhanced following the delay of a week.

Recall of Information

If persons assume that ingroups are similar to themselves and outgroups are relatively dissimilar, then they may very well recall such information more readily. Similarly, if persons assume outgroups are more homogeneous than ingroups, their recall of information about the outgroup may be less rich and less differentiated than their recall of ingroup information.

In a series of experiments, Rothbart and his colleagues reported that the categorization of persons into an ingroup and an outgroup is sufficient to bias subjects' recall of information about the groups (Howard & Rothbart, 1980). In their first study, subjects were divided into two groups using the dot-estimation procedure employed by Tajfel and his associates (Tajfel et al., 1971). Subjects were then provided with a list of positive and negative traits to be assigned to the two groups. As expected, subjects assigned more positive items to the ingroup and, consequently, more negative items to the outgroup than vice versa. In two other experiments subjects were provided with both positive and negative traits about the groups. When later asked to recall which items belonged with the respective groups, subjects recalled more negative statements about the outgroup and fewer negative statements about the ingroup than was actually the case. This finding fits nicely with an experiment reported by Rothbart, Evans, and Fulero (1979). Persons in their experiment were better able to recall statements that confirmed their expectations about a group than statements that disconfirmed or were unrelated to their expectations. (See the chapter by Rothbart for a more detailed presentation.) Given that we expect outgroups to be relatively dissimilar to ourselves, recall of information about the ingroup and outgroup may accentuate alleged intergroup differences.

In a recently completed experiment (Wilder, 1980b) modeled after one presented earlier (homogeneity of beliefs), subjects completed several tasks including an attitude inventory that tapped their opinions on a variety of issues (e.g., politics, art). After completing these tasks, subjects were divided into two groups and assigned to separate rooms where they received feedback about the opinions of ingroup and outgroup members as well as brief demographic descriptions of these persons. Following an interpolated task, subjects were asked to recall the information that had been presented to them. They then were given a list of information and were asked to identify with whom each piece of information had been associated.

Results showed that subjects were better able to recall information indicating ingroup similarities and outgroup dissimilarities relative to themselves. This finding complements results demonstrating that persons expect ingroup members to be more similar to themselves than outgroup members (Allen & Wilder, 1979). Moreover, on the recognition task, subjects made more false identifications of characteristics that indicated ingroup similarity and outgroup dissimiliarity to themselves. Once the groups were established, subjects maintained clear distinctions between the groups.

Information Preference

The research reviewed in the foregoing indicates that the establishment of ingroup/outgroup categories affects the manner in which persons infer beliefs and recall past behaviors of others. The recall data suggest that the categorization process actively influences what information about the group will be most accessible to us. We might expect to find similar effects when persons are given the opportunity to select among several kinds of information about members of ingroups and outgroups. Specifically, we hypothesized that persons would express a preference for information that is consistent with expectations about ingroups and outgroups (Wilder & Allen, 1978).

If a person desires stability in her or his social relations (Heider, 1958), information that is consistent with the person's definition of the social situation should be useful because it reinforces and stabilizes one's perception of the situation. Thus, in an intergroup setting a person should prefer information indicating that ingroup members are similar to oneself and that outgroup persons are dissimilar. This pattern of information preference is consistent with and serves to strengthen perceived differences between the ingroup and outgroup.

In Wilder and Allen's (1978) study, subjects were divided into two groups, allegedly on the basis of their painting preferences but actually by random assignment. After completing an attitude inventory, they were given an opportunity to see information indicating (relative to their own attitudes) their similarity with the ingroup, dissimilarity with the ingroup, similarity with the outgroup, or dissimilarity with the outgroup. Appropriate choices were also available for subjects in a control condition who were not categorized into groups. Subjects rank ordered their preferences for viewing each of the four types of available information. We hypothesized that when divided into two groups, subjects would prefer information indicating their similarity with the ingroup and dissimilarity with the outgroup. But there would be no preference for one kind of information over another when subjects were not divided into groups. Results supported both predictions; when an ingroup/outgroup categorization was created, persons chose to view information that would augment intergroup differences.

Results of the experiment are consistent with studies reported earlier in which subjects' recall of information was affected by the group membership of the target persons. In those experiments subjects recalled fewer individual characteristics of outgroup members than of ingroup members (Wilder, 1980b). Taken together, these findings indicate that persons act to maintain differences between cognitive categories—in this case, ingroups and outgroups.

The literature reviewed to this point has dealt with categorization effects upon a person's expectations and interpretations of the behavior of group members. In the next section a considerable body of work is summarized that has investigated categorization effects on behavior directed at ingroups and outgroups. This research has focused on intergroup bias—either prejudiced beliefs or behavioral discrimination.

Intergroup Bias

Most explanations of intergroup bias have assumed the existence of some tangible reason for negative reactions to an outgroup. Bias has been attributed to a variety of factors including competition between groups, exploitation induced by the larger social and economic system, assumptions of belief dissimilarity, and child-raising practices of parents (Allport, 1954; Ashmore, 1970; Rokeach, 1960). All these explanations regard intergroup bias, whether at the level of attitude (prejudice) or behavior (discrimination), as a response likely to be fostered in either a specific set of persons (Adorno, Frenkel-Brunswik, Levinson, & Sanford, 1950), a specific culture (Pettigrew, 1959; Simpson & Yinger, 1965), or a specific set of situational conditions (Campbell, 1967). Tajfel (1969) has proposed that intergroup bias may be a more general phenomenon, a direct product of the categorization process. He has argued that the mere existence of different social groups is sufficient to foster biased behavior. In particular, persons favor groups of which they are members (ingroups) at the expense of groups to which they do not belong (outgroups).

To test his strong assertion, Tajfel devised a paradigm in which subjects are assigned to one of two groups on the basis of a trivial criterion (e.g., preference for the paintings of two artists, estimation of dots on slides). Although subjects believe they have been divided into groups on the basis of their judgments, actual group assignment is random. Each subject is also given a code number to keep his or her identity hidden. Later, subjects are told that they will have the opportunity to divide rewards among others in the experiment. They are provided with a booklet of reward matrices; two of the more common are illustrated here.

These numbers are rewards for:
Member no. _____ of _____ group   1   2   3   4   5 6 7 8 9 10 11 12 13 14
Member no. _____ of _____ group   14 13 12 11 10 9 8 7 6   5   4   3   2   1

These numbers are rewards for:
Member no. _____ of _____ group   7 8 9 10 11 12 13 14 15 16 17 18 19
Member no. _____ of _____ group   1 3 5   7   9 11 13 15 17 19 21 23 25

The numbers in the top row depict the number of points (worth some monetary amount) that are to be awarded to the person whose code number appears in the top line at the left of the matrix. The bottom row of numbers are the points that may be awarded to the person whose code number appears on the bottom line at the left. Subjects are required to circle only one vertical pair of numbers in each matrix. Subjects are generally asked to divide rewards between two members of the ingroup, between two members of the outgroup, and between a member of the ingroup and a member of the outgroup. Note that in the first matrix depicted, the total number of points is held constant at 15, so any points awarded to one person is at the expense of the other person. In the second matrix the total number of points varies, so that an increase in points to one person results in an increase in points to the other person. Note that the differential advantage enjoyed by the person on the top line decreases as the total rewards increase. This matrix is of considerable interest because it pits two possible response strategies against each other. If I simply want to maximize the benefit for the person described on the top line, I should choose a combination toward the right end of the scale. On the other hand, if I want to favor that person by maximizing her or his advantage over the other person, I should choose a combination at the left end of the scale. (A fuller description of these and other matrices can be found in Tajfel et al., 1971). It is important to remember that each subject's own code number never appears in a matrix; consequently, a subject's decisions cannot directly benefit herself or himself.

In a conceptually similar paradigm (Rabbie & Horwitz, 1969), subjects are divided into groups at the experimenter's whim. They then tell one another a few biographical facts about themselves and are given an opportunity to earn a prize. The prize, however, is arbitrarily awarded to one of the two groups. As part of the dependent measures, subjects evaluate members of the ingroup, members of the outgroup, the ingroup as a whole, and the outgroup as a whole on several traits. These are presented as bipolar scales, and subjects are asked to indicate the extent to which the others possess such characteristics as responsibility, consideration, openness, soundness of judgment, and so forth.

Regardless of the specific paradigm, results from these studies have consistently shown that subjects discriminate in their behavior—they assign more positive traits (Rabbie & Horwitz, 1969; Rabbie & Wilkens, 1971; Wilson & Miller, 1961) and rewards (Allen & Wilder, 1975; Tajfel et al., 1971) to the ingroup than to the outgroup. (See Brewer, 1979, for a comprehensive review of this literature and a description of the paradigms currently in use.) As an example, consider a study by Billig and Tajfel (1973) in which half of the subjects were assigned code numbers in the 40s and half in the 70s. Half of the subjects were then explicitly assigned to one of two groups on the basis of the code numbers (one group of 40s and one of 70s); the remaining subjects were not assigned to groups. Subjects then divided rewards among the other persons in the experiment. When divided into two groups, subjects discriminated in favor of their ingroup at the expense of the outgroup. But when subjects were not explicitly categorized into groups, they did not show substantial bias in the assignment of rewards. Thus, when subjects regarded one another as group members, they behaved differently from when they viewed each other as individuals. These findings have been replicated in one form or another in many experiments (Brewer & Silver, 1978; Doise, Csepeli, Dann, Gouge, Larsen, & Ostell, 1972; Doise & Sinclair, 1973; Kahn & Ryen, 1972; Rabbie & Horwitz, 1969; Rabbie & Wilkens, 1971; Tajfel & Billig, 1974). Ingroup preference has been shown to occur even in the absence of competition or direct contact between groups.

These findings are interesting for a number of reasons. First, they demonstrate that intergroup bias may be induced by very minimal manipulations. Even so, the division of subjects into categories must have a minimum, if unimportant, rationale. Thus, in the Billig and Tajfel (1973) experiment described previously subjects who were arbitrarily given different code numbers, but who were not explicitly assigned to a ''group'', did not display the bias typically found in other studies using this paradigm. Similarly, Rabbie and Horwitz (1969) failed to find bias when the groups were explicitly created by chance (flip of the coin). But discrimination did occur when the experimenter arbitrarily assigned them to groups. In the latter situation, subjects may have inferred that the experimenter had some reason or ulterior motive for partitioning them as he did, and that his reason reflected a significant difference between the groups.

Second, the bias observed in the minimal group research occurs even when subjects cannot benefit directly from the manner in which they divide the rewards. Thus, one cannot simply dismiss the findings as a mere demonstration of self-interest. In the experimental paradigm developed by Tajfel (1970), for instance, subjects are given the opportunity to divide rewards between two ingroup members, two outgroup members, or an ingroup member and an outgroup member. The various ingroup and outgroup members are represented by their code numbers. The subject's own code number never appears on these dependent measures, so one never has the opportunity to reward oneself.

Third, most subjects do not display strong ingroup favoritism. Although subjects show a consistant pattern of ingroup favoritism on the measures, very few subjects (less than 10% in my research) maximize the ingroup's gain at the expense of the outgroup. In general, subjects give a few more points (money) or a little higher rating on trait scales to the ingroup. For example, when given the opportunity to divide 15 points, subjects generally award 9 or 10 points to their own group and 5 or 6 points to the other group. Few subjects award 14 to their ingroup and only 1 to the outgroup. But the significant finding is that this bias, though relatively small, appears to be a stable phenomenon that occurs across age groups, nationalities, and sex.

Finally, in many of these experiments subjects act not simply to reward the ingroup, but to maintain a relative advantage for the ingroup over the outgroup (Allen & Wilder, 1975; Billig & Tajfel, 1973; Tajfel et al., 1971). Subjects ensure that the ingroup is treated more favorably than the outgroup even if this results in the ingroup obtaining less than the maximum amount of reward. For example, when given the choice between awarding 7 points to the ingroup and 1 point to the outgroup or 12 points to the ingroup and 11 points to the outgroup, subjects prefer the 7/1 alternative to the 12/11 choice even though this decision does not maximize ingroup outcomes. The 7/1 decision does, however, maximize the difference between the ingroup and the outgroup.

That intergroup bias may be fostered simply by structuring a situation so that persons are members of different groups has two interesting implications for the study of intergroup relations. First, intergroup discrimination may be created without any apparent justification (such as competition between groups). Discrimination may be an unavoidable product (or covariate) of categorizing the environment into ingroups and outgroups. Second, contrary to some theories of intergroup relations (Allport, 1954; Ashmore, 1970), discrimination may not be a product of irrational thought but may be a consequence of one's attempt to organize and simplify the environment.

Several explanations have been offered to account for ingroup/outgroup bias in the minimal group situations. These explanations have focused on three different levels of psychological analysis—cultural norms (societal level), social identity (interpersonal level), and cognitive process (intrapersonal level). As such, they are not very amenable to "critical" tests pitting one against another. Moreover, given the lack of research in this area, one cannot determine whether any one hypothesis has substantially more support than the others. Suffice it to say that social behavior has many causes and is most likely overdetermined in any situation (Campbell, 1967). To the extent that these explanations appear plausible, they should all be assumed to be viable at this time.

Cultural Norm Hypothesis.   Tajfel (1970) proposed a normative explanation of bias in the minimal group situation. Presumably persons are socialized in our culture to favor groups to which they belong at the expense of outgroups. In support of this argument, Tajfel cited evidence indicating that young children express ingroup favoritism even though they have little knowledge of the groups they evaluate. In these investigations Tajfel had grade school and preschool children rate the attractiveness of several nationalities. Subjects favored their own nations, as well as allies, over traditional enemies.

In an intergroup relations experiment using Tajfel's procedure, Allen and Wilder (1975) reported that subjects expected others in the ingroup and outgroup to behave the same way they did (i.e., to show ingroup favoritism in the distribution of rewards). This might appear to be supportive of a normative explanation, but subjects also reported that their preferred tactic would have been equality in the distribution of rewards. Contrary to a normative explanation, subjects did not feel that they should have divided rewards unequally.

Findings from another study (Dion, 1973) also failed to support a normative explanation. If discrimination against the outgroup is normative, socially sanctioned behavior, then one would expect greater discrimination the more closely the subject is identified with the ingroup. Dion (1973) failed to find support for this prediction; subjects in highly cohesive groups were no more biased against the outgroup than were subjects in groups low in cohesiveness.

Social Identity Hypothesis.   A second explanation posits that discrimination in an intergroup setting reflects a desire for positive social identity (Billig & Tajfel, 1973; Turner, 1975). When categorized into novel groups, subjects are uncertain about their social identity relative to others in the situation. One way of establishing a positive social identity for oneself and one's ingroup is to behave differentially toward the outgroup. One such behavior that differentiates the groups is, of course, ingroup favoritism at the expense of the outgroup. This explanation assumes that subjects actively engage in a social comparison process—evaluating their identity or well-being relative to the outgroup. The social identity hypothesis can explain the curious finding that subjects often act to maximize the difference between the groups rather than simply maximizing benefits for the ingroup.

Cognitive Differentiation Hypothesis.   A more basic explanation uses a gestalt or perceptual analogy to analyze the intergroup setting (Dion, 1979a; Wilder, 1978c). Social categorization divides the environment into two mutually exclusive categories—ingroup and outgroup. Inasmuch as these categories are initially differentiated in a nonoverlapping manner, persons expect to encounter information that emphasizes the differences between the groups. Furthermore, given the opportunity, persons may act to differentiate between the groups. Intergroup discrimination is one way (indeed the only way in the studies of intergroup relations in the minimal group setting) of maintaining the cognitive differentiation between the groups. To the extent that subjects perceive themselves as a unit with the ingroup (Heider, 1958), they will act to favor the ingroup over the outgroup. Thus, ingroup/outgroup bias may be a consequence of normal categorization processes.

One implication of this argument is that persons should be sensitive to information that differentiates between ingroups and outgroups; in particular, to information that emphasizes positive aspects of the ingroup and negative aspects of the outgroup (Wilder & Allen, 1978). In accord with this reasoning, Campbell (1967) has argued that behavior an ingroup member would be punished for is particularly likely to be noticed and integrated into the outgroup stereotype. Thus, not only do we perceive the outgroup as different from the ingroup, but we may be prone to notice and attribute undesirable characteristics to the outgroup. Most of the research cited in this chapter is consistent with the differentiation explanation of bias.

If the differentiation hypothesis has merit, then techniques that alter the categorization should affect intergroup bias. In particular, discrimination should be lessened if the categories of ingroup and outgroup are changed. The third part of this chapter is concerned with techniques that can be used to alter the ingroup/outgroup categorization.

REDUCING INTERGROUP BIAS THROUGH A CHANGE IN CATEGORICAL STRUCTURE

An overview of the research presented in the first two parts of this chapter reveals a consistent pattern of outcomes across studies. When among others, the behavior of a person categorized as a group member (as opposed to an individual among an aggregate) is judged to be less informative about her or him, is attributed less to dispositional and more to situational causes, is considered more homogeneous and similar to other group members' beliefs, is recalled less accurately, and is perceived to be less credible and less independent of the behavior of the other group members. In short, the group member is attributed fewer unique personal characteristics than the person not categorized into a group; in this sense the group member is relatively deindividuated. If a group member is more deindividuated than a person not categorized into a group, then one might expect the group member to be a more likely target of bias.

To apply this argument to the intergroup bias data, it must be argued that members of the outgroup are relatively more deindividuated than members of the ingroup. First, from a perceptual standpoint, the person is immersed in her or his ingroup whereas the outgroup is psychologically less differentiated. Recall that the outgroup was considered to be homogeneous and generally dissimilar to the ingroup (Allen & Wilder, 1979; Wilder, 1980a). In addition, persons recalled more detailed information about fellow ingroup members than about members of the outgroup. Second, we assume that fellow members of our ingroup believe and behave more similarly to ourselves than do outgroup members. Inasmuch as we consider ourselves to be unique individuals (Fromkin, 1973), we may also believe that others like us (members of the ingroup) are more unique than members of the less differentiated outgroup. Third, because we perceive ingroup members to be more similar to ourselves than outgroup members, we may be more confident in predicting other characteristics of the ingroup than in forecasting characteristics of the outgroup. In short, we should have greater confidence in predicting the cognitive structure of ingroup than of outgroup persons. Fourth, if we assume that persons interact more frequently with ingroup than outgroup members, then we should have more direct knowledge of ingroup members. Such knowledge would include a variety of differentiating characteristics (e.g., diversity of physical appearance, behaviors, nuances of speech). Having less contact with the outgroup, we should not encounter as much individuating information. In essence, categorization encourages a relatively more deindividuated view of the outgroup than of the ingroup.

LeVine and Campbell (1972) have summarized some cross-cultural data that is consistent with the deindividuation argument. In separate investigations Middleton (1960) and Swartz (1961) reported that unfamiliar outgroups were regarded as less human than more familiar outgroups. For example, the Trukese categorize remote groups of New Guinea with loathsome animals such as sharks (Swartz, 1961). In a similar vein, outgroups are frequently regarded as immoral, as people who do not observe conventional standards of civilized behavior (Dollard, 1938).

Consequences of Deindividuation

Deindividuation of persons has been shown to have severe negative consequences for them. Persons who are relatively deindividuated are more likely to be targets of aggression than are persons of whom we have greater knowledge. For example, Milgram's (1965) research on obedience has demonstrated that anonymity of the victim facilitates aggressive interaction with her or him. Subjects in his research gave more severe shocks to victims when they had fewer cues that could individuate them (i.e., when the victims were out of sight in the next room) than when they could either see or touch them. On the other hand, persons are more likely to help victims when they know something about them (Emswiller, Deaux, & Willits, 1971).

Deindividuation of outgroup members is a device that has been used by film makers to control the audience's sympathies when portraying conflict between groups. An example of this occurs in the "Odessa steps" sequence of Sergei Eisenstein's film, *Potemkin*.[3] As the government troops (bad persons) march down the seemingly endless steps of Odessa toward their peasant victims (good persons), we see whole rows and columns of soldiers at once. They march uniformly, in perfect cadence, with their faces always hidden. No individual soldier emerges from the mass. The peasants in the film, on the other hand, are presented individually, in close-ups. We see many of them a second and third time during the sequence, expressing strong emotions. We witness their individual involvement with the conflict. In one instance a woman is shot in the face,

---

[3] I am indebted to Warren Cooper for suggesting this example.

her glasses are shattered and tilt over her nose. In another a baby sits on the steps crying as the rows of boots approach. These examples illustrate the skill with which Eisenstein manipulates our sympathies by deindividuating one group (soldiers) and individuating another (peasants).

If deindividuation of target persons lessens our regard for them, then individuation of those persons may enhance our favorability toward them. Although direct experimental evidence for this latter prediction is scant, some anecdotal evidence suggests that individuation encourages a more favorable or sympathetic response. Zimbardo (1970) reported that guards in Nazi concentration camps treated Jews more leniently when they knew their names than when they were anonymous members of the Jewish outgroup.

Returning to the ingroup/outgroup literature, individuation of outgroup members may mediate a reduction of bias for any of several reasons. First, individuation of the outgroup breaks down the simple perception of the outgroup as a homogeneous unit. It changes the situation from intergroup to interindividual relations. Because the group categories are no longer as accurate and, therefore, as useful in summarizing information, the maintenance of a distinction between the groups is less important. Second, individuation of outgroup members focuses attention on these persons and may enable one to notice points of similarity between oneself and the individuated members of the outgroup. Any perceived similarity may facilitate a positive reaction. Third, if attention is focused on the individuated outgroup members, one should be more prone to take their role and, perhaps, empathize with them. Putting oneself in their place should encourage a sympathetic or, at minimum, a more tolerant response to them.

If the mere creation of group categories is sufficient to create intergroup bias, then techniques that alter the ingroup/outgroup categorization should be effective in reducing such bias (Ryen, 1976). Several tactics will be suggested to lessen the ingroup/outgroup distinction. All these techniques result in the individuation of outgroup members. They involve a change in the perception of the outgroup, so that it is no longer viewed as a relatively undifferentiated unit but rather as a more heterogeneous collection of individuals. These proposals are organized under four headings for ease of presentation: (1) characteristics of the perceiver (or ingroup member) that affect her or his likelihood of categorizing others into groups; (2) relationship of the perceiver to the ingroup; (3) relationship among the outgroup members; and (4) characteristics of the situation in which the groups interact.

Characteristics of the Perceiver

This section focuses on characteristics of the perceiver that influence whether or not he or she will categorize another into an outgroup. These factors may be ordered in terms of their relative stability or permanence. Beginning with the most stable and proceeding to the more fleeting, they are the perceiver's cognitive complexity, cognitive set, level of arousal, and focus of attention.

Cognitive Complexity.   The use of categories to encode information appears to be common to all cultures (Rosch & Lloyd, 1978). Yet cultures differ in the complexity and richness of the categories used to classify stimuli (e.g., the difference between Eskimos and Americans in discrimination of snow). Just as there are differences across cultures in the complexity of categories, persons within any culture of group may vary in the richness of the categories they employ to organize stimuli.

As part of his theory of personality, Kelly (1955) hypothesized that a person's behavior is a product of her or his construction of reality. To the extent that persons differ in the categories they use to construct a representation of the environment, their interpretations of and responses to the environment should also differ. From this general framework several investigators have proposed a stable difference among persons in their style of handling information (e.g., Schroeder, Driver, & Streufert, 1967). Persons who are high in cognitive complexity make fine discriminations among stimuli and organize stimuli into subclasses within categories. On the other hand, persons who are low in complexity have difficulty handling complex and ambiguous information. They try to organize the environment into a few simple categories, thereby obscuring both differences and subtle similarities among stimuli that the cognitively complex individual might note.

Research on cognitive complexity is relatively sparse, and difficulties are compounded by the lack of a universally accepted measure of the concept (Bannister & Mair, 1968). Nevertheless, cognitive complexity seems to be an individual-difference variable of relevance to the question of social categorization. Persons with low complexity should be particularly prone to categorize others into simple "us–them" categories. Tendencies to overlook differences among elements in a category should increase the likelihood of deindividuating outgroup persons. Thus, relative to cognitively complex persons, individuals with low complexity should be more likely: (1) to view an interpersonal interaction as an ingroup/outgroup situation; and (2) to discriminate in favor of the ingroup over the outgroup.

Although no direct evidence relevant to these hypotheses has been gathered, some studies suggest the predicted negative association between cognitive complexity and intergroup bias (Coffman, 1962; Gardiner, 1972). Glock, Wuthnow, Piliavin, and Spencer (1975) assessed several individual-difference variables in a field study of interracial prejuduce in three New Jersey communities. In all three communities they reported that the only personality variable significantly related to degree of prejudice was the person's level of "cognitive sophistication" (Gough, 1957). Cognitively sophisticated persons displayed less prejudice than cognitively unsophisticated persons.

Curiously, there are circumstances in which the cognitively complex person may be expected to display greater bias against an outgroup than the cognitively simple individual. Consider the following situation. Suppose it is determined that a cognitively complex and a cognitively simple individual are equally prejudiced against a particular group. Suppose, further, that both encounter a member of the outgroup who does not fit the negative stereotypes of the group. The cognitively complex person is hypothesized to possess a more differentiated view of the outgroup. Moreover, the complex person should be more flexible; that is, better able to adapt to novel or unexpected information. The complex perceiver can, therefore, integrate information that contradicts her or his expectations without drastically altering her or his existing conception of the outgroup. As a result, the complex perceiver should persist in the categorization of the stimulus person as an outgroup member and respond to the person as such. The cognitively simple perceiver, on the other hand, should find an exception to her or his expectations more difficult to account for, because of her or his rigid, narrow conception of the outgroup. The cognitively simple perceiver may, therefore, be more likely either to alter her or his conception of the outgroup (i.e., make the outgroup more favorable) or to decide that the target person is not really a member of the outgroup after all and does not merit a biased response. This argument is purely speculative at this point, but does serve as a reminder that variables may not be unidirectional in their effects.

Cognitive Set.   The study of the effects of perceptual set on cognitive performance has a long history in psychology. For instance, Kulpe (cited in Sherif, 1936) performed a series of studies investigating the influence of Aufgabe (task set) on perception. Subjects were presented with stimuli about which different aspects could be recalled (e.g., number of letters, colors, patterns). Subjects recalled more aspects of the stimuli emphasized by the Aufgabe and with greater accuracy than items not made salient. Similarly, one might expect a person's set to perceive herself or himself as part of a group to affect her or his categorization of other persons.

Intuitively, persons who are highly cognizant of their own membership in a group should be prone to categorize others into groups. When a person's membership in a group is salient, he or she will be particularly sensitive to the relationship of others to his or her ingroup. Dimensions critical to membership in the ingroup should, therefore, be salient in perceiving others. An alternative argument that leads to the same prediction is based on a model of limited attention (Kahneman, 1973). This is essentially a distraction interpretation. To the extent a person focuses on her or his own membership in a group, the person will be less able to focus on the behavior of others in the environment. The person will be relatively unable to make fine differentiations among individuals, increasing the likelihood that they will be categorized into simple groups.

In a test of this prediction, subjects were either explicitly categorized into groups and interacted with their fellow group members to emphasize the categorization, or they were not organized into groups at all (Wilder, 1979). They then viewed a videotape of four persons engaged in two tasks—a simple motor task and a discussion of a legal case. Subjects who had been explicitly categorized into a group were more likely to judge the four stimulus persons as members of a common, interdependent group than were subjects who had not been categorized into a group. Thus, salient group membership may encourage a "group set," so to speak, on the part of the perceiver. It is unclear at this time whether these results were due to sensitivity for group cues in the behavior of others or simply to distraction resulting from the subject's membership in a group.

An implication of this study is that cues that discourage a "group set" on the part of the perceivers should decrease the likelihood of categorizing others in the environment as a group. For example, a person wearing a uniform of a particular group may feel more identified with that group at that particular moment (in part, perhaps, because others will categorize her or him with that group) and may be likely to organize others into groups relevant to that ingroup. Removal of the uniform (group cue) should lessen the salience of that group and decrease the likelihood of categorizing others into relevant outgroups.

Level of Arousal.   Another relatively unstable state of the perceiver that may affect categorization is the perceiver's level of arousal. Kahneman (1973) has observed that heightened arousal narrows one's focus of attention and decreases one's capacity to process information from the environment. In short, heightened arousal should foster less precise discriminations and the use of fewer categories in person perception. Turning to the ingroup/outgroup situation, one would predict that aroused persons should oversimplify their social environment by collapsing others into groups and failing to note fine distinctions among them. Intuitively, it seems that aroused persons (e.g., anger, grief) often respond to others on the basis of superficial characteristics. In these situations a person is more likely to view others simply as being "with me" (ingroup) or "against me" (outgroup).

To test this hypothesis we manipulated subjects' level of arousal and observed its effects on their categorization of others into groups (Wilder, Cooper, & Thompson, 1980). Arousal was operationally defined as threat of embarrassment for performing childish behaviors. As part of the instructions, the experimenter stated that pictures would be taken of subjects in "unusual situations" to be used as stimuli in a future experiment concerned with effects of disconfirmed expectations on impression formation. Subjects in the arousal condition were told that they would pose for a series of pictures in a playpen while holding a rattle in one hand, holding a bottle in the other, and sucking on a pacifier. To emphasize the reality of this impending embarrassment, subjects were shown pictures of others posing in the manner just described, the aforementioned props were placed in full view of the subjects on a nearby table, and a playpen was placed in the corner of the room. In the control condition, subjects were given the same cover story, but they were told the photographs would be taken of them wearing a rubber mask. Because this procedure disguised their identities, we expected that subjects would not become aroused at the prospect of having their pictures taken. Subjects in the arousal condition rated themselves more anxious and more embarrassed than subjects in the corresponding control condition.

Following the arousal manipulation, subjects in all conditions viewed a videotape of four persons discussing a legal case. For half of the subjects in each condition, the persons on the tape gave opinions that were basically in agreement with one another. For the remaining subjects, one person on the tape disagreed with the others and gave a contrary opinion. Thus, the experiment was a 2 × 2 factorial with level of arousal and consensus of opinions on the tape being the dependent factors. On the postexperimental questionnaire, subjects were asked to estimate the similarity among the jurors on the videotape, to state whether they appeared to be a group or a collection of independent individuals, and to recall as much of their behaviors as possible.

Subjects in the arousal conditions regarded the stimulus persons as more similar to each other and were more likely to categorize them as a group than were subjects in the control conditions. Not unexpectedly, subjects who viewed the unanimous confederates judged them to be more similar and more likely to be a group than subjects who viewed the tape with a dissenter. On the recall measure, subjects in the arousal conditions made more errors in recalling the opinions and descriptions of the confederates than subjects in the control conditions. Perhaps the aroused subjects were so preoccupied with the impending embarrassing situation that they failed to make or to retain the fine discriminations among the stimulus persons that the control subjects were able to report. Finally, subjects in the dissent conditions were more accurate and complete in their recall of the deviant's behavior than were subjects in the unanimous conditions. This finding is consistent with the attention literature (Kahneman, 1973; Taylor & Fiske, 1978), inasmuch as the dissenter's behavior made him quite salient to subjects, regardless of their level of arousal.

In summary, results from this experiment demonstrated that increasing the arousal (in this case anxiety at the prospect of embarrassment) of persons restricts their attention and/or ability to make fine discriminations among target persons. An implication of this finding is that a decrease of arousal should encourage a more individuated perception of stimulus persons, thereby lessening the probability of categorizing them into a simple group. It is unclear at this point whether arousal in this study affected the subject's range of attention so that he or she noticed fewer characteristics of the stimulus persons or whether arousal affected the subject's ability to recall information about the stimulus persons. Further research in this area might explore, on a more molecular level, the processes behind these findings.

Attention and Information. As suggested in the preceding paragraphs, narrowing the perceiver's attention should make it more difficult to notice or to retain differences among target persons. Stated alternatively, narrowing of attention should result in the gathering of less information from the target's behavior and a greater propensity to perceive the target in terms of relatively simple categories. On the other hand, increasing one's attention toward a target person should enable one to discover more individuating facets of the target's behavior, making simple categorizations less likely to occur.

An experimental test of this hypothesis was devised using the paradigm employed in a previously discussed experiment involving units of behavior (Wilder, 1979). In that study, subjects partitioned an actor's behavior into what they judged to be meaningful units of action. The actor was either a group member or an individual independent of those about him. The actor's behavior was judged to be less informative (i.e., divided into fewer units) when the actor was a member of a group than when he or she was unrelated to the others. In the present experiment (Wilder 1979) subjects observed a videotape of four persons who were either members of a common group (group conditions) or unrelated to one another (aggregate conditions). Crossed with the group/aggregate manipulation was the instructional set given to subjects. They were told either to divide a target person's behavior into many fine units (i.e., look for many meaningful acts in her or his behavior) or to partition the behavior into naturally occurring units (i.e., whatever they felt was appropriate).

Data from this 2 × 2 design revealed that subjects in the group condition were more likely to perceive the stimulus person as independent of the others and recalled more specific information about her or his appearance and behavior when they focused closely (divided the behavior into many units) than when they divided the behavior into normal size units. Indeed, subjects in the group condition who used fine units did not differ from subjects in the aggregate conditions in their reaction to the target person. When using fine units, subjects in the group condition recalled more cues that differentiated the actor from the rest of the group than when they used normal units. In summary, when fine units were employed, the target person was perceived to be relatively independent of the others even when he or she was a group member. Thus, the categorization of persons into a group may be disrupted if the perceiver can be induced to scrutinize the behavior of those persons closely, thereby gleaning additional unique information about them.

Several explanations can be offered for these findings. Perhaps focusing closely on the actor simply distracted the subjects from other group members on the tape. Consequently, the actor appeared more unique because the similar behavior of the others was overlooked. Alternatively, focusing closely on the actor may have enabled subjects to notice information that differentiated the actor from others, information that otherwise may have been missed. This latter expla-

nation is consistent with the finding that subjects recalled more unique information (information that differentiated the actor from the others) in the fine-unit
conditions than in the natural-unit conditions.

Relationship of Perceiver to Ingroup

The more a person feels attracted to or identifies with the ingroup, the greater
should be the person's favoritism of the ingroup. It stands to reason that the more
a person likes or feels a part of a group, the more the person should value and
want to reward the group. Moreover, persons attracted to ingroups with norms of
ingroup favoritism should favor the ingroup all the more as a means of satisfying
the expectations of the group. It would follow, then, that techniques that reduce a
person's identification with the ingroup should lessen ingroup favoritism. One
such technique involves a decrease in contact with the ingroup. Less contact with
the ingroup should make it less salient and reduce the likelihood of forming
strong attachments to its members.

Studies of contact between groups have focused on interaction with the outgroup following contact (Amir, 1969, 1976; Riordin, 1978). Little attention has
been paid to how contact with the outgroup affects ingroup relationships. Given a
finite amount of time for social interactions, the more contact there is with the
outgroup, the less time should be available for contact with the ingroup. Success
of some intergroup contact situations, therefore, may be due to a concomitant
decrease in ingroup contact and lessening of ingroup identification.

Some of the categorization research suggests that a person's relationship with
the ingroup affects behavior toward outgroups. Allen and Wilder (1975) varied
the attitudinal similarity of the ingroup and outgroup to subjects in their experiment. Subjects displayed more ingroup favoritism when the ingroup was attitudi-
nally similar to themselves than when it was dissimilar. But the similarity of the
outgroup had no effect on their behavior. In a similar vein, Dion (1973) reported
that manipulation of ingroup cohesiveness affected intergroup behavior; subjects
displayed ingroup favoritism when the ingroup was highly cohesive but failed to
discriminate when ingroup cohesiveness was low. In another study Dion (1979b)
manipulated the status of the group members. Subjects in the equal-status
groups evaluated their ingroup more positively than the outgroup; no such bias
occurred in the unequal-status group. Other researchers have examined effects of
ingroup failure on intergroup bias (Dion, 1979b; Kahn & Ryen, 1972). They
reported that ingroup failure coupled with outgroup success eliminated ingroup
favoritism and even resulted in some outgroup favoritism. Finally, Gerard and
Hoyt (1974) found that ingroup favoritism increased as the size of the ingroup
decreased from four to two persons. In short, the research briefly reviewed here
indicates that a person's relationship to the ingroup can have a significant impact
on behavior toward an outgroup, quite apart from the behavior of the outgroup.

In a recent experiment, Wilder and Thompson (1980) tested the hypothesis that reducing contact with the ingroup lessens identification with and favoritism of the ingroup. Females were recruited from two colleges situated a few miles from each other, Douglass College and Rutgers College. Subjects were chosen from these populations because they represented mutually exclusive groups who had some well-formed (though not necessarily well-informed) impressions of one another.

Pretesting revealed that, relative to themselves, Rutgers women thought Douglass women were more concerned with their appearance, more studious, and more worried about grades. Douglass women believed Rutgers women were more interested in "good times" and were less feminine. Our pretesting had shown no marked hostility or animosity between the groups, but there was some intergroup rivalry such that most subjects clearly preferred the college they were attending. Each group rated their college as a friendlier and generally better place to be.

Five subjects from each college were recruited for each experimental session. Subjects were informed that the experimenters had been asked by the university administration to compare the performance of Douglass and Rutgers students on a variety of cognitive tasks. Groups were randomly assigned to one of five conditions. They either interacted for one or two half-hour sessions with the ingroup and for one or two sessions with the outgroup. In addition, some subjects were assigned to a control condition in which they interacted only with the ingroup. Each of the contact sessions was designed to promote cooperative interaction because cooperative behavior has been shown to be effective in reducing intergroup bias (Amir, 1969). At the conclusion of the experiment, subjects completed a questionnaire that assessed their feelings about members of both groups as well as their recollections of what had occurred during the experiment. In addition, subjects divided earnings between the ingroup and the outgroup on a reward matrix similar to that used in previous research (Wilder, 1978c).

Analysis of the reward distribution indicated main effects for both amount of ingroup and amount of outgroup contact. Increasing contact with the outgroup in the cooperative setting of this experiment facilitated a reduction of ingroup/ outgroup bias. Subjects were less biased when outgroup contact was high than when contact was low. Turning to the effect of ingroup contact, subjects were less biased when ingroup contact was low than when ingroup contact was high. These results support the hypothesis that a reduction in contact with the ingroup may be an effective means of reducing ingroup/outgroup bias.

Findings from this study suggest a method of reducing intergroup bias in situations where cooperative contact with the outgroup is not feasible. Under such circumstances, one might attempt to reduce contact among ingroup members. If the ingroup members associate with each other less, their group membership may be less salient and, more importantly, their identification with the ingroup may be weakened. As a result, ingroup favoritism should decrease.

Relationship of Target Person to Outgroup

Members of an outgroup who wish to reduce discrimination directed at themselves may attempt to remove the group label that has been attached to them. If they can behave so as not to be categorized into the outgroup, they should be spared the negative attributions associated with that category. One way a person may differentiate herself or himself from the outgroup would be to behave in a manner contrary to that expected of the outgroup. Alternatively, a person might reveal personal information that is individuating, information that accentuates unique qualities of oneself. Such information should make it difficult for an observer to respond to the person according to simplistic stereotypes of the outgroup. Two sets of experiments have examined each of these techniques.

Individuation Through Dissent.   Dissenting from the behavior of the majority of the outgroup should enhance the salience of an individual outgroup member (Taylor & Fiske, 1978). As argued in the discussion of behavior units and categorization, the closer the perceiver scrutinizes the dissenter, the more likely he or she will discern individuating characteristics that further distinguish the dissenter from the rest of the outgroup (or from the perceiver's stereotypes of the outgroup). In addition, dissent partitions a person from her or his group by abrogating the unit relationship between them (Heider, 1958).

In the first of three experiments (Wilder, 1978c), the efficacy of dissent was investigated using a variation of the Tajfel (1970) paradigm for intergroup research. Subjects were artibrarily categorized into two groups by the experimenter. Each group was led to a different room. Subjects were told that the members of the outgroup were adjudicating two legal cases and that they would be evaluating the outgroup's performance later in the experiment. Subjects then worked on a couple of filler tasks until the outgroup had finished deliberating the cases. Feedback from the outgroup indicated that either all members agreed on both cases (unanimous condition), one member dissented on both cases (dissent condition), or feedback was obtained from only one person (alone condition).[4] Subsequently, subjects completed dependent measures that included six reward matrices of the kind described earlier.

Analysis of the data indicated that subjects in the unanimous and alone conditions displayed significantly greater ingroup favoritism than subjects in the dissent condition. Overall, subjects in the dissent condition divided rewards almost

---

[4]The alone condition was included as a control. Any differences between the unanimous and dissent conditions could have been attributed to dissent or to the specific positions taken by the dissenter. To control for the latter interpretation, in the alone condition subjects were given feedback only about the behavior of one outgroup member. This person behaved identically to the dissenter in the dissent condition. If the dissent and alone conditions differed (as the analysis showed), then the effect of dissent could not have been attributed to the specific positions taken by the dissenter but rather to the act of disrupting unanimity.

equally between the ingroup and the outgroup. Moreover, subjects were more likely to describe the outgroup as an aggregate of independent individuals than as a single unit in the dissent condition than in the other conditions. Evidently, the dissent altered the perception of the group from a simple to a more differentiated category.

Individuation Through Disclosure of Information.   Another method of individuation may be employed quite independently of the behavior of other outgroup members. This technique consists of disclosing personal information about oneself. Information that is relatively unique to a person should encourage a more complex and differentiated view of her or him. Such information should prevent or counter overly simplified categorizations. Because information that makes a person stand out from others in the group is highly dependent on the expectations the observer has about the group, information that may be distinctive in one group situation may be commonplace in another. As a trivial example, a short person in a photography club may not be particularly distinctive, but the same person on a basketball team would be quite distinctive. Other characteristics, such as personal idiosyncrasies, should be highly distinctive in most situations.

In two experiments Wilder (1978c) varied the distinctiveness of information subjects had about members of an outgroup and measured the impact of this information on measures of ingroup/outgroup bias. Subjects in these experiments were divided into two groups and were instructed to perform several problem-solving tasks. On one of these tasks, subjects in all conditions received highly critical feedback from the outgroup. Later, subjects discovered that they did not have enough information to complete another task. They were permitted to send a message to the other group requesting assistance to complete the task. The message the groups received in reply from the outgroup constituted the experimental manipulation.

Groups of subjects were assigned to one of four conditions, with some receiving all the help they had requested (cooperative condition), others receiving no help whatsoever (uncooperative condition), others receiving partial help from half of the outgroup acting as a deindividuated unit (partially cooperative-group condition), and, finally, some receiving partial help from half of the outgroup acting as individuals (partially cooperative-individual condition). Specifically, feedback in the partially cooperative-group condition came from the entire outgroup; the message was signed "Group B." But in the partially cooperative-individual condition, the assistance came in the form of individual notes signed with the initials of those helping (e.g., "M. L."). The primary dependent measure of interest was a reward matrix that subjects used to divide earnings between the ingroup and the outgroup.

As expected, subjects showed the most ingroup favoritism on the reward distribution task when the outgroup was uncooperative and the least bias when the outgroup was fully cooperative. (These conditions were included to set the range of bias expected to be observed in the experiment.) The partially cooperative conditions fell in between. Significantly less ingroup favoritism occurred when the outgroup was individuated (partially cooperative-individual condition) than when they responded as a group (partially cooperative-group condition), even though the outgroup's behavior did not differ between the two conditions. When assistance came from outgroup members presented in a more individuated manner, bias against them did not differ substantially from the amount of bias observed when the outgroup completely cooperated.

Some anecdotal evidence is consistent with these results. Recently, Warren Cooper and I have begun investigating crisis situations in which persons may be readily categorized into an outgroup. One such situation is that of being held hostage. Hostage situations often involve two mutually exclusive groups—the hostages and their captors. Indeed, hostages are frequently chosen because they represent an outgroup despised by their captors. In examining the hostage literature, we have read several accounts of hostages receiving more favorable treatment when they have acted in a manner that individuates themselves from the narrow category of outgroup member. Consider, for instance, the case of Gerard Vaders.

In December, 1975, Mr. Vaders was held hostage on a train commandered by South Moluccans near Groningen, Netherlands (Ochberg, 1977). At one point when their demands were not being met, the terrorists decided to execute Vaders. They gave him an opportunity to dictate a final letter to his family. In that letter Vaders talked about his life, his accomplishments and shortcomings. Although he talked about his family and his hopes for them, it is important to note that he did not gush or plead for sympathy. When he had finished dictating the letter, his captors decided not to execute him after all. Instead, they ushered another hapless hostage out and shot him without allowing him to compose a farewell letter.

Relationship of Ingroup to Outgroup

A fourth set of techniques for reducing the effect of categorization involves a change in the perception of the outgroup's relationship to the ingroup. If the outgroup can be made to appear more similar to the ingroup, then any discrimination based on perceived differences should be lessened.

Change of Ingroup/Outgroup Dimension. A change in perception of the outgroup can be accomplished in two ways. First, the outgroup may be recategorized so that it becomes part of the ingroup. This would necessitate the elimination of cues that demarcate the ingroup/outgroup boundary, virtually an impossible task between groups where boundaries are based on distinctive physical cues or long tradition.

Alternatively, one might change the relevant dimension of categorization so that a new group category supercedes the original basis of differentiation. For example, one might attempt to reduce friction between black and white workers by arguing that their problems are not due to racial characteristics but rather to the effects of the economic system beyond the control of either group. Thus, one attempts to make both blacks and whites perceive each other as members of the same group (workers) in opposition to a capitalist outgroup (which may also include both blacks and whites). The important point here is that the recategorization involves a change in the ingroup/outgroup boundary so that the former outgroup becomes part of the ingroup, and a new outgroup is brought into play. In addition, the criteria for distinguishing between ingroup and outgroup members change. In the example, the ingroup/outgroup dimension changes from race to economic class.

The success of any attempt to recategorize the groups on another dimension should be dependent on how important the current categorization is to the perceiver. The more investment the perceiver has in the present intergroup structure, the harder it should be to recategorize the groups. Similarly, one might expect perceivers who are relatively flexible in their cognitive operations (e.g., greater cognitive complexity) to be more able to recategorize groups along different dimensions.

A recent experiment by Commins and Lockwood (1978) is relevant to this change-of-dimension hypothesis. Employing Tajfel's (1970) paradigm, the experimenters crossed two dimensions of intergroup differentiation: religious affiliation of the subjects (Protestant, Catholic) and dot estimation (overestimators, underestimators). Subjects (average age of 15) were selected from Catholic and Protestant schools in Northern Ireland. In the Catholic condition all subjects were Catholics and were divided into groups of "underestimators" and "overestimators" allegedly on the basis of the dot-estimation task. The same method was employed for groups in the Protestant condition. In the Mixed condition, half of the subjects were Catholics and half were Protestants; they were assigned to groups in the same manner as in the other conditions. Because subjects did not know the identity of fellow ingroup members, those in the Mixed condition had no way of knowing how many Protestants and Catholics were in each group. Subjects in all conditions completed a set of reward matrices as the dependent measures.

Data from the matrices showed that subjects in the Catholic and Protestant conditions displayed the same amount of ingroup favoritism over the outgroup. But subjects in the Mixed condition were somewhat (though not significantly) less biased in the division of rewards between the groups. For the Catholic and Protestant conditions, religion was an irrelevant dimension, inasmuch as members of both groups shared the same affiliation. Any ingroup favoritism was due solely to the categorization manipulation. But in the Mixed condition, categorization on the basis of religion and dot estimation overlapped. It was highly likely that some ingroup and outgroup members for the dot-estimation task were outgroup and ingroup members, respectively, for the religion category. Findings from the Commins and Lockwood (1978) experiment appear to be consistent with the arguments presented above. Ingroup favoritism was reduced when the ingroup and outgroup boundaries were somewhat unclear, and members of an outgroup could also be members of another ingroup. Although additional evidence is needed, the Commins and Lockwood study suggests that recategorization of an ingroup and outgroup can lessen bias.

In a review of ethnocentrism research, LeVine and Campbell (1972) cited several studies showing less intergroup conflict in societies where persons were members of several overlapping social groups as compared with societies where groups were relatively independent of one another. A good example of this situation was reported by Murphy (1957). The Mundurucu of Brazil have a matrilocal society; following marriage, men reside with the families of their brides. Consequently, a man has ties among many homes—ties with his parents, with his wife's family inasmuch as he is now living with them, and with his brothers who also may be married and living with new families. Thus, a complex network of family bonds is one consequence of a matrilocal society. On the other hand, in a patrilocal system a man remains with his parents following marriage, so the probability of his forming strong ties outside his family is reduced. Interestingly, in comparing the two kinds of societies, Murphy (1957) found more conflict in groups using the patrilocal arrangement. This finding is consistent with the argument that bias between groups should be greater to the extent ingroups and outgroups are sharply divided with little overlap.

Change in Judgment of Outgroup.   A change in perception of the outgroup may also occur when a more distant outgroup is introduced to the situation (Thompson, Wilder, & Cooper, 1979). The original outgroup should be viewed as more similar to the ingroup and treated more favorably in the presence of the new, more distant outgroup than if that outgroup were not salient. What we hypothesized is similar to the assimilation/contrast effects reported in perceptual judgments (Eiser, 1971; Sherif, 1967).

Subjects were randomly assigned to one of four conditions in yet another ingroup/outgroup experiment. In the moderate-disagreement condition they were divided into two groups. The groups were asked to adjudicate a legal case and received feedback indicating that members of the outgroup moderately disagreed with their views. The extreme-disagreement condition was identical to the preceding one with the exception that feedback from the outgroup indicated that they disagreed quite strongly with the ingroup. The third condition (split-group) was designed to be a composite of the first two conditions. Subjects were informed that the outgroup was not unanimous in its opinion; half of the outgroup differed moderately and half differed sharply from the ingroup's position. The moderate and extreme factions gave the same responses as the outgroup allegedly made in the moderate and extreme-disagreement conditions, respectively. Finally, in the moderate-and-extreme condition, subjects were divided into three groups. Additional subjects participated in these sessions, so group size was the same as in the other conditions. Subjects received feedback indicating that one outgroup differed moderately and one differed extremely from the ingroup. The split-group and moderate-and-extreme conditions were identical with the exception that there was only one outgroup in the former condition and two outgroups in the latter condition. Thus, the difference between the ingroup and outgroup(s) was varied systematically on a single dimension—opinions about a legal case. Later, subjects were given the opportunity to divide rewards between members of the ingroup and members of the outgroup(s).

We hypothesized that subjects in the moderate-and-extreme condition would display less bias toward the moderate outgoup than subjects in the moderate-disagreement condition, even though the moderate outgroup expressed the same position in both conditions. Bias directed at the outgroup was not expected to decrease in the split-group condition even though subjects were exposed to the same range of opinions as in the moderate-and-extreme condition. Of critical importance was the fact that opinions in the split-group condition emanated from a single outgroup. Given that the moderate and extreme persons were all members of the same outgroup, the moderate members could not be easily separated from the more extreme members and assimilated in the direction of the ingroup.

Results supported these hypotheses. Significant bias was directed against the outgroup in the moderate-disagreement, extreme-disagreement, and split-group conditions. Similarly, subjects in the moderate-and-extreme groups condition discriminated against the extreme outgroup when dividing rewards, but bias directed at the moderately different outgroup was significantly reduced. Indeed, subjects in this condition did not differ reliably from a strategy of equality when dividing rewards between the ingroup and the moderate outgroup. Results of this experiment indicated that an outgroup may be treated more favorably when a more extreme outgroup is introduced to the setting.

An implication of this research is that an outgroup may also be judged more distant by the introduction of a new group. Thus, if a new outgroup were introduced that was even closer to the ingroup than the original outgroup, the original outgroup might be perceived as more distant than before. Such a change in judgment may enhance discrimination directed at the first outgroup. For example, the immigration of a group that is more similar to a nation's population than other recent immigrants may foster more bias directed at the earlier immigrants, who are now judged to be more different (or whose differences are more apparent) than before the last group arrived. Quite apart from a shift in judgment, however, this reaction might also be due to an increase in the salience of cues distinguishing the ingroup from the first outgroup caused by the introduction of the new outgroup.

The arguments in the preceding paragraphs imply that lessening the perceived distance between ingroups and outgroups should ameliorate intergroup bias. But one might also argue that decreasing perceived distance between groups also increases the potential threat of one group to the other. Thus, if two groups are very similar, they may perceive one another as potential rivals for the same goals, the same recruits, the same symbols. In short, the social identity of the groups may be threatened precisely because they are similar to each other. Based on arguments presented here and elsewhere (Brewer & Campbell, 1976; LeVine & Campbell, 1972), the possibility for tension should be augmented if several similar groups are viewed by one another as distinct. On the other hand, if there is a more remote outgroup to focus attention on, the groups may perceive themselves as a single unit in response to the new threat. In this case tensions among the groups should be lessened, and hostilities should be focused on the more extreme outgroup. The preceding example is reminiscent of the notion that external threats unite groups. Presumably, groups quickly settle or put aside disputes among themselves when they are faced with a common threat (LeVine & Campbell, 1972; Sherif, 1967; Sumner, 1906; White, 1949). It would be interesting to determine if these utilitarian changes in the favorability of the outgroup also produce relatively permanent cognitive changes on the part of ingroup members (e.g., changes in stereotypes, perception of more similarities and fewer differences with the outgroup). If the latter sort of changes can occur, then there is some hope that external crises may serve a positive function in the long run—that of fostering better intergroup relations with allied outgroups.

CONCLUSIONS, CONSIDERATIONS, AND CAVEATS

In the spirit of the other chapters in this book, I have argued that the categorization process can have a significant impact on intergroup relations. The first part of the chapter was devoted to a discussion of consequences of categorizing persons into groups on a perceiver's interpretation of their behavior. The behavior of group members was judged to be less informative about them and less dispositionally caused than the behavior of persons not organized into a group. In addition, group members were assumed to be more similar to one another and less credible than persons not so categorized. In these investigations subjects observed others who were either members of a common group or independent of one another. Subjects themselves were not categorized into a group.

The second part of the chapter considered effects of categorization in an ingroup/outgroup setting; that is, when the perceiver was a member of a group. In these experiments subjects were divided into two (or more) mutually exclusive groups on the basis of a relatively trivial criterion. In most of these studies subjects did not interact with members of either their alleged ingroup or the outgroup. The mere creation of an intergroup situation encouraged persons to make certain assumptions about the groups. These assumptions may be justified on the basis of past experience but also may be quite incorrect for any particular instance. Thus, ingroup members assumed that they were relatively similar to one another and dissimilar to the outgroup members who, in turn, were also thought to be similar to each other. Furthermore, persons assumed that the outgroup was more homogeneous than their ingroup. Persons acted to confirm these assumptions by preferring to have, and by remembering better, information that emphasized ingroup similarities and outgroup dissimilarities relative to themselves. When given the opportunity, persons differentiated between the groups by favoring ingroups over outgroups on trait ratings and reward distributions even when they had no knowledge of whom they were rating in the two groups. Indeed, in several experiments persons chose to differentiate between the ingroup and the outgroup even if their actions did not maximize ingroup benefits.

Explanations of categorization effects on intergroup bias have been offered from three different perspectives, with each claiming some supportive data: social norm, social identity, and cognitive differentiation. It was noted that these explanations are interrelated and, therefore, are best regarded as complementary rather than mutually exclusive. The focus of this chapter has been on cognitive differentiation, which emphasizes the role of categorization processes. If categorization into groups is sufficient to create some of the bias observed in the intergroup literature, then tactics that alter the categorization should be helpful in reducing bias.

In the third part of the chapter, several variables were considered that influence one's likelihood of categorizing others as an outgroup. First, several elements pertaining to the perceiver were identified. These included one's focus of attention (organization of the outgroup's behavior into action units), cognitive set (salience of ingroup membership), level of arousal, and cognitive complexity. Second, the relationship between the perceiver and her or his ingroup was found to affect behavior toward the outgroup. Greater contact with the ingroup fostered increased intergroup bias. Third, the behavior of the outgroup members affected the stability of the outgroup category. Dissent and individuation of outgroup members made them appear to be less of a group, resulting in a decrease of ingroup favoritism. Finally, perception of the outgroup was affected by the presence of other groups in the social field. Salience of an outgroup that differed sharply from the ingroup benefited a more moderate outgroup. Discrimination against the moderate outgroup was significantly reduced in the presence of the more extreme outgroup.

Despite (or perhaps because of) the consistency of many of the findings reported in this chapter, one must be careful not to overextend these outcomes. On the one hand, one might be tempted to conclude that, inasmuch as categorization is endemic to us, so also will intergroup bias always be with us. Alternatively, one might conclude that discrimination may be eliminated by merely removing or replacing intergroup distinctions. Unfortunately, most intergroup situations are not as simple as the paradigms used in the research reported here. We have stripped away many variables (e.g., the person's history of interaction with the groups, group norms, the history of interaction between the groups) in order to examine the effects of categorization at its most fundamental level. It would appear, therefore, that findings reported here may be generalized most directly to situations where persons either are encountering others for the first time or where the groups are relatively distant and have little direct contact. In the first circumstance the perceiver must devise an initial structure for the situation. In the latter case the perceiver may easily select and integrate information about the outgroup as he or she desires, for the reality of distant outgroup members does not impinge greatly.

One rather disturbing finding that can be applied to many intergroup situations concerns the self-fulfilling nature of categorization. The research reviewed here indicates that, once established, persons act to maintain (and even enhance) intergroup differences. Thus, perceiving others as an outgroup may encourage us to assume, to search for, and to remember information that accentuates differences between groups. In this manner the process becomes recursive. The categorization of persons into an outgroup leads me to assume that they are similar to one another and dissimilar from me; they are homogeneous, unlike the varied individuals in my group; their behavior is more due to characteristics of their group, unlike my behavior, which reflects my individuality; consequently, they are less independent and credible than my group; and so forth. This repetitive pattern may not continue indefinitely, but it may not reverse itself unless some element (such as those discussed in the foregoing) is introduced to break the cycle. Note that much of this argument assumes that we are usually unaware of cognitive processes involved in categorization (Nisbett & Wilson, 1977).

Having cautioned the reader against overgeneralizations, I shall disregard my admonition and extend the research reported here to other attempts to understand intergroup behavior. Research reviewed here has implications for two intuitive and fairly well-supported hypotheses—the belief-similarity explanation of bias (Rokeach, 1960) and the hypothesis that intergroup contact can decrease bias (Amir, 1969).

According to Rokeach (1960), intergroup bias stems largely from the assumption that outgroup members possess dissimilar and, perhaps, threatening beliefs. To reduce bias one must be assured that the outgroup does share one's beliefs and values. The categorization research provides a nice complement to Rokeach's theory. The assumption that outgroups have dissimilar beliefs appears to be an immediate outcome of organizing persons into groups. Moreover, once this assumption is made, it is self-perpetuating in that our behavior may easily sustain it. To break this pattern, then, one would be advised to counteract assumptions of dissimilar beliefs between different groups as soon as possible (providing, of course, that these assumptions are untrue).

One way in which assumptions about belief similarity may be tested is through direct contact with the outgroup. In a review of the contact literature, Amir (1969, 1976) concluded that contact can be effective under "favorable" circumstances. Quite favorable circumstances are ones in which contact occurs among persons of equal status in a cooperative environment (Sherif, 1967).

These circumstances focus on the content of the interaction—who are the persons; what are they doing? To this I propose to add the question of the form of contact—what is the structure of the contact situation?

The categorization research suggests that the structure of contact between the groups will be an important factor in the success or failure of the contact. One would expect contact that allows the group boundaries to remain highly salient (thereby emphasizing the ingroup/outgroup categorization) to be less effective than contact that mixes individuals of both groups. Consider, for example, contact between two groups where each group sits at a separate table wearing identification tags. Although the setting may be designed to induce cooperation between the groups, ingroup identification should be salient throughout the interaction. Such circumstances would encourage a perception of the outgroup members as a single unit, and not as a more individuated set of persons.

Contrast the preceding setting with one in which contact occurs among individuals of the two groups. Returning to the example, suppose members of both groups intermingle with one another at the tables and group identification labels are removed. The boundary between the groups would be less salient in this situation. Furthermore, perception of the outgroup as a homogeneous unit should be abandoned as more information is obtained about individual members of the outgroup. Persons should notice more individuating characteristics of one another, characteristics that may encourage a more sympathetic or humane reaction when next confronted with an intergroup evaluation.

A study by Chadwick-Jones (1962) is relevant to these speculations. Chadwick-Jones examined the effects of contact with Italians working in Great Britain on British attitudes toward Italians. Subjects were divided into three categories commensurate with the kind of contact they had with Italians. Britons who were isolated from Italians responded with indifference or unclear attitudes about them. Apparently, these subjects had insufficient contact to develop strong attitudes. Those persons having some contact by virtue of living closer to Italians were the most disapproving of them. For sake of argument, let us suppose that I am particularly likely to notice the group membership of persons who are members of groups with which I have relatively infrequent contact. If I have a history of little contact with a particular category of stimuli, I should not have the expectation of encountering an element of that category. Consequently, when one does happen my way, I should be especially likely to notice it as an example of that category of stimuli (Taylor & Fiske, 1978). If this does occur, then one should view outgroup members with whom one has little interaction as elements of a category rather than as more complex, individuated persons. Based on the individuation research, intergroup bias should be especially prone to occur under these circumstances. On the other hand, Chadwick-Jones reported that subjects who had frequent face-to-face contact with outgroup members were able to differentiate among individual members of the Italian outgroup and expressed more positive attitudes toward them.

As a final note, it should be remembered that the categorization phenomena presented in this and other chapters are of interest for several reasons. First, in their own right, they provide a partial answer to the questions of how we notice, encode, integrate, and recall information. Second, these phenomena provide clues toward the unraveling of social behavior of a more complex nature, such as intergroup relations. In this respect they have forced us to broaden perspectives and even to reconsider some of our assumptions of social interaction. In so doing they have added vitality to our endeavors.

REFERENCES

Adorno, T. W., Frenkel-Brunswik, E., Levinson, D. J., & Sanford, R. N. *The authoritarian personality.* New York: Harper, 1950.

Allen, V. L. Social support for nonconformity. In L. Berkowitz (Ed.), *Advances in experimental social psychology* (Vol. 9). New York: Academic Press, 1975.

Allen, V. L., & Wilder, D. A. Categorization, belief similarity, and intergroup discrimination. *Journal of Personality and Social Psychology, 1975, 32,* 971–977.

Allen, V. L., & Wilder, D. A. Group categorization and attribution of belief similarity. *Small Group Behavior,* 1979, *10,* 73–80.

Allport, G. W. *The nature of prejudice.* Cambridge, Mass.: Addison–Wesley, 1954.

Allport, G., & Postman, L. *The psychology of rumor.* New York: Holt, 1947.

Amir, Y. Contact hypothesis in ethnic relations. *Psychological Bulletin, 1969, 71,* 319–341.

Amir, Y. The role of intergroup contact in change of prejudice and ethnic relations. In P. A. Katz (Ed.), *Towards the elimination of racism.* New York: Pergamon Press, 1976.

Asch, S. E. Effects of group pressure upon the modification and distortion of judgment. In H. Guetzkow (Ed.), *Groups, leadership and men.* Pittsburgh, Pa.: Carnegie Press, 1951.

Ashmore, R. D. The problem of intergroup prejudice. In B. E. Collins, *Social psychology.* Reading, Ma.: Addison-Wesley, 1970.

Bales, R. F. A theoretical framework for interaction process analysis. In D. Cartwright & A. Zander (Eds.), *Group dynamics: Research and theory.* Evanston, Ill.: Row & Peterson, 1953.

Bannister, D., & Mair, J. M. M. *The evaluation of personal constructs.* New York: Academic Press, 1968.

Barker, R. G. (Ed.). *The stream of behavior.* New York: Appleton-Century-Crofts, 1963.

Billig, M. *Social psychology and intergroup relations.* New York: Academic Press, 1976.

Billig, M., & Tajfel, H. Social categorization and similarity in intergroup behavior. *European Journal of Social Psychology,* 1973, *3,* 27–52.

Brewer, M. B. In-group bias in the minimal intergroup situation: A cognitive–motivational analysis. *Psychological Bulletin,* 1979, *86,* 307–324.

Brewer, M. B., & Campbell, D. T. *Ethnocentrism and intergroup attitudes: East African evidence.* New York: Halsted Press, 1976.

Brewer, M. B., & Silver, M. Ingroup bias as a function of taste characteristics. *European Journal of Social Psychology,* 1978, *8,* 393–400.

Bruner, J. S. Social psychology and perception. In E. E. Maccoby, T. M. Newcomb, & E. L. Hartley (Eds.), *Reading in social psychology.* New York: Holt, Reinhart & Winston, 1958.

Campbell, D. T. Enhancement of contrast as a composite habit. *Journal of Abnormal and Social Psychology,* 1956, *53,* 350–355.

Campbell, D. T. Common fate, similarity and other indices of the status of aggregate persons as social entities. *Behavioral Science,* 1958, *3,* 14–25.

Campbell, D. T. Stereotypes and perception of group differences. *American Psychologist,* 1967, *22,* 812–829.

Cantor, N., & Mischel, W. Traits as prototypes: Effects on recognition memory. *Journal of Personality and Social Psychology,* 1977, *35,* 38–48.

Carmichael, L., Hogan, H. P., & Walter, A. A. An experimental study of the effect of language on the reproduction of visually perceived form. *Journal of Experimental Psychology,* 1932, *15,* 73–86.

Carroll, J. S., & Payne, J. W. (Eds.). *Cognition and social behavior.* Hillsdale, N.J.: Lawrence Erlbaum Associates, 1976.

Cartwright, D., & Zander, A. *Group dynamics* (3rd ed.). New York: Harper & Row, 1968.

Cattell, R. B. New concepts for measuring leadership, in terms of group syntality. *Human Relations,* 1951, *4,* 161–184.

Chadwick-Jones, J. K. Intergroup attitudes: A stage in attitude information. *British Journal of Sociology,* 1962, *13,* 57–63.

Coffman, T. L. *Personality structure, involvement, and the consequences of taking a stand.* Unpublished doctoral dissertation, Princeton University, 1962.

Cohen, C. *Cognitive basis of stereotyping.* Paper presented at the meeting of the American Psychological Association, San Francisco, August 1977.

Commins, B., & Lockwood, J. The effects of intergroup relations of mixing Roman Catholics and Protestants: An experimental investigation. *European Journal of Social Psychology,* 1978, *8,* 383–386.

DeLamater, J. A definition of "group." *Small Group Behavior,* 1974, *5,* 30–44.

Dion, K. L. Cohesiveness as a determinant of ingroup–outgroup bias. *Journal of Personality and Social Psychology,* 1973, *28,* 163–171.

Dion, K. L. Intergroup conflict and intergroup cohesiveness. In W. G. Austin & S. Worchel (Eds.), *The social psychology of intergroup relations.* Monterey, Calif.: Brooks/Cole, 1979. (a)

Dion, K. L. Status equality, sex composition of group and intergroup bias. *Personality and Social Psychology Bulletin,* 1979, *5,* 240–244. (b)

Doise, W., Csepeli, G., Dann, H., Gouge, C., Larsen, K., & Ostell, A. An experimental investigation into the formation of intergroup representations. *European Journal of Social Psychology,* 1972. *2,* 202–204.

Doise, W., & Sinclair, A. The categorization process in intergroup relations. *European Journal of Social Psychology,* 1973, *3,* 145–147.

Dollard, J. Hostility and fear in social life. *Social Forces,* 1938, *17,* 15–25.

Eiser, J. R. Enhancement of contrast in the absolute judgment of attitude statements. *Journal of Personality and Social Psychology,* 1971, *17,* 1–10.

Emswiller, R., Deaux, K., & Willits, J. Similarity, sex and requests for small favors. *Journal of Applied Social Psychology,* 1971, *1,* 284–291.

Feldman, W. S., Higgins, E. T., Karlovak, M., & Ruble, D. M. Use of consensus information in causal attributions as a function of temporal presentation and availability of direct information. *Journal of Personality and Social Psychology,* 1976, *34,* 694–698.

Fromkin, H. L. *The psychology of uniqueness: Avoidance of similarity and seeking of differentness.* West Lafayette, Ind.: Krannert Graduate School of Industrial Administration, 1973.

Gardiner, G. S. Complexity training and prejudice reduction. *Journal of Applied Social Psychology,* 1972, *2,* 326–342.

Gerard, H. B., & Hoyt, M. F. Distinctiveness of social categorization and attitude toward ingroup members. *Journal of Personality and Social Psychology,* 1974, *29,* 836–842.

Glock, C. Y., Wuthnow, R., Piliavin, J. A., & Spencer, M. *Adolescent prejudice.* New York: Harper & Row, 1975.

Gough, H. G. *California psychological inventory manual.* Palo Alto, Calif.: Consulting Psychologists Press, 1957.

Hansen, R. D., & Lowe, C. A. Distinctiveness and consensus: The influence of behavioral information on actors' and observers' attributions. *Journal of Personality and Social Psychology*, 1976, *34*, 435–443.

Harvey, J. H., Arkin, R. M., Gleason, J. M., & Johnston, S. Effect on expected and observed outcome of an action on the differential causal attributions of actor and observer. *Journal of Personality*, 1974, *42*, 62–77.

Heider, F. *The psychology of interpersonal relations*. New York: Wiley, 1958.

Homans, C. G. The human group. New York: Harcourt, 1950.

Howard, J. W., & Rothbart, M. Social categorization and memory for in-group and out-group behavior. *Journal of Personality and Social Psychology*, 1980, *38*, 301–310.

Jones, E. E., & Davis, K. E. From acts to dispositions: The attribution process in person perception. In L. Berkowitz (Ed.), *Advances in experimental social psychology* (Vol. 2). New York: Academic Press, 1965.

Jones, E. E., & McGillis, D. Correspondent inferences and the attribution cube. A comparative reappraisal. In J. Harvey, W. Ickes, & R. Kidd (Eds.), *New directions in attribution research*. Hillsdale, N.J.: Lawrence Erlbaum Associates, 1976.

Kahn, A., & Ryen, A. H. Factors influencing the bias towards one's own group. *International Journal of Group Tensions*, 1972, *2*, 33–50.

Kahneman, D. *Attention and effort*. Englewood Cliffs, N.J.: Prentice-Hall, 1973.

Kelley, H. H. Attribution theory in social psychology. In D. Levine (Ed.), *Nebraska Symposium on Motivation*. Lincoln, Neb.: University of Nebraska Press, 1967.

Kelly, G. A. *The psychology of personal constructs*. New York: Norton, 1955.

Knowles, E. S., & Bassett, R. L. Groups and crowds as social entities: Effects of activity, size, and member similarity on nonmembers. *Journal of Personality and Social Psychology*, 1976, *34*, 137–145.

Köhler, W. Physical gestalten. In W. D. Ellis (Ed.), *A source book of Gestalt psychology*. New York: Humanities Press, 1967.

Krech, D., & Crutchfield, R. S. *Theory and problems of social psychology*. New York: McGraw–Hill, 1948.

LeVine, R. A., & Campbell, D. T. *Ethnocentrism: Theories of conflict, ethnic attitudes, and group behavior*. New York: Wiley, 1972.

Lewin, K. *Resolving social conflicts*. New York: Harper, 1948.

McArthur, L. A. The how and what of why: Some determinants and consequences of causal attributions. *Journal of Personality and Social Psychology*, 1972, *22*, 171–193.

Mead, M. *Cooperation and competition among primitive peoples*. New York: McGraw-Hill, 1937.

Merton, R. K. *Social theory and social structure*. Glencoe Ill.: Free Press, 1957.

Middleton, J. *Lugbara religion*. London: Oxford, 1960.

Milgram, S. Some conditions of obedience and disobedience to authority. *Human Relations*, 1965, *18*, 57–76.

Miller, G. A. The magical number seven, plus or minus two: Some limits on our capacity for processing information. *Psychological Review*, 1956, *63*, 81–97.

Murphy, R. F. Intergroup hostility and social cohesion. *American Anthropologist*, 1957, *59*, 1018–1035.

Newcomb, T. M. Social psychological theory; integrating individual and social approaches. In E. P. Hollander & R. G. Hunt (Eds.), *Current perspectives in social psychology*. New York: Oxford University Press, 1963.

Newtson, D. Attribution and the unit of perception of ongoing behavior. *Journal of Personality and Social Psychology*, 1973, *28*, 28–38.

Newtson, D. Foundations of attribution: The unit of perception of ongoing behavior. In J. Harvey, W. Ickes, & R. Kidd (Eds.), *New directions in attribution research*. Hillsdale, N.J.: Lawrence Erlbaum Associates, 1976.

Nisbett, R. C., & Borgida, E. Attribution and psychology of prediction. *Journal of Personality and Social Psychology*, 1975, *32*, 932–943.

Nisbett, R. C., & Wilson, T. D. Telling more than we know: Verbal reports on mental processes. *Psychological Review*, 1977, *84*, 231–259.

Ochberg, F. The victim of terrorism: Psychiatric considerations. *Terrorism: An International Journal*, 1977, *1*, 1–22.

Orvis, B. R., Cunningham, J. D., & Kelley, H. H. A closer examination of causal inference: The roles of consensus, distinctiveness, and consistency information. *Journal of Personality and Social Psychology*, 1975, *32*, 605–616.

Pettigrew, T. Regional differences in anti-Negro prejudice. *Journal of Abnormal and Social Psychology*, 1959, *59*, 28–36.

Rabbie, J. M., & Horwitz, M. Arousal of ingroup–outgroup bias by a chance win or loss. *Journal of Personality and Social Psychology*, 1969, *13*, 269–277.

Rabbie, J. M., & Wilkens, G. Intergroup competition and its effect on intragroup and intergroup religion. *European Journal of Social Psychology*, 1971, *1*, 215–234.

Riordin, C. Equal-status interracial contact: A review and revision of the concept. *International Journal of Intercultural Relations*, 1978, *2*, 161–185.

Rokeach, M. *The open and closed mind: Investigations into the nature of belief systems and personality systems.* New York: Basic Books, 1960.

Rosch, E., & Lloyd, B. B. *Cognition and categorization.* Hillsdale, N.J.: Lawrence Erlbaum Associates, 1978.

Ross, L., Bierbrauer, G., & Hoffman, S. The role of attribution processes in conformity and dissent: Revisiting the Asch situation. *American Psychologist*, 1976, *31*, 148–157.

Rothbart, M., Evans, M., & Fulero, S. Recall for confirming events: Memory processes and the maintenance of social stereotypes. *Journal of Experimental Social Psychology*, 1979, *15*, 343–355.

Ruble, D. N., & Feldman, N. S. Order of consensus, distinctiveness, and consistency information and causal attributions. *Journal of Personality and Social Psychology*, 1976, *34*, 930–937.

Ryen, A. H. *Intergroup attitudes as a function of group proximity and task orientation.* Paper presented at the Midwestern Psychological Association, Chicago, May 1976.

Schroder, H. M., Driver, M. J., & Streufert, S. *Human information processing.* New York: Holt, Rinehart & Winston, 1967.

Sherif, M. *The psychology of social norms.* New York: Harper Books, 1936.

Sherif, M. *Social interaction process and products.* Chicago: Aldine, 1967.

Simpson, G. E., & Yinger, J. M. *Racial and cultural minorities* (3rd ed.). New York: Harper & Row, 1965.

Stotland, E., Cottrell, N. B., & Laing, O. Group interaction and perceived similarity of members. *Journal of Abnormal and Social Psychology*, 1960, *61*, 335–340.

Stotland, E., Zander, A., & Natsoulas, T. Generalization of interpersonal similarity. *Journal of Abnormal and Social Psychology*, 1961, *62*, 250–256.

Sumner, W. G. *Folkways.* New York: Ginn, 1906.

Srull, T. K., & Wyer, R. S. Category accessibility and social perception: Some implications for the study of person memory and interpersonal judgments. *Journal of Personality and Social Psychology*, 1980, *38*, 841–846.

Swartz, M. J. Negative ethnocentrism. *Journal of Conflict Resolution*, 1961, *5*, 75–81.

Tajfel, H. Cognitive aspects of prejudice. *Journal of Social Issues*, 1969, *25*, 79–97.

Tajfel, H. Experiments in intergroup discrimination. *Scientific American*, 1970, *223*, 96–102.

Tajfel, H. The roots of prejudice: Cognitive aspects. In P. Watson (Ed.), *Psychology and race.* Chicago: Aldine, 1973.

Tajfel, H., & Billig, M. Familiarity and categorization in intergroup behavior. *Journal of Experimental Social Psychology*, 1974, *10*, 159–170.

Tajfel, H., Billig, M., Bundy, R., & Flament, C. Social categorization and intergroup behavior. *European Journal of Social Psychology*, 1971, *1*, 149–178.

Tajfel, H., Sheikh, A. A., & Gardner, R. C. Content of stereotypes and the inferences of similarity between members of stereotyped groups. *Acta Psychologica,* 1964, *22,* 191–201.

Tajfel, H., & Wilkes, A. L. Classification and quantitative judgment. *British Journal of Social Psychology,* 1963, *54,* 101–114.

Taylor, S. E., & Fiske, S. T. Salience, attention, and attribution: Top of the head phenomenon. In L. Berkowitz (Ed.), *Advances in experimental social psychology* (Vol. 10). New York: Academic Press, 1978.

Taylor, S. E., Fiske, S. T., Etcoff, N. L., & Ruderman, A. J. Categorical and contextual basis of person memory and stereotyping. *Journal of Personality and Social Psychology,* 1978, *36,* 778–793.

Thompson, J. E., Wilder, D. A., & Cooper, W. E. Shift in judgment of an outgroup following the introduction of a more different outgroup. Paper presented at the meeting of the American Psychological Association, New York, September 1979.

Turner, J. C. Social comparison and social identity: Some prospects for intergroup behavior. *European Journal of Social Psychology,* 1975, *5,* 5–34.

Tversky, A., & Gati, I. Studies of similarity. In E. Rosch & B. B. Lloyd (Eds.), *Cognition and categorization.* Hillsdale, N.J.: Lawrence Erlbaum Associates, 1978.

Wells, G. L., & Harvey, J. H. Do people use consensus information in making causal attribution? Journal of Personality and Social Psychology, 1977, *35,* 279–293.

Wells, G. L., & Harvey, J. H. Naive attributor's attributions and predictions: What is informative and when is an effect an effect? *Journal of Personality and Social Psychology,* 1978, *36,* 483–490.

White, L. A. *The science of culture: A study of man and civilization.* New York: Farrar & Straus, 1949.

Wilder, D. A. Perception of groups, size of opposition, and social influence. *Journal of Experimental Social Psychology,* 1977, *13,* 253–268.

Wilder, D. A. Homogeneity of jurors: The majority's influence depends upon their perceived independence. *Law and Human Behavior,* 1978, *2,* 363–376. (a)

Wilder, D. A. Perceiving persons as a group: Effects on attributions of causality and beliefs. *Social Psychology,* 1978, *1,* 13–23. (b)

Wilder, D. A. Reduction of intergroup discrimination through individuation of the outgroup. *Journal of Personality and Social Psychology,* 1978, *36,* 1361–1374. (c)

Wilder, D. A. *Effects of perceiving persons as a group on the information conveyed by their behavior.* Unpublished manuscript, Rutgers University, 1979.

Wilder, D. A. *Predictions of belief homogeneity and similarity as a function of the salience of an outgroup following social categorization.* Manuscript submitted for publication, 1980. (a)

Wilder, D. A. *Ingroup–outgroup categorization and information recall.* Manuscript submitted for publication, 1980. (b)

Wilder, D. A., & Allen, V. L. Group membership and preference for information about other persons. *Personality and Social Psychology Bulletin,* 1978, *4,* 106–110.

Wilder, D. A., Cooper, W. E., & Thompson, J. *The facilitation of categorical judgments through arousal.* Manuscript submitted for publication, 1980.

Wilder, D. A., & Thompson, J. Intergroup contact with independent manipulation of in-group and out-group interaction. *Journal of Personality and Social Psychology,* 1980, *38,* 589–603.

Wilson, W., & Miller, N. Shifts in evaluations of participants following intergroup competition. *Journal of Abnormal Social Psychology,* 1961, *63,* 428–431.

Zander, A., Stotland, E., & Wolfe, D. Unity of groups, identification with group, and self-esteem of members. *Journal of Personality,* 1960, *28,* 463–478.

Zimbardo, P. The human choice: Individuation, reason, and order versus deindividuation, impulse, and chaos. In W. Arnold and D. Levine (Eds.), *Nebraska Symposium on Motivation,* 1970, *17,* 237–307.

8 Cognitive and Dyadic Processes in Intergroup Contact

Terrence L. Rose
University of California, Santa Barbara

Legislative and judicial decisions have opened the way for desegregation in this country and political forces have pushed for similar reforms in other nations. But the jurisdiction of such decisions is in fact limited, applying only to the policies of social institutions or systems of subordinate institutions. Translating a decision or policy into a viable set of procedures or program that is effective and receives public support is a more difficult process than deciding on the policy itself.

School busing programs provide but one example of an instance where social policies have been hindered by problems of translation into a viable social program for reform. Those opposed to busing are quick to criticize these desegregation programs as being ineffective and poorly conceived. But given the climate of strong opposition that surrounds these programs, it is doubtful whether any program could ever be successful. It is perhaps more fitting to ask what outcomes might be expected given the implementation of these programs at the level of overt compliance. This question has been posed repeatedly over the years. More simply phrased, we might ask what can be expected when members of social groups are placed in proximity to each other? This is the question of intergroup contact and is the focus of this chapter.

Accompanying the promise of equal opportunity, desegregation programs have offered the hope that by associating with each other more frequently, the members of different racial and ethnic groups would come to be less prejudiced toward each other and live side by side in a truly integrated society. Studies have been conducted in order to evaluate whether such programs do indeed lead to reductions in prejudice. This large body of research has been reviewed by several authors (Allport, 1954; Amir, 1969, 1976; Ashmore, 1970; Cook, 1962, 1969; Harding, Proshansky, Kutner, & Chein, 1969; Katz, 1970). There also have been reviews dealing with the effects of contact within specific settings (Armor, 1972; Carithers, 1970; Katz, 1964). This chapter does not once again review this body of research. Instead, it focuses on the conceptual problems that have impeded progress in this research area and how the adoption of new conceptual strategies could further our understanding of intergroup contact.

The first part of the chapter discusses the conceptual perspective that has been adopted by researchers in the past. It shows how this research has tended to focus on a limited range of issues for investigation and how it has been limited by the absence of theoretical models of intergroup contact. It is argued that these problems could be overcome by adopting a different orientation—one that focuses on the psychological processes operating in the contact setting and borrows the research and theory currently available in cognitive and social psychology.

The alternative orientation adopted in this chapter is best described as an information-processing approach to the study of intergroup contact. The emphasis is upon the flow of information within the contact setting and the way in which it is processed by the interactants. Intergroup contact is viewed as a potential learning experience in which new information about the members of different social groups can be acquired and used to test the validity of one's social stereotypes and expectancies. However, the individual's partner is not the only social stimulus in the contact setting. The person may acquire information about himself or herself as well through the observation of his or her own behavior and the way in which the partner responds. In this way the individual may not only come to learn about the partner but may also come to question or revise his or her own self-view.

In developing this perspective toward the study of intergroup contact, an attempt is made to specify the cognitive and dyadic processes mediating intergroup interactions and how the nature of such interactions comes to determine the amount and quality of information processed by the individuals involved. The emphasis is therefore on cognitive processes and their subsequent effects on behavior.

The role of cognitive processes in intergroup behavior and perception has received increased attention in recent years (see Hamilton, 1979, and the other contributions to the present volume). Much of this research is considered in relation to intergroup interaction. However, it will become apparent that the beginnings of an information-processing approach were available much earlier but were simply not systematically applied to the study of intergroup contact. The present chapter seeks to apply this research and theory as a means of demonstrating how an information-processing approach to contact could advance theory, systematize research strategies, and integrate contact research with more recent developments in psychology.

THE LIMITATIONS OF PAST RESEARCH

The Traditional Orientation Toward Contact

Research on intergroup contact began with field studies designed to test whether contact per se would result in favorable changes in intergroup attitudes. It soon became apparent that existing prejudices could, depending on circumstances, either increase or decrease following intergroup contact. Researchers began to realize the necessity of adopting a more detailed analysis of this issue and of formulating more complex hypotheses.

Following the publication of Allport's (1954) classic book, *The Nature of Prejudice,* the strategy taken by most researchers was one of distinguishing among different types of contact and the settings in which they might occur. The goal of this approach was to identify and isolate aspects of the contact setting or variables that moderate the outcomes of intergroup contact (Amir, 1969, 1976; Cook, 1962). As a result of Allport's (1954) original statement and subsequent work by researchers in the field, a number of important moderating variables have been identified that can be used for classifying different contact settings. For example, Amir (1969) suggests that contact will result in increasingly favorable relations between different social groups when: (1) contact is between individuals of equal status; (2) contact occurs in a social climate where authorities and norms support intergroup interaction; (3) the interaction is intimate rather than casual or superficial; (4) contact is pleasant for the interactants and occurs in a rewarding context rather than being unpleasant, involuntary, or tension laden; (5) the interactants cooperate with each other in achieving common, superordinate goals rather than competing against each other for resources and adopting mutually exclusive goals; and (6) the members of each group view the other group and its members favorably prior to actual interaction. Thus, there appears to have been some progress made by utilizing this approach. However, there are also certain limitations of this approach. These are considered before moving on to a discussion of more recent research.

Attitudes, Behavior, and the Range of Research

In most of the research on intergroup contact aspects of the contact setting, such as the intimacy of interaction or its pleasantness, have been conceptualized as the independent variable or antecedent condition, whereas attitude change has been viewed as the dependent variable or consequence of contact. Most studies have compared the attitudes of individuals within a segregated setting with those in a similar, but desegregated, environment, or changes in intergroup attitudes have simply been examined before and after desegregation.

One of the main problems with this strategy of research is that it arbitrarily restricts the range of issues addressed by empirical research and, consequently, the applicability of this research. Prejudice may reflect itself in both the attitudes and behavior of the individual and each of these needs to be studied to understand fully the nature of intergroup contact. Few studies in the contact literature have sought to determine the factors and processes responsible for different forms of intergroup behavior by systematically observing ongoing interactions between the members of different social groups. Instead, it typically has been assumed that particular forms of interaction would take place. Even when attitudes were viewed as resulting from a particular quality of interaction, there was normally little empirical evidence that contact was, for example, intimate, pleasant, or conducive of equal status relationships (Cagle, 1973). In some studies, verbal reports of the frequency of contact (Deutsch & Collins, 1951) or other retrospective reports of these interactions have been obtained. But relying on the subject's memory of his or her own behavior is a questionable strategy, inasmuch as the subject's ability to remember information is limited and may be neither accurate nor unbiased in describing these past events.

Thus, rather than studying behavior within the contact setting as an issue in itself, most researchers have simply treated the interval of time prior to the administration of attitudinal measures as a singular event and relied upon their intuitions in assessing the type of interaction that actually took place during this interval of time. Future studies of intergroup contact need to direct more attention to the patterns of behavior characteristic of intergroup interactions and the way in which personal relations develop and change through time. A greater emphasis on dyadic processes in the contact setting could foster this type of research by directing attention to the study of event sequences during interaction.

The importance of broadening contact research to include studies of intergroup behavior, as well as studies of attitudinal changes, is apparent when one begins to ask practical questions about the applicability of past research. For example, consider the proposition that intimate contact is more effective than superficial forms of interaction in reducing prejudice. How does one bring about such encounters, especially among highly prejudiced persons who might resist such attempts? Simply putting people next door to each other will not guarantee the development of intimate relationships. Cagle (1973) has argued that studies of desegregated housing projects—such as the classic studies of Deutsch and Collins (1951) and Wilner, Walkley, and Cook (1952)—though sometimes viewed as demonstrating the efficacy of intimate contact, objectively offer no basis for such a conclusion. In fact, Cagle aruges that these settings seem to elicit few intimate interracial relationships, a conclusion consistent with other studies of desegregated neighborhoods (Bradburn, Sudman, Gockel, & Noel, 1971; Hamilton & Bishop, 1976). Given the absence of studies designed to observe systematically interracial face-to-face interaction, this issue is difficult to resolve completely.

A similar problem exists with other factors, such as the relative status of the interactants. Simply stipulating that two people have equal status in a setting will not guarantee that the interactants adopt a similar view and treat each other as equals. Black and white students, for example, may officially be afforded equal status by the school's administrative staff, but treated differentially by teachers (Rubovitz & Maehr, 1973) and differ in status within informal social groups with their peers. A number of studies have found that white subjects tend to dominate task-related interactions and appear to have higher status within interracial work groups (Cohen, 1972; Katz & Benjamin; 1960, Katz, Goldston, & Benjamin, 1958). Researchers need to verify that the conditions they presume to be operative in a given setting are indeed present.

More work also needs to be done in which these factors are studied as dependent, as well as independent variables. Recent work has been directed toward the study of techniques for promoting equal-status participation in classroom settings (Cohen, Lockheed, & Lohman, 1976) and, thus, like the studies of Katz and his colleagues, has come to treat equal status as a dependent measure rather than simply an antecedent of attitude change. Similar studies need to be conducted in which other conditions, such as the intimacy or pleasantness of contact, are also treated as outcomes rather than being treated solely as preconditions for attitude change. Consistent with this change in emphasis, attitudes need to be treated as the antecedents, as well as the outcomes, of intergroup contact.

This goal could be facilitated by treating contact as an ongoing process of interaction rather than as a static event. The reciprocal nature of empirical relationships would be more clearly apparent if construed within a framework of event sequences. The present chapter takes this approach. Existing attitudes and beliefs about one's partner, the setting, and so forth constitute the immediate causes of behavior in the contact setting. These beliefs allow one to anticipate the other's behavior and regulate one's actions in line with these expectancies. But one is also responsive to the interaction context and will sample information during the interaction as a basis for accommodation to the particular setting. Interpersonal interaction is the result of existing beliefs and newly acquired information being brought to bear on the regulation of one's behavior. What this implies is that the interactants' behaviors will be shaped by their existing beliefs but, in addition, the contact setting may also provide information that could force these beliefs to change. Past research has focused predominantly on how attitudes change in response to new information, but the interactants' existing attitudes may also profoundly affect the quality of interaction that develops in the contact setting.

The present approach also differs from that seen in past research by considering the processes that might explain changes in intergroup attitudes and the initiation of certain types of interaction. For example, if intergroup contact serves as a basis for acquiring new information relevant to existing stereotypes and intergroup attitudes, then it is necessary to go beyond the measurement of attitudes and consider how incoming information is processed by the individual. That is, one must consider how the information is encoded and transformed from a physical code to one consistent with knowledge in long-term memory. One must also consider *which* aspects of the available information are attended to, how this new information is incorporated into memory, and how it then comes to affect existing beliefs. Encoding, retrieval, and judgment are all relevant cognitive processes that affect the processing of new information and its integration with one's existing knowledge. Thus a series of interrelated processes must be understood if attitude change is to be adequately explained. A similar type of process analysis needs to be developed to understand how different patterns of interaction develop.

Studies of intergroup contact have paid little attention to the processes underlying intergroup interactions and their subsequent effects on attitudes; the present orientation focuses more specifically on these underlying processes. Adopting a process orientation will require a fundamental shift in the focus of research and a corresponding change in the methodological techniques that are employed (Taylor, 1976). But there are advantages to this approach. One of these is the effect it would have on future theoretical development in this research area.

Theory and the Specification of Processes

Amir's (1969) review of the contact literature indicates that certain empirical relationships have been found between aspects of the contact setting and the outcomes of intergroup contact. However, the development of theoretical models for explaining these findings and for relating them to each other within a general conceptual framework has not received sufficient attention. Amir (1976) has argued that the relative absence of theory in the contact literature has limited our understanding of intergroup relations. But the problem has not simply been the absence of theoretical ideas; it has more often been the failure to apply systematically those that have been available (Ashmore, 1970). Rarely have empirical findings either been predicted from or interpreted within an explicit theoretical framework, and even less frequently have researchers attempted to devise tests that would differentiate among competing hypotheses from different theories. However, this strategy of pitting different theoretical predictions against each other seems essential for theoretical refinement and the development of systematic programs of research (Platt, 1964).

This assessment of the contact literature as being largely atheoretical in emphasis is supported by two observations. First, a survey of this research shows that it has been concerned almost exclusively with the discovery of those aspects of the contact setting that are associated with favorable changes in intergroup attitudes. Thus, as discussed in the previous section, the range of issues studied has been restricted to a small subset of those that are potentially interesting, and the emphasis has been on the discovery of main effects rather than the specification of more complex relationships. There has been little interest in how, or if, various aspects of contact influence each other in important ways or interact to produce their observed effects on intergroup attitudes. However, a conceptual analysis of intergroup interaction would seem to suggest a variety of ways in which these different variables might be related.

A second indication of the need for theoretical guidance in this area of research is that, even though a variety of factors have been found that are believed to moderate the outcomes of intergroup contact, little is known about the intervening variables and psychological processes mediating these relationships. It is important, however, to specify the processes underlying empirical findings, inasmuch as the same outcome typically can be ascribed to a variety of different processes. For example, in a classic field experiment, Sherif, Harvey, White, Hood, and Sherif (1961) found that campers belonging to different groups were biased in favor of their own group; they typically chose members of their own group on a sociometric task and rated the products of their own group's members as superior to those of the other group. Sherif et al. explain these biases favoring the ingroup as resulting from competition among the groups and argues that tasks designed to induce cooperation between the members of the two groups served to reduce these evaluative biases. According to these authors, when two groups are competitively interdependent, favoritism is displayed toward members of the ingroup and against members of the outgroup, because whereas the ingroup shares one's own goals and helps one accomplish these goals, members of the outgroup adopt opposing goals that hinder one's success. With cooperative interdependence these evaluative biases diminish because one's own goals are shared by the members of each group. However, this explanation in terms of group interdependence is not the only reasonable explanation for these findings. Recent research indicates that ingroup favoritism may result even when the members of different groups are not in competition with each other. Rather than being a function of the interdependence among groups, this favoritism may result from cognitive processes of categorization and depend more on the salience of group membership (Brewer, 1979).

These comments suggest that in order to understand fully the nature of intergroup contact, it is necessary to consider the processes underlying empirical findings. Obviously though, before these processes can be specified and the relationships between different variables explicated, an initial theoretical framework is needed, and, as we have seen, such a framework is not yet available. How then are we to bolster theoretical development in this area of research? The answer being offered here, and one that has been suggested before (Ashmore, 1970), is to apply existing theoretical perspectives in psychology to the study of intergroup contact. This would not only provide theoretical perspectives for those working on issues of intergroup relations, but it would help to make the findings from future research in this area more relevant to other lines of research in psychology. In the remainder of this chapter it is shown how existing research and theory in social and cognitive psychology can be applied to the study of intergroup contact and how this approach leads to the generation of theoretical predictions and new issues for empirical study.

THE INFORMATIVENESS OF CONTACT

Contact has often been viewed as a means for acquiring information about a group's members that could lead to changes in group stereotypes (Ashmore, 1970) or incorrect assumptions of belief incongruence (Rokeach, Smith, & Evans, 1960). Each of these views implies that, by interacting with members of another group, the individual may come to learn that his or her existing beliefs are either false or exaggerated, revise these beliefs in light of newly acquired information and, as a result, come to act in a more positive manner toward the group's members.

When intergroup contact is viewed from this perspective it becomes important to recognize that information about a social group and its members may be obtained in a variety of ways. Changes in intergroup attitudes have generally been assumed to result from the information acquired during direct face-to-face interactions between the members of different social groups. However, a study by Hamilton and Bishop (1976) shows that attitudes may change in the absence of such interaction. These investigators examined a number of comparable white suburban neighborhoods in which a new family came to occupy the house of a departing family. In some cases the new family was black, whereas in other cases the newcomers were white. Hamilton and Bishop found that, after one year's time, the residents having black neighbors showed a decrease in prejudicial attitudes, whereas those acquiring new white neighbors increased on this same measure of racial prejudice. However, there was also evidence obtained that these changes in prejudice were not the result of face-to-face interaction with the black neighbors. Interracial interactions were extremely infrequent and attitude change was completely independent of actual interaction!

Clearly, even in the absence of face-to-face interaction, intergroup attitudes could change due to the acquisition of new information about a group and its members. It is important to distinguish between different channels of communication and recognize that face-to-face interaction is not a necessary condition for changes in intergroup attitudes. Information about a group also may be obtained through secondary sources, such as the media or the conversation that takes place among friends or acquaintances. Hamilton and Bishop (1976), in fact, obtained evidence that information about the new black neighbors was transmitted through neighborhood discussion and that these discussions paralleled changes in prejudice. That is to say, discussions about the newcomers were mostly negative at first but, with time, they became increasingly favorable; they were, like the residents' attitudes, mostly positive in tone after one year.

Despite the seemingly high correspondence between neighborhood discussion about the new black neighbors and prejudicial attitudes toward blacks, there was no evidence that these changes in attitudes were the direct result of neighborhood discussion. In interpreting their findings Hamilton and Bishop suggested that the reduced prejudice found in the integrated neighborhoods was neither the result of actual interaction nor discussions that occurred between the older residents. Rather, they attributed these changes to the lack of information that would have confirmed negative expectancies and fears about what effects would be brought about by neighborhood integration. That is, fearing changes in their property values, increased violence in the neighborhood, or other negative events, the residents' attitudes may have changed simply because these events did not come to pass. This interpretation, then, points to still another form of communication —one that does not require any interaction between the members of different groups. When different racial or ethnic groups are placed in proximity to each other—such as occurs with desegregation programs—the members of each group may observe each other's behavior and notice the occurrence or lack of occurrence of certain events. In this way they may acquire new information about each other even if they choose to avoid intergroup interactions.

Whether information about a social group is provided through face-to-face interaction, passive observation of its members, or indirectly through secondary sources, there will be common cognitive processes involved in the assimilation of this information by the individual. This is not meant to suggest that information acquired through these different means will be equally accurate, as easily assimilated into the person's existing knowledge base, or equally effective at changing prejudicial beliefs. The information available through one channel of communication may differ in certain ways from that available through a different one, both in terms of content and processing demands. And, as suggested above, it is important to distinguish between these different channels of communication. However, underlying the assimilation of and accomodation to new information are certain common processes. The present section examines these processes and the implications they have for the study of intergroup contact.

The Constructivist Approach

According to Rokeach et al. (1960), prejudice is caused by the anticipation of belief incongruence. That is to say, people are assumed to be prejudiced against a different racial or ethnic group because they expect its members to hold beliefs different from their own. Underlying this approach is the assumption shared by a variety of theories (Byrne, 1969; Heider, 1958) that people like those who share their views and dislike those who hold opposing beliefs or attitudes.

The theory of Rokeach et al., and other approaches adopted by those studying intergroup contact (Ashmore, 1970), lead one to expect that incorrect beliefs about a social group and its members may be changed simply by presenting the individual with information contradicting these erroneous beliefs. Intergroup contact is but one means of accomplishing this task. However, as pointed out by Dienstbier (1972), Rokeach et al.'s theory only deals with the effect of perceived belief differences on prejudice while assuming that the perception of belief differences is unaffected by existing prejudice. Dienstbier (1972) has argued against this assumption and shown that the relationship between prejudice and perceptions of belief incongruence is best viewed as being reciprocal in nature. In other words, prejudice does not only *result from* differences in beliefs but may *result in* the perception of belief differences as well.

Dienstbier (1972) obtained support for this view in two experiments. In each of these studies the subjects watched an interview take place on a television monitor. The picture of the monitor was sufficiently distorted so that it was possible to tell some of the subjects that the interviewee was white while telling other subjects that he was black. All the subjects watched exactly the same interview. In support of his argument, Dienstbier (1972) found that, even though all subjects watched exactly the same sequence of events, those who thought the interviewee was black felt his beliefs were more dissimilar to their own than the subjects who thought that he was white.

These results suggest that the subjects' perceptions of the interviewee were not simply a function of the actual information conveyed but were systematically biased by the subjects' beliefs about his group membership. Dienstbier (1972) interpreted these findings as due to the subjects' prejudice causing the perception of belief differences and as demonstrating the importance of considering reciprocal causal relations between prejudice and the perception of belief incongruence. However, similar effects have been found in studies of impression formation (Kelley, 1950), suggesting that such biases represent a more general phenomenon that is not restricted to cases of intergroup perception. These biases, then, appear to be caused not by prejudice per se but, rather, reflect the role one's existing beliefs or expectations play in the processing of new information. In the discussion that follows it is argued that greater consideration be given to the cognitive processes underlying such biases and a recognition of the similarities between intergroup perception and more general cognitive phenomena.

The perspective adopted here is what has come to be called the "constructivist" approach to information processing. This approach can be contrasted with that adopted by earlier investigators studying intergroup contact and prejudice from an informational perspective (Rockeach et al., 1960). These earlier approaches tended to assume that new information is acquired through a simple and rather passive learning process. As a result of this orientation, instead of studying the way new information is processed by the individual, researchers tended to focus primarily on the validity (or lack thereof) of the individual's existing intergroup beliefs and the extent to which intergroup contact provided information contradicting these beliefs. It is, of course, essential to consider the actual information available for processing by the individual. However, it is just as essential to consider the processes involved in the acquisition of that new information.

It is becoming increasingly apparent from research in cognitive psychology that learning is not a passive process and that the information that is remembered is not simply a verbatim reproduction except for what is lost through a passive forgetting process. This was demonstrated nearly half a century ago by Bartlett (1932), who found that, in trying to reproduce written passages from memory, his subjects not only committed errors of omission but distorted the content and meaning of the passages while adding to their reproductions new information that was not contained in the passages. These findings suggested that Bartlett's subjects were not simply storing a veredical copy of the passages but instead were actively forming some internal representation of them.

More recent research suggests that, in forming such internal representations of incoming information, people may preserve the meaning while forgetting the exact form in which it was presented. For example, Sachs (1967) found that when given an immediate recognition test her subjects were able to distinguish between a sentence they had just read and other sentences that differed either in syntax or meaning. However, when the subjects were tested for their ability to recognize the sentence following the presentation of other, intervening material, they were still able to distinguish between the original sentence and others differing in meaning, but they now had difficulty distinguishing it from sentences differing only in syntactic structure. Thus, what was stored in long-term memory appeared to be a representation that preserved its meaning but not its exact form.

In the process of encoding and storing incoming information, certain aspects of it may be lost; errors will then occur when the subsequent task requires that this information be retained (Bransford & Franks, 1971). The individual appears to extract the information from the stimulus array that is meaningful to him or that is relevant to the task at hand (Lingle, Geva, Ostrom, Leippe, & Baumgardner, 1979; Morris, Bransford, & Franks, 1977). Consequently, it may not be sufficient to know what information is simply available to the individual for processing; if predictions are to be made about what will be learned or which existing beliefs, if any, will be changed after the receipt of new information, it is necessary to know how the information comes to be processed. It is for this reason that we must consider the cognitive processes operating within the interactants during intergroup contact and not simply the information available for processing.

In the process of encoding information, the individual not only selects particular aspects of the available information for storage in memory, but also imposes upon the information an organizational structure. In other words, rather than storing each piece of information (e.g., the separate behaviors of an actor or the separate sentences in a story) as a separate unit, the information is integrated into an organized representation that specifies the relationships existing between these separate pieces of data.

Hamilton, Katz, and Leirer (1980) investigated the role of higher-level organizational processes that operate when the perceiver attempts to form an impression of another person. They presented a series of sentence predicates to subjects and asked them to form an impression of the person they supposedly described. Each sentence described a discrete action performed by the person and was drawn from one of four different content categories (e.g., social activities, athletic activities, etc.). Evidence for an organizational process was obtained by presenting the sentence predicates in a random order and then measuring the extent to which these items were clustered according to the a priori categories in free recall. As predicted by Hamilton et al., the items were organized to a greater extent than expected by chance, indicating that the subjects had indeed imposed an organizational structure on the information. This finding of categorical clustering in free recall would not have been possible unless the subjects possessed these concepts or categories in memory prior to performing the task. Thus, one implication of this finding is that, in forming an impression of an actor, the perceiver forms an organized representation—the impression—around existing concepts in memory.

Other research shows that the organization of incoming information around such concepts facilitates memory for this information (Bransford & Johnson, 1972; Dooling & Mullet, 1973). For example, Bransford and Johnson (1972) found that subjects who were presented with the theme underlying a written passage before reading it recalled more of the passage than subjects who either were not given the theme or who were given the theme only after reading the passage. Thus, providing the theme of the passage to the subjects enabled them to access an existing concept in memory as a basis for organizing the content of the passage.

At this point the question naturally arises as to how one's existing knowledge is represented in memory and how it is used in processing new information. Rumelhart and Ortony (1977) have provided a model of comprehension and memory that deals with these issues. It relies on the concept of *schemata,* which they define as:

> data structures for representing the generic concepts stores in memory. They exist for generalized concepts underlying objects, situations, events, sequences of events, actions and sequences of actions. . . . A schema contains, as part of its specification, the network of interrelations that is believed to generally hold among the constituents of the concept in question [p. 101].

Rumelhart and Ortony (1977) discuss the properties of schemata at length and the interested reader is referred to their paper. The notion of schemata provides a general framework that incorporates the important, overlapping features of the various approaches toward this issue of representation that have appeared in recent years.

Schemata are thought to play a fundamental role in the processing of information and are invoked during attentional, encoding, retrieval and higher-level thought processes. However, they result in information being processed selectively, and consequently biases inevitably result from their application. In the discussion that follows, we consider how these biases arise and the implications they have for the study of intergroup contact.

Biases in Memory

One function of schemata is to provide a basis for the organization of incoming information. That is to say, by organizing separate pieces of data around a schema or category in memory, an integrated representation may be constructed that links the separate pieces of data together. This process reduces the amount of work necessary for the retrieval of the information at a later point in time, because the location of one piece of information quickly leads to the location of other information that is connected to it within this integrated representation. It also enhances comprehension because the schema provides a context for the interpretation of incoming information and specifies the relationships existing between the separate pieces of data encountered by the individual (Bransford & Johnson, 1972).

However, the organization of information around categories also results in significant biases in memory. For example, Taylor, Fiske, Etcoff, and Ruderman (1978) had subjects observe a simulated group discussion in which half of the group's members were black and half were white. They found that when the subjects were later asked to recall which member of the group had made certain comments during the discussion, the subjects committed more within-group than between-group errors. In other words, subjects were able to remember accurately whether a black or white member had made the comment but were less accurate in identifying exactly which member had made the remark.

This finding suggests that the subjects were organizing the information around categories of group membership or racial origin. The significance of this research is that it shows one basis for the development of stereotypes. That is, if one can remember only the race of an individual but not his or her individual identity, it is a short step before erroneously concluding that the act or attribute of this one person is characteristic of the group as a whole. This categorization strategy might also lead to embarrasing or otherwise unpleasant consequences if its utilization becomes apparent to one's partner in the contact setting. That is, confusing one's partner with other members of the same group suggests that members of the group are seen as being the same—evidence that one is indeed prejudiced.

When two separate pieces of information are not directly related to each other, the schema also may aid in the organization of this information through the generation of inferences that tie them together (Kintsch, 1976). When we focus on interpersonal perception in intergroup settings, two types of structural representations may be especially important in this process. One of these consists of the stereotypes (Brigham, 1971) or set of organized beliefs in memory pertaining to the target person's racial or ethnic group. These stereotypes mediate inferences about the target person on the basis of group membership. Another basis for making inferences about a person is one's implicit personality theory. People will readily infer the presence of additional traits in a person based on those traits the person is known to possess. The evidence for these implicit personality theories is extensive (Schneider, 1973). Both stereotypes and implicit personality theories may be viewed as schemata and a basis for making inferences and organizing incoming information.

These belief systems allow people to make inferences about others when their knowledge of them is limited. However, their utilization in the processing of new information may also result in systematic biases. Studies suggest that the inferences people make come to be stored in memory along with the information actually presented (Kintsch, 1976). These inferences may then be confused with what was actually encountered, leading to systematic biases in recognition or recall (Bower, 1977; Bransford, Barclay, & Franks, 1972). This process of inferential elaboration provides one explanation for the biased perceptions of Dienstbier's (1972) subjects, inasmuch as it is reasonable to assume that the subjects simply went beyond the information contained in the target person's behavior and made inferences about him or her consistent with their stereotypes and implicit personality theories.

This process of inferential elaboration should serve to distort the perceiver's memory for an actor's behavior in line with his or her existing beliefs or expectancies about the actor. A similar outcome appears to result from the selective attention, encoding, and/or retrieval of information. Pichert and Anderson (1977) have shown that the perspective adopted by subjects in reading a story influences which aspects of the story can later be recalled. Specifically, they found that the likelihood of a particular idea being recalled was a direct function of its importance in terms of the perspective adopted in reading the story. Moreover, subjects who adopted different perspectives recalled more items related to their own, as opposed to the other perspective. Pichert and Anderson (1977) felt that this perspective manipulation led subjects to invoke different schemata as a basis for encoding the story that they read.

The relevance of this research for the study of intergroup contact would be more apparent if the individual's perspective were, more specifically, a configuration of stereotypic beliefs about some social group. Recent research suggests that stereotypes may indeed act as schemata and bias recall in a similar manner. For example, Rothbart, Evans, and Fulero (1979) found that information about a stimulus person was more likely to be recalled when it was related to an experimentally created stereotype descriptive of his or her social group than when it was unrelated to the stereotype. Thus, it appears that stereotypes may bias an individual's recollection of past events by acting as a perspective for selectively processing incoming information.

This cognitive bias might not only distort the person's memory for a single actor's behavior, but over more extended periods of time and more extended contact with the members of a group, it could result in the erroneous belief that existing stereotypes have been confirmed when objectively they have not. This conclusion is suggested by studies of covariation judgments in which subjects are presented with stimulus pairs and then asked to recall the actual degree of association or covariation between the various stimuli represented in these pairs. These studies have consistently found that stimuli are recalled as co-occurring with greater frequency when they are associated together in long-term memory than when they are unassociated (Chapman, 1967; Chapman & Chapman, 1967, 1969; Tversky & Kahneman, 1973).

The relevance of this research to issues of intergroup perception is seen in a study by Hamilton and Rose (1980; see also the chapter by Hamilton in this volume). These investigators had subjects read through a series of sentences in which the members of different occupational groups were described by trait adjectives that were either stereotypic of the person's group or unrelated to the group's stereotype. Hamilton and Rose found that, even though each trait had actually described each group's members an equal number of times, those traits stereotypic for a group were recalled as describing the group's members more often than the remaining trait adjectives. This result is consistent with the studies cited previously. However, the stereotypic traits were also recalled as describing members of their associated group more often than the members of the other occupational groups. Thus, if one views stereotypes as implicit beliefs about the correlation between categories of group membership and psychological attributes, it is seen that the subjects' stereotypes were, in effect, subjectively confirmed in the absence of any substantiating evidence. These studies suggest that over repeated encounters with the members of different groups, the tendency to recall schema-related information better than information unrelated to the schema may result in the erroneous perception of correlational relationships expected on the basis of stereotypic beliefs. One obvious conclusion from this research is that the person's existing beliefs and expectations about a group may be relatively unaffected as a result of intergroup contact and, in fact, they may actually be bolstered even when they have objectively been disconfirmed.

Unfortunately, the locus of this cognitive bias(es) is not clear from the research cited up to this point, for a number of different processes may account for these effects. However, it is apparent from other research that schema-based biases may occur either at the time of encoding new information (Zadny & Gerard, 1974) or during its retrieval (Anderson & Pichert, 1978; Snyder & Uranowitz, 1978). This is to be expected, inasmuch as schemata play an integral part in attentional, encoding, and retrieval processes. The important point to be made here is that biases in information processing can serve to undermine the potential of intergroup contact to disconfirm erroneous social stereotypes. Earlier approaches to the study of intergroup contact failed to appreciate this problem, because they overlooked the effect existing beliefs have on the processing of new information.

Biases in Information Seeking

The research discussed in the last section demonstrates biases in the assimilation and retention of the information available for processing. However, it is also important to recognize the active role the individual plays in determining the type of information to which he or she is exposed. Within the contact situation, each of the interactants may regulate their own behavior in order to elicit certain types of information from their partners. They may directly solicit information through questioning, or they may adopt a strategic approach of acting in such a way as to elicit informative responses from their partners. In each case, biases may emerge in the way information comes to be sampled.

Wilder and Allen (1978; see also the chapter by Wilder) have shown that, once a basis is available for categorizing people into groups, the individual tends to prefer information that maximizes between-group differences while minimizing within-group differences. This finding has a number of implications. For example, this bias in information seeking should serve to heighten the perception that the members of an outgroup are different from oneself and might discourage the desire for intergroup interaction (Byrne, 1969). Secondly, treating another as a member of a group rather than as an individual can undermine the potential of developing a satisfactory relationship.

Biases in information seeking may also enhance the likelihood of stereotypic beliefs being confirmed during interaction. Snyder and Swann (1978; see also the chapter by Snyder in this volume) have shown that people tend to test their hypotheses about others in a biased fashion. The subjects in these studies were provided with an initial hypothesis about a partner and were then allowed to test this hypothesis by soliciting information from him or her. Snyder and Swann found that subjects tended to adopt the strategy of seeking mainly confirmatory evidence—a strategy that would promote the perpetuation of erroneous hypotheses. This tendency to focus exclusively on confirming cases of a hypothesis has been noted before in studies of correlational judgments (Jenkins & Ward, 1965) and seems to reflect a profound departure from the prescriptions of normative theories of hypothesis testing.

This research suggests that the individual appears to sample information in a biased manner as well as processing it in a biased manner once it becomes available. However, it is unclear whether such an obviously biased form of hypothesis testing as that employed by Snyder and Swann's subjects (i.e., direct questioning) would occur in intergroup settings when the interactants wish to test the validity of their social stereotypes. If the individual's negative stereotypes become apparent to his or her partner, this could elicit hostility and disrupt an ongoing interaction. This strategy could have other aversive effects for the person as well. However, more subtle biases of this type might occur in the contact setting and, in some cases, one person's negative beliefs may actually be accepted to be true by his or her partner. These issues are discussed more fully later in this chapter.

Biases of Interpretation and Attribution

Up to this point we have regarded the objective information as offering evidence either for or against the individual's existing stereotypic beliefs, and argued that cognitive biases may lead to the selective sampling, encoding, retention, and retrieval of confirming information at the expense of disconfirming information. However, in many cases, the information may be ambiguous and its implications unclear. When this state of affairs exists, both one's behavior in the contact setting and the effect of this information on one's current beliefs will depend on the way in which the information is interpreted. Of course, this would always be the case, but when the information is ambiguous there is greater margin for error and misinterpretation.

The ambiguity of information is something that must be dealt with constantly in our daily experiences. How a perceiver interprets an actor's behavior will depend on the context in which it occurs. The context in this case includes: (1) the environmental setting in which the behavior occurs, including the behavior of other actors in the setting; and (2) the behaviors performed by the actor prior to the enactment of his or her current response. However, the context of an act includes more than these external events; it also includes the context that is brought to the setting by the perceiver in the form of existing knowledge and assumptions (Broudy, 1977). This includes the perceiver's beliefs and prior knowledge of the actor as well as knowledge of the setting in which the actor is observed. The total context of an act is best viewed as the product of the interaction between these internal and external contextual configurations.

The role of the surrounding context in the interpretation of an actor's behavior is seen in a study by Snyder and Frankel (1976). These investigators had subjects watch an actor on a television monitor; the actor was said to be taking part in an interview. In line with an elaborate cover story, subjects saw only the video portion and had no access to the verbal content of the "interview." Although all subjects watched the same videotaped sequence, some were told that the topic of the interview was sex, and in this case the subjects were given a list of interview questions regarding sexual values and preferences. Other subjects were told instead that the interview concerned political matters and were given a set of questions relevant to this topic. This variation in the instructions given to the subjects served as a manipulation of the environmental context surrounding the actor's behavior; however, the context could only exist because of the subjects' assumptions and prior knowledge about what these different topics imply for the actor's behavior.

Snyder and Frankel found that when the actor was thought to be discussing sexual matters, the subjects judged her as being more upset and uncomfortable than when she was thought to be discussing political issues. Thus, the context had a strong effect upon the subjects' interpretations and categorization of the actor's nonverbal behavior.

One reasonable interpretation of this finding is that the contextual information served to elicit different schemata for processing the actor's behavior. The subjects in the sexual-discussion group, for instance, may have been led to draw on their knowledge of how people typically behave in discussing sexual matters publicly, noting that such discussions are often accompanied by hesitancy, embarassment, and other manifestations of emotional arousal. These expectations could then have biased their perceptions in two ways. First, signs of discomfort and nervousness in the actor would have been anticipated by these subjects and, consequently, these behavioral cues should have been more readily noticed and encoded than when they were not initially anticipated, as in the political-discussion group. Secondly, nonverbal behavior is ambiguous, that is, susceptible to multiple interpretations. Thus, nonverbal behaviors that were categorized as signs of nervousness in the sexual-discussion group may have been categorized as signs of, say, involvement in the political-discussion group.

The schema approach to information processing suggests that the way in which an act is categorized will depend on the schemata employed. People are thought to employ those schemata or categories that are most accessible before they invoke alternative schemata as a basis for interpreting an actor's behavior. The relative accessibility of different schemata, however, is complexly determined by a combination of "event driven" and "conceptually driven" processing. Bobrow and Norman (1975) describe these types of processing as follows: "Conceptually driven processing tends to be top-down, driven by motives and goals, and fitting input to expectations; event driven processing tends to be bottom-up, finding structures in which to embed the input [p. 140]." These two processes operate simultaneously to determine the configuration of schemata utilized in the interpretation and storage of incoming information. These processes are discussed in detail by Rumelhart and Ortony (1977).

The notion of conceptually driven processing helps explain why the individual's perception and memory of events is often biased in line with his or her expectancies. That is, the individual's expectancies are mediated by highly accessible schemata, and these schemata tend to be employed in processing new information before others are invoked; only when the information cannot be incorporated with these primary structures will others be sought. However, as noted above, an actor's behavior will often be ambiguous and hence can be categorized in a number of different ways. The relative accessibility of different categories will determine how it is eventually categorized. Two potentially bias-ing factors that affect the relative accessibility of different schemata or categories are the frequency (Tversky & Kahneman, 1973) and recency (Higgins, Rholes, & Jones, 1977) of activation.

If stereotypes or categories of group membership are highly accessible during intergroup interaction, then we might expect biased interpretations occasionally to arise such that the same behavior that might be performed by a member of one's own group might be given a different interpretation when performed by someone from a different racial or ethnic group. The nature of such biases would depend on the structure of the schema or category residing in long-term memory and the exact nature of the actor's behavior, but given the undesirable implica-tions of many stereotypes, we might expect these biases to result in overly negative impressions rather than overly favorable ones.

Support for this line of reasoning comes from a study by Duncan (1976). He found that similar actions performed by black and white actors were categorized differently by white observers: The mild shove of a white actor was typically labeled as "playing around" or "dramatizing," whereas the black actor's be-havior was more often viewed as "aggressive behavior" or "violent behavior." This is precisely what would be expected if the black actor's behavior came to be categorized in terms of prevalent stereotypes. Unfortunately, this cognitive bias would probably serve to enhance the stereotype and retard any favorable effects of intergroup contact.

Integrally related to this categorization process is the process of attribution in which a perceiver seeks to uncover the causal factors underlying an actor's behavior and thereby explain the act's occurrence. This attribution process re-quires more than the mere categorization of an actor's behavior; it also requires that inferences be made about the actor's intentions, motives, and goals in the setting (Heider, 1958; Jones & Davis, 1965). The perceiver goes beyond a simple comprehension of what type of behavior has occurred in order to under-stand why it occurred. As with the categorization process discussed above, however, these inferences about why an actor behaved as he or she did are constrained by the context in which the act takes place and the schemata that are accessible when these inferences are made.

The role of context in the attribution process is evident in studies that have systematically varied the situational context in which an act occurs. These studies have shown that behavior is attributed mainly to internal dispositions of the actor (e.g., personality traits, attitudes, values) rather than situational factors when the act is freely chosen (Jones & Harris, 1967) and performed in the absence of, or in spite of, situational constraints (Jones, Davis, & Gergen, 1961). Thus, the per-ceiver appears to consider the external context in forming an impression of an actor and explaining his behavior.

However, the perceiver does not appear to give proper weight always to the context or the situational factors constraining an actor's behavior. This phenomenon was first noted by Heider (1958) and has since been labeled the "fundamental attribution error" (Ross, 1977). It is reflected in the tendency to overattribute behavior to internal, dispositional causes relative to situational factors. This bias in the attribution process might serve to distort further one's perception of his or her partner in the contact setting over and above that caused by biases in the categorization process discussed previously. Not only might one see an act as violent, for example, but one would also be prone to see one's partner as being violent by nature (see Snyder & Frankel, 1976).

One way to overcome this bias is to have the observer emphathize with the actor and adopt the actor's own point of view in the attribution process. Studies have shown that when observers are told to empathize with an actor, they typically arrive at attributional judgments more like those the actor invokes for explaining his or her own behavior (Gould & Sigall, 1977; Regan & Totten, 1975). Inducing such a shift in perspective would appear to be one way, then, of minimizing the fundamental attribution error and promoting a better understanding between the interactants.

These empathy-induced shifts in attribution may be understood as resulting from a shift in the way the available information comes to be processed; that is, by instructing the observer to adopt the actor's perspective and empathize with him or her, the observer probably comes to access different systems of existing knowledge for making attributional judgments than he or she would have otherwise. These knowledge structures then act as constraints upon the observer's attributional inferences. However, in the case where the members of different groups interact with each other for the first time, it may be difficult for them effectively to adopt their partner's point of view. Rather than truly adopting the other's perspective, the interactants may adopt a point of view that is really different. True empathic understanding requires knowledge of how the other reacts and thinks in response to a particular set of conditions, and this may only be possible as the interactants become more familiar with each other and come to know each other more intimately (Levinger & Snoek, 1972).

The individual's perspective establishes a set of constraints upon attributional judgments, presumably by altering the accessibility of different schemata in long-term memory. However, when stereotypic beliefs are highly accessible in the setting they too may constrain attributional inferences and bias the way in which the individual comes to interpret the partner's behavior. A number of studies have demonstrated that attributional inferences may be biased by the individual's existing beliefs or evaluative orientation toward another person (Dion, 1972; Regan, Straus, & Fazio, 1974; Taylor & Jaggi, 1974). Particularly relevant to the present chapter is the study by Taylor and Jaggi (1974). These investigators asked Hindu subjects to make attributional judgments for desirable and undesirable behaviors performed by Hindu and Muslim actors. Taylor and Jaggi found that their Hindu subjects tended to attribute desirable behaviors to characteristics of the actor if he or she was also Hindu, while attributing undesirable behaviors to situational factors. However, when the actor was Muslim, the subjects showed the reverse pattern: They attributed desirable behaviors to situational factors and undesirable behaviors to dispositions of the actor.

This finding suggests that the individual's stereotypic beliefs about a group could be further bolstered through biases in attribution. However, unlike many of the cognitive biases discussed earlier, this type of bias might not only distort the person's memory of what occurred within the contact setting, but would also affect how the person construes the partner's intentions and goals as interaction takes place. This could affect the nature of the interaction that develops and determine whether the contact setting promotes or retards the development of better intergroup relations. This line of reasoning is consistent with a number of studies that show attributional inferences influence the person's subsequent behavior; that is to say, the person's behavior is not a function of objective events but rather the interpretation given to those events (see Bem, 1972; Ickes & Kidd, 1976, for research showing the effect of attributional judgments on behavior).

The research reviewed in this section points to a system of cognitive processes that could very well undermine the potential of intergroup contact to reduce existing prejudices. It demonstrates that the individual's perceptions, recollections, and judgments of others may be biased by existing beliefs and stereotypes and that rather than providing new information that will discredit erroneous stereotypes, intergroup contact may only provide ambiguous data that is distorted to conform to and bolster these beliefs. The operation of these biases may help explain why some studies have found an intensification or polarization of intergroup attitudes following contact rather than systematic changes across different individuals (Guttman & Foa, 1951; Mussen, 1950). Some authors, in fact, have argued that polarization effects rather than systematic changes in the direction of existing attitudes are what most studies of intergroup contact actually have found (Amir, 1976; Guttman & Foa, 1951).

Earlier, it was noted that information about a social group may be obtained in a variety of different ways. In each case we would expect biases of the type specified in this section to occur; that is, new information will be assimilated to the person's existing knowledge base regardless of the channel through which it is encountered. However, it is important to recognize that different channels of communication also differ in important ways. For example, when information is received secondhand, it may well have passed from one source to another numerous times. This allows for the possibility of distortions being introduced at each link in the chain of communication. Thus, as the information travels there may be a compounding of the various biases discussed in this section (Allport & Postman, 1945; Bartlett, 1932) and, consequently, secondhand information may be especially inaccurate.

In the sections that follow, the focus is on face-to-face interaction as a channel of communication. Here, too, there are relatively unique features to consider in adopting an information-processing approach. For example, there are greater cognitive demands placed on the perceiver, inasmuch as he or she must not only categorize and make judgments about the other's behavior but must also plan his or her own behavior at the same time. Face-to-face interaction would therefore seem more difficult than other forms of observation that are unilateral in the flow of information. On the other hand, the interactants can each solicit specific information from their partners. This might reduce the likelihood of misunderstandings being perpetuated over time and unclear aspects of the situation remaining unclear or being distorted in line with the perceiver's assumptions.

The sections that follow examine the nature of intergroup interactions. Are they typically different or similar to the type of interactions that develop between members of the same social group? Are they likely to promote or retard favorable intergroup relations? In examining these questions a cognitive perspective is retained. An attempt is made to specify some of the cognitive processes that serve to regulate the interactants' behavior in the contact setting. It is also shown how the person's stereotypic beliefs and existing expectations regarding intergroup interactions may influence the quality of interactions that develop. Finally, one especially important question that is raised is the extent to which we can expect those type of interactions to develop that typically have been seen as conducive of favorable intergroup relations, most specifically, intimate interactions that result in the formation of close intergroup relationships.

THE QUALITY OF INTERRACIAL INTERACTIONS

In his review of the contact literature, Ashmore (1970) noted the tendency to misperceive the behavior of others and, as a result, fail to revise, adequately, prejudicial attitudes following intergroup contact. He suggests that it is not enough to have contact with members of a group whose behavior is inconsistent with existing stereotypes; the contact must be frequent and intimate enough to preclude perceptual distortion.

Ashmore (1970) suggests that such distortions may be overcome most effectively when the interactants are cooperatively interdependent and when they are placed into an intimate relationship with each other. When two people share common goals they should be less likely to misperceive the other's behavior, because such distortions could undermine their chances of reaching their shared goal. They must accurately assess the other's behavior, abilities, and personality to ensure effective integration of their individual efforts. They must also remain open to information from each other and, consequently, they are more likely to be susceptible to social influence attempts of the other. In general, cooperative interdependence is expected to promote each person's receptiveness to information from the other and facilitate the development of homogeneity of behavior and attitudes. The end result is a minimization of perceptual distortion and actual differences between the interactants.

These elements are present whenever two people enter into a close interpersonal relationship in which each person is dependent on the other for his or her outcomes (Thibaut & Kelley, 1959). However, other effects also may occur when two people come to be close friends. Attraction to a member of a minority group not only may make one more open to information from the other, but this attraction may generalize to other members of the group. Moreover, a developing friendship may lead to interaction in settings other than those necessary for the accomplishment of group goals. Broadening the range of contact may then provide a greater range of information about the other and lessen the possibility of situation-specific attitude change (Ashmore, 1970).

These considerations suggest that cooperative interdependence and intimate relationships that promote such interdependence could promote favorable relationships between the members of different social groups and lessen the biases discussed in the previous section. However, there are other reasons to expect the formation of intimate intergroup relationships to foster a reduction in prejudicial beliefs and behavior.

One of these reasons is integrally related to a distinction typically made in the contact literature between intimate and superficial contact (Amir, 1969). Earlier conceptualizations often viewed the contact *setting* as being either intimate or superficial and stressed the importance of intimate contact in promoting positive intergroup relations. However, intimacy might better be conceptualized as the attainment of a particular state in an ongoing relationship (Levinger & Snoek, 1972; Thibaut & Kelley, 1959) rather than a property of the setting itself. Certain environments may promote the development of intimate relationships better than others but they are not inherently intimate or superficial. For example, within the most superficial settings two friends may break out of the roles they each play in these settings and behave as they might in other contexts. The question addressed in the present chapter is not so much how different settings promote or inhibit the development of intimate relationships, but how the formation of intimate relationships between the members of different social groups may reduce intergroup prejudice.

Given this distinction between settings and relationships there is another basis for espousing the virtues of intimacy. When an intimate relationship is fostered between two people, each becomes familiar with various aspects of the other's personality. In more superficial relationships the range of knowledge acquired about the other is restricted largely because that interaction is confined to a limited number of social contexts. That this difference may have significant implications for the study of intergroup contact is suggested by results reported by Gurwitz and Dodge (1977). They found that stereotyped attributions to a target person were less frequent when evidence disconfirming the stereotype for her social group was concentrated in the description of a single group member rather than dispersed across different members of the group. However, the opposite relationship was found when the evidence confirmed stereotypic beliefs about the target person's social group: Information dispersed across different members of the group enhanced stereotypic attributions to the target person to a greater extent than when the same information was conveyed in the description of a single group member.

Because an intimate intergroup relationship offers the possibility of multiple disconfirmations of the stereotype from the behavior of only one member of the group, Gurwitz & Dodge's findings suggest that such relationships may be more effective in changing that stereotype. Superficial relationships, in contrast, would have greater potential to confirm the stereotype, because with a larger number of superficial relationships, it is likely that there could be multiple confirmations of the stereotype across different members of the group.

There is yet another reason for favoring the development of intimate rather than more superficial relationships between the members of different groups. With superficial contact the members of each group are likely to have little information about each other except for that conveyed by surface characteristics, such as the other's skin color, physical attractiveness, dress, or language. Given only these types of information, however, it is reasonable to expect that a perceiver will tend to categorize others using these distinctive characteristics and differentiate people along traditional group lines, such as race, ethnicity, social class, and sex. In essence, then, surface contact would serve to prime or activate (see Higgins et al. 1977) categories of group membership and evoke stereotypic schemata for processing the behavior of others. In other words, by limiting intergroup interaction to more superficial forms and inhibiting the development of intimate relationships, it is more likely that people will continue to think about others in terms of their group membership. With more intimate relationships a more differentiated view develops of others in which a variety of categories can be used to process their behavior. The reason this is important is that the biases in information processing discussed earlier result from the application of schemata in long-term memory. To the extent stereotypes and categories of group membership are accessible during intergroup interaction, these stereotypes may be bolstered and the other's behavior misperceived in line with these stereotypes. The reasoning offered here suggests that this process would more likely with less intimate contact between the members of different social groups.

These considerations suggest a number of possible bases for the efficacy of intimate relationships between members of different social groups to reduce existing intergroup prejudice. The question that arises at this point is to what extent can we expect such relationships to develop when the members of different social groups are placed in desegregated contexts.

The Development and Maintenance of Interpersonal Relationships

One particularly useful approach to the study of interpersonal relationships is Thibaut and Kelley's (1959) theory of social exchange. Thibaut and Kelley propose that dyadic interaction and the development of interpersonal relationships are a function of the rewards and costs expected from the relationship. If relatively unfavorable outcomes are expected the individual will avoid intimate encounters with others and discourage the development of potential relationships with them. On the other hand, if relatively favorable outcomes are expected, then greater intimacy will be desired and attempts will be made to initiate or expand the relationship beyond its current state. Changes in an ongoing relationship and the development of new relationships depend on the individuals' current level of satisfaction and the availability of more favorable alternatives.

In order for each member of a dyad to know what outcomes are available from a relationship they must possess some information about the other that will enable them to forecast and predict what these outcomes might be. In the case where no real relationship yet exists, one tends to rely heavily on social stereotypes invoked by the physical characteristics of the person (Levinger & Snoek, 1972). When a relationship already exists, information acquired in past interactions can be used to guide future interactions.

According to Thibaut and Kelley (1959) initial interactions tend to be highly uniform and stereotyped in that most people behave similarly in such settings. Such interactions are characterized by formality, constraint, and politeness and consequently are conventional and highly predictable. As a result, they offer a limited amount of information that can be used to forecast the outcomes potentially available from a relationship. Although normative, socially desirable behavior is relatively uninformative about the other person (Jones & Davis, 1965), Thibaut and Kelley suggest that these forms of interaction are functional for the actor. They allow him to enter into a potentially unstable relationship and gain additional information without incurring heavy costs. With increasing confidence in the viability of a new relationship, the members of the dyad shift from the self-presentation strategies characterizing initial interactions to more revealing patterns of behavior. This shift is necessary because new information must be acquired that will allow the interactants to predict the other's behavior and respond in such a way as to maximize the available outcomes. It is also necessary in order to reduce any remaining uncertainty about the stability of present outcomes and those that are likely to become available in the future. What this implies is that with increasing interaction and increased commitment to a relationship there should be a corresponding increase in the amount of self-disclosure between the interactants (Chaikin & Derlega, 1976). Eventually, the members of the dyad may each obtain an extensive knowledge base for predicting the other's behavior and forecasting the outcomes associated with various types of interaction.

Within interracial settings perhaps one of the most salient features of the other person would be his or her race. Given that this is so, it is likely that inferences made about the other would be influenced by the stereotype of his or her racial group. If the stereotype is favorable, then positive outcomes would probably be expected from a relationship with members of the group. However, if the stereotype is unfavorable, as it is for most racial stereotypes, then negative outcomes would be forecast. One prediction, then, from Thibaut and Kelley's

(1959) framework is that interracial interaction typically might be avoided. Evidence for this proposal comes from studies of desegregated neighborhoods that show that interracial contact tends to be less frequent than contact between the members of the same racial group (Bradburn et al., 1971; Hamilton & Bishop, 1976).

One would also expect on this basis that, in cases where contact is unavoidable, the members of interracial dyads would be less likely to develop an intimate relationship and might actively avoid an expansion of the relationship beyond its current state. One manifestation of this avoidance would be the display of few signs of intimacy or acceptance in interracial interactions. This strategy of interaction would help the reluctant individual to discourage the development of the relationship. One way of measuring the degree of acceptance or intimacy afforded another person is through nonverbal indices of immediacy (Mehrabian, 1969). Word, Zanna, and Cooper (1974) utilized a number of these nonverbal measures in an experiment where white subjects played the role of interviewers and interviewed either black or white job applicants. These investigators found that less nonverbal immediacy was displayed and less time was spent in the interviews with the black job applicants. Thus, less intimacy was displayed toward the black than white job applicants and the interracial setting was avoided relative to the intraracial one.

Another way of measuring the amount of intimacy during interaction is by measuring the amount of self-disclosure between the interactants (Chaikin & Derlega, 1976). Chaikin, Derlega, Harris, Gregorio, and Boone (1973; cited in Chaikin & Derlega, 1976) obtained evidence of both avoidance and restricted communication in interracial dyads. They had white subjects converse with a black or white confederate, who either disclosed highly personal information about himself or who was relatively impersonal. Consistent with other research (Derlega, Harris, & Chaikin, 1973), the subjects reciprocated a white confederate's personal disclosures and revealed more personal information about themselves when he was more intimate with them. However, when the confederate was black, the subjects failed to match his disclosure level and were actually somewhat less intimate when he was more intimate with them. Thus, there is less self-disclosure within interracial settings than typically is found between members of the same racial group, at least in the initial stages of a relationship. As a consequence of this restricted flow of communication, there is little information available to the interactants that they might use to predict effectively the other's future behavior. Uncertainty would therefore remain high and the relationship would be unlikely to develop beyond its current state.

In failing to reciprocate the other's personal disclosures of information, or in failing to initiate a process of mutual self-disclosure, a white actor may be viewed by the black as cold and unfriendly (Chaikin & Derlega, 1974). This appraisal would receive additional confirmation if the white also displayed signs of nonverbal rejection, as was seen in the study by Word et al. (1974). The ultimate outcome of this process would be the confirmation of the black's negative beliefs about whites. Moreover, having formed a negative impression of the actor and feeling rejected by him or her, it is likely that signs of rejection would be reciprocated by the black. This reaction could then serve as confirmation of the white actor's initial beliefs, leading to a self-fulfilling prophecy (Merton, 1948) and further undermining the future development of the relationship.

Support for this line of reasoning was obtained in a second experiment by Word et al. (1974). White confederates, acting as interviewers, were trained to behave in either a more or less immediate fashion toward white subjects, who role-played job applicants. In a high immediacy condition the confederates modeled their nonverbal behavior after those subjects who had interviewed white job applicants in the previous study and thus acted in a relatively accepting manner. In the low immediacy condition the confederates modeled the behavior displayed toward black job applicants in the previous study and were relatively unaccepting on a nonverbal level. Word et al. found that the nonverbal behavior of the less immediate interviewer resulted in a reciprocal pattern of nonverbal rejection by the subjects. These subjects also liked the interview less, performed less effectively in the setting, and showed greater signs of discomfort or uneasiness compared to subjects in the high immediacy group.

This study provides but one demonstration of how self-fulfilling prophecies may originate during interpersonal interaction. Studies have demonstrated the operation of self-fulfilling prophecies in a variety of contexts (Jones, 1977) and have shown that these patterns of interaction may originate from the stereotypes of the interactants (see chapter by Snyder in this volume). These studies clearly show that an actor may, without realizing his or her own part in this process, elicit confirmation of his or her existing beliefs by constraining the partner's behavior and precluding alternative responses.

The emergence of a self-fulfilling prophecy during interaction represents a case in which an individual receives a biased sample of information about another person and is misled into thinking his or her erroneous expectancies about the other are correct. Thibaut and Kelley (1959) have presented an informational analysis of dyadic interaction in which they discuss how information becomes biased by strategies of self-presentation. They suggest that when favorable outcomes are expected from a relationship the members of a dyad will each try to portray themselves in a favorable light so as to encourage the other's interest; this will not be the case when negative outcomes are forecast. In other words, when people expect relatively favorable outcomes, they will try to act in such a way as to convince a partner that the relationship will be a rewarding one for him or her in return. This strategy of self-presentation obviously results in a biased sample of information being provided. However, Thibaut and Kelley suggest that this enables the development of the relationship beyond its current state by stimulating a greater exchange of information between the members of the dyad.

One way of encouraging another's interest is to demonstrate that one possesses those characteristics that are valued by the other. An illustration of this process has been supplied by Zanna and Pack (1975). They found that when women perceived a male partner as being highly desirable, they portrayed themselves as being consistent with his view of the "ideal woman." However, when he was not seen as being a desirable partner, the women acted in ways consistent with their true beliefs. Thus it appears as though the women's predictions regarding the outcomes available from any potential relationship with the male target person resulted in a pattern of self-presentation that was biased. This probably would have served to attract the more desirable target person to the relationship, but it also resulted in a distorted representation of these women's typical attitudes and behavior.

A number of other strategies for encouraging the interest of a potential partner are available to a person. For example, one might adopt similar attitudes, conform to a partner's requests, or otherwise display a liking for the partner and what he or she stands for. In each case one may be viewed as acting in such a way as to convince a prospective partner that, by establishing or developing a mutual relationship, he or she will be able to obtain favorable outcomes.

When the individual holds negative racial stereotypes about the members of a social group and these are salient during intergroup interaction, one would expect few instances of such behavior. Unfavorable or unacceptable outcomes would be inferred and, rather than encouraging friendships with the group's members, any potential relationships would be discouraged. Interaction might occur in such cases, but unless the person received new information more favorable in nature, or individuating information that might discourage reliance on group stereotypes (see the chapter by Wilder in this volume), the interaction would probably remain formal, constrained, and uninformative for the interactants, or possibly degenerate into unpleasant interaction through the processes already discussed. Only when favorable outcomes are expected from the relationship will the person actively seek the other's interest and an expansion of the relationship. Thus Thibaut and Kelley's framework provides a basis for predicting discriminatory behavior.

Verbal Acceptance and Reverse Discrimination in Interracial Settings

The studies of interracial interaction reviewed in the previous section were presented as though their findings reflected manifestations of racial prejudice and deliberate attempts by the subjects to avoid more intimate relations with members of a different racial group. Although such reactions might be expected from highly prejudiced persons, the subjects in this research have been college students who represent perhaps one of the most liberal populations in the United States. Rather than freely espousing extremely negative stereotypes of blacks, these individuals are reluctant to express such beliefs (Sigall & Page, 1971) and typically score low on measures of racial prejudice.

A series of studies by Dutton and his colleagues (Dutton, 1976) has shown that people who considers themselves unprejudiced tend to guard this self-image and actually may "bend over backwards" to demonstrate to themselves that they adhere to egalitarian values. In two studies it was shown that when these individuals were threatened by the suggestion that they might be prejudiced, they responded by showing preferential treatment to the member of a discriminated minority group (Dutton & Lake, 1973; Dutton & Lennox, 1974). This pattern of behavior appears to be especially likely when the person is in a position to be publicly evaluated (Dutton & Yee, 1974). According to these authors, the reverse discrimination exhibited by these subjects represents an attempt to discredit this threatening inference about themselves. That is, by responding very favorably toward a member of the minority group in question, the subjects may provide themselves with new data that disconfirms the implication that they hold discriminatory attitudes.

Other research suggests that, rather than discouraging the interest of black partners, the liberal white may try very hard to gain their acceptance. For example, Poskocil (1975) has shown that white subjects express more liberal racial attitudes in interracial than all-white "discussion groups." This attempt to gain the other's acceptance and approval may represent still another method gaining assurance that one is lacking in racial prejudice.

A similar phenomon is apparent in laboratory studies of aggression (Donnerstein & Donnerstein, 1972; Donnerstein, Donnerstein, Simon, & Ditrichs, 1972). For example Donnerstein et al. found that direct aggression by white subjects was stronger when displayed toward black than white victims but only when the subjects' identities remained anonymous. If the black victim knew the aggressor's identity or could later retaliate, the subjects inhibited direct expressions of aggression and actually aggressed against him or her less than they did toward a white victim. These findings provide additional evidence that under certain conditions people will inhibit displays of preference for their own group's members and actually respond more favorably toward members of a different racial group.

These findings would seem to indicate that, at least under some conditions, the white person may actually go out of the way to gain a black partner's liking and approval. But will such attempts be successful? Poskocil (1975, 1977) suggests that such attempts will often fail to elicit a black person's approval: Rather than being a sign of friendship and acceptance these overtures are likely to be perceived as signs of white hypocrisy and guilt. As we have seen, this perception appears to have some basis. That is, although the white person may show overt agreement, compliance, and preferential treatment toward the black partner, he or she may also fail to reciprocate the latter's attempts at more intimate exchanges (Chaikin et al., 1973), display nonverbal signs of rejection (Word et al., 1974), and seek escape from the interaction (Word et al., 1974).

Furthermore, once the person has reasserted his or her egalitarian values, less compliance actually may be seen in response to another request from a member of the same minority group (Dutton & Lennox, 1974). The person may act prejudiced when not under evaluative pressures (Donnerstein & Donnerstein, 1972; Donnerstein, et al., 1972; Dutton & Yee, 1974) and, when under such pressures, may simply substitute less direct signs of prejudice for more direct forms (Donnerstein & Donnerstein, 1972; Donnerstein, et al., 1972).

This conflictual quality present in the white's behavior is also evident in findings reported by Weitz (1972). She examined nonverbal (voice quality, behavioral measures) and verbal measures of acceptance toward black and white "interaction partners," and found that all of these measures were positively correlated when the subject's partner was white; however, when the partner was black, there was an inverse relationship between the nonverbal and verbal measures. In other words, those subjects displaying the most direct form of acceptance also showed the least acceptance on behavorial and nonverbal measures. In discussing this finding, Weitz (1972) emphasized the negative outcomes of verbal acceptance accompanied by nonverbal restraint:

> For the black in real interracial interaction, the above pattern leads to a situation of conflicting cues: positive verbal approach coupled with negative voice tone and behavior. For the white, this conflicted situation doubtlessly leads to anxiety and discomfort, and perhaps even to a tendency to avoid interracial contact [p. 17].

Weitz interpreted this finding using the concept of *ambivalence* (Katz, 1970). Ambivalence refers to a state of conflict that results when a person holds both positive and negative attitudes toward the same person, group, or object. Weitz proposes that her subjects were ambivalent toward their black partners and that they tended to repress their hostile feelings toward them. Weitz maintains that this repressed affect then was expressed through less easily monitored or consciously controlled channels. Thus positive affect was expressed verbally while repressed hostility toward the partner "leaked out" through less controllable nonverbal and behavioral channels.

Accompanying the ambivalence notion is the concept of *amplification* (Katz, 1970). Katz proposes that when the person has ambivalent attitudes toward another person his or her responses toward this person will be exaggerated in magnitude. Thus the person who is ambivalent toward blacks should display more favorable reactions toward a black partner than someone who holds uniformly positive attitudes toward that person's racial group. Similarly, when unfavorable reactions are performed, these should be more extreme than those performed by persons holding uniformly unfavorable attitudes toward the other's racial group.

This framework provides one basis for interpreting the findings reviewed thus far. It can account for Weitz's findings and those cases of reverse discrimination discussed earlier. Poskocil (1977) has suggested that some black people in interracial settings adopt a similar interpretation of white people's behavior. They construe the white person's exaggerated verbal acceptance as signs of guilt, his or her nonverbal behavior as evidence of concealed racism, and generally views expressions of liking and acceptance as insincere.

However, these findings may be interpreted in other ways. In the sections that follow some of these alternatives are discussed. It is shown how these findings may be conceptualized in terms of cognitive processes and their affective consequences rather than conflict between different motivational or affective states. On the other hand, it should be kept in mind that, regardless of how we interpret these patterns of behavior, the consequences of intergroup contact will be determined by the way in which the interactants construe the situation. Given conflicting cues and apparent signs of rejection by the other, the individual is likely to find the contact setting unpleasant, avoid the development of a more intimate relationship, and receive confirmation of negative stereotypes held about the other group. Thus, these findings suggest a number of obstacles to be contended with if intergroup contact is to be implemented as a basis for reducing prejudice. Simply placing the members of different groups together will not insure the development of intimate intergroup relationships.

Self-Evaluation as a Source of Discomfort

One feature common to most of these studies of interracial behavior is the evaluative atmosphere of the setting. The subjects in these studies seem to act more favorably toward members of a different racial group than members of their own group mainly when others are present who could potentially judge their behavior (Donnerstein & Donnerstein, 1972; Donnerstein et al., 1972; Dutton & Yee, 1974; Poskocil, 1975) or when information is received that threatens their self-images (Dutton & Lake, 1973; Dutton & Lennox, 1974). When the subjects' anonymity has been emphasized and there is no suggestion that they may be prejudiced, this favorability toward the outgroup is normally absent and preferential treatment is afforded members of their own group instead (Donnerstein & Donnerstein, 1972; Dutton & Yee, 1974). It appears, then, that people behave differently depending on whether or not they are placed in the position of being evaluated either by others or by themselves.

But what process is responsible for this differential pattern of behavior? One conceptual framework that can be used to answer this question is Duval and Wicklund's theory of objective self-awareness (Duval & Wicklund, 1972; Wicklund, 1975). Duval and Wicklund argue that the person may alternate between a state of *subjective self-awareness*—in which attention is directed outward towards the external environment—and a state of *objective self-awareness*—in which attention is turned inward upon oneself as an object. Theoretically, these are mutually exclusive attentional states; that is, the person may shift from one state to another but cannot focus his or her attention simultaneously on both external and internal stimuli.

While in the state of objective self-awareness, one views oneself as an object of evaluation and judges one's behavior against those standards that are salient. The outcome of this self-focused state is one's awareness of potential discrepancies between one's actual behavior and ideal standards of how to behave. According to Duval and Wicklund, one will generally fail to meet these standards in practice and thus will experience an unpleasant affective state resulting from this unfavorable self-appraisal. In order to reduce this unpleasant state one is expected either to shift to a state of subjective self-awareness or try to bring behavior in line with one's standards. The former strategy leads to such actions as distraction through self-stimulation (e.g. nervous habits), displacing attention away from those stimuli arousing self-focused attention, or simply fleeing the situation. The latter strategy results in behavior change and highlights the role of objective self-awareness in the process of self-regulation of behavior. A large body of literature has developed that provides construct validity for the concept of objective self-awareness and support for the theory's predictions (Wicklund, 1975).

Certain conditions that have been present in those studies of interracial behavior discussed earlier probably would have encouraged subjects to focus attention upon themselves and thus may be viewed as manipulations of objective self-awareness (Wicklund, 1975). For example, in order to supply the suggestion that they had deviated from their own professed standards of racial tolerance and egalitarianism, Dutton and his colleagues (Dutton & Lake, 1973; Dutton & Lennox, 1974) led some subjects to believe that they were hearing their own hearts beat as they watched a series of slides. Donnerstein et al. (1972) employed a manipulation of anonymity that also would have moderated the subjects' focus of attention. In this study the subjects either were assured that their responses would remain anonymous or were required to perform their responses nonanonymously with a videocamera aimed at them throughout the experiment. In a similar vein, Dutton and Yee (1974) used the presence or absence of an audience to manipulate the subjects' anonymity.

If it is true that objective self-awareness has been elicited in subjects and that they have been responding to standards of interracial acceptance present in these experimental settings, then the theoretical framework of Duval and Wicklund (1972) provides an alternative interpretation for the findings reviewed earlier. Instances of reverse discrimination, verbal acceptance, and compliance exhibited by white subjects toward their black partners may be viewed as attempts to behave in a manner consistent with these standards. Findings of nonverbal rejection or constraint may reflect the negative affect accompanying objective self-awareness when the individual fails to meet these standards. And because verbal acceptance and nonverbal constraint would both be expected to increase with the perceived discrepancy between actual and ideal patterns of behavior, the theory seems to predict the inverse relationship between verbal acceptance and nonverbal immediacy found by Weitz (1972).

This theoretical framework may also be used to explain the findings of Chaikin et al. (1973). As described earlier, these investigators found normal patterns of reciprocal self-disclosure breaking down when white subjects interacted with a black partner but not in those cases where their partner was white. One might expect such disruptions of normal patterns of interaction when one or both of the interactants are made objectively self-aware. Besides putting him or her on guard, so to speak, self-focused attention would serve to direct the individual's attention away from the external environment and his or her partner. Consequently, he or she is likely to be unresponsive to verbal and nonverbal cues provided by the other and fail to perform more typical patterns of behavior guided by these cues, such as reciprocation of the other's personal disclosures. This process, then, may explain why the person caught in self-conscious deliberation appears inhibited and shows a lack of spontaneity in behavior. It would also explain the lack of intimacy seen in interracial dyads not as an avoidance of intimate interracial interactions but as the result of the individual's failure to encode adequately the other's behavior. This interpretation is consistent with the assumption that objective and subjective self-awareness are mutually exclusive states and receives some support from recent research (Vallacher, 1978).

Earlier in this chapter it was suggested that interracial settings might tend to be avoided and more intimate relationships fail to develop between the members of different racial groups because of the constrained and unpleasant nature of interracial interactions. The discussion in this section suggests that the constraint and discomfort accompanying some interracial encounters may be the outcome of cognitive processes involved in the self-regulation of behavior, rather than the manifestation of either prejudice per se or of ambivalent motives.

The discussion in this section also highlights the importance of considering self-perception processes and the way in which changes come about in beliefs about oneself. Earlier it was argued that the contact setting may provide information relevant to one's stereotypic schemata and thereby facilitate changes in existing prejudicial beliefs. However, each individual also possesses a cognitive structure for representing knowledge of self, that is, a self-schema (Markus, 1977), and this structure may undergo change as well. Through self-observation, social comparison processes (Suls & Miller, 1977), or an awareness of others' evaluations, one may acquire information that either supports or contradicts this self-schema. This information may then either bolster one's self-schema, force it to be modified, or as discussed in this section, lead to behavioral change and self-regulation strategies aimed at its preservation.

Novelty and Uncertainty in Interracial Settings

Thibaut and Kelley (1959) argue that people are initially uncertain about entering into a new relationship because they are not sure of either the acceptability or stability of future outcomes available from the relationship. This uncertainty is to some extent present in all relationships whether they are current or prospective ones, but the novelty and "strangeness" of new relationships accentuates this uncertainty, resulting in formal and constrained interactions.

The extent of uncertainty present will tend to be moderated by the type of interaction and the setting in which it takes place. Settings differ in their familiarity and the extent to which they are structured to limit the range of possible interactions. In highly structured settings, norms typically prescribe how the person should behave and there are specific roles that come to be occupied by the interactants. People can rely on their knowledge of these norms and role requirements in guiding their behavior by staying within the bounds of the role. They can also be relatively certain that others will behave according to convention and thus can easily anticipate their behavior.

In less structured or less routine settings, however, there is greater variability in the way different people behave. It is only as the relationship between two people progresses, and their familiarity with each other increases, that stable and predictable patterns of interaction develop. The patterns of behavior that do develop will tend to be more personalized and less widely accepted than the cultural norms governing behavior in more structured or routine settings, and these stable patterns of behavior will only emerge as there is mutual accommodation of each person's behavior to that of his or her partner (Levinger & Snoek, 1972; Thibaut & Kelley, 1959). What eventually results is a set of shared contractual norms between the interactants that is relatively unique to their relationship.

These considerations suggest that uncertainty should be most prevalent when clear normative prescriptions governing behavior are absent and when in the earlier phases of an emerging or changing relationship. In these situations people are uncertain about the potential outcomes available from a relationship and how to behave in order to insure satisfactory outcomes. They will be less able to anticipate the partner's behavior and less certain how their own behavior will be interpreted and responded to by the partner than in more familiar settings. Thus, people are uncertain because they are forced to deal with a novel situation but, with time they will acquire information that will enable them to forecast future outcomes and guide their behavior.

Another way of conceptualizing this process is in terms of schemata. That is, rather than viewing relationships as progressing due to the adoption of shared contractual norms, we could choose to view this process as one of constructing new schemata for controlling one's own behavior in the relationship and comprehending that of one's partner. Similarly, rather than viewing different settings in terms of whether or not there are clear norms and roles, we could differentiate settings in terms of whether or not one possesses schemata for these settings that will help to structure one's perceptions and guide one's behavior. Langer (1978) calls these cognitive structures or schemata *scripts*. She presents research findings suggesting that social interaction may, in some cases, proceed in a relatively automatic fashion, without much conscious thought or attention on the part of the interactants and argues that this is because the interactants' behavior is under the control of well-rehearsed scripts.

According to Langer (1978), "when encountering a novel situation, for which, by definition, they have no script," or "when experiencing a negative or positive consequence that is sufficiently discrepant with the consequences of prior enactments of the same behavior [p. 56]," people will come to engage in conscious thought and deliberation. However, when behavior comes to be regulated in a more conscious manner, the interaction is expected to lose its spontaneous quality and become unpleasant for the individuals involved. The absence of well-rehearsed scripts and the necessity of engaging in conscious thought increases the demands placed on their cognitive facilities, makes interaction more difficult and effortful and, consequently, less pleasant as well. In other words, the interactants must exert more effort to comprehend each other's behavior and must consciously think through their actions and coordinate them with their partner's.

These considerations suggest that interactions occurring within novel settings or during the earlier phases of a relationship might be uncomfortable for the interactants and highly constrained because of the presence of added uncertainty and conscious thought. Thibaut and Kelley (1959) propose that the uncertainty and constraint characterizing such encounters will be all the more prevalent when the members of a dyad belong to different racial or ethnic groups. Due to segregation the members of different groups are unlikely to have had much experience interacting with each other, except within very specific contexts, and thus intergroup contact is likely to be an especially novel experience for many people. Clearly, though, intergroup interactions will differ from intragroup interactions only if the other's group membership is a salient attribute for the actor; otherwise the actor would be no more uncertain of how to behave, and no less spontaneous in behavior, than he or she would with a stranger belonging to his or her own social group.

At least in interracial settings, however, it is not unreasonable to expect that the interactants will be extremely aware of their different group membership, inasmuch as there are highly distinctive physical differences serving to differentiate the members. The other's physical characteristics would tend to stand out and attract the individual's attention (Langer, Taylor, Fiske, & Chanowitz, 1976) and this would make it likely that he or she would categorize the partner in terms of racial background. Yet the question remains as to why differences in physical features, or other distinctive aspects such as language or dress, should heighten uncertainty, conscious deliberation, and behavioral constraint. One explanation is that differences in physical appearance, or expected differences in beliefs (Rokeach et al., 1960) or personality characteristics inferred on the basis of these physical differences, could enhance uncertainty by suggesting to the interactants that their past experiences are not applicable in the contact setting.

This doubt could then lead each individual to adopt a strategy of exercising caution and thinking through his or her actions before their execution. The person also might wish to wait until a relatively larger amount of information about the partner has become available before initiating a response. This strategy could be disruptive, however, because it would have the effect of restricting the flow of information between the interactants and heightening perceptions of shared rejection. Both of these outcomes would serve to inhibit the relationship's development.

One could also view this process in terms of the application of scripts or schemata. Thus, even in novel settings interaction could still proceed with little conscious thought and uncertainty if a well-rehearsed schema can be substituted in the absence of one specifically designed for the current setting or particular relationship at hand. In other words, one way to deal with a novel situation or new relationship is to treat it as though it is a familiar one. This process may be more difficult to implement, however, in interracial settings. The adoption of a conservative decision rule for releasing behavioral control to an established schema would force the individual to think through his or her behavior consciously. And the presence of highly distinctive cues (i.e. the other's physical attributes) would serve to distract the individual's attention away from those cues capable of engaging these existing schemata.

This discussion suggests that the novelty of interracial encounters might underlie their apparent constraint. Being uncertain and opting for a more thoughtful consideration of what his or her partner's motives are in the setting and how one should behave, the individual's behavior may become inhibited and less spontaneous. This inhibition of behavior may then prevent the development of the relationship by restricting communication and mutual self-disclosures between the interactants (Chaikin et al., 1973). The interaction also would tend to be unpleasant for the interactants due to the uncertainty and conscious deliberation responsible for their inhibited behavior. Moreover, in perceiving the other's hesitancy and constraint in the setting, the individual receives ambiguous information that may be construed as signs of rejection and possibly serve as confirmation of negative social stereotypes. People will not necessarily avoid relationships with others simply because they appear to be different (Byrne, 1969), but this avoidance may arise unless they are assured that others will like them despite these dissimilarities (Walster & Walster, 1963). This assurance is unlikely to be forthcoming given the scenario presented here.

The novelty of interracial encounters also might be an important factor in the arousal of objective self-awareness. One who has had little experience in interracial settings not only would be uncertain as to what a partner's attitudes are and what type of behavior can be expected from him or her; one probably would be uncertain as to one's own attitudes as well. Even though a person may view oneself as a fair-minded egalitarian, tolerant of other social groups, this self-image, and other attitudes that one holds relevant to intergroup contact, need not rest upon a firm foundation; and when the person has had little chance to interact with the members of different racial and ethnic groups, it is unlikely that they do. For example, rather than possessing a well-elaborated set of schemata that have grown out of extensive interracial experiences, the average white American is more likely to adopt relevant beliefs and attitudes as a result of secondhand information and, in constructing a self-schema relevant to this domain, may simply assume that he or she has those attributes that are socially desirable.

However, because of the lack of firsthand knowledge of other groups and himself vis-à-vis these groups, the person may be especially susceptible to the state of objective self-awareness. Vallacher (1978) found that subjects less certain of their self-image in a particular domain were more affected by a manipulation of objective self-awareness, suggesting that the unexperienced person might be especially likely to become self-conscious in intergroup settings. Moreover, once the person becomes self-focused, discomfort would be more likely given this lack of experience because one would be more likely to behave in ways inconsistent with one's attitudes (Regan & Fazio, 1977). Thus, the novelty of interracial contact might lead to both conflictual, inconsistent behavior and a heightened self-awareness of these inconsistencies by the interactants.

SUMMARY AND RECOMMENDATIONS

The research in this chapter seems to sound a pessimistic note over the voices of researchers who have espoused the virtues of intergroup contact. The research in the earlier part of this chapter suggests that the interactants' stereotypic beliefs and expectancies may bias the way in which the information available in the contact setting is processed, such that, even when there is little objective evidence for these stereotypes, the persons may come to feel that they have received confirmation. Biases in the way information is sampled, encoded, stored, and retrieved all tend to bolster one's existing beliefs. It is therefore essential to consider the beliefs of the interactants prior to their meeting if one is to predict the quality of interaction that will emerge and what the subsequent attitudes of the interactants will be. If they each hold unfavorable views of the other, interaction is likely to be unpleasant and their subsequent attitudes even more unfavorable than before.

However, certainly under some circumstances people's attitudes will change in response to new information despite these biases. Future research should be directed toward finding those conditions that facilitate these changes and minimize the biases discussed in this chapter. Little is known about how stereotypes and other types of knowledge structures change over time. Some ideas have appeared recently that attempt to deal with this issue (see Rumelhart & Norman, 1978; also see the chapter by Taylor in this volume), but our knowledge of learning processes—as opposed to processes of comprehension and memory—is lacking.

Amir's (1969) review of the contact literature suggests that pleasant, equal status and intimate contact tends to promote favorable intergroup relations, and in the latter part of this chapter it was argued that erroneous stereotypes would be expected to show the greatest revision when intimate, as opposed to more superficial, relationships come to be formed between the members of different social groups. However, the available research on interraical behavior suggests that interracial settings are more likely to be unpleasant than pleasant and that the interaction characterizing such settings is more likely to discourage than foster the formation of intimate relationships. The exact reason for this is yet to be determined, and it is still unclear whether the different findings reviewed here are all the outcome of the same process or the product of different processes. However, a number of different explanations for these findings were offered in order to show how existing theoretical perspectives in psychology could be applied to the study of intergroup contact.

One factor that appears to be important regardless of the theoretical perspective adopted is the salience of group categories. Before one can obtain differential patterns of behavior between intergroup and intragroup interactions, the individuals involved must come to categorize each other in terms of their group membership. All the findings discussed in this chapter seem to occur because categories of racial or ethnic group membership are highly salient for subjects. People will continue to categorize others regardless of what we do, but if different categories or schemata can be elicited, different biases in the processing of information and different patterns of interaction can be promoted. Research is needed that will help us understand how different schemata gain precedence over others. This should help us to specify how we can get people to categorize others in terms of attributes besides their racial or ethnic origin and perhaps how to treat each other as unique human beings rather than the members of a particular social group. Wilder (in this volume) discusses this issue in greater detail.

Another factor that appears to underlie many of the findings reviewed in this chapter is the novelty of intergroup contact. The arousal of objective self-awareness, the inconsistency of white subjects' behavior toward blacks, and the discomfort accompanying interracial encounters may all be interpreted as being the outcome of uncertainty, arising from a lack of experience in interracial settings and a lack of familiarity with the members of different racial groups. However, if the novelty of such encounters does indeed underlie these findings, then one way to minimize these problems and make interracial interaction more rewarding for the interactants, would be to introduce a greater amount of structure into such settings. Perhaps it is best to limit initial encounters to settings where there are clearer norms and roles, or well-rehearsed schemata for guiding one's behavior. This would reduce uncertainty and the cognitive demands placed on the interactants.

If problems arise in intergroup settings partly because of their novelty then it is possible that, with time, these problems could be overcome as intergroup encounters become less avoidable and more frequent. As the novelty of contact diminishes, people might learn to interact more spontaneously and effectively in intergroup settings and be better able to achieve favorable outcomes from relationships that extend beyond racial or ethnic boundaries. Moreover, as interaction becomes less constrained, it might persist long enough so that the interactants could acquire the information about each other that is necessary before the abandonement of stereotypic beliefs can occur. A recent study of Locksley, Borgida, Brekke, and Hepburn (1980) suggests that very little information actually may be required about a person before one will cease stereotyping and respond to him or her not as a member of a category but as a unique individual.

It should be kept in mind that the research findings discussed in this chapterr often have been limited to conditions of minimal information and where no prior interactions have taken place between the members of different groups. The body of research on intergroup behavior and intergroup interactions has focused largely on first encounters and relied on single-session laboratory experiments. More of this type of research is necessary if we are to understand dyadic processes in detail. However, future research also needs to focus on the way in which information about a person is acquired across multiple sessions and the way in which patterns of interaction and relationships change over time (Levinger & Snoek, 1972). Longitudinal studies of intergroup encounters are clearly called for if we are to shed light on the magnitude of the problems discussed in this chapter.

Past research on intergroup contact has often been guided by a concern with the effectiveness of social programs designed to reduce prejudice and promote favorable intergroup relations. Those programs that are implemented should indeed be evaluated and further efforts toward social reform encouraged. Furthermore, in the process of evaluating current social programs, it often may be the case that a valuable data base is generated that could be used to assess the generalizability of laboratory findings. However, past research generally has not been guided by theoretical models of intergroup interaction. The present chapter has attempted to show how intergroup contact may be studied in terms of the psychological, mainly cognitive, processes that operate within the individual. It is hoped that this perspective toward the study of intergroup contact will help the discipline progress and become more integrated with other areas of inquiry in psychology.

ACKNOWLEDGMENTS

Preparation of this chapter was supported in part by NIMH Grant 29418 (David L. Hamilton, principal investigator). I would like to thank David Hamilton for his helpful comments on earlier drafts of this chapter.

REFERENCES

Allport, G. W. *The Nature of Prejudice*. Reading, Mass.: Addison-Wesley, 1954.

Allport, G. W., & Postman, L. J. The basic psychology of rumor. *Transactions of the New York Academy of Sciences*, 1945, Series II, VIII, 61–81.

Amir, Y. Contact hypothesis in ethnic relations. *Psychological Bulletin*, 1969, *71*, 319–342.

Amir, Y. The role of intergroup contact in change of prejudice and ethnic relations. In P. A. Katz (Ed.), *Towards the Elimination of Racism*. New York: Pergamon Press, 1976.

Anderson, R. C., & Pichert, J. W. Recall of previously unrecallable information following a shift in perspective. *Journal of Verbal Learning and Verbal Behavior*, 1978, *17*, 1–12.

Armor, D. J. The evidence on busing. *The Public Interest*, 1972, *28*, 90–126.

Ashmore, R. D. Solving the problem of prejudice. In B. E. Collins, *Social Psychology*. Reading, Mass.: Addison-Wesley, 1970.

Bartlett, F. C. *Remembering: A study in Experimental and Social Psychology*. London: Cambridge University Press, 1932.

Bem, D. J. Self-perception theory. In L. Berkowitz (Ed.), *Advances in Experimental Social Psychology*, (Vol. 6). New York: Academic Press, 1972.

Bobrow, D. G., & Norman, D. A. Some principles of memory schemata. In D. G. Bobrow & A. Collins (Eds.), *Representation and Understanding: Studies in Cognitive Sciecne*. New York: Academic Press, 1975.

Bower, G. *Injecting life into deadly prose*. Paper presented at the annual meeting of the Western Psychological Association, Seattle, 1977.

Bradburn, N. M., Sudman, S., Gockel, G. L., & Noel, J. R. *Side by Side*. Chicago: Quadrangle books, 1971.

Bransford, J. D., Barclay, J. R., & Franks, J. J. Sentence memory: A constructive versus interpretive approach. *Cognitive Psychology*, 1972, *3*, 193–209.

Bransford, J. D., & Franks, J. J. The abstraction of linguistic ideas. *Cognitive Psychology*, 1971, *2*, 331–350.

Bransford, J. D., & Johnson, M. K. Contextual prerequisites for understanding: Some investigations of comprehension and recall. *Journal of Verbal Learning and Verbal Behavior*, 1972, *11*, 717–726.

Brewer, M. B. Ingroup bias in the minimal intergroup situation: A cognitive–motivational analysis. *Psychological Bulletin*, 1979, *86*, 307–324.

Brigham, J. C. Ethnic stereotypes. *Psychological Bulletin*, 1971, *76*, 15–38.

Broudy, H. S. Types of knowledge and purposes of education. In R. C. Anderson, R. J. Spiro, & W. E. Montague (Eds.), *Schooling and the Acquistion of Knowledge*. Hillsdale, N.J.: Lawrence Erlbaum Associates, 1977.

Byrne, D. Attitudes and attraction. In L. Berkowitz (Ed.), *Advances in Experimental Social Psychology* (Vol. 4). New York: Academic Press, 1969.

Cagle, L. T. Interracial housing: A reassessment of the equal-status contact hypothesis. *Sociology and Social Research*, 1973, *57*, 342–355.

Carithers, M. W. School desegregation and racial cleavage, 1954–1970: A review of the literature. *Journal of Social Issues,* 1970, *26,* 25–47.

Chaikin, A. L., & Derlega, V. J. Liking for the norm breaker in self-disclosure. *Journal of Personality,* 1974, *42,* 117–129.

Chaikin, A. L., & Derlega, V. J. Self-disclosure. In J. W. Thibaut, J. T. Spence, & R. C. Carson (Eds.), *Contemporary Topics in Social Psychology.* Morristown, N.J.: General Learning Press, 1976.

Chaikin, A. L., Derlega, V. J., Harris, M. S., Gregorio, D., & Boone, P. *Self-disclosure in biracial dyads.* Unpublished manuscript, Old Dominion University, 1973.

Chapman, L. J. Illusory correlation in observational report. *Journal of Verbal Learning and Verbal Behavior,* 1967, *6,* 151–155.

Chapman, L. J., & Chapman, J. P. Genesis of popular but erroneous psychodiagnostic observations. *Journal of Abnormal Psychology,* 1967, *72,* 193–204.

Chapman, L. J., & Chapman, J. P. Illusory correlation as an obstacle to the use of valid psychodiagnostic signs. *Journal of Abnormal Psychology,* 1969, *74,* 271–280.

Cohen, E. Interracial interaction disability. *Human Relations,* 1972, *25,* 9–24.

Cohen, E. G., Lockheed, M. E., & Lohman, M. R. The center for interracial cooperation: A field experiment. *Sociology of Education,* 1976, *49,* 47–58.

Cook, S. W. The systematic analysis of socially significant events: A strategy for social research. *Journal of Social Issues,* 1962, *18,* 66–84.

Cook, S. W. Motives in a conceptual analysis of attitude-related behavior. In W. J. Arnold & D. Levine (Eds.), *Nebraska Symposium on Motivation.* Lincoln, Neb.: University of Nebraska Press, 1969.

Derlega, V. J., Harris, M. S., & Chaikin, A. L. Self-disclosure reciprocity, liking, and the deviant. *Journal of Experimental Social Psychology,* 1973, *9,* 277–284.

Deutsch, M., & Collins, M. E. *Interracial Housing: A Psychological Evaluation of a Social Experiment.* Minneapolis, Minn.: University of Minnesota Press, 1951.

Dienstbier, R. A. A modified belief theory of prejudice emphasizing the mutual causality of racial prejudice and anticipated belief differences. *Psychological Review,* 1972, *79,* 146–160.

Dion, K. K. Physical attractiveness and evaluations of children's transgressions. *Journal of Personality and Social Psychology,* 1972, *24,* 207–213.

Donnerstein, E., & Donnerstein, M. White rewarding behavior as a function of the potential for black retaliation. *Journal of Personality and Social Psychology,* 1972, *24,* 327–334.

Donnerstein, E., Donnerstein, M., Simon, S., & Ditrichs, R. Variables in interracial aggression: Anonymity, expected retaliation, and a riot. *Journal of Personality and Social Psychology,* 1972, *22,* 236–245.

Dooling, D. J., & Mullet, R. L. Locus of thematic effects in retention of prose. *Journal of Experimental Psychology,* 1973, *97,* 404–406.

Duncan, B. L. Differential social perception and the attribution of intergroup violence: Testing the lower limits of stereotyping of blacks. *Journal of Personality and Social Psychology,* 1976, *34,* 590–598.

Dutton, D. G. Tokenism, reverse discrimination, and egalitarianism in interracial behavior. *Journal of Social Issues,* 1976, *32,* 93–107.

Dutton, D. G., & Lake, R. A. Threat of own prejudice and reverse discrimination in interracial situations. *Journal of Personality and Social Psychology,* 1973, *28,* 94–100.

Dutton, D. G., & Lennox, V. L. Effect of prior "token" compliance on subsequent interracial behavior. *Journal of Personality and Social Psychology,* 1974, *29,* 65–71.

Dutton, D. G., & Yee, P. The effect of subject liberalism, anonymity, and race of experimenter on subject's rating of oriental and white photos. *Canadian Journal of Behavioral Science,* 1974, *6,* 332–341.

Duval, S., & Wicklund, R. A. *A Theory of Objective Self-Awareness.* New York: Academic Press, 1972.

Gould, R., & Sigall, H. The effects of empathy and outcome on attribution: An examination of the divergent-perspectives hypothesis. *Journal of Experimental Social Psychology,* 1977, *13,* 480–491.

Gurwitz, S. B., & Dodge, K. A. Effects of confirmations and disconfirmations on stereotype-based attributions. *Journal of Personality and Social Psychology,* 1977, *35,* 495–500.

Guttman, L., & Foa, U. G. Social contact and intergroup attitude. *Public Opinion Quarterly,* 1951, *15,* 43–53.

Hamilton, D. L. A cognitive–attributional analysis of stereotyping. In L. Berkowitz (Ed.), *Advances in Experimental Social Psychology* (Vol. 12). New York: Academic Press, 1979.

Hamilton, D. L., & Bishop, G. D. Attitudinal and behavioral effects of initial integration of white suburban neighborhoods. *Journal of Social Issues,* 1976, *32,* 47–67.

Hamilton, D. L., Katz, L. B., & Leirer, V. O. Organizational processes in impression formation. In R. Hastie, T. Ostrom, E. Ebbesen, R. Wyer, D. Hamilton, & D. Carlston (Eds.), *Person Memory.* Hillsdale, N.J.: Lawrence Erlbaum Associates, 1980.

Hamilton, D. L., & Rose, T. L. Illusory correlation and the maintenance of stereotypic beliefs. *Journal of Personality and Social Psychology,* 1980, *39,* 832–345.

Harding, J., Proshansky, H., Kutner, B., & Chein, J. Prejudice and ethnic relations. In G. Lindzey & E. Aronson (Eds.), Handbook of Social Psychology (Vol. 5). Reading, Mass.: Addison-Wesley, 1969.

Heider, F. *The Psychology of Interpersonal Relations.* New York: Wiley & Sons, 1958.

Higgins, E. T., Rholes, W. S., & Jones, C. R. Category accessibility and impression formation. *Journal of Experimental Social Psychology,* 1977, *13,* 141–154.

Ickes, W. J., & Kidd, R. F. An attributional analysis of helping behavior. In J. H. Harvey, W. J. Ickes, & R. F. Kidd (Eds.), *New Directions in Attribution Research* (Vol. 1). Hillsdale, N.J.: Lawrence Erlbaum Associates, 1976.

Jenkins, H. M., & Ward, W. C. Judgment of contingency between responses and outcomes. *Psychological Monographs,* 1965, *79* (1, Whole No. 594).

Jones, E. E., & Davis, K. E. From acts to dispositions: The attribution process in person perception. In L. Berkowitz (Ed.), *Advances in Experimental Social Psychology* (Vol. 2). New York: Academic Press, 1965.

Jones, E. E., Davis, K. E., & Gergen, K. J. Role playing variations and their informational value for person perception. *Journal of Abnormal and Social Psychology,* 1961, *63,* 307–310.

Jones, E. E., & Harris, V. A. The attribution of attitudes. *Journal of Experimental Social Psychology,* 1967, *3,* 1–24.

Jones, R. A. *Self-Fulfilling Prophecies.* Hillsdale, N.J.: Lawrence Erlbaum Associates, 1977.

Katz, I. Review of evidence relating to effects of desegregation on the intellectual performance of Negroes. *American Psychologist,* 1964, *19,* 381–399.

Katz, I. Experimental studies of Negro–white relationships. In L. Berkowitz (Ed.), *Advances in Experimental Social Psychology* (Vol. 5). New York: Academic Press, 1970.

Katz, I., & Benjamin, L. Effects of white authoritarianism in biracial work groups. *Journal of Abnormal and Social Psychology,* 1960, *61,* 448–456.

Katz, I., Goldston, J., & Benjamin, L. Behavior and productivity in biracial work groups. *Human Relations,* 1958, *11,* 123–141.

Kelley, H. H. The warm–cold variable in first impression of personality. *Journal of Personality,* 1950, *18,* 431–439.

Kintsch, W. Memory for prose. In C. N. Cofer (Ed.), *The Structure of Human Memory.* San Francisco: W. H. Freeman, 1976.

Langer, E. J. Rethinking the role of thought in social interaction. In J. H. Harvey, W. J. Ickes, & R. F. Kidd (Eds.), *New Directions in Attribution Research* (Vol. 2). Hillsdale, N.J.: Lawrence Erlbaum Associates, 1978.

Langer, E. J., Taylor, S. E., Fiske, S., & Chanowitz, B. Stigma, staring and discomfort: A novel-stimulus hypothesis. *Journal of Experimental Social Psychology*, 1976, *12*, 451–463.

Levinger, G., & Snoek, J. D. *Attraction in Relationship: A New Look at Interpersonal Attraction*. Morristown, N.J.: General Learning Press, 1972.

Lingle, J. H., Geva, N., Ostrom, T. M., Leippe, M. R., & Baumgardner, M. H. Thematic effects of person judgments on impression organization. *Journal of Personality and Social Psychology*, 1979, *37*, 674–687.

Locksley, A., Borgida, E., Brekke, N., & Hepburn, C. Sex stereotypes and social judgment. *Journal of Personality and Social Psychology*, 1980, *39*, 821–831.

Markus, H. Self-schemata and processing information about the self. *Journal of Personality and Social Psychology*, 1977, *35*, 63–78.

Mehrabian, A. Some referents and measures of nonverbal behavior. *Behavior Research Methods and Instrumentation*, 1969, *1*, 203–207.

Merton, R. K. The self-fulfilling prophecy. *Antioch Review*, 1948, *8*, 193–210.

Morris, C. D., Bransford, J. D., & Franks, J. J. Levels of processing versus transfer appropriate processing. *Journal of Verbal Learning and Verbal Behavior*, 1977, *16*, 519–533.

Mussen, P. H. Some personality and social factors related to changes in children's attitudes toward Negroes. *Journal of Abnormal and Social Psychology*, 1950, *45*, 423–441.

Pichert, J. W., & Anderson, R. C. Taking different perspectives on a story. *Journal of Educational Psychology*, 1977, *69*, 309–315.

Platt, J. R. Strong inference. *Science*, 1964, *146*, 347–353.

Poskocil, A. *White racial attitudes in a liberal milieu as a function of group racial composition*. Paper presented at the annual meeting of the American Psychological Association, Chicago, 1975.

Poskocil, A. Encounters between black and white liberals: The collision of stereotypes. *Social Forces*, 1977, *55*, 715–727.

Regan, D. T., & Fazio, R. On the consistency between attitudes and behavior: Look to the method of attitude formation. *Journal of Experimental Social Psychology*, 1977, *13*, 28–45.

Regan, D. T., Straus, E., & Fazio, R. Liking and the attribution process. *Journal of Experimental Social Psychology*, 1974, *10*, 385–398.

Regan, D. T., & Totten, J. Empathy and attribution: Turning observers into actors. *Journal of Personality and Social Psychology*, 1975, *32*, 850–856.

Rokeach, M., Smith, P. W., & Evans, R. I. Two kinds of prejudice or one? In M. Rokeach, *The Open and Closed Mind*. New York: Basic Books, 1960.

Ross, L. The intuitive psychologist and his shortcomings: Distortions in the attribution process. In L. Berkowitz (Ed.), *Advances in Experimental Social Psychology*. New York: Academic Press, 1977.

Rothbart, M., Evans, M., & Fulero, S. Recall for confirming events: Memory processes and the maintenance of social stereotypes. *Journal of Experimental Social Psychology*, 1979, *15*, 343–355.

Rubovits, P. C., & Maehr, M. L. Pygmalion black and white. *Journal of Personality and Social Psychology*, 1973, *25*, 210–218.

Rumelhart, D. E., & Norman, D. A. Accretion, tuning and restructuring: Three modes of learning. In J. W. Cotton & R. L. Klatzky (Eds.), *Semantic Factors in Cognition*. Hillsdale, N.J.: Lawrence Erlbaum Associates, 1978.

Rumelhart, D. E., & Ortony, A. The representation of knowledge in memory. In R. C. Anderson, R. J. Spiro, & W. E. Montague (Eds.), *Schooling and the Acquisition of Knowledge*. Hillsdale, N.J.: Lawrence Erlbaum Associates, 1977.

Sachs, J. D. S. Recognition memory for syntactic and semantic aspects of connected discourse. *Perception and Psychophysics*, 1967, *2*, 437–442.

Schneider, D. J. Implicit personality theory: A review. *Psychological Bulletin*, 1973, *79*, 294–309.

Sherif, M., Harvey, O. J., White, B. J., Hood, W. R., & Sherif, C. W. *Intergroup Conflict and Cooperation: The Robbers Cave Experiment.* Norman, Okla.: University Book Exchange, 1961.

Sigall, H., & Page, R. Current stereotypes: A little fading, a little faking. *Journal of Personality and Social Psychology,* 1971, *18,* 247–255.

Snyder, M., & Swann, W. B. Hypothesis-testing processes in social interaction. *Journal of Personality and Social Psychology,* 1978, *36,* 1202–1212.

Snyder, M., & Uranowitz, S. Reconstructing the past: Some cognitive consequences of person perception. *Journal of Personality and Social Psychology,* 1978, *36,* 941–950.

Snyder, M. L., & Frankel, A. Observer bias: A stringent test of behavior engulfing the field. *Journal of Personality and Social Psychology,* 1976, *34,* 857–864.

Suls, J. M., & Miller, R. L. (Eds.). *Social Comparison Processes.* Washington, D.C.: Hemisphere, 1977.

Taylor, D. M., & Jaggi, V. Ethnocentrism and causal attribution in a South Indian context. *Journal of Cross-Cultural Psychology,* 1974, *5,* 162–171.

Taylor, S. E. Developing a cognitive social psychology. In J. S. Carroll & J. W. Payne (Eds.), *Cognition and Social Behavior.* Hillsdale, N.J.: Lawrence Erlbaum Associates, 1976.

Taylor, S. E., Fiske, S. T., Etcoff, N. C., & Ruderman, A. J. Categorical and contextual bases of person memory and stereotyping. *Journal of Personality and Social Psychology,* 1978, *36,* 778–793.

Thibaut, J. W., & Kelley, H. H. *The Social Psychology of Groups.* New York: Wiley, 1959.

Tversky, A., & Kahneman, D. Availability: A heuristic for judging frequency and probability. *Cognitive Psychology,* 1973, *5,* 207–232.

Vallacher, R. R. Objective self-awareness and the perception of others. *Personality and Social Psychology Bulletin,* 1978, *4,* 63–67.

Walster, E., & Walster, G. W. Effect of expectancy to be liked on choice of associates. *Journal of Abnormal and Social Psychology,* 1963, *67,* 402–404.

Weitz, S. Attitude, voice and behavior: A repressed affect model of interracial interaction. *Journal of Personality and Social Psychology,* 1972, *24,* 14–21.

Wicklund, R. A. Objective self-awareness. In L. Berkowitz (Ed.), *Advances in Experimental Social Psychology* (Vol. 8). New York: Academic Press, 1975.

Wilder, D. A., & Allen, V. L. Group membership and preference for information about others. *Personality and Social Psychology Bulletin,* 1978, *4,* 106–110.

Wilner, D. M., Walkley, R. P., & Cook, S. W. Residential proximity and intergroup relations in public housing projects. *Journal of Social Issues,* 1952, *8,* 45–69.

Word, C. O., Zanna, M. P., & Cooper, J. The nonverbal mediation of self-fulfilling prophecies in interracial interaction. *Journal of Experimental Social Psychology,* 1974, *10,* 109–120.

Zadny, J., & Gerard, H. B. Attributional intentions and informational selectivity. *Journal of Experimental Social Psychology,* 1974, *10,* 34–52.

Zanna, M. P., & Pack, S. J. On the self-fulfilling nature of apparent sex differences in behavior. *Journal of Experimental Social Psychology,* 1975, *11,* 583–591.

9 Extending the Stereotype Concept

Thomas F. Pettigrew
University of California, Santa Cruz

INTRODUCTION

Cognitive social psychology has become one of the most exciting subfields of the discipline in recent years. Led by the writers of the other chapters of this volume, this challenging perspective not only contributes to social psychological theory but is of direct importance to the many practical applications of the discipline.

The excitement generated by these advances in both theory and practice is annually demonstrated at the meetings of the American Psychological Association. Of late, the sessions where Ashmore, Hamilton, Rothbart, Snyder, Taylor, Wilder, and their colleagues are delivering papers have been characterized by standing-room-only crowds. Admittedly, social psychology has been marked throughout its short history with sweeping fads, some of which left little permanent trace. But I believe that the view advanced persuasively in these pages has a lasting significance for the discipline's thinking and future directions. And this chapter presents the reasons for this belief by placing the central thrust of this volume in a larger context.

Cognitive social psychology draws its inspiration from several sources. Most immediately, the significant and impressive progress made in recent years in cognitive psychology has had a lasting effect on the thinking of this new cohort of social psychologists.[1] Not only many of their ideas, but some of their experi-

---

[1]As we note later in Table 9.1, this influence is indicated by the fact that 9% of all the published references cited in the previous chapters of this volume are from cognitive psychology sources—far more than from any other subfield outside of social psychology.

mental designs have been shaped by the exemplars furnished by cognitive psychologists. In turn, cognitive social psychologists provide direct tests in the social world for the often highly abstract, noninteractive phenomena of cognitive psychology.

But this is only part of the "sociology-of-knowledge" context within which this new school of thought should be interpreted. For the question remains as to why the work of cognitive psychologists should find such fertile soil so quickly for application in social psychology. The narrow answers to this question are obvious. All the authors in this book are located in psychology departments where they have daily contact with those engaged in the cognitive psychology enterprise. More importantly, there is a long and important cognitive tradition within experimental social psychology. It is basically a Gestaltist tradition that stems from Lewin, Heider, and Asch through "the new look in perception" of Bruner and others to the modern work of Kelley, Jones, Tajfel, and others. And as experimental social psychologists, the writers of this volume are very much part of this tradition.

But the broader answer to this question is the one on which this chapter focuses. The advances of cognitive psychology have been seized upon with such vigor in large part because they provide an important means by which to attack the core issues of social psychology. And these core issues are shared by the diverse wings of the discipline. Consequently, the work reported in this book unites—often unwittingly, perhaps—the discipline's far-flung branches. This chapter discusses these various branches—experimental social psychology, symbolic interactionism, and contextual social psychology; and it maintains that, in spite of basic epistemological differences between them, the research findings and basic theory evolving in the three wings are converging. Central to this convergence is the work of cognitive social psychologists as reported in these pages.

A fundamental insight of social psychology shared by all three branches is that whatever human beings perceive as "real" is in fact real in its social consequences. Thus, the stuff of social cognition, from stereotypes to misattributions, is not just of psychological interest at the microbehavioral level; it also constitutes a critical (perhaps the most critical) mediation between the microindividual and the macrosocial levels of analyses. And if one grants that the specification of such mediators is the unique task of social psychology, then it is hardly surprising that the work described in this book helps to unite the varied perspectives within the discipline.

This chapter, then, reviews the preceding papers in this broader perspective. And it takes the view that the concept of stereotype, which is provided with new breadth and potency by this book, has been fashioned into a significant explanatory mediator between individual and social phenomena.

THE THREE WINGS OF SOCIAL PSYCHOLOGY

Social psychology is an interstitial field.[2] Like physical chemistry and biochemistry, it has emerged from its two parent disciplines with a distinctive focus. Textbooks provide a vast array of definitions. Yet virtually all interpretations broadly regard social psychology as the study of the mediational processes between the individual and social systems, between the psychological and the sociological levels of analyses. That the field is still evolving out of its two root disciplines is made clear by the awkwardness of its present-day structure in higher education. Social psychologists are found in both psychology and sociological departments, often with little or no communication between them. In addition, the discipline is rent by three quite diverse subgroups, which have limited cross-communication.[3] All three of these major wings focus on specifying mediational processes, but in sharply different ways. Indeed, the many contrasts between the field's wings make any convergence among them all the more interesting.

Experimental Social Psychology

The most mobilized and, perhaps, the most prestigious of the three clusters is experimental social psychology. It is the dominant influence behind this volume. Based almost entirely within psychology departments, this wing stresses controlled laboratory experimentation on individual psychological processes as the mediators of social and situational effects. Like its parent discipline, experimental social psychology relies heavily on internal states as explanations (e.g., attitudes, attributions, dissonance, expectations, and, of course, stereotypes) and typically reduces the social world to the level of the individual. Increasingly over recent decades, this wing has stressed situational factors at the expense of personality factors—a move that aligns its interests closer to those of symbolic interactionists. And increasingly over these same years, experimental social psychologists have favored cognitive over motivational and learning considerations—a move that aligns its interests closer to those of both of the other wings.

The mobilization of experimental social psychology derives from its organization within the American Psychological Association and its concentration in a few journals—*The Journal of Personality and Social Psychology, The European*

---

[2]Parts of this section have appeared previously in Pettigrew (1980a).

[3]For example, as we note in Table 9.1, only 2% of the citations in this volume are drawn from symbolic interactionist sources. And this is true in spite of the fact that the present authors are unusually sophisticated about the other wings of the discipline and that most of the volume's content treats major concerns of the symbolic interactionist wing.

Journal of Social Psychology, and *The Journal of Experimental Social Psychology* (and to a lesser extent, *The Journal of Personality* and *The Journal of Applied Social Psychology*). Indeed, roughly half of the articles cited in the previous chapters appeared in one of these five journals (Table 9.1). Inspection of these journals reveals the trade-offs that typify research in this area. Not only is it overwhelmingly characterized by laboratory experimentation, but college students predominate as subjects (Helmreich, 1975). Sampling procedures for subject selection are rarely employed. And, surprisingly, individual differences are generally ignored and considered simply "error." (Taylor and Wilder provide refreshing exceptions to this tendency in their chapters in this volume.) Experiments in this tradition often employ experimental confederates, programmed scripts, and contrived roles and situations. In short, the ability to make tight, causal inferences about a specific situation (internal validity) is maximized at the expense of the ability to generalize the results confidently (external validity).

TABLE 9.1.
Sources of Previous Chapters' Published References[a]

	Journals	Chapters and Books	Total
Social Psychology			
Experimental Social Psychology[b]	50.3% ⎱	⎰	⎰
Contextual Social Psychology[c]	8.3% ⎰	⎱ 57.4%	⎱ 58.2%
Symbolic Interactionism[d]	1.5%	3.2%	2.1%
Additional Areas			
Cognitive psychology[e]	6.8%	12.8%	8.9%
Other psychology[f]	24.3%	12.8%	20.2%
Other sociology[g]	6.2%	6.4%	6.3%
General (anthropology, philosophy, etc.)[h]	2.7%	7.4%	4.4%
Totals	100.1%	*100.0%*	100.1%
(*n*)	(338)	(188)	(526)

[a] Note that this table does not provide a base line of the sizes of the universes of all possible publications available under each of the categories. This is important because experimental social psychology probably publishes more journal articles (though not more books) than the other two wings.

[b] E.g., *Journal of Personality and Social Psychology* and *Journal of Experimental Social Psychology.*

[c] E.g., *Social Psychology Quarterly* and *Journal of Social Issues.*

[d] *Social Problems* and SI papers in other journals.

[e] *Verbal Learning and Verbal Behavior* and *Cognitive Psychology.*

[f] E.g., *Psychological Bulletin* and *Psychology Review.*

[g] E.g., *Social Forces* and *American Sociological Review.*

[h] E.g., *American Anthropologist.*

Kurt Lewin, the brilliant German transplant, is the acknowledged modern father of this branch of social psychology. Recent trends, however, are importantly the work of third-generation Lewinians who are the students of such Lewinians as Leon Festinger. Generally missing, unfortunately, from the original tradition are Lewin's interestes in natural groups, situational measurement, action research, and close coordination between laboratory research and applied field work.

Consequently, this wing of the field has borne the brunt of harsh criticism, not the least of which has emanated from experimental social psychologists themselves. Charges of faddism, triviality, narrowness, and limited generalizability have been hurled repeatedly over the past fifteen years. Tartly commenting on recent theories of this branch, Ivan Steiner (1974), for instance, writes: "On reading these models the . . . man from Mars might conclude that earthlings never accept the prefabricated verdict of social reality [p. 103]."

But the proof, after all, is in the pudding: How well do the principles generated by experimental social psychologists apply in fact to the "real world," to such vital applications as intergroup relations? For the most part, I believe these principles do usefully generalize. Indeed, this book contains an impressive demonstration of how the work of this wing can be forcefully brought to bear on a concept that has long been a proven weapon in the explanatory arsenal of intergroup relations specialists. Moreover, we shall note how many of the contentions advanced in these chapters coincide with the findings and theories of the other wings of social psychology. Put bluntly, the so-called "crisis" in experimental social psychology has been exaggerated; and the social cognition work represented in this volume furnishes further evidence for this conclusion.

Symbolic Interactionism (SI)

Smaller in number but also highly mobilized, symbolic interactionists are concentrated on the West Coast and found almost exclusively in sociology departments. They reject with equal vigor both John Watson's behavioralist reductionism and Emile Durkheim's "sociologism." Instead, they trace their thought back to William James, John Dewey, Charles Cooley, and especially to George Herbert Meade and "the Chicago school" of the 1920s and 1930s. Herbert Blumer (1969), a leader of this wing, and his Berkeley students named and institutionalized the symbolic interaction tradition. As the label implies, this wing emphasizes face-to-face interaction and symbolism; hence, its principal concerns include social communication, roles, the self, identity, collective behavior, and deviance (Lindesmith, Strauss, & Denzin, 1977). It is particularly directed at the study of social problems, as indicated by the fact that its chief publication outlet is *Social Problems*. Unique among the wings, social interactionism considers at length such basic questions as how social problems are socially constructed and recognized by society in the first place (Spector and Kitsuse, 1977).

Symbolic interactionists believe that process is the appropriate focus rather than static relationships between individual or structural variables. Thus, they typically utilize field observation, open-ended interviewing, and unobstrusive methods, and they are suspicious of both experimental and survey methods for doing violence to the subtle, reflexive processes of human interaction. The trade-off for symbolic interactionism, then, is a surrendering of research rigor in order to get close to the action and concerns of the real world; it thereby risks internal validity to achieve external validity.

House (1977) and others criticize symbolic interactionists for throwing out the baby with the bath water. In rejecting the extremes of Watson and Durkheim, this subgroup is accused of having unduly spurned quantitative methods, causal analysis, and macrosociology. Mark Snyder's findings, reported in Chapter 6, support many of the core contentions of symbolic interactionism, even though he used experimental methods in the laboratory that are disparaged by this wing. With greater communication among the three subgroups of social psychology in the future, there is no reason why symbolic interactionist theory (as opposed to methodological dogma) would not become central to a united discipline.

Contextual Social Psychology

This wing of the discipline is the least mobilized and the least recognized, though it may well be the largest in sheer numbers. Yet its consistent attention to individual factors in the context of macrostructural factors clearly distinguishes it from the other two subgroups. Its proponents are found in both sociology and psychology departments as well as in interdisciplinary programs. Hence, they have more communication with the other types of social psychologists. And its chief journal outlets, *Social Psychology Quarterly* (formerly *Sociometry*) and the *Journal of Social Issues,* are among the few publications where articles drawn from all three wings appear. Various labels have been applied to this group over the years: social structure and personality, psychological sociology, etc. But its necessarily interdisciplinary focus makes it difficult to define. The term "contextual" is coined here in order to emphasize this subgroup's most distinctive characteristic—namely, its consistent simultaneous use of individual and social variables in both its theory and research.

More narrowly, many of the social psychologists who share this approach can be traced to having been students, teachers, or both at such interdisciplinary programs as the former interdepartmental social psychology program at the University of Michigan and the former Department of Social Relations at Harvard University. And, like the present author, contextual social psychologists are prone to write chapters that attempt to integrate the various parts of the discipline.[4]

Contextual social psychology shares with the other subgroups the emphasis on cognitive factors at the individual level of analysis that marks this volume. Moreover, it shares with experimental social psychology a concern for quantitative methods and with symbolic interactionism a concern for real-world data and applied problems. But it is more interested in general personality and social structural considerations, and it more explicitly seeks to specify the mediators that operate between these levels. This combination of concerns usually dictates the use of quasi-experimental or nonexperimental methods, especially small group studies and surveys using probability samples. More of a balanced trade-off is struck, then, between maximizing both external and internal validity than in the other wings. Overall, however, contextual social psychology is the wing least characterized by particular empirical methods.

House (1977) points out that this subgroup's focus constitutes major concerns for many leading social theorists of the past: Max Weber's "Protestant ethic," Emile Durkheim's "anomie," and Karl Marx's "alienation"—to mention but a few. Perhaps it is easiest to define the wing by specifying a few of its modern-day adherents. In sociology, contextual social psychologists include Merton, Stouffer, Lazarsfled, Inkeles, Bales, Lenski, Sewell, Gamson, Schuman, Rainwater, Runciman, and James Davis. In psychology, they include Cantril, Sherif, Newcomb, Brewster Smith, Rokeach, Riecken, Kelman, Donald Campbell, Angus Campbell, Back, Kahn, Kenneth B. Clark, Harding, David Sears, and the writer. Note how many of these social psychologists are best known for applications of the field to evaluation research, electoral politics, international relations, and intergroup relations. This fact is not an accident. Contextual social psychology is in large part a product of applied research. In particular, the applications of social science during World War II shaped its character and led directly to the founding of the interdisciplinary programs at Michigan, Harvard, and elsewhere. Intergroup relations, prejudice, and stereotypes, then, have been traditionally studied within social psychology by those in its contextual wing. The focus of this volume, then, is itself a symptom of the convergence of the wings when experimentalists bring their analyses to bear on this venerable topic of contextual social psychology.

---

[4]House (1977), both a product and a teacher of social psychology in sociology at the University of Michigan, affords another example of this phenomenon. And the present writer has engaged in this pastime on previous occasions (Pettigrew, 1967).

THE INTELLECTUAL CONTEXT OF THESE COGNITIVE
ANALYSES

It is instructive to check first on the proximate influences shaping the first eight chapters of this volume. Table 9.1 provides an ordering of the citations. Not surprisingly, experimental social psychological references predominate, followed by other psychological citations. Cognitive psychology references are especially frequent, and sociological references, including symbolic interactionist sources, are relatively rare. Moreover, the few references cited from the other two wings are concentrated in those chapters that directly impinge on them—Snyder for symbolic interactionism and Rose for contextual social psychology.

A more finely grained analysis within the cognitive references reveals more interesting trends. Bartlett is cited only twice, though his ground-breaking *Remembering* (1932) had great influence in early social psychological work on social perception.[5] More remarkable, perhaps, is the almost total absence of reference to the so-called "new look in perception." A movement in the late 1940s and 1950s, this perspective drew from Bartlett, Freud, and the Gestaltists to emphasize the directing role of motivation in shaping and biasing social perception. Its acknowledged leader, Jerome Bruner, receives but one mention.

Admittedly, the writer betrays his age by recalling the now not-so-"new look," for it was in fashion during his undergraduate and graduate days. Part of the failure of this movement to influence the present work could simply reflect the relative youth of the other authors and the strong bias in the discipline for the latest, most contemporary thought and sources. But I believe the reason is deeper. The cognitive analysis advanced in this volume reflects the trends in social psychology of the past generation away from motivational explanations, and these analyses stem from more purely Gestaltist roots than they do from either the Bartlett or Freudian traditions.

These intellectual roots are nowhere clearer than in the handling of motivation. For most of the authors, the only nod to motivational concerns involves a prefatory mention of the need for human beings to possess a stable, meaningful perceptual world. The exceptions to this statement are noteworthy. In describing the three principal orientations to stereotypes, Ashmore and Del Boca include motivational issues under the psychoanalytic approach. And Rothbart reports experimental results that hark back to the "new look in perception" perspective. In supporting the contentions of Kanouse and Hanson (1971) concerning the greater influence of negative information, Rothbart finds that undesirable traits are far more likely to be utilized in group descriptions regardless of the frequency

---

[5]One indication of this early influence of Bartlett was an excerpt drawn from his seminal volume that was reprinted in the field-shaping *Readings in Social Psychology*, edited originally by Newcomb and Hartley (1947).

of the traits in the population.[6] Rothbart sees this finding as clear support for a model that posits greater motivation to avoid negative than to enhance positive consequences. Finally, Ashmore explicitly mentions the need to extend the analysis of motivational influences on cognition beyond that of the perceiver simply seeking ''to make sense out of the social environment.'' But he views this issue as ''a complication,'' and leaves its handling to others.

Put bluntly, without denying the role of motivational factors, present-day cognitive social psychology is primarily interested in seeing how far it can successfully push a purely cognitive analysis. Hamilton (Chapter 4) summarizes this central point: ''explanations of phenomena related to stereotyping need not *necessarily* include reference to the perceiver's prejudicial attitudes or to the motivational functions served by stereotypic beliefs.'' In my opinion, it is this identifying characteristic of cognitive social psychology that is at once its great strength and its great weakness. It is a strength in that cognitive mediators lie at the heart of social psychological analyses of all three wings, and this present movement bids to make a major contribution at this critical point. The many new insights and perspectives brought to the traditional concept of stereotype in this volume constitute a solid demonstration of this contribution. At the same time, this single-minded concentration on one-third of the psychological triumvirate of affect, cognition, and conation leaves many of these fascinating analyses incomplete. One can readily agree that the single-minded strategy makes sense at this early point in the discipline's development, that the ''new look'' strategy of attempting to join affect and cognition was premature. Yet at some point, more rounded analyses will be required. Snyder points the way by showing the intimate connections between cognition and behavior in human interaction. The discerning reader can find further intriguing suggestions throughout this book for some of the directions these more complete analyses might take.

One approach in this direction would involve a deeper look at the often posited human need and search for meaning, understanding, and predictability. This human need is relied on heavily by all three wings of the discipline— another convergence of note. Symbolic interactionists, using different terminology, assume it in their discussions of the symbolic meanings of human action. Contextual social psychologists have found it useful in devising microlevel explanations of social phenomena. Four decades ago, for example, Hadley Cantril (1941) postulated the human need for meaning as central to his explanation of the rise of such social movements as Nazism in situations of great threat and ambiguity. And more recently the need for stability and meaning has been invoked to explain the continuation of ethnic identification in the United States in the face of withering ethnic cultural and institutional life (Pettigrew, 1978).

---

[6]Similarly, Hamilton reports that Hamilton and Gifford (1976, Experiment 1), in their illusory correlation studies, noted a strong bias among their subjects to assign negative behaviors.

Yet, as Berkowitz (1969, pp. 87–88) points out, this presumed motive has consistently suffered from vague terminology and analytic imprecision. Clearly, meaning has instrumental value, for without it we are lost in "an unorganized chaotic universe." And meaning has reinforcing properties comparable to the satisfaction of biological drives (Munsinger, 1964). On many grounds, then, further theoretical and empirical work on this heavily-relied-upon human motive seems indicated and promising for linking motivational and cognitive considerations of particular importance to social psychology.

EXTENDING THE CONCEPT OF STEREOTYPE

Prejudice and intergroup relations have been studied within the discipline largely by contextual social psychologists. Allport's (1954) basic conceptual scheme has stood the test of time and still shapes the field. And, as Taylor (Chapter 3, this volume) correctly points out, a principal reason why Allport's analysis of intergroup prejudice has held up is that he made basic cognitive processes central to his formulation. Allport's Gestalt leanings helped him to project the field's future trends, for we have seen how it has been largely Gestalt influence via Fritz Heider that has shaped progress in recent years (Pettigrew, 1979).

Allport (1954) held prejudice to consist of irrationally based, negative attitudes against social groups and their members. Prejudice, then, has two key components—one cognitive (irrationally based), the other affective (negative attitudes against social groups). In treating the cognitive aspect of prejudice, intergroup relations specialists traditionally have stressed the overgeneralization, oversimplification, and distortion of reality that is often involved. And the chief concept employed since the 1920s in this realm has been that of "stereotype." As Ashmore and Del Boca (Chapter 1, this volume) make clear, the use of the term was typically narrow both empirically and conceptionally. Literally dozens of investigations trod the Katz and Braly (1933) research path without deviation. And few of them bothered to define the concept beyond the initial Lippmann (1922) notion of "pictures in our heads."

Moreover, in their zeal to demonstrate the logical errors of bigots, many of these early writers implied that the cognitive distortions represented by stereotypes were somehow a uniquely aberrant feature of prejudice. This emphasis was snugly consistent with the dominant progressive thought on race relations during the 1940s. This was the Human Relations Era, where intergroup problems were defined in terms of prejudiced people who needed to have their intergroup attitudes altered. Social structure was ignored; problems of discrimination were assumed to be correctable only after "the hearts and minds of men" were modified first. This psychological reductionism was typified by the work on *The Authoritarian Personality* (Adorno, Frenkel-Brunswik, Levinson, & Sanford, 1950), and even characterized sociological work in race relations (Pettigrew, 1980b). The assumption of aberrant cognitive processes, then, was simply a consistent part of the larger definition of the problem as consisting of "sick," prejudiced people.

Allport (1954) was one of the first to counter this view, to maintain that the cognitive distortions associated with prejudice were actually the product of "natural" and universal cognitive processes. And the reader must have noticed that this is a favorite point of cognitive social psychologists, for each chapter in this volume furnishes persuasive evidence for Allport's contention. But these analyses go far beyond both Allport and contemporary work in intergroup relations by expanding the concept of stereotype and demonstrating its direct connection with a host of other concepts and phenomena. Drawing together the various threads of the analysis, these expansions and connections can be briefly summarized.

1. *Stereotypes are a Direct Function of Categorization Processes.* Inspired by the work of Tajfel (1969), virtually all of the authors make use of this perspective. But it is Taylor and Wilder who explicitly pursue its implications.

2. *Stereotypes are Individually, Not Consensually, Held.* Ashmore and Del Boca distinguish the concept from its more sociological usage of generalized group images that pervade a given culture. They suggest that "cultural stereotype" be employed for the latter meaning, a useful suggestion that would avoid considerable confusion in the present literature.[7]

3. *Stereotypes Consist of Patterns of Traits Rather Than Individual Traits Considered One at a Time.* Ashmore and Del Boca insist that stereotypes are not simply trait attributions but actually *Gestalt* attributions—an often overlooked point of considerable significance that is firmly supported by relevant evidence. And this specification represents a convergence with symbolic interactionism. Reaching back to James and its other philosophical roots, SI insists that symbolic social meanings necessarily come in "packaged chunks" rather than isolated items, that single-trait analyses are precisely the type of "Wat-

---

[7]This need for conceptual clarity reoccurs often between the wings of social psychologists. Those few social psychologists who assume a top-down, marcro-to-micro perspective, most of whom were socialized in sociology, typically define key concepts in terms external to individuals. The great majority of social psychologists who assume a bottom-up, micro-to-macro perspective, including virtually all of those socialized in psychology, typically define key concepts in terms internal to individuals ("integumented" in Allport's terms). Thus, a few sociological social psychologists have proposed that personality be conceived of as the sum total of roles played by an individual, a notion that other social psychologists would wish to define separately—in the manner that Ashmore and Del Boca suggest for separating "cultural stereotype" from the internal concept of "stereotype." The general acceptance of such useful distinctions would enhance cross-wing communication within the discipline.

sonianism" that does violence to how human beings perceive and react to one another.

4. *Stereotypes Have Both Potency and Evaluative Dimensions.*   Ashmore demonstrates empirically that stereotypes are best conceptualized as trait patterns of varying potency ("soft" female versus "hard" male) embedded in evaluative structures. Two examples are provided of the importance of distinguishing between these two Osgood dimensions. Ashmore notes how the same trait (sentimental) attributed to females is evaluated negatively by men (i.e., inept) and positively by women (i.e., nurturant). And Ashmore and Del Boca cite the Saenger and Flowerman (1954) study that showed that both "Jews" and "Americans" were judged as "aggressive" but the evaluative meanings of the trait were different for the two Gestalts. Once again, symbolic interactionists can supply numerous additional examples. Thus, "deviants" and "straights" frequently agree on the differentiating features of their contrasting life styles but place these features in entirely different evaluative contexts.

5. *Stereotypes Are Implicit Personality Theories Applied to Social Group Membership.*   Ashmore discusses at length the theoretical and empirical implications of connecting these two disparate concepts.

6. *Stereotypes Are Perceived Correlations Between Social Groups and Attributes.*   Hamilton demonstrates this perspective with his studies of the illusory correlation phenomenon applied to stereotypes. But to gain consistency with Ashmore's aforementioned Point 3, it is more precise to state that stereotypes are perceived correlations between social groups and *patterns* of attributes—a refinement that fits with a number of Hamilton's empirical results.

7. *Stereotypes Are Essentially Schemata.*   Hamilton notes that both stereotypes and schemata are conceptualized as involved with the encoding, interpretation, retention, and retrieval of information. And he draws out the implications of this similarity in this volume and elsewhere (Hamilton, 1979).

8. *Stereotypes of a Global Nature Often Evolve Into a Set of Specific, Subtype Stereotypes.*   Coming from different empirical directions, both Ashmore and Taylor arrive at this significant conclusion. We pursue this phenomenon further in later discussion and find yet another convergence with symbolic interactionism.

9. *Stereotypes Can Be Fused When the Target Is Classified Under Two Relevant Group Labels* (e.g., rich Chicano).   Ashmore emphasizes this little-studied phenomenon on the basis of Cohen's (1977) conclusion that "human memory involves multiple, cross-cutting categorizations of the same informa-

tion.'' Like an efficient, fast-retrieval library, cross-classification is often effectively utilized in human memory. Straightforward as this may sound, few investigators in the stereotype literature have allowed for this possibility, much less
studied it systematically.

10. *Stereotypes Are Strongly Influenced by the Salience of the Group Member
and the Structure of the Intergroup Situation.*   Here the discussions by Taylor,
Rothbart, Wilder, and Rose are all highly relevant.

Taylor's focus on token representation fits with much of what has been established in the intergroup relations research literature for some years. Two examples suffice. The massive study of American education, *The Equal Educational
Opportunity Survey* (Coleman, Campbell, Hobson, McPartland, Mood, Weinfeld, & York, 1966, pp. 333–334), found that black children who were the sole
members of their race in their classrooms rendered extreme achievement test
scores. Beyond the greater variance in scores that would be expected on the basis
of their relatively small numbers and without any apparent selection explanation,
black children playing ''the solo role'' in their classrooms performed either
extremely well or poorly relative to similar black children in other school settings. One is tempted to speculate that peer acceptance was an important
mediator of this effect; those who were accepted may have tended to perform
well, those rejected may have tended to perform badly. On the basis of such field
data, race relations specialists have strongly recommended against tokenism
(Pettigrew, 1975).

Another example of an apparent solo effect occurred in the 1960s when black
youth began to enroll for the first time at traditionally all-white southern state
universities. After a few ''trial'' years but while the numbers of black students
were still token at best, an interesting political phenomenon swept these southern
campuses. Suddenly, popular black students were being elected president of the
student government at a dozen or so of these schools.[8] Relative power and threat
issues are involved here, of course. But in support of the possibility that these
events also reflected the ''pet'' role of tokenism delineated by Kanter (1977),
there are virtually no black student government presidents on these campuses today now that the proportions of blacks in the student bodies have risen significantly.

11. *Stereotypes Directly Shape Social Interaction.*   In Snyder's words,
stereotypes mediate ''between the domain of thought and the domain of action.''

---

[8]A comparable effect may also characterize certain forms of politics off the campus as well. Thus,
the only black U.S. Senator of the 20th century, Edward Brooke, was elected from Massachusetts,
where black voters constitute less than 3% of the electorate. And many statewide offices held by
black public figures today are in states, such as Washington, where the black population represents a
token proportion.

And his ingenuous investigations dramatically prove the point. We later discuss these studies further.

12. *Stereotypes Constitute a Critical Component of the Larger Process of Deindividuation of Those Categorized as Outgroup Members.* This important connection made by Wilder allows a link to be made between the microlevel concept of stereotype and the more extreme acts of discrimination and even genocide against hated outgroups.

13. *Stereotypes are Extremely Persistent; They Resist Alteration Because of Basic Cognitive Processes as Well as the Extensive Social Support They Typically Receive.* Together with the demonstration that intergroup stereotypes are natural phenomena, the stubborn persistence of stereotypes and the many reasons for this persistence are major themes running throughout this volume. Indeed, there is almost "overkill" on the point. One begins to wonder how stereotypes ever shift, given the multitude of reasons for their tenacity. Because it is critical for both theory and application, we turn to discuss this issue at length.

THE PERSISTENCE AND MODIFICATION OF STEREOTYPES

Stereotype Persistence

Stereotypes are overdetermined. Early social learning and strong motivational processes often underlie them as well as cognitive biases. Indeed, each of the three orientations to the study of stereotypes listed by Ashmore and Del Boca—the sociocultural, psychodynamic, and cognitive approaches—provides abundant reasons for the remarkable resilience of most (but not all) group stereotypes.

The preceding chapters provide a vast array of cognitive biases that are implicated in this phenomenon as well as ways in which they shape interaction so as to restrict disconfirming information. We have seen repeated demonstrations of how these biases structure the way information is sampled, encoded, stored, and retrieved so that stereotypes not only go unchallenged but frequently are strengthened. Recall Rothbart's point that in acting on our intergroup beliefs we systematically restrict disconfirming evidence. Indeed, argues Rothbart, our lack of responsiveness to the disconfirming evidence that does confront us is probably necessary, given the requirement of prior expectations for smooth social interaction. And Snyder adds to this reasoning the fact that we actually see and meet only specific cases (if any) of the stereotyped outgroup. Little wonder, then, that stereotypes about the *general* case prove to be so impervious to change.

Such cognitive considerations often interact with social structural phenomena to enhance these effects further. Consider the differential access of white Americans today to various segments of the black American world. Black poverty and despair are largely beyond the purview of most whites. But the enlarged black middle class, with its new opportunities in formerly all-white institutional settings, is highly conspicuous to whites. This *differential association* process lends visible support to the comfortable contention widely held among whites that racial injustice was basically corrected during the civil rights era of the 1960s. In short, it is often the case in American society that the social selection of experiences combines with perceptual selection to create larger intergroup biases than even the impressive research herein reported can demonstrate.

Consider, too, the social support rendered group stereotypes by the mass media. *All in the Family* is only an extreme example of the typical 30-minute situation-comedy program favored by commercial television. Without the opportunity to develop characterizations in depth and with the need to appeal to mass audiences, the scripts of such shows necessarily must rely on widely shared cultural stereotypes. Other mass media forms, even the news, further this process. Rothbart, in demonstrating the particular salience of extreme cases, notes that the media accentuate the dramatic and the extreme. "News," after all, is in large part defined by the mass media as that which is sensational and surprising.

In addition, the many factors specified by Hamilton in the illusory correlation phenomenon are also congruent with mass media presentations. Recall his emphasis on the fact that usually "the *nonoccurrence* of an event class is hardly noticeable." And combine this with the much discussed fact that the mass media bias their presentations less from what they repetitively issue forth than from the enormous amount of life experience, news, and other potential content that they systematically exclude. Similarly, the potency of negative instances—which are more likely to be seen as "newsworthy" than positive instances—further enhances the media's support of prevailing cultural stereotypes. Indeed, the very basis of illusory correlations—the biasing effects of sequential information—is itself a necessary characteristic of mass media presentations. And children are among the biggest consumers of the most stereotyped medium of all—television; Hamilton stresses how the illusory correlation is most likely to aid in the development of stereotypes among the young. Moreover, the research literature on the effects of the mass media suggests that these effects are greatest on subjects (such as Vietnam) about which the public does not have prior attitudes and beliefs—a point consistent with Hamilton's suggestion that the illusory correlation phenomenon is likely to be strongest for little-known groups. Finally, such situational comedies as *All in the Family* necessarily exploit the type of associative links and genuine group differences that further exacerbate the development of group stereotypes. Writers for the mass media understand all too well the force of Hamilton's felicitous expression: "I wouldn't have seen it if I hadn't believed it!" And critics of the media who maintain that television is a major source for social support of negative intergroup stereotypes may well have a strong point apart from any intended biasing of content by media personnel,

There are, then, many points at which the purely cognitive analyses advanced in these pages converge with well-studied phenomena in the contextual social psychological and sociocultural traditions. But the analyses of this volume go further, with Snyder, Wilder, and Rose applying these cognitive ideas to areas specialized in by the other branches of social psychology. Thus, Snyder demonstrates one of the most fundamental components of symbolic interactionism (SI)—the thoroughly recursive nature of human interaction.[9] And he does it by employing methods that orthodox SI theory has argued could not do justice to the ongoing flow of interaction.

This convergence on a central proposition of the discipline becomes even more intriguing when Snyder shows how this basic property of interaction provides yet another basis for the perpetuation of social stereotypes. At least on first encounters, his data suggest that intergroup contact often may not affect overgeneralized stereotypes in part because of two restrictive processes: *reconstruction* (selective memory for those facts that confirm stereotypes); and *behavioral confirmation* (the shaping of interactants' behaviors so that they do in fact confirm the initial stereotype).

The first of these processes, reconstruction, harks back to Bartlett (1932), received emphasis during "the new look in perception," and follows, too, from the emphasis of the 1960s on the consistency principle and much of the work of symbolic interactionists over recent decades. The second, behavioral confirmation, has often been noted in American black–white relations. For instance, students of the continuing tensions between white police and black communities note that self-fulfilling prophecies are often invoked. The police, aware of their status as hated outsiders in the ghetto, anticipate violence from a black suspect. The suspect in turn anticipates police harrassment. Both act on their assumptions and make them correct. Black suspects in time are in fact more likely to resort to violence with the police, and the police are more likely to harass citizens in the ghetto and use firearms on black suspects. The ingenious research of Word, Zanna, and Cooper (1974), described by Snyder, demonstrates that this same process of behavioral confirmation can also take place in less dramatic settings—as in interviewing for employment. Whites often discriminate against black people without full awareness, though the effect of limiting black life chances and choices is just the same. Breaking such self-fulfilling cycles, as Snyder notes, is no mean task—especially in the context of racism that has marked American black–white relations for three-and-a-half centuries.

Similarly, Wilder's array of studies suggests that "perceiving others as an outgroup may encourage us to assume, to search for, and to remember information that accentuates differences between groups." Wilder's evidence is particu-

---

[9]Snyder is quite aware of the links between his work and that of the symbolic interactionists and cites several relevant SI references. But in other parts of the volume, classic SI statements are advanced with only experimental social psychological references. Rose, for example, writes that "the person's behavior is not a function of objective events but rather the interpretation given to those events." Meade or Blumer could not have said it more succinctly.

larly compelling because of the manner in which his experiments systematically vary a number of critical ingroup–outgroup dimensions of great interest to contextual social psychologists (e.g., perceived aggregates versus genuine groups, contact within the ingroup, dissent within the outgroup, and the larger intergroup context of more extreme outgroups).

In his application of cognitive analyses to the extensive literature on intergroup contact, Rose reaches similar conclusions to those of Wilder. Allport's (1954) optimal conditions for stereotype-breaking and prejudice-reducing contact are not easy to attain, or at least do not characterize most black–white contact in contemporary America. (However, there is considerable evidence that these contact conditions describe a far higher proportion of interracial contacts than prior to the Civil Rights Movement). And Rose makes a strong case for systematically applying cognitive, as well as the more traditional situational analyses, to the evaluation of intergroup contact.

Finally, a number of the authors mention causal attributional factors as furnishing yet additional resiliency to stereotypes. Pettigrew (1979) has expanded these and similar ideas into a generalized system of hypotheses labeled "the ultimate attribution error." Briefly stated, the ultimate attribution error operates when negative acts by outgroupers are seen to be caused by permanent dispositions and positive acts by outgroupers are explained away in a variety of situational and transitory ways. Two interrelated phenomena, then, constitute the ultimate attribution error:

1. When people perceive what they regard as a negative act by a member of a disliked outgroup, they are more likely to attribute it dispositionally, often as genetically determined, in comparison to the attribution of the same act by an ingroup member.

2. When people perceive what they regard as a positive act by a member of a disliked outgroup, they are morely likely to discount it, in comparison to their attribution of the same act by an ingroup member, in one or more of four ways, as the result of: (1) an exceptional case ("She is certainly bright and energetic—not like other Chicanas."); (2) luck or special advantage ("He either made it through dumb luck or affirmative action—he could never have done it on his own."); (3) unusually high motivation and effort ("Jewish students make better grades just because they study so hard."); and (4) manipulable situational context ("What could the cheap Scot do but pay the whole check after the waiter handed it to him and we all looked at him in silence?"). Moreover, these tendencies are held to be enhanced when: (1) the perceivers are prejudiced; and (2) highly involved; (3) the group memberships are salient; and (4) the groups have histories of conflict with developed and negative stereotypes.

A recently completed experimental test of this attributional means of maintaining social stereotypes illustrates how it can work in black—white interaction

(Pettigrew, Jemmott, & Johnson, 1980). White college students observed both black and white confederates of the experimenters conduct a quiz game patterned after Ross and his colleagues (Ross, Amabile, & Steinmetz, 1977). In such situations, the questioners are seen as far more knowledgeable than the hapless contestants even though the questioners have the enormous situational advantage of asking questions taken from their own idiosyncratic stores of information. A script of the same questions and answers was used in all conditions. Yet the "good" performances of the black questioners were significantly more often attributed to "luck," and the "poor" performances of black contestants attributed to less general knowledge and college preparation. Furthermore, those subjects who revealed on a questionnaire greater prejudice toward the mentally ill more often responded in this fashion.

Stereotype Modification

These numerous reasons why stereotypes are so resistant to change raise the question as to how stereotypes are *ever* modified. This volume has advanced a number of interesting answers to this query. Given the "naturalness' of the cognitive biases shown to underlie stereotypes, all these suggestions necessarily relate to influencing the content and context of relevant incoming information. For example, Taylor calls for intergroup situations where group membership is less salient. The solo role is her case in point. Token group representation has long been opposed by intergroup specialists largely on the grounds of the severe difficulties it can create for minority members. Taylor adds to this reasoning the point that little significant alteration in stereotypes among majority members can be anticipated in such situations. Even though individuation may occur, Allport's (1954) "refencing" of stereotypes is likely to be triggered and the solo representative regarded as "a special case."

In viewing intergroup contact from an information-processing perspective, Rose extends Taylor's emphasis on reducing group salience. In general, he adopts a somewhat more negative view of what even optimal intergroup contact can accomplish than I do (Pettigrew, 1971). I believe this results from his focusing on the typical discomfort and novelty of initial encounters between previously separated groups. Positive change from contact is likely to be a long-term process, and little longitudinal work has been conducted by contextual social psychologists in this research literature. But that which is available casts doubt upon Rose's gloomy assumptions that intimate relationships under pleasant conditions are not likely for even intergroup contact that meets Allport's stringent conditions.

Nonetheless, intergroup specialists support Rose's suggestion that initial contact settings possess clear norms and roles. Those desegregated public schools that have adopted openly "racial" rules to ensure the full participation of all races in all activities have tended to have greater success in attaining "genuine integration" (Pettigrew, 1971, 1975). At first blush, this finding may appear to be a contradiction to the low-saliency strategy of Taylor and Rose. But actually, if one adopts the necessary longitudinal perspective, these explicitly racial practices are required to distribute the races throughout the school's social structure. Without such rules of operation, there often occurs such racially salient and symbolic maldistributions as all-black basketball teams and all-white school newspaper staffs.

Wilder offers additional possibilities. He reasons that any feature that reduces the effects of group categorization will reduce undifferentiated stereotyping of and discriminatory behavior toward outgroups. Focusing on the maximization of *individuation,* Wilder provides an extensive tour of the possibilities. At the level of the perceiver, he shows that lowering arousal and discouraging "group set" aid individuation. At the level of the perceiver's relationship to the ingroup, he shows that a variety of techniques that lessen a person's ingroup identification fosters individuation. Here he makes the interesting point that outgroup contact may induce individuation of outgroup members in part because it acts to reduce ingroup contact. This suggestion deserves to be studied systematically in future field research on the contact hypothesis. And it raises issues concerning the connections between the categorization analyses of this volume and social evaluation and comparison theory in social psychology (Pettigrew, 1967).

Wilder next analyzes the structure and behavior of the outgroup. Individuation is enhanced by any process that makes categorization of the outgroup's members difficult, that abrogates "the unit relationship between them." He considers internal dissent within the outgroup and the disclosure of personal information by an outgroup member. But herein lies a dilemma for minority groups wishing to reduce the hostility directed toward them. Through internal dissent made known to the outside, the adoption of the majority culture, and other methods, a minority could follow Wilder's advice. But in so doing, the group surrenders its pride, its distinctiveness, its culture, even its ability to mobilize effectively to use the political process and other means for redress of grievances. There is, then, always a tension between "selling out" and "buying in," between gaining acceptance of the group and developing group pride, distinctiveness, and political mobilization.

This tension also relates to Wilder's suggestions concerning the relationship between the ingroup and outgroup. He points out that outgroups can sometimes be recategorized as part of the ingroup or more often as part of a more inclusive category based on a different dimension ("workers," "Americans"). Important here is a fundamental consideration of consensus theory in social theory—namely, the critical significance of overlapping social groupings that establish cross bonds within such diverse societies as that of modern America. Without such cross bonds, Parsons and other sociologists have argued, the structural basis of societal consensus is severely limited and widespread intergroup conflict is likely. Given its central importance in social theory, cross-bonding group identifications deserve considerably more empirical and theoretical attention in social psychology than they have received. And this holds true as well for the closely related problem of group boundaries and how they are perceived (Pettigrew, 1978).

A final proposal by Wilder involves the potentially positive effects of a distant and threatening third group on ingroup—outgroup perceptions and relations. In social-judgment theory terms (Sherif & Hovland, 1961), the introduction of a new and extreme anchor redefines the judgmental continuum and shifts the perception of the old outgroup from the latitude of rejection to that of acceptance. Examples of this phenomenon abound in the intergroup relations literature. In the 1950s, the court-oriented National Association for the Advancement of Colored People (NAACP) was viewed by many whites as an extremist, militant black organization. But once the 1960s brought the violent rhetoric of the Black Muslims, Black Panthers, and similar groups onto the racial scene, the NAACP became seen more realistically as a middle-of-the-road, "responsible" black group despite its actually having in absolute terms moved toward greater militancy. Or, in the stereotype literature, the image of the cunning and cruel Japanese dominated white American thought during World War II. But once Japan became a democratic ally against "the red threat," the basic stereotype of the Japanese improved with remarkable alacrity in national survey data.

These examples suggest that most of the means discussed in this book for modifying stereotypes and improving intergroup relations are dependent on the larger social structural context. These means are the mediators at the individual level of these larger social changes, but they are unlikely to be achieved without major structural alterations. Rothbart (Chapter 5, this volume) puts it bluntly: "if we wish to change our stereotypes of the inferiority of women and blacks, we would do well to change *first* their inferior social and economic status."[10] And in this same vein Snyder (Chapter 6) reminds us that: "Often, changes in stereotypes appear to have been accompanied by (and, perhaps, precipitated by) organized social movements to mobilize members of stereotyped groups to ameliorate their circumstances and, at the same time, to dispel negative stereotypes about these groups." He suggests that these organized social movements may increase the visibility of "the general case," though this possibility would largely be mediated by the mass media and their attendant biases.

There is considerable indirect evidence in contextual social psychology in support of Rothbart's emphasis on actual social change and Snyder's on the role of social movements. For example, consider the longitudinal data of Fig. 9.1 on the willingness to vote for "a qualified woman" for President of the United

---

[10]Interestingly, almost precisely the same point was made forcefully three-quarters of a century ago by the highly influential sociological social psychologist, W. I. Thomas (1907): "The world of modern intellectual life is in reality a white man's world. Few women and perhaps no blacks have ever entered this world in the fullest sense [p. 468]."

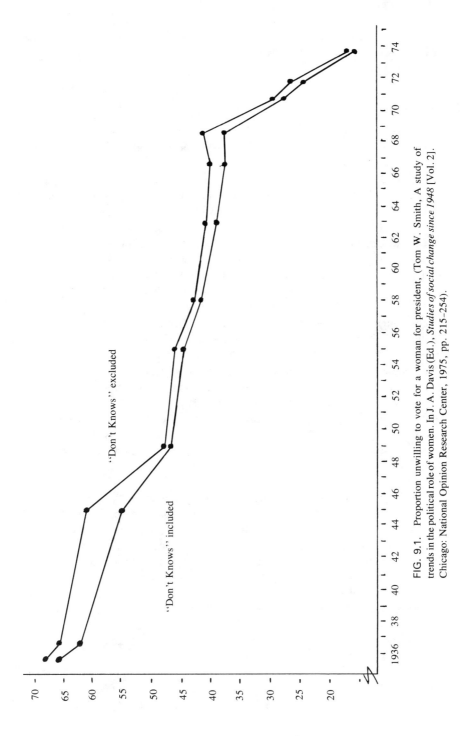

FIG. 9.1. Proportion unwilling to vote for a woman for president, (Tom W. Smith, A study of trends in the political role of women. In J. A. Davis (Ed.), *Studies of social change since 1948* [Vol. 2]. Chicago: National Opinion Research Center, 1975, pp. 215–254).

"Don't Knows" excluded

"Don't Knows" included

States. Observe the first drop in resistance during World War II, when traditional sex roles were challenged by large numbers of women working in war factories and joining the newly formed WAC and WAVE units in the Armed Services. But observe the more dramatic drop in resistance coincident with the rise of the Feminist Movement. And other analyses of these same data by Ferree (1974) show that this 1969–1974 shift took place among both sexes, but particularly among women themselves. That this unusually large and rapid shift reflects basic change among both sexes in the image of women would be consistent with Ashmore's finding that the stereotype of women had less clarity among his college student subjects than that of males. Comparable shifts occurred in survey data on racial attitudes and beliefs at the time of the Civil Rights Movement. Thus, during just the three years from 1963 to 1966 at the height of the Movement, the percentage of white Americans who believed that blacks "smell different" dropped from 60 to 52 and the percentage who believed that they "have looser morals" dropped from 55 to 50 (Brink and Harris, 1967). Over a longer time span, the percentage of whites who agreed that "Negroes are as intelligent as white people" rose from only 42 in 1942 to about 80 by the 1960s (Hyman & Sheatsley, 1964). Most of this fading of the antiblack stereotype occurred after—and not before—such major structural alterations as public school desegregation had taken place in the respondents' communities (Hyman and Sheatsley, 1964). And recent models demonstrate that most of this change reflects actual "conversion" of white cohorts who lived through the years of the Movement rather than a "replacement" of the more bigoted elderly by the more tolerant young (Taylor, Sheatsley, & Greeley, 1978). It has also been shown that dramatic events, such as the tragic assassination of Dr. Martin Luther King, Jr. in 1968, can have a profound effect on racial attitudes and beliefs (Riley & Pettigrew, 1976). Consistent with this book's analyses, however, these effects of King's death were greatest for those types of whites who already possessed more open attitudes toward racial change prior to the murder.

Finally, the Hamilton and Bishop (1976) study of neighborhood desegregation in New Haven has been cited throughout the book as evidence for the fact that normative change itself can erode antiblack beliefs even when little or no interracial contact has taken place. This is a well-documented phenomenon throughout the race relations literature that gives some ray of optimism for the future modification of negative social stereotypes. For example, consider the responses of national samples to the standard survey question: "Do you think white students and Negro students should go to the same schools, or to separate schools?" In 1942, only 30% of white Americans favored "same schools." But by 1956, the percentage had risen to 49; by 1963, to 63; by 1965, to 67; by 1970, to 74; by 1972, to 86; and by 1976, to 83 (Greeley & Sheatsley, 1974; Hyman & Sheatsley, 1964; Taylor et al., 1978). Note that these samples of adults had rarely gone themselves to desegregated schools, but were reflecting the many structural changes going on around them. Public commitment is also involved.

Many of those sampled had sent their children without themselves having the interracial contact. Indeed, one recent study shows that it is the parents of public school children who are directly affected by school desegregation who evince the greatest positive change at the time of a court order (Jacobson, 1978).

SUBGROUP STEREOTYPES

What is a realistic goal for modifying negative social stereotypes? The old Human Relations Movement mentioned earlier often sought to eliminate group stereotypes altogether. Allport (1954) knew that was unrealistic, and lowered his goal to the replacement of negative with positive group stereotypes. His popularly written book, *The Nature of Prejudice,* was designed to be his contribution toward that end. It may not be too cynical, on the basis of the present analyses, to set our practical sights one more notch lower.[11] Group stereotypes will be forever with us. And it seems that negative stereotypes are likely to predominate, considering their apparent greater salience and information value (Kanouse & Hanson, 1971). But global, undifferentiated group stereotypes need not be permanent fixtures. And the analyses of both Ashmore and Taylor provide encouragement for this significant possibility.

Because categorization derives from learning and experience, Taylor holds that increasing familiarity with an outgroup should lead to an increasing number of substereotypes. Female subtypes can include mother, princess, showgirl, castrator, career woman, and so on. Indeed, Taylor suspects that the subcategories for either sex actually come to encompass the full range of human attributes. Such a complete system, obviously, cannot be disconfirmed. Moreover, she points out that the usual assessment of trait lists seeking global stereotypes will not uncover this level of stereotyping. Hence, much of the apparent fading of the stereotype of black Americans in survey data in recent decades probably masks the decomposition of the broad "id" stereotype into specific substereotypes often based on social class position.

Ashmore agrees. But rather than narrowly identifying the subcategories with just social roles, as does Taylor, he believes they probably come at various levels of breadth and acceptance—general cultural subtypes, those only recognized within a particular subculture (as in the rich characterizations of Yiddish), and those "that are completely idiosyncratic." At the cultural level, there is here a

---

[11]The word "cynical" is used purposely, because scientific judgments of social possibilities are highly colored by the political times in which they are rendered (Bramson, 1961). The optimism for extensive social change in race relations that characterized social science during the 1950s and 1960s, for example, has been replaced by a generally dour view of the possibilities in recent years. And this dour view is reflected in this volume, too, especially by Rose. If we overshot with our enthusiasm in past decades, we may be too cynical today in understating the possibilities for change.

further convergence with symbolic interactionist thought. In the work of Orrin Klapp (1963, 1964, 1969) in particular, there is a developed literature on the great wealth of cultural types ("heroes, villains, and fools") that receive extensive mass media publicity. These projected types are held to be critical for identity development in a mass society. And they supply the cultural content and assumptions that undergird widely shared implicit personality theories and subcategory stereotypes. Some of these cultural types in the occupational sphere—the quiet, reserved librarian, the loquacious, aggressive salesperson—have been exploited in studies reported here by Hamilton and others.

The theoretical and practical importance of this phenomenon of subcategory stereotyping suggests that this is an area that begs for intense conceptual and empirical attention during the 1980s. Together with the new, more ambivalent and ambiguous behavioral forms of racism and sexism that are emerging (Dutton, 1976; Gaertner, 1973; Pettigrew, in press), this subcategorization process may more subtly capture the more complex nature of intergroup relations in post-Movement America. Pointing to such future work, the somewhat contrasting formulations of the process by Taylor and Ashmore deserve comment.

Taylor's analysis is both more ambitious and speculative. By attaching the subcategories to social roles, she implies that they are to some degree situation specific. And by tying in these subcategories with a middle and basic level of person perception in Roschian terms, she supplies for future workers an explicit specification of the phenomenon for testing. Taylor may well be right on both counts, but it seems premature at this point to narrow our view of this process. And there is potentially a conceptual conflict between perceiving stereotypes at any level as, on the one hand, implicit *personality* theories (Ashmore) and, on the other hand, *social role* components (Taylor). Personality, after all, is the concept devised to explain consistencies in behavior of a given individual across different situations. And social role is the concept devised to explain consistencies in behavior in a given situation across different individuals. To be sure, indicators of the two concepts typically covary. Particular personalities are often attracted to particular social roles, and role participation socializes its occupants and shapes personality development. But sociologists are quick to point out that most social roles are far from being personality specific for their effective execution. A wide range of personalities apparently successfully enacts given roles, though with contrasting stylistic flourishes. Subcategory stereotypes seem to cover both perceived personality types and perceived role types, and sociological work in this area cautions us not to confuse the two—even though they are complexly interwoven. The contradiction of conceiving of these substereotypes in both personality and role terms is probably more apparent than real. But conceptual clarity demands a subtle model that allows for the complexity of dealing at both of these levels.

To make this point more concretely, think of the new subcategory stereotypes that are now emerging for black Americans. The rapid growth in recent decades of the black middle class and the increased class stratification this has created within black America has led to a new need for many whites to distinguish among black people. Many of these new subcategories, as Taylor would suspect, assume occupational role forms—"the affirmative-action worker," "the striving new professional," etc. And many appear to involve implicitly racist personality theories—"the father-absent teenager," "the shiftless welfare mother," etc. Most of the new forms appear to blend both personality and role components, but the dominant feature seems to be class position and the assumptions that derive from it. Black middle class respondents often report that they have learned to emit numerous class cues from clothes to language whenever dealing with whites, regardless of role or situation.

Such considerations raise the question as to whether or not this process of substereotyping constitutes any improvement in intergroup thinking and relations. Taylor expresses her reservations on this score. I am a bit more sanguine, for many of the subcategory stereotypes are evaluatively positive even if often patronizing. At the least, a variety of stereotypes affords a far greater degree of interactional flexibility in intergroup relations than the older Procrustean images. This point, too, requires detailed research. But, perhaps, the greater range of potential evaluations afforded by substereotypes helps to account for Ashmore's failure to find a clear evaluative difference between his male and female images.

INDICATED FUTURE DIRECTIONS

The perspective presented in this volume invites further work in many directions. A number of these directions have already been commented on: longitudinal cognitive studies on how social stereotypes are modified; more attention to how individuals adapt cognitively to cross-bonding, overlapping memberships and the boundaries between groups; and further conceptualization and empirical work on the process of developing subcategory stereotypes. The chapter closes by mentioning briefly further possibilities at all three levels of social psychological concern—individual differences, interpersonal interaction, and sociocultural considerations.

Individual Differences.   Like most of experimental social psychology in recent years, the principal thrust of this volume has been on the universal and the generic rather than the individual and unique. But Wilder and Taylor present interesting data on individual differences that offer promise for further effort in this direction.

Wilder looks at motivational arousal and cognitive set and finds that unaroused subjects without a "group set" are less likely to employ group categorizations. But Taylor fails to find any differences across sex and race of subjects in the tendency to organize information by sex and race categories. Nor does she find any tendency for her subjects to stereotype members of an outgroup more than of their ingroup. But she did obtain strikingly specific and contrasting results from two diverse measures related to sex roles. Using the Bem Sex Role Inventory, she finds that highly sex-typed men and women used sex as an organizing category in perception more than androgynous subjects though they did not recall any greater amount of information. A Feminism scale tapping traditional or liberal sex-role conceptions, however, did not yield this outcome. But Taylor reports just the opposite result for the favorability ratings of female participants in her procedure. In this dependent measure of sexism, androgynous people were just as prejudiced as sex-typed people, but those who believed in traditional roles for women were more likely to rank higher the equated performances of men over women.

These interesting results pinpoint motivational influences on cognition in the manner of the old "new look in perception." But more directly relevant to this volume's analysis, perhaps, would be research on individual differences in cognitive styles, abilities, and aptitudes directly. And there are a variety of much used measurement instruments that can be utilized, ranging from field dependence and ideational fluency (Ekstrom, French, Harman, & Derman, 1976) to category width (Pettigrew, 1958) and cognitive complexity (Bieri, Atkins, Brir, Leaman, Miller, & Tripodi, 1966). Immodestly, the point can be illustrated with my own measure. Generalized individual tendencies to employ either broad or narrow categories across content should be centrally related to the present analyses that revolve around the process of categorization. But, as Wilder suggests for cognitive complexity, the relationship is not likely to be simple. Broad categorizers, it can be hypothesized, should use fewer, but more global, group stereotypes. Yet these expansive categories should resist disconfirmation more rigorously than those of narrow categorizers who typically seek categories free of negative instances.

Interpersonal Interaction.   Many suggestive leads at this level have been advanced in these pages. Suffice it here to add one general suggestion that is relevant to most social psychological areas of study.

The discipline, in my view, is too focused on what Emile Durkheim termed *mechanical solidarity*—the bonds of social life that derive from similarity. Social psychology has for too long almost ignored the equally critical other side of the coin, *organic solidarity*—the bonds of social life that derive from interdependent differences (as in complimentary roles). Some (though not all) of the pessimism of many social psychological analyses of intergroup relations can be traced to this near-exclusive attention to mechanical solidarity. With similarity as the chief binding principle, the contrasts of different groups by definition restricts social psychological theory and remedial suggestions. Perhaps the singular focus on similarity in the person-perception area represents the extreme case in point. Sherif is one of the few social psychologists to focus on interdependence and difference in the intergroup area. Hopefully, future work in this and other domains of social psychology will follow his lead.

Sociocultural Considerations.   If we wish to claim human universality for cognitive analyses, it is obviously necessary to prove it through cross-cultural testing. And because intergroup conflict and negative stereotypes are to be found, unfortunately but significantly, throughout the world, there is no dearth whatsoever of research sites. Cognitive anthropologists are active in this realm. And the innovative cross-cultural work of Eleanor Rosch (1975, 1977) provides an impressive model of what social psychologists can contribute to this area of study.

REFERENCES

Adorno, T. W., Frenkel-Brunswik, E., Levinson, D. J., & Sanford, R. N. *The authoritarian personality.* New York: Harper & Row, 1950.

Allport, G. W. *The nature of prejudice.* Reading, Mass.: Addison–Wesley, 1954.

Bartlett, F. C. *Remembering: A study in experimental and social psychology.* Cambridge, England: Cambridge University Press, 1932.

Berkowitz, L. Social motivation. In G. Lindzey & E. Aronson (Eds.), *The handbook of social psychology* (Vol. 3, 2nd ed.). Reading, Mass.: Addison–Wesley, 1969.

Bieri, J., Atkins, A. L., Brir, S., Leaman, R. L., Miller, H., & Tripodi, T. *Clinical and social judgment: The discrimination of behavioral information.* New York: Wiley, 1966.

Blumer, H. *Symbolic interactionism.* Englewood Cliffs, N.J.: Prentice–Hall, 1969.

Bramson, L. *The political context of sociology.* Princeton, N.J.: Princeton University Press, 1961.

Brink, W. & Harris, L. *Black and white: A study of U.S. racial attitudes today.* New York: Simon and Schuster, 1967.

Cantril, H. *The psychology of social movements.* New York: Wiley, 1941.

Cohen, G. *The psychology of cognition.* New York: Academic Press, 1977.

Coleman, J. S., Campbell, E. Q., Hobson, C. J., McPartland, M., Mood, A. M., Weinfeld, F. D., & York, R. L. *Equality of educational opportunity.* Washington, D.C.: U.S. Government Printing Office, 1966.

Dutton, D. G. Tokenism, reverse discrimination, and egalitarianism in interracial behavior. *Journal of Social Issues,* 1976, *32* (2), 93–107.

Ekstrom, R. B., French, J. W., Harman, H. H., & Derman, D. *Manual for kit of factor-referenced cognitive tests.* Princeton, N.J.: Educational Testing Service, 1976.

Ferree, M. M. Women for president: Changing responses. *Public Opinion Quarterly,* 1974, *38,* 390–399.

Gaertner, S. Helping behavior and racial discrimination among liberals and conservatives. *Journal of Personality and Social Psychology,* 1973, *25,* 335–341.

Greeley, A. M., & Sheatsley, P. B. Attitudes toward racial integration. In L. Rainwater (Ed.), *Social problems and public policy: Inequality and justice.* Chicago: Aldine, 1974.

Hamilton, D. L. A cognitive–attributional analysis of stereotyping. In L. Berkowitz (Ed.), *Advances in experimental social psychology* (Vol. 12). New York: Academic Press, 1979.

Hamilton, D. L., & Bishop, G. D. Attitudinal and behavioral effects of initial integration of white suburban neighborhoods. *Journal of Social Issues,* 1976, *32,* 47–67.

Hamilton, D. L., & Gifford, R. K. Illusory correlation in interpersonal perception: A cognitive basis of stereotypic judgments. *Journal of Experimental Social Psychology,* 1976, *12,* 392–407.

Helmreich, R. Applied social psychology: The unfulfilled promise. *Personality and Social Psychology Bulletin,* 1975, *1,* 548–560.

House, J. S. The three faces of social psychology. *Sociometry,* 1977, *40,* 161–177.

Hyman, H. H., & Sheatsley, P. B. Attitudes toward desegregation. *Scientific American,* July 1964, *211,* 16–23.

Jacobson, C. K. Desegregation rulings and public attitude changes: White resistance or resignation? *American Journal of Sociology,* 1978, *84,* 698–707 (reprinted in Pettigrew, 1980b).

Kanouse, D. E., & Hanson, L. R. Negativity in evaluations. In C. E. Jones, D. E. Kanouse, H. H. Kelley, R. E. Nisbett, S. Valins, & B. Weiner (Eds.), *Attribution: Perceiving the causes of behavior.* Morristown, N.J.: General Learning Press, 1971.

Katz, D., & Braly, K. Racial stereotypes in one hundred college students. *Journal of Abnormal and Social Psychology,* 1933, *28,* 280–290.

Kanter, R. M. Some effects of proportions on group life: Skewed sex ratios and responses to token women. *American Journal of Sociology,* 1977, *82,* 965–990.

Klapp, O. E. *Heroes, villains and fools.* Englewood Cliffs, N.J.: Prentice- Hall, 1963.

Klapp, O. E. *Symbolic leaders: Public dramas and public men.* Chicago: Aldine, 1964.

Klapp, O. E. *Collective search for identity.* New York: Holt, Reinhart & Winston, 1969.

Lindesmith, A. R., Strauss, A. L., & Denzin, N. K. *Social psychology* (5 ed.). New York: Holt, Rinehart & Winston, 1977.

Lippmann, W. *Public opinion.* New York: Harcourt, Brace, Jovanovitch, 1922.

Munsinger, H. L. Meaningful symbols as reinforcing stimuli. *Journal of Abnormal and Social Psychology,* 1964, *68,* 665–668.

Newcomb, T. M., & Hartley, E. L. (Eds.). *Readings in social psychology.* New York: Holt, Rinehart & Winston, 1947.

Pettigrew, T. F. The measurement and correlates of category width as a cognitive variable. *Journal of Personality,* 1958, *26,* 532–544.

Pettigrew, T. F. Social evaluation theory: Convergences and applications. In D. Levine (Ed.), *Nebraska Symposium on Motivation, 1967.* Lincoln, Neb.: University of Nebraska Press, 1967.

Pettigrew, T. F. *Racially separate or together?* New York: McGraw-Hill, 1971.

Pettigrew, T. F. (Ed.), *Racial discrimination in the United States.* New York: Harper & Row, 1975.

Pettigrew, T. F. Three issues in ethnicity: Boundaries, deprivations, and perceptions. In M. Yinger and R. Cutler (Eds.), *Modern social issues.* New York: Basic Books, 1978.

Pettigrew, T. F. The ultimate attribution error: Extending Allport's cognitive analysis of prejudice. *Personality and Social Psychology Bulletin,* 1979, *5,* 461–476.

Pettigrew, T. F. Social psychology's potential contributions to an understanding of poverty. In V. T. Covello (Ed.), *Poverty and Public Policy: An Evaluation of Social Science Research.* Boston: Hall, 1980(a).

Pettigrew, T. F. (Ed.), *The sociology of race relations: Reflection and reform.* New York: Free Press, 1980(b).

Pettigrew, T. F. *New patterns of racism: American race relations since the 1960s.* Cambridge, Mass.: Harvard University Press, in press.

Pettigrew, T. F., Jemmott, J., & Johnson, J. *The questioner effect: Testing the ultimate attribution error.* Manuscript in preparation, University of California, Santa Cruz, 1980.

Riley, R. T., & Pettigrew, T. Dramatic events and attitude change. *Journal of Personality and Social Psychology,* 1976, *34,* 1004–1015.

Rosch, E. Universals and cultural specifics in human categorization. In R. Brislin, S. Bochner, & W. Lonner (Eds.), *Cross-cultural perspectives on learning.* New York: Halsted Press, 1975.

Rosch, E. Human categorization. In N. Warren (Ed.), *Advances in cross-cultural psychology* (Vol. 1). London: Academic Press, 1977.

Ross, L. D., Amabile, T. M., & Steinmetz, J. L. Social roles, social control, and biases in social-perception processes. *Journal of Personality and Social Psychology*, 1977, *35*, 485–494.

Saenger, G., & Flowerman, S. Stereotype and prejudicial attitudes. *Human Relations*, 1954, *7*, 217–238.

Sherif, M., & Hovland, C. I. *Social judgment, assimilation and contrast effects in communication and attitude change*. New Haven, Conn.: Yale University Press, 1961.

Spector, M., & Kitsuse, J. I. *Constructing social problems*. Menlo Park, Calif: Cummings, 1977.

Steiner, I. D. Whatever happened to the group in social psychology? *Journal of Experimental Social Psychology*, 1974, *10*, 94–108.

Tajfel, H. Cognitive aspects of prejudice. *Journal of Social Issues*, 1969, *25*(4), 79–97.

Taylor, D. G., Sheatsley, P. B., & Greeley, A. M. Attitudes toward racial integration. *Scientific American*, June 1978, *238*, 42–49.

Thomas, W. I. The mind of woman and the lower races. *American Journal of Sociology*, 1907, *12*, 435–469 (reprinted in part in Pettigrew, 1980b).

Word, C. O., Zanna, H. P., & Cooper, J. The nonverbal mediation of self-fulfilling prophecies in interracial interaction. *Journal of Experimental Social Psychology*, 1974, *10*, 109–120.

10

Stereotyping and Intergroup Behavior: Some Thoughts on the Cognitive Approach

David L. Hamilton
University of California, Santa Barbara

The social psychological study of stereotyping and intergroup behavior has had a somewhat unusual place in the history of this discipline. Whereas most of the "traditionally important" topics in social psychology are concerned with *processes* (e.g., attitude change, interpersonal attraction, impression formation, conformity, bargaining), research on stereotyping and intergroup behavior has focused on the effects of ethnicity as a *stimulus* variable, merely noting the consequences of this stimulus property for various outcome measures. Although this distinction is perhaps a bit overdrawn, it is not difficult to cite instances in the research literature that lend some validity to this view. For example, whereas most research on person perception has been concerned with the processes by which a perceiver combines and integrates disparate pieces of information about a target person in making judgments of that person (Hamilton, 1980), studies of stereotypes have focused largely on the content of subjects' stereotypic conceptions of various racial, religious, and national groups (cf. Brigham, 1971, for a review). Similarly, whereas research on attitude change has studied the processes mediating the effects of such variables as communicator characteristics, message characteristics, and recipient's prior beliefs on subsequent attitudes, studies of intergroup attitudes have been primarily concerned with the effects of one situational variable—whether or not the setting provides for intergroup contact—on attitude change, with little direct attention aimed at examining possible mediating processes (Amir, 1976; Rose, Chapter 8, this volume). Thus, there has been a failure to recognize the inherent interrelationship between the study of stereotyping and intergroup behavior and the investigation of basic social psychological processes. Rather, the tendency has been to consider sex, race, and ethnicity as "special topics" within the field. The unfortunate consequence is that research on these topics has become somewhat divorced from research and theorizing in mainstream social psychology.

The chapters comprising this volume represent a departure from this trend. The research discussed by these authors reflects the most current developments in social cognition research in general, and the effects of cognitive structures on social information processing in particular, and applies this framework to an understanding of intergroup perception and interaction. As such, the findings reported in these chapters simultaneously increase both our knowledge of basic cognitive processes and our understanding of issues of considerable social significance. In this regard, the present volume is somewhat unique, for although a number of recent books have addressed the remarkable explosion of interest in social cognition that has occurred in the last few years (Hastie, Ostrom, Ebbesen, Wyer, Hamilton, & Carlston, 1980; Higgins, Herman, & Zanna, 1981; Nisbett & Ross, 1980; Wyer & Carlston, 1979), this is the first instance in which this orientation has been applied to a single social issue. Hopefully, this kind of integrative analysis will become more common in the future.

In the preceding chapter Pettigrew has discussed these contributions in the context of their place within the broader frameworks of social psychology as a discipline and of previous research on intergroup relations. In this chapter I comment more specifically on the cognitive orientation reflected in this volume, offering some views on the recent developments in this approach and noting some potentially useful avenues for further investigation.

THE COGNITIVE APPROACH IN HISTORICAL PERSPECTIVE

Although the research summarized in this volume represents the most current advances in this area of investigation, the conceptual orientation underlying this work is not new. As Ashmore and Del Boca pointed out in Chapter 1, recognition of the important role of cognitive mediators in stereotyping and intergroup interaction can be traced at least as far back as Lippmann (1922). Certainly Gordon Allport, in his classic book *The Nature of Prejudice* (Allport, 1954), stressed the importance of categorization and other cognitive processes in understanding perceptions of outgroups. In the following years papers by Campbell (1956, 1967), Secord (1959), Tajfel (1969), Vinacke (1957), and others periodically offered restatements of the cognitive viewpoint. Yet despite its long history, it is also clear that this approach has experienced considerable development in recent years. As the chapters comprising this volume indicate, there was a flurry of activity during the 1970s in which this approach was more richly articulated and more broadly extended than ever before. And the research stimulated by these developments has provided a solid empirical base for many of the postulates of the cognitive viewpoint, as is well documented in the diverse array of findings reported in the preceding chapters.

What factors account for this dramatic increase of interest in the cognitive determinants and mediators of intergroup perception and interaction? A number of contributing factors can be identified, but I think two are of utmost importance, one being contextual and one being specific to the substantive domain.

As Pettigrew (Chapter 9) observes, the contributors to this volume (and other contemporary researchers investigating the cognitive bases of stereotyping and intergroup behavior) come primarily from a background in mainstream experimental social psychology. As such, they come from an ideological tradition, the Zeitgeist of which has become, over the past two decades, progressively more cognitive in its focus. From its origins in the work of its founder, Kurt Lewin, experimental social psychology has attached considerable importance to theorizing about and the investigation of cognitive mediating processes. Moreover, the revolution that occurred in cognitive psychology during the late 1960s and early 1970s had, by the mid-1970s, begun to have an impact on cognitively oriented social psychologists. Both the theoretical concepts and the research methodologies of cognitive psychology were applied by these investigators in their efforts to understand the cognitive processes underlying phenomena of social psychological interest, and the term "social cognition" emerged to refer to research at the intersection of these two subdisciplines. Whereas social psychological theories had always posited cognitive mediators in explaining the phenomena of interest (e.g., attitude change, attraction, impression formation), now the emphasis shifted to the direct investigation of those cognitive processes. For the researcher with substantive interests in stereotyping and intergroup behavior, the application and extension of the cognitive psychologists' concepts and research tools to identifying and studying the cognitive foundations of these phenomena was a natural step. That this effort has been fruitful is documented in the preceding chapters.

The more specific catalyst for the resurgence of interest in a cognitive approach to this domain is found, I believe, in the work of Henri Tajfel. In a series of studies conducted during the 1960s, Tajfel and his colleagues (Tajfel, 1969, 1970; Tajfel, Billig, Bundy, & Flament, 1971; Tajfel, Sheikh, & Gardner, 1964; Tajfel & Wilkes, 1963) demonstrated that the mere categorizations of persons into ingroup and outgroup can have dramatic consequences at both the perceptual and behavioral level. Such differentiation itself can produce accentuated perceptions of within-group similarity and between-group dissimilarity and can lead to behavioral preference for ingroup members and discrimination against outgroup members. These experiments have stimulated a considerable amount of research by others on ingroup–outgroup differentiation (see Brewer, 1979b, for a review of this literature) and hence are important in their own right. For the present discussion, however, they are important for another reason. What this work demonstrated is that judgmental and behavioral phenomena reflecting the differential perception of and response to ingroup and outgroup members can be the consequence of categorization processes alone and need not reflect preexisting prejudicial attitudes or motivated self-interest. That is, the discriminatory behavior evidenced by Tajfel's subjects occurred in the absence of conditions typically thought to underlie intergroup discrimination—prior hostile attitudes toward the outgroup, intergroup competition, opportunity for personal gain as a result of discriminatory behavior, and so forth.

These findings suggested the more general principle that, at least under some circumstances, aspects of our cognitive functioning may, by themselves, constitute the bases for stereotyping and intergroup discrimination. And indeed, within a few years research drawing on a number of cognitive principles had been reported by several authors providing evidence in support of this viewpoint (Hamilton & Gifford, 1976; Langer, Taylor, Fiske, & Chanowitz, 1976; Rothbart, Fulero, Jensen, Howard, & Birrell, 1978; Taylor, Fiske, Close, Anderson, & Ruderman, 1975). Simultaneously, evidence began to appear indicating that stereotypes, as cognitive structures, can influence how information about group members is processed and its implications for interpersonal behavior (Hamilton, 1977; Rothbart, Evans, & Fulero, 1979; Snyder, Tanke, & Berscheid, 1977; Word, Zanna, & Cooper, 1974). Thus the notion suggested by Tajfel's experiments—that the judgmental and behavioral phenomena from which stereotypic beliefs and prejudicial attitudes are typically inferred can occur as manifestations of our normal cognitive functioning—soon received considerable empirical support.

SOME UNRESOLVED ISSUES FOR THE COGNITIVE APPROACH

The research reported by the contributors to this volume provides an impressive body of findings regarding the role of cognitive processes in stereotyping and intergroup interaction. Hopefully this collection of chapters will stimulate other researchers to extend these lines of investigation, as well as to determine the limitations of and boundary conditions on the phenomena described by the present authors. In this section I offer a few thoughts and speculations regarding some of the implications of the findings that have been reported and suggest some possible avenues of inquiry that may be fruitful.

The Nature of Stereotypic Concepts

As Ashmore and Del Boca (Chapter 1) have discussed, the concept of stereotype has been defined in a variety of ways by social scientists, various authors including different properties of stereotypes in their definitions. Most researchers who adopt a cognitive perspective would at least be comfortable with Ashmore and Del Boca's definition of a stereotype as "a set of beliefs about the personal attributes of a group of people" and would regard questions concerning the validity, appropriateness, and rigidity of those beliefs as empirical issues to be investigated rather than as defining properties of the construct.

Research on stereotypes has focused almost exclusively on the first part of this definitional statement, that is, on the nature of the beliefs comprising one's stereotype of a particular group. An important theme that emerges from several of these chapters is that the latter part of this statement also deserves attention. Specifically, if we are to understand the nature of stereotypes as they are held and used by perceivers, we also need to consider the "group of people" to which those beliefs are applied by the observer. Traditionally, researchers have investigated their subjects' stereotypic beliefs about very large classes of people—about blacks and whites, about women and men, etc. Findings reported by both Ashmore (Chapter 2) and Taylor (Chapter 3) suggest that, at least for some purposes, such classifications may represent categories of persons that are too broad to capture adequately the actual nature of perceivers' conceptions of these groups. The results of Ashmore's hierarchical clustering analyses indicated that, although subjects' conceptions of males and females could be clearly differentiated (in terms of hard-minded versus softhearted characteristics), meaningful subgroups of males and females were clearly evident in the cognitive structures of these subjects. These subgroups were often characterized by quite different patterns of attributes. For example, in one analysis, female perceivers differentiated between two types of women, one of which was characterized as weak, excitable, temperamental, nervous, and confused, whereas another subgroup was described as poised, idealistic, cautious, and tactful. These same subjects distinguished between men who are conservative, formal, and unemotional and those they perceived as vain, reckless, mischievous, and loud. Given that subjects make such clear distinctions among subcategories of females and males, one might question the extent to which the more generalized characterizations of women and men accurately represent their stereotypic conceptions of these groups.

A similar argument has been made by Taylor (Chapter 3). Her research has shown that as the race or sex composition of a group becomes increasingly unbalanced, the perceived contribution or impact of a minority person on the group discussion increases. For example, the "solo" black was seen as having played a more significant role in the group process than was the same stimulus person (i.e., same person in the stimulus slides, same voice on the tape) in a racially balanced group. Taylor reports that subjects' evaluations of a stimulus person on stereotypic traits did not vary strongly with the manipulation of group composition but that their characterizations of that person's role in the group did. Moreover, their descriptions of these minority persons reflected differentiated conceptions of subtypes within the broader race and gender categories. Taylor argues that for groups with whom the perceiver has some familiarity the most significant amount of stereotyping occurs at this subtype level—that females will be perceived not in terms of a set of traits comprising the stereotype of women in general, but rather in terms of one or another of the subcategories of females (e.g., motherly type, bitch, showgirl) that the perceiver has developed as a result of past experience. Stereotypes, then, are viewed as multilevel conceptions of groups, similar to current thinking about levels of categorization in object classification (Rosch, 1978). Taylor proposes that "males" and "females" are superordinate categories that, although generally distinguishable in terms of a number of properties, are too broad to be optimally useful. Nested within these superordinate categories are lower-order subcategories (possibly at several levels), which are more functional because of their greater articulation of objects (persons) within a category while still providing meaningful differentiations between different categories.

Evidence recently reported by Brewer (1979a) on stereotypes of the elderly converges nicely with this viewpoint. Brewer proposed that the category "old person" is a superordinate category, and that people have more meaningful stereotypes of several different subtypes of elderly persons (e.g., grandmotherly types, elder statesmen, senior citizens). To investigate this possibility, a set of 30 photographs of elderly persons was developed, 10 of which were selected by the researchers as representing each of the three subtypes just noted. These photographs were presented to subjects who were instructed to sort them into categories as they thought appropriate. A free-sort cluster analysis that compares the obtained clustering with an a priori classification scheme indicated that the subjects' sortings conformed significantly with the researchers' prespecified categories. Thus, the subjects did not perceive the stimulus photographs simply as a sample of "old people" but rather as three meaningful subgroups of elderly persons. The next step in the research was to determine whether distinct stereotypic conceptions were associated with these subgroups. In this study, subjects were shown a subset of three photographs and were asked to indicate, on an adjective checklist, which attributes the three persons had in common. Some subjects were shown three photographs selected from a single cluster, whereas others were shown a set containing one photograph from each of the three subgroups. Subjects who judged the categorically homogeneous sets checked significantly more traits as characteristic of all three persons than did those shown the heterogeneous sets, and there was more consensus in the traits assigned among subjects in the former group. In addition, there was considerable agreement in the traits checked for two different sets of photographs selected from the same cluster, but little overlap in attributes checked for sets representing different clusters. Thus the clusters of photographs correspond to psychologically meaningful categories in subjects' conceptions of elderly persons. Compared to their judgments of the heterogeneous sets (representing "old people in general''), subjects' stereotypes of the three subgroups were fairly well articulated and clearly differentiated from each other. Cantor and Mischel (1979) report similar findings regarding subjects' conceptions of certain personality types.

Conceptualizing stereotypes as multilevel conceptions of groups, and recognizing that stereotyping can occur at any of these levels, would seem to represent a significant advance in our thinking about the nature of stereotypes. If perceivers, in processing information about members of some broad class of persons (blacks, women, old people), have and use well-differentiated subordinate categories corresponding to subgroups of individuals, a researcher's analyses based on measures reflecting only the superordinate categories would likely lead to inappropriate conclusions about the nature of the subjects' stereotypes and the extent to which stereotyping has occurred. In addition, one's interpersonal interactions with an outgroup member are likely to differ depending on the particular subgroup that person is perceived as belonging to. Thus it becomes important to know not only one's beliefs about the superordinate categories used in classifying persons into broad groups, but also the nature of the subordinate level categories in one's cognitive structure, the beliefs associated with each one, and the degree of differentiation among them. Future research on stereotyping, perhaps drawing further from the cognitive literature on levels of categorization, will need to pursue these issues.

This view of stereotypic concepts does not imply that *all* stereotyping occurs at subordinate levels of categorization that differentiate among various subtypes of members of the broader groups that have traditionally been the focus of investigation. Certainly, in the case of outgroups for whom one has little knowledge or experience, analyses at the superordinate level at appropriate, if only because the perceiver does not have a basis for making differentiations among subcategories of that group. For most Americans, Belgians are Belgians, and even though some may know that there are two important and distinct subpopulations in Belgium (Flemish-speaking and French-speaking), most of us do not have sufficient familiarity with these subgroups to have well-articulated and differentiated stereotypic conceptions of them. In such cases stereotyping would take place at the superordinate level, occurring in a diffuse, undifferentiated manner, assuming common characteristics shared by members of a large class of persons. As one becomes increasingly familiar with members of the group, through information acquired about them and/or from first-hand experiences, differentiations among subgroups of individuals would presumably become apparent, resulting in the development of subordinate level categories. Conceivably this process could continue for several levels, to the point that each of several subtypes consists of a relatively small, homogeneous group of persons. Obviously, the process by which such multilevel structures emerge, and the determinants of differentiations among subcategories, is an important avenue for future research. The need for developmental research on these issues is also apparent.

Difficulties of Disconfirmation, and Other Problems of Change

A second theme that recurs throughout this volume concerns the role of cognitive processes in the maintenance and change of stereotypic beliefs. The cognitive biases evidenced in several of these research programs converge toward the same outcome; for the most part, their effect is to perpetuate preexisting beliefs and to reduce their openness to change. Findings reported by Hamilton (Chapter 4) and Rothbart (Chapter 5) indicate that stereotypic expectancies can influence how new information about group members is processed, such that prior beliefs are maintained in the face of nonconfirming information. Snyder's research (Chapter 6) documents that stereotypic beliefs can influence one's interactions with another person, resulting in the behavioral confirmation of those expectancies. And Rose (Chapter 8) discusses a variety of processes that could affect interactions between members of different groups, most of which would create the conditions for the maintenance of prior expectancies and undermine the potentially beneficial effects of intergroup contact.

Given these findings, the question immediately arises, how can these biasing effects be overcome? The answer to this question remains elusive. One would have to concede that researchers in this tradition have been more successful in demonstrating the existence of such biases than in uncovering means of counteracting them. One of the difficulties is that we are dealing with cognitive processes that are, for the most part, useful to the individual in coping with and adapting to a complex stimulus world. The mechanisms that produce these biases presumably are highly functional in many contexts. The problem, then, is to find means of altering or circumventing, in one circumstance, processes that have become habitual because of their adaptive value in many other circumstances. In view of the significance, both theoretical and practical, of the issue, the need for research on this topic is obvious. In the following comments I highlight some of the points made by the contributors that might facilitate future thinking on this problem.

Let us begin by considering the levels of categorization view of social stereotypes discussed in the preceding section. According to this perspective, increased knowledge of and familiarity with a group results in the fragmenting of a global stereotype of that group into differentiated conceptions of subgroups, such that stereotyping would most commonly occur with regard to smaller, more homogeneous categories of persons. Presumably, as one continues to acquire information about group (and subgroup) members, this process can result in the differentiation of more and more subgroups at a particular level, and perhaps additional levels of subgroups within subgroups. As Taylor (Chapter 3) points out, disconfirmation of stereotypic concepts thus becomes difficult, for any particular individual can be perceived as belonging to one or another subcategory (or, if not, a new subtype can be established). If stereotyping involves the attribution of psychological characteristics to human groups (Tajfel, 1969), then the total amount of stereotyping has not been reduced. Persons are still being categorized into (sub)groups, and all the consequences of the categorization process for intergroup perception, discussed by Taylor (Chapter 3) and Wilder (Chapter 7), would still hold. The stereotyping is simply occurring with regard to smaller groupings of persons.

But it is important to recognize the significance of the changes that result from this process. To change from stereotyping in terms of gross categorizations of persons (females versus males, blacks versus whites, etc.) to a reliance on more specific subtypes of group members is not a trivial difference. One of the primary characteristics of stereotypic beliefs, noted by many authors (see Ashmore & Del Boca, Chapter 1), is that they represent gross overgeneralizations applied to all members of a social category. To the extent that one makes meaningful differentiations among subgroups within a larger class of persons, then one's statements about members of a subtype will constitute less sweeping characterizations. For example, to say that career women are characterized by attributes A, B, and C whereas housewives are X, Y, and Z still constitutes stereotyping, and such descriptions are still overgeneralizations (in that, for example, not all housewives are Xish), but the number and diversity of individuals assumed to possess a certain trait is greatly reduced in comparison to more traditional assumptions that all members of the superordinate category (i.e., women) are the same. Moreover, assuming that many of the subordinate differentiations have at least some basis in reality, the degree of inaccuracy of stereotypic statements at this level will be less than that of comparable statements at the superordinate level. So there seems to be some gain as the perceiver moves to lower levels of categorization in construing others in terms of their group memberships. The limiting case of this process, of course, would be when each individual is seen as unique and hence is not categorized with others at all. Although there certainly are contexts in which such individuality is maintained in processing information about others, for many purposes this is cognitively unfeasible, and conceptually grouping others into categories is virtually necessary (Cantor & Mischel, 1979).

According to the levels of categorization view, conceptualization will be most likely to occur at a level for which (1) the categories at that level are richly articulated (i.e., the objects in any given category share a number of attributes in common), and (2) the categories at that level are meaningfully differentiated (i.e., objects in different categories do not share a large number of attributes in common). If stereotyping can occur at any of several levels of categorization, and if it is preferable that people's conceptions of groups reflect a heterogeneous set of subtypes within any global group categorization, then the question becomes, how can we get perceivers to develop and use subordinate levels of classification in processing information about others? This is an issue about which we can do little more than speculate, but any means of "breaking down" the categories currently used by a perceiver would serve this end. Wilder (Chapter 7) reports research showing that individuation of outgroup members can highlight their heterogeneity, thereby overcoming the assumed similarity of outgroup members and hence lead to reductions in ingroup/outgroup bias. Increased familiarity with members of a stereotyped group would also provide a basis for recognizing that they don't all share the same attributes, and thus lead to differentiations among subtypes. Additional research on methods of inducing persons to establish subordinate levels of more specific categorizations is needed. Once such methods can be identified, their effectiveness in changing the nature and, in particular, the consequences of one's stereotypes can be evaluated.

An alternative to breaking down existing conceptual categories is to change the attribute on which the perceiver's categorization of others is based. Any individual is a member of numerous "groups" according to which perceptions of him or her might be organized. For example, Tom is male, black, over 30, a college graduate, a salesman, and lives in Atlanta. These "surface" characteristics alone provide several possible bases for categorization—one might construe Tom as part of the over–30 generation, or as a salesman, or as a southerner. But the typical perceiver would, of course, respond to Tom first as a black and, having categorized him as such, be sensitive to ways in which Tom differs from the perceiver's conception of whites and infer that Tom is likely to have a number of characteristics assumed to be shared by blacks. In other words, among the several available cues that might call up prototypes or be the basis for categorization, race would likely be dominant. If the perceiver could be induced to utilize other cues instead of (or at least in addition to) race, then the influence of racial stereotypes would be reduced. This would seem to be a difficult task in that the cues on which most major stereotypes are based (e.g., race, sex, age, etc.) are physically prominent and difficult for a perceiver to ignore. Nevertheless, Wilder (Chapter 7) cites some evidence indicating that ingroup/outgroup biases are somewhat reduced when multiple group memberships of the participants are apparent. In addition, results reported by Taylor (Chapter 3) suggest that androgynous persons do not use gender categories in encoding information about a mixed-sex group of stimulus persons, whereas sex-typed individuals do. Although these findings are largely suggestive, they do indicate that additional work on this problem may be fruitful.

Thus far in our discussion of changing stereotypic beliefs we have focused on the categorization process and how changes in it might alter the nature and use of one's stereotypes. The process of change—for example, breaking down a subordinate category into subtypes—would begin with the recognition that incoming stimulus information about a group member doesn't "fit" well with existing categories and the assumptions associated with them. However, research discussed by several authors in this volume (Hamilton, Chapter 4; Rothbart, Chapter 5; Wilder, Chapter 7; Rose, Chapter 8) indicates that information that disconfirms stereotypic expectancies does not have as much impact on prior beliefs as one might logically expect that it should. If disconfirming information about a group member is not construed as incongruent with existing conceptions of the group, the change process would not begin.

In discussing this issue, Rothbart (Chapter 5) distinguishes between two possible means by which disconfirming information might come to have an impact on stereotypic beliefs, which he calls the "bookkeeping" model and the "conversion" model. According to a bookkeeping model, the person would be viewed as a conscientious processor of information, weighing the balance of confirming and disconfirming evidence as it is progressively accumulated. As information incongruent with prior beliefs is acquired, the person presumably would make revisions in those beliefs accordingly, and if enough disconfirming evidence were accumulated, then a meaningful change in one's stereotypic expectations would gradually come about. In some ways, efforts to reduce prejudice through increased intergroup contact are based on this view of the change process: As one has more and more interaction with outgroup members, the invalidity of one's stereotypic beliefs will become increasingly apparent, and change in those beliefs and attitudes will follow. This is certainly a reasonable conception of how change occurs and is probably an accurate description for many circumstances. People do acquire and accumulate knowledge as a result of their experiences, and it would be surprising if that knowledge had no bearing on one's beliefs and attitudes. But this is a highly rational conception of the information processor, probably too much so. If there is a common theme running through the chapters of this volume, it is that our cognitive systems do not treat incoming information in such an equal-handed fashion. We are neither equally open to nor equally responsive to confirming and disconfirming information. As these research programs have shown, there are a number of obstacles that undermine the effectiveness of stereotypically incongruent information and result in its having less impact than it "ought" to have.

In addition to this "bookkeeping" view of belief change, Rothbart proposes a "conversion" model of the change process, a view "that change is more catastrophic than gradual, and that a few highly salient, critical instances play a dominant role in the disconfirmation process." This statement actually contains two interesting ideas. One is that under some conditions change does not occur gradually through successive revision of one's beliefs, based on the accumulation of information over time, but rather that there is an all-or-none character to the change process. The second is that change results from the differential impact of a small number of disconfirming instances, sufficiently dramatic and occurring in close temporal proximity so that their occurrence cannot easily be discounted.

Rothbart thus presents two quite different views of the change process. Both are quite plausible, and both probably have some degree of validity. The contrast between them, however, is interesting when one considers the accumulated research on the disconfirmation of stereotypic beliefs. Most of this research implicitly seems to adopt the "bookkeeping" view of how change is likely to be brought about. In laboratory experiments, subjects are typically given a series of stimulus items about a person or members of a group, a subset of which contains information incongruent with stereotypic expectations. In field studies it is assumed that, over time, interactions with outgroup members will provide some experiences that disconfirm one's prior beliefs. In both settings it is presumed that those disconfirming instances will lead to revisions in one's stereotypic beliefs or intergroup attitudes.

In contrast, it is difficult to find reports of research designed to evaluate the conversion view of the change process. Two recent papers, however, are suggestive. Riley and Pettigrew (1976) reported two studies in which survey data were analyzed to determine the impact of a single, dramatic event on racial attitudes. In one case, for example, surveys conducted in Texas over a period of several months in 1968 revealed a favorable shift in racial attitudes immediately following the assassination of Martin Luther King, Jr., a change that was not evident over a comparable period prior to the assassination and that remained stable for several months thereafter. Although the amount of attitude change observed in these data would not qualify as evidence for a "conversion" process, these findings do indicate that a single, highly salient incident can have a strong impact on long-term attitudes.

A second, quite different, finding relevant to this question comes from a laboratory experiment reported by Gurwitz and Dodge (1977). Subjects in this study read information about three females, all of whom were members of the same sorority. For some subjects, the material presented contained items of information incongruent with the prevailing stereotype of sorority members. In one condition, each of the three descriptions included one disconfirming item, whereas in another condition all three disconfirming items described one of the women. The subjects' task was to make a number of inferences about a fourth woman who belonged to the same sorority. Subjects made less stereotypic inferences about the target person when the disconfirming items all described one person, instead of being dispersed throughout the three descriptions. This intriguing result can be viewed as consistent with Rothbart's suggestion that disconfirming information will have more impact when it occurs in a condensed form that will make its incongruency more salient. It is also consistent with Wilder's (Chapter 7) proposal that reducing the perceived homogeneity of a group's members will result in a reduction in stereotyping.

The problem of how to change stereotypic beliefs and prejudicial attitudes has been a persisting dilemma throughout the history of research on intergroup relations. Similarly, the problem of understanding the differential processing of confirming and disconfirming information has been a difficult task for social cognition researchers (Hastie, 1981). Both problems are destined to continue to be foci of research attention in the future. The bookkeeping and conversion views of the change process represent quite different approaches to implementing change, and determining the circumstances under which each is likely to be effective remains an important avenue of investigation in increasing our understanding of the change process.

Group Stereotypes and Interactions With Individuals

There is an interesting dichotomy in the research literature on intergroup relations that warrants further attention. The extensive literature on stereotypes has, for the most part, been concerned with people's conceptions of *groups*. This work has focused on the attributes assumed to be characteristic of persons belonging to various groups, the persistence of those beliefs over time, and their resistance to new information (Brigham, 1971; Ehrlich, 1973; Hamilton, 1979). A second body of research has investigated the behavior of majority group persons in interaction with *individuals* who belong to a minority group. For example, studies of interracial interactions (Dutton, 1976; Gaertner, 1976; Katz, 1970) document the differential responses of whites in interaction with black and white others.

There is an implicit assumption that the phenomena investigated in each domain have implications for the phenomena studied in the other domain. That is, it is assumed that the nature of one's stereotypic beliefs about a *group* will influence one's judgments of and behavior towards *individual* members of that group, and correspondingly, that one's interactions with outgroup members ought to have some bearing on one's perceptions of and beliefs about that group. But the nature and extent of these influences remain unclear.

Consider the latter relationship first, that one's interactions with members of a stereotyped group will influence one's stereotypic beliefs about the group as a whole. Certainly the movement toward desegregation has been based, at least in part, on this assumption, and it is doubtful that the sizable changes in racial and sex role attitudes that have occurred in the last two decades would have come about if there were not some validity to this view. Still, it is not uncommon for a person to have reasonably good relationships with certain blacks, for example, as friends or coworkers, while still maintaining predominantly negative attitudes toward blacks as a group. And the accumulated research on the effects of intergroup contact has led some (Amir, 1976) to question how widespread such effects are likely to be. Impressive findings of change in intergroup attitudes following contact are occasionally countered by findings of no change, and perhaps more frequently by results indicating that the changed attitudes are limited to certain members of the outgroup, to certain types of interaction, or to certain settings. In the literature on interracial contact there has been considerable discussion (Allport, 1954; Ashmore, 1970) of the conditions under which interactions with individual members of an outgroup will have an impact on one's generalized beliefs about that group as a whole. A remaining problem for the cognitive viewpoint is the determination of how the qualifying conditions influence cognitive mediators such that change in one's stereotypic beliefs occurs under some conditions, but not under others.

What about the opposite relationship, the influence of stereotypic beliefs on one's judgments of and interactions with a member of the stereotyped group? Certainly one of the major advances in stereotyping research during the last decade has been the demonstration that stereotypes influence such diverse processes as the interpretation of an outgroup member's behavior (Duncan, 1976), one's causal attributions for the person's behavior (Deaux, 1976; Wilder, Chapter 7), the retention of information about group members (Cohen, 1977; Hamilton, Chapter 4; Rothbart, Chapter 5) and one's own behavior in interaction with an outgroup member (Snyder, Chapter 6; Word et al., 1974). And interestingly, Rose's (Chapter 8) analysis of why intergroup contacts and interactions might not alter stereotypic beliefs and attitudes focuses on the effects of those stereotypes on the interaction itself.

Despite this impressive array of findings, the picture is not entirely clear here, either. For example, Mann (1967) reported finding numerous inconsistencies between subjects' attributions of traits to a stereotyped group and their attribution of those same traits to a randomly selected member of the group about whom subjects had no additional information. In other words, attributes assumed to be characteristic of the group were not necessarily assumed to be characteristic of the individual. In a similar vein, Locksley, Borgida, Brekke, and Hepburn (1980) found that stereotypic beliefs (e.g., that males are more assertive than females) may have little influence on judgments of an individual when relevant behavioral information is available. When subjects were provided with just one behavioral episode demonstrating assertive behavior, male and female target persons were rated equivalently on this dimension. In this case, then, subjects' prior beliefs had little impact on their judgments of an individual stimulus person.

Stereotypes are generalized conceptions of groups. When one learns about or interacts with a member of that group, one develops a conception of that individual person, with his or her group membership being a potential ingredient of that impression or representation of the person. The question then becomes, how are conceptions of groups linked to conceptions of individuals belonging to those groups? As noted earlier, recent stereotyping research has enlightened us a good deal regarding how group concepts have a bearing on one's conception of and behavior toward an individual, although the Mann and Locksley et al. findings indicate that our understanding of the mediating processes is not complete. Even less is known about how one's conceptions of individuals, derived from personal experiences, feed into one's conception of the groups of which those individuals are a part.

The Role of Affect in a Cognitive Approach

The cognitive orientation emphasized in this volume focuses on the information-processing mechanisms by which knowledge and beliefs are acquired and utilized by the human judge. As a consequence, the person portrayed by this approach is one who is actively coping with incoming stimuli, continually attending to, encoding, and interpreting information, representing it in knowledge structures, and retrieving it from memory. As we have seen throughout these pages, the processes employed may not always resemble "optimal" information processing, and the person's judgments and behavior may reflect the consequences of the biases inherent in one's cognitive system. But the person is seen as one who is adapting to a complex stimulus world through the use of cognitive mechanisms and strategies that have proved to be functional in the past.

This approach, then, gives us a view of a thinking, cognizing person, but not of a feeling person. Yet if there is any domain of human interaction that history tells us is laden with strong, even passionate, feelings, it is in the area of intergroup relations. And this point makes clear the fact that the cognitive approach, despite the rich and varied advances that it has made in recent years, is by itself incomplete. This assertion certainly is not surprising, even for the cognitively oriented researcher, for it has never been in doubt. Nor does it undermine the usefulness of a single-minded pursuit of a particular point of view. Pushing the cognitive (or any other) approach as far as it can go, to determine both its potentialities and its limits, is a worthwhile enterprise, as is clearly documented in the work of the present contributors. I believe, however, that we are now at a point where integrative efforts toward determining the relationship between the cognitive and affective domains are appropriate and, in fact, will become of increasing importance.

How this integration is to be achieved is unclear and in this discussion I provide no solutions to what I believe will be a complex and challenging problem (see Fiske, in press, for a more extended discussion of this topic). I merely offer some thoughts on two aspects of this issue that suggest potentially useful approaches one might take to investigating this question. In discussing these two approaches, it is useful to differentiate between two possible conceptions of what "affect" might mean when viewed within a cognitive framework. First, we might consider the role of the person's *affective state* in processing information and think about how differences in amount of affect or emotional involvement might influence the various cognitive processes that have been studied by researchers in this tradition. Second, we might consider one's *affective response* to the information received, and think about how that affective component is processed and represented in relation to the cognitive component of one's response.

As Ashmore and Del Boca indicated in Chapter 1, there is a large body of literature that emphasizes the need-fulfilling functions of stereotypic beliefs and prejudicial attitudes. In this orientation these beliefs and attitudes are viewed in terms of their role in the overall personality functioning of the individual. Consequently the focus of this work has been on individual differences and the relationship of personality variables to prejudice and discrimination (Ashmore & Del Boca, 1976). Yet it seems highly likely that these relationships are mediated by the effect of such variables—whether they be transient affective or need states, or more stable personality characteristics—on the cognitive processes of interest to social cognition researchers. What influence do these variables have on selective attention to stimuli and on which stimuli are salient to the observer? on the categorization process in perceiving others? on how information about group members is organized and represented in memory? on the retention and retrieval of information about group members? Recently, research relevant to some of these questions has been reported. For example, Wilder (Chapter 7) has investigated the effects of certain perceiver characteristics (e.g., arousal) on the categorization process, and there is a growing number of studies concerned with the effects of mood state and affective involvement on memory (Bower, Monteiro, & Gilligan, 1978; Dutta, Kanungo, & Freibergs, 1972; Isen, Shalker, Clark, & Karp, 1978). Still, we have only begun to investigate the complexities of these processes. The answers to the questions posed above not only would be of interest in their own right but also would increase our knowledge of the mechanisms by which these "noncognitive" variables have their influence on important outcome variables, such as one's judgments of and behavior toward outgroup members.

A second approach to integrating the cognitive and affective domains considers affect not as an independent variable but as a component of one's response to incoming information about a person or group. In this sense, affect refers primarily to one's evaluation of (or affective response to) the object or objects to which the acquired information pertains. The question at issue concerns the relationship between one's cognitive representation of information about a person or group (e.g., what is retained in memory) and one's evaluative response to (e.g., one's judgment of) that person or group. Our ability to evaluate this question, however, is limited by the fact that surprisingly few studies have included both cognitive and affective measures among their dependent variables.

Intuitively it seems plausible that there would be strong linkages between these cognitive and affective components, and that each might have some effect on the other. For example, strong preexisting evaluative opinions about a group may influence the processing of information about members of that group—what aspects of the information are attended to, how it is organized in memory, what and how much is retained, and so forth. Likewise, it seems reasonable to assume that the way in which information about persons or groups is represented in memory would have considerable bearing on one's subsequent judgments of those target persons. These considerations suggest that measures of cognitive variables and measures of affective variables ought to show somewhat parallel patterns of results. Evidence to this effect is in fact available from a few studies. For example, Hamilton and Gifford (1976; see Hamilton, Chapter 4) found that an illusory correlation bias in processing information about members of two groups had similar influences on measures of retrieval of information from memory (i.e., memory for group memberships, frequency estimates) and on measures reflecting affective reactions (evaluative trait ratings). And Reyes, Thompson, and Bower (1980) reported that manipulation of the vividness of the information describing a person both increased subjects' recall of that information and influenced subsequent judgments of the stimulus person. These findings are consistent with the view that the cognitive and affective components are strongly related to each other—either because one's affective response will influence the cognitive processing of information, or because one's affective response is based on the cognitive representation of the processed information, or both.

However, there are a number of findings that are unsettling for this point of view. In the impression-formation literature, for example, studies have found different primacy/recency functions for recall and evaluative judgments (Anderson & Hubert, 1963; Dreben, Fiske, & Hastie, 1979; Riskey, 1979). In the attribution literature, certain manipulations that consistently produce strong attribution effects appear to have little influence on recall measures (McArthur, 1981; Taylor & Fiske, 1978). And in a recent paper Zajonc (1980) argues specifically against the view that evaluative judgments follow from a cognitive analysis of stimulus characteristics. He proposes that affective judgments are primary, immediate, and in many cases independent of cognitive processing of information, and he cites a variety of findings that are consistent with his argument.

It may be, however, that the issue is more complicated than is suggested by the preceding discussion. In most of these studies, evaluations of a stimulus person were examined in relation to one's recall of the stimulus information describing that person. But as information processors we are cognitively quite active. In addition to "taking in" some portion of the information presented, we elaborate on that information, draw inferences from it, and use these processes to develop organized cognitive representations of persons or groups (Hamilton, 1981). Moreover, these self-generated cognitions would seemingly play a role in shaping our evaluations of target persons or groups. If so, then evidence regarding the relationship of evaluative judgments to memory for the stimulus information alone may underestimate the extent to which the cognitive and affective domains are actually linked.

Several studies provide evidence supporting this view. For example, Jaccard and Fishbein (1975) have shown that evaluative ratings of a stimulus person can be predicted more accurately from the stimulus information provided *and* the inferences about the person one makes on the basis of that information than from the stimulus information alone. Similarly, in attitude research Greenwald (1968) has found that opinion measures, taken after subjects read a persuasive communication, were predicted more accurately by the subjects' self-generated cognitions while reading the communication than by their retention of the communication content. And findings reported by Ostrom, Lingle, Pryor, and Geva (1980) suggest that the cognitive representation a perceiver forms in making a judgment of a stimulus person is used as the basis for subsequent evaluative judgments, and not the stimulus information on which that impression was originally based. The results of these studies indicate, once again, that greater attention to cognitive mediating processes is called for.

The general question of the relationship between the cognitive processing and representation of the information contained in a stimulus and one's evaluative or affective response to that stimulus is certain to be a continuing issue in the social cognition literature. The cognitive and affective domains are clearly linked in important ways, but the nature and extent of those relationships remain unknown. Findings from future research on this issue will have important implications for our understanding of people's conceptions of and interactions with members of stereotyped groups.

TOWARD CONCEPTUAL INTEGRATION

The goal of this book has been to present a current statement of the cognitive approach to the investigation of stereotyping and intergroup behavior. We have brought together some of the major contemporary contributors to this orientation and provided them the opportunity to present their research in an integrated, programmatic fashion and to discuss their findings in the context of earlier work in this tradition. The final two chapters have discussed these contributions in the framework of the broader literature on intergroup relations and with a view to remaining, unresolved issues. The present volume, then, should be considered a "progress report"—a statement of the current status of the cognitive viewpoint, in terms of its conceptual developments and its empirical foundations. We trust that our knowledge of the cognitive underpinnings of these phenomena will continue to grow as other investigators extend the work of these authors, and we hope that the efforts represented in these pages will contribute to that further development of the cognitive viewpoint.

However, as Ashmore and Del Boca summarized in their introductory chapter, the cognitive approach is but one of three historically important orientations to the study of stereotyping and intergroup behavior. The sociocultural and psychodynamic approaches also have rich histories and have stimulated much of the research and theorizing in this field. These three perspectives are most appropriately viewed as complementary, rather than competing, approaches. Like the three apocryphal blind men describing an elephant, each orientation provides a partial understanding of the processes that underlie intergroup perceptions and interactions. Each one offers its own mediating constructs, each focuses attention on its own research questions, and each suggests its own strategies for action toward change. They provide partially overlapping, sometimes conflicting, but largely complementary explanations for a range of phenomena too diverse and complex for any one of them to account for thoroughly.

Recognition of this point suggests that our criteria for "further development of the cognitive viewpoint" ought to include not only the clarification of issues specific to this approach but also the extension of this viewpoint to its intersection with the sociocultural and psychodynamic perspectives. Points of contact between approaches should be identified and investigated. These points of contact should include areas where two approaches overlap or can be brought together, as well as issues where they "lock horns." This strategy offers several potential benefits for progress in this field. First, in order to investigate and compare two approaches to some issue, it is necessary that the respective positions on that issue be stated unambiguously and in researchable terms. Thus, this strategy can result in a more precise clarification of each of the individual orientations. Second, to the extent that such integrative and comparative efforts are successful, our knowledge and understanding of stereotyping and intergroup behavior will grow considerably. And finally, by identifying and empirically pursuing the intersections between approaches, we may establish the foundation from which a more integrated theoretical framework can emerge. We hope that the next "progress report" will be able to report significant advances in this direction.

ACKNOWLEDGMENT

Preparation of this chapter was supported in part by NIMH Grant 29418.

REFERENCES

Allport, G. W. *The nature of prejudice*. Reading, Mass.: Addison–Wesley, 1954.

Amir, Y. The role of intergroup contact in change of prejudice and intergroup relations. In P. A. Katz (Ed.), *Towards the elimination of racism*. New York: Pergamon Press, 1976.

Anderson, N. H., & Hubert, S. Effects of concomitant verbal recall on order effects in personality impression formation. *Journal of Verbal Learning and Verbal Behavior*, 1963, *2*, 379–391.

Ashmore, R. D. Solving the problem of prejudice. In B. E. Collins, *Social psychology*. Reading, Mass.: Addison–Wesley, 1970.

Ashmore, R. D., & Del Boca, F. K. Psychological approaches to understanding intergroup conflict. In P. A. Katz (Ed.), *Towards the elimination of racism*. New York: Pergamon Press, 1976.

Bower, G. H., Monteiro, K. P., & Gilligan, S. G. Emotional mood as a context for learning and recall. *Journal of Verbal Learning and Verbal Behavior*, 1978, *17*, 573–585.

Brewer, M. B. *A cognitive model of stereotypes of the elderly*. Paper presented at a symposium on "Perceptions of the aged: Basic studies and institutional implications," American Psychological Association Convention, New York, 1979. (a)

Brewer, M. B. Ingroup bias in the minimal intergroup situation: A cognitive-motivational analysis. *Psychological Bulletin*, 1979, *86*, 307–324. (b)

Brigham, J. C. Ethnic stereotypes. *Psychological Bulletin*, 1971, *76*, 15–38.

Campbell, D. T. Enhancement of contrast as a composite habit. *Journal of Abnormal and Social Psychology*, 1956, *53*, 350–355.

Campbell, D. T. Stereotypes and the perception of group differences. *American Psychologist*, 1967, *22*, 817–829.

Cantor, N., & Mischel, W. Prototypes in person perception. In L. Berkowitz (Ed.), *Advances in experimental social psychology* (Vol. 12). New York: Academic Press, 1979.

Cohen, C. *Cognitive basis of stereotyping*. Paper presented at the American Psychological Association Convention, San Francisco, 1977.

Deaux, K. Sex: A perspective on the attribution process. In J. H. Harvey, W. J. Ickes, & R. F. Kidd (Eds.), *New directions in attribution research* (Vol. 1). Hillsdale, N.J.: Lawrence Erlbaum Associates, 1976.

Dreben, E. K., Fiske, S. T., & Hastie, R. The independence of evaluative and item information: Impression and recall order effects in behavior-based impression formation. *Journal of Personality and Social Psychology*, 1979, *37*, 1758–1768.

Duncan, B. L. Differential social perception and attribution of intergroup violence: Testing the lower limits of stereotyping of blacks. *Journal of Personality and Social Psychology*, 1976, *34*, 590–598.

Dutta, S., Kanungo, R. N., & Freibergs, V. Retention of affective material: Effects of intensity of affect on retrieval. *Journal of Personality and Social Psychology*, 1972, *23*, 64–80.

Dutton, D. G. Tokenism, reverse discrimination, and egalitarianism in interracial behavior. *Journal of Social Issues*, 1976, *32* (2), 93–108.

Ehrlich, H. J. *The social psychology of prejudice*. New York: Wiley, 1973.

Fiske, S. T. Social cognition and affect. In J. H. Harvey (Ed.), *Cognition, social behavior, and the environment*. Hillsdale, N.J.: Lawrence Erlbaum Associates, 1981.

Gaertner, S. L. Nonreactive measures in racial attitude research: A focus on "liberals." In P. A. Katz (Ed.), *Towards the elimination of racism*. New York: Pergamon Press, 1976.

Greenwald, A. G. Cognitive learning, cognitive response to persuasion, and attitude change. In A. G. Greenwald, T. C. Brock, & T. M. Ostrom (Eds.), *Psychological foundations of attitudes*. New York: Academic Press, 1968.

Gurwitz, S. B., & Dodge, K. A. Effects of confirmations and disconfirmations on stereotype-based attributions. *Journal of Personality and Social Psychology*, 1977, *35*, 495–500.

Hamilton, D. L. *Illusory correlation as a basis for social stereotypes*. Paper presented at a symposium on "Cognitive biases in stereotyping," American Psychological Association Convention, San Francisco, 1977.

Hamilton, D. L. A cognitive–attributional analysis of stereotyping. In L. Berkowitz (Ed.), *Advances in experimental social psychology* (Vol. 12). New York: Academic Press, 1979.

Hamilton, D. L. Person perception. In L. Berkowitz, *A survey of social psychology* (2nd ed.). New York: Holt, Rinehart & Winston, 1980.

Hamilton, D. L. Cognitive representations of persons. In E. T. Higgins, C. P. Herman, & M. P. Zanna (Eds.), *Social cognition: The Ontario Symposium*. Hillsdale, N.J.: Lawrence Erlbaum Associates, 1981.

Hamilton, D. L., & Gifford, R. K. Illusory correlation in interpersonal perception: A cognitive basis of stereotypic judgments. *Journal of Experimental Social Psychology*, 1976, *12*, 392–407.

Hastie, R. Schematic principles in human memory. In E. T. Higgins, C. P. Herman, & M. P. Zanna (Eds.), *Social cognition: The Ontario Symposium*. Hillsdale, N.J.: Lawrence Erlbaum Associates, 1981.

Hastie, R., Ostrom, T. M., Ebbesen, E. B., Wyer, R. S., Jr., Hamilton, D. L., & Carlston, D. E. *Person memory: The cognitive basis of social perception*. Hillsdale, N.J.: Lawrence Erlbaum Associates, 1980.

Higgins, E. T., Herman, C. P., & Zanna, M. P. *Social cognition: The Ontario Symposium*. Hillsdale, N.J.: Lawrence Erlbaum Associates, 1981.

Isen, A. M., Shalker, T. E., Clark, M., & Karp, L. Affect, accessibility of material in memory, and behavior: A cognitive loop? *Journal of Personality and Social Psychology*, 1978, *36*, 1–12.

Jaccard, J. J., & Fishbein, M. Inferential beliefs and order effects in personality impression formation. *Journal of Personality and Social Psychology*, 1975, *31*, 1031–1041.

Katz, I. Experimental studies of Negro–white relationships. In L. Berkowitz (Ed.), *Advances in experimental social psychology* (Vol. 5). New York: Academic Press, 1970.

Langer, E. J., Taylor, S. E., Fiske, S. T., & Chanowitz, B. Stigma, staring, and discomfort: A novel-stimulus hypothesis. *Journal of Experimental Social Psychology*, 1976, *12*, 451–463.

Lippmann, W. *Public opinion*. New York: Harcourt, Brace, Jovanovitch, 1922.

Locksley, A., Borgida, E., Brekke, N., & Hepburn, C. Sex stereotypes and social judgment. *Journal of Personality and Social Psychology,* 1980, *39,* 821–831.

Mann, J. W. Inconsistent thinking about group and individual. *Journal of Social Psychology,* 1967, *71,* 235–245.

McArthur, L. Z. What grabs you? The role of attention in impression formation and causal attribution. In E. T. Higgins, C. P. Herman, & M. P. Zanna (Eds.), *Social cognition: The Ontario Symposium.* Hillsdale, N.J.: Lawrence Erlbaum Associates, 1981.

Nisbett, R., & Ross, L. *Human inference: Strategies and shortcomings of social judgment.* Englewood Cliffs, N.J.: Prentice-Hall, 1980.

Ostrom, T. M., Lingle, J. H., Pryor, J. B., & Geva, N. Cognitive organization of person impressions. In R. Hastie, T. M. Ostrom, E. B. Ebbesen, R. S. Wyer, Jr., D. L. Hamilton, & D. E. Carlston (Eds.), *Person memory: The cognitive basis of social perception.* Hillsdale, N.J.: Lawrence Erlbaum Associates, 1980.

Reyes, R. M., Thompson, W. C., & Bower, G. H. Judgmental biases resulting from differing availabilities of arguments. *Journal of Personality and Social Psychology,* 1980, *39,* 2–12.

Riley, R. T., & Pettigrew, T. F. Dramatic events and attitude change. *Journal of Personality and Social Psychology,* 1976, *34,* 1004–1015.

Riskey, D. R. Verbal memory processes in impression formation. *Journal of Experimental Psychology: Human Learning and Memory,* 1979, *5,* 271–281.

Rosch, E. Principles of categorization. In E. Rosch & B. B. Lloyd (Eds.), *Cognition and categorization.* Hillsdale, N.J.: Lawrence Erlbaum Associates, 1978.

Rothbart, M., Evans, M., & Fulero, S. Recall for confirming events: Memory processes and the maintenance of social stereotypes. *Journal of Experimental Social Psychology,* 1979, *15,* 343–355.

Rothbart, M., Fulero, S., Jensen, C., Howard, J., & Birrell, P. From individual to group impressions: Availability heuristics in stereotype formation. *Journal of Experimental Social Psychology,* 1978, *14,* 237–255.

Secord, P. F. Stereotyping and favorableness in the perception of Negro faces. *Journal of Abnormal and Social Psychology,* 1959, *59,* 309–315.

Snyder, M., Tanke, E. D., & Berscheid, E. Social perception and interpersonal behavior: On the self-fulfilling nature of social stereotypes. *Journal of Personality and Social Psychology,* 1977, *35,* 656–666.

Tajfel, H. Cognitive aspects of prejudice. *Journal of Social Issues,* 1969, *25* (4), 79–97.

Tajfel, H. Experiments in intergroup discrimination. *Scientific American,* 1970, *223,* 96–102.

Tajfel, H., Billig, M. G., Bundy, R. P., & Flament, C. Social categorization and intergroup behavior. *European Journal of Social Psychology,* 1971, *1,* 149–178.

Tajfel, H., Sheikh, A. A., & Gardner, R. C. Content of stereotypes and the inference of similarity between members of stereotyped groups. *Acta Psychologica,* 1964, *22,* 191–201.

Tajfel, H., & Wilkes, A. L. Classification and quantitative judgment. *British Journal of Psychology,* 1963, *54,* 101–114.

Taylor, S. E., & Fiske, S. T. Salience, attention, and attribution: Top of the head phenomena. In L. Berkowitz (Ed.), *Advances in experimental social psychology* (Vol. 10). New York: Academic Press, 1978.

Taylor, S. E., Fiske, S. T., Close, M., Anderson, C., & Ruderman, A. *Solo status as a psychological variable: The power of being distinctive.* Unpublished manuscript, Harvard University, 1975.

Vinacke, W. E. Stereotypes as social concepts. *Journal of Social Psychology,* 1957, *46,* 229–243.

Word, C. O., Zanna, M. P., & Cooper, J. The nonverbal mediation of self-fulfilling prophecies in interracial interaction. *Journal of Experimental Social Psychology,* 1974, *10,* 109–120.

Wyer, R. S., Jr., & Carlston, D. E. *Social cognition, inference, and attribution.* Hillsdale, N.J.: Lawrence Erlbaum Associates, 1979.

Zajonc, R. B. Feeling and thinking: Preferences need no inferences. *American Psychologist,* 1980, *35,* 151–175.

Author Index

Numbers in *italics* indicate pages with complete bibliographic information.

A

Abelson, R. P., 66, *81*
Abrahams, D., 192, *212*
Abramson, L. Y., 121, *142*
Adorno, T. W., 7, 10, 26, *32*, 228, *253*, 312, *329*
Alfert, E., 208, *210*
Allen, V. L., 84, *113*, *114*, 223, 225, 227, 230, 231, 232, 233, 241, *253*, *257*, 274, *302*
Alloy, L. B., 121, *142*
Allport, G. W., 7, 10, 11, 29, *32*, 83, *113*, 152, 157, *179*, 209, *210*, 219, 228, 231, *253*, 260, 261, 279, *298*, 312, 313, 319, 320, 325, *329*, 334, 345, *351*
Amabile, T. M., 320, *331*
Amir, Y., 241, 242, 251, *253*, 260, 261, 264, 279, 281, 296, *298*, 333, 345, *351*
Anderson, C., 90, 92, *114*, 336, *353*
Anderson, J., 163, *179*
Anderson, N. H., 101, *113*, 163, 170, *179*, *180*, 349, *351*
Anderson, R. C., 272, 273, *298*, *301*
Arber, S., 208, *211*
Arkin, R. M., 221, *255*
Armor, D. J., 260, *298*
Aronson, E., 192, *212*
Asch, S. E., 11, 16, *32*, 41, 53, *79*, 152, *179*, 213, *253*
Ashmore, R. D., 3, 13, 17, 19, 21, 24, 25, *32*, 37, 38, 39, 40, 41, 42, 43, 45, 47, 50, 52, 58, 66, 72, 76, *79*, *80*; *81*, 106, *113*, 228, 231, *253*, 260, 264, 265, 266, 267, 280, 281, *298*, 345, 347, *351*
Atkins, A. L., 328, *329*

B

Backman, C. W., 19, *35*, 198, *211*
von Baeyer, C. L., 196, 197, *210*
Bakan, D., 54, *79*
Bales, R. F., 215, *253*
Bandura, A., 193, *210*
Bannister, D., 236, *253*
Barclay, J. R., 185, *210*, 272, *298*
Barker, R. G., 220, *253*
Bartlett, F. C., 185, *210*, 269, 279, *298*, 310, 318, *329*
Bassett, R. L., 216, *255*
Baumgardner, M. H., 269, *301*
Bayton, J. A., 208, *212*
Beach, L. R., 66, *79*, 122, *143*
Bee, H., 9, 13, *34*, 37, 38, 42, 56, *81*
Bem, D. J., 78, *79*, 279, *298*
Bem, S. L., 99, 100, *113*, 197, *210*
Ben-Horin, D., 25, *32*
Benjamin, L., 263, *300*
Bennett, S. M., 42, *81*
Berkowitz, L., 312, *329*
Berman, J. S., 134, *143*, 192, *210*
Berscheid, E. S., 67, *81*, 116, 120, *144*, 192, 193, 194, 203, *210*, *212*, 336, *353*

355

Subject Index